Action Research

Models, Methods, and Examples

A volume in
Applied Research Methods in Education and the Social Sciences
Jerry W. Willis, *Series Editor*

Action Research

Models, Methods, and Examples

edited by

Jerry W. Willis
St. John Fisher College

Claudia L. Edwards
St. John Fisher College

INFORMATION AGE PUBLISHING, INC.
Charlotte, NC • www.infoagepub.com

Library of Congress Cataloging-in-Publication Data

Action research : models, methods, and examples / edited by Jerry W. Willis,
St. John Fisher College; Claudia Edwards, St. John Fisher College.
   pages cm. – (Applied research in education and the social sciences)
 ISBN 978-1-62396-655-3 (pbk.) – ISBN 978-1-62396-656-0 (hardcover) –
ISBN 978-1-62396-657-7 (e-book) 1. Social problems–Research. 2. Action
research. 3. Action research–Case studies. 4. Action research in
education. 5. Action research in education–Case studies. I. Willis, Jerry
W.
 HN29.A33 2014
 303.3'72–dc23

                                                              2014011094

Printed in the United States of America

CONTENTS

SECTION I

INTRODUCTION

SECTION II

ACTION RESEARCH MODELS AND APPROACHES

PREFACE

The idea for this book came from a doctoral course the two editors taught on action research. We felt a need for a book that would broadly and comfortably introduce students, practitioners, and applied researchers to action research even if they were unfamiliar with that approach to doing research in the field, including their own work environment. There are already many very good books dedicated to a particular type of action research, and we used one of those books in the course. If you prefer a particular model of action research there are probably several books about that model. If you want a book about using action research in a particular setting, such as schools, hospitals, or businesses, there are probably a number of books written for researchers and practitioners in that setting. In fact, there are hundreds of books about action research and they approach the topic from an amazing range of perspectives and angles.

The diversity of books about action research is a testament to the popularity of this form of applied, real-world research. It is also an indication of how diverse and broad the concept of action research is. There are action research models for many different levels—from one individual doing a self-study to improve his or her professional practice to models that facilitate institutional or even cultural or national/international change. There are also models of action research (AR) based on different worldviews/paradigms such as positivism, interpretive theory, and critical theory.

AR models designed for different levels, and based on different worldviews, explain much of the diversity in what we call action research, but there is also a third continuum of differences. That is the purpose of an

Action Research, pages vii–ix
Copyright © 2014 by Information Age Publishing
All rights of reproduction in any form reserved.

action research project. Some AR models were designed to quickly find technical and prescriptive solutions to relatively straightforward problems of professional practice. However, like Kurt Lewin's original version of AR, some contemporary models have as one goal, a better understanding of a problem, or building ways of addressing more complex issues of practice. Still others have the goal of emancipation. Action research models designed to address different purposes further add to the diversity of AR.

We edited this book and contributed three introductory chapters because we did not feel there were book-length treatments of action research that both address the diversity of AR as a concept and are suited to both novice and experienced applied researchers. We wrote the first three chapters with the goal of exposing readers to the diversity of the action research concept. The goal of those chapters is to broaden a reader's view of what action research is. The chapters lay the foundation for understanding the many different approaches to AR and how to approach the process of choosing a model or approach to use in your own action research.

The remaining 10 chapters in the book expand and deepen that foundation. Each is an overview of a real action research project. Taken together these ten chapters illustrate the way many different ways of doing AR were actually implemented. We asked the authors to tell the story of their action research project as it really happened. Some AR books present a somewhat abstract and theoretical explanation of what AR should be, but what AR *should be* according to theory can vary significantly from what really happens in practice. The theoretical picture of a particular form of AR is usually simpler, clearer, and acknowledges fewer problems than the picture presented through descriptions of actual AR projects. Descriptions of actual projects tend to be more complex, more ill-structured, and to include discussion of more unanticipated problems than theory-based descriptions. That is why the last ten chapters in this book tell complex stories. They are not clean stories of simple action research. In fact, there may not be such a thing as "simple" action research projects. These chapters present a more complex picture of AR; they provide ill-structured stories that almost always include problems that must be dealt with.

We selected these chapters so that each represents several types of action research. For example, Chapter 4, written by Dr. La-Kacia Walker-Floyd, is an example of action research that focuses on one individual (the author of the chapter) and has the goal of better understanding as well as improving her work as an online college instructor. That chapter is roughly based on interpretive theory and a major AR method was participatory action research journaling. In contrast, Chapter 6, by Dr. Shankar Shankaran, describes an action research project designed to facilitate change in a large, technical/engineering organization. It uses a positivist foundation. Chapters 11 and 12 are even broader in focus; they are action research projects that attempt to change how a society (in Kenya and in Malawi) deals with a widespread problem. Both these chapters are examples of participatory AR which is often based on critical theory.

Taken together the last 10 chapters in the book illustrate how particular teams used AR models based on a variety of paradigms to address many levels as well as many purposes. Taken together we hope the two parts of this book provide readers with a broad understanding of what AR is and how it can be used for many different purposes.

—Jerry W. Willis and Claudia L. Edwards

SECTION I

INTRODUCTION

CHAPTER 1

THE TWISTS AND TURNS OF ACTION RESEARCH HISTORY

Jerry Willis and Claudia L. Edwards
St. John Fisher College

ABSTRACT

This chapter introduces the book and action research which is a large and diverse family of applied research methods, ideologies, paradigms, and procedures. We trace the modern history of action research, beginning with Kurt Lewin in the 1940s, and look at the political and cultural trends that interacted with action research ideas from the forties to date.

If a group is engaged in "research" it may be doing any of several hundred types of work. There are that many, and more, types of research, including action research, archaeological digs, autoethnography, biographical research, case study research, clinical trials research, computational modeling, consumer research, content analysis, correlational research, cross cultural research, design research, dialectical research, DNA analysis, ethnographic research, experimental research, field research, *geisteswissenschaft*

Action Research, pages 3–20
Copyright © 2014 by Information Age Publishing
All rights of reproduction in any form reserved.

research, genealogical research, hermeneutic research, history research, interview research, judicial research, literary criticism, marketing research, meta-analytic research, narrative inquiry research, neuroimaging research, operations research, psychometric research, quasi experimental research, regression research, *reviews of research,* survey research, tests and measurement research, *verstehen* research, and *naturwissenschaft* research. This list is by no means comprehensive, and many types of research mentioned, such as interviewing, are actually groups of research methods rather than a single method. However, the list does illustrate the extraordinary range of human activities that are called research. Admittedly, some types of research in this list are relatively esoteric while others are widely used, but a quick search on Amazon.com will turn up quite a few books and articles that deal with each of them.

This book is about one type of research in the list above—action research. Action research is a family of methods for doing research in the field rather than in a laboratory setting. It is often done by practicing professionals rather than research professionals, and the reasons for doing it are typically very practical rather than theoretical. In this introductory chapter, the focus is on exploring both the history of AR and its conceptual and philosophical foundations. Chapter 2 continues the exploration of AR and discusses common characteristics of AR as well as common types of AR. However, before we begin that exploration it is important to put AR in a broader context.

WAYS OF KNOWING

That broader context is research as a way of understanding our physical, social, and psychological world. Figure 1.1 illustrates one way of presenting a big picture of the human enterprise we call *research.*

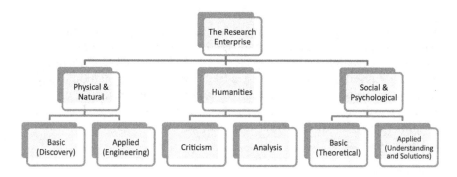

Figure 1.1　A big picture depiction of the research enterprise.

Research is one of many ways of seeking knowledge and understanding. There are also many other ways, such as asking someone you trust, relying on the statements of an authority such as the government or a religious institution, or going to a palm reader or astrologer. You may consider some of those ways of knowing to be totally bogus, but it is important to note that each of them is valued and relied upon by others (who may consider your preferred ways of knowing to be bogus). These and many other alternatives to research have been, and continue to be, used by significant numbers of people who seek knowledge, answers, and solutions.

Research is distinguished from most other ways of knowing by its emphasis on the collection and analysis of data. Almost every definition of research has as a core concept the idea that humans can better understand their world, or make better decisions, if they systematically collect data and carefully analyze it. This general definition applies to virtually all forms of research—whether it involves a historian trying to uncover the ancient origins of the Slavic peoples of Eastern Europe or a physicist studying the conductive characteristics of different compounds when they are cooled to absolute zero.

The idea that you and I, as humans, can better understand something by systematically collecting and analyzing data is a relatively new idea in Western thinking. It began in earnest with the ancient Greeks and it blossomed in the Enlightenment. In fact, we are still under the influence of Enlightenment thinking because it made the case that humans have the capacity to study their surroundings and use their powers of observation and reasoning to draw inferences, develop solutions, and explain phenomena. This is humanism in its broadest sense—the idea that humans do not need to rely on the gods of Olympus or other superhuman sources to understand the world. Humans have the capacity to do that themselves, and research is one of their most important ways of knowing.

Since the Enlightenment, the West has built a huge and multifaceted structure around the concept of research and it has created many different families, subgroups, and specializations of research. One convenient way of dividing up research is illustrated by the middle level in Figure 1.1. It organizes research into three diverse cultures, one for the physical and natural sciences, one for the humanities, and a third for the social and psychological disciplines. These three huge "cultures" of research traditions and methodologies began to emerge, and diverge, during and after the Enlightenment. Today, the ideas and methods of research are so diverse that a research chemist, for example, needs very different training and experiences than a psychologist or a research industrial engineer.

The differences across the research cultures have emerged in part because members of those cultures subscribe to different ways of doing research and have different reasons for doing it. Overall, the diversity across cultures (and within cultures) is probably good, but it can be a barrier when researchers from different cultures or subcultures try to communicate or collaborate. The cultural differences are so great that it takes little effort to find someone from, for example, a physical science such as chemistry who argues that what researchers in the humanities do is not research at all because it is not what physical scientists do. Or, you can find researchers in psychology who publicly proclaim that what scholars in the humanities do is not "really" research because it does not adhere to the version of the scientific method that has dominated American psychology for over a hundred years. These arguments about whether the work in a particular discipline is or is not "real" research have been going on for centuries. Baron C. P. Snow, the British novelist and physicist, added considerable fuel to that argumentative fire when he delivered his *Two Cultures* lecture at Cambridge University in 1959. In it, he asserted there are two "cultures" in modern universities—scientists and "literary intellectuals"—and that British higher education, in contrast to the American system, had favored the humanities (literary intellectuals) over the scientific disciplines. He felt this was a serious mistake and proposed that the sciences be better treated in funding, support, and respect. He also urged the two cultures to learn to communicate and collaborate. His book, *The Two Cultures* (1959), and his 1968 follow-up, *The Two Cultures: And a Second Look*, have been immensely influential in focusing attention on the fact that the logic, focus, and questions of researchers in diverse disciplines are quite different. Figure 1.1 is an expansion of Snow's two cultures concept. His scientific disciplines were the natural and physical sciences, and his "literary intellectuals" culture has been divided into two cultures—the humanities and the social and psychological disciplines. These three divisions seem to better represent the cultures operating in American higher education today. They are all part of a broad and diverse approach to knowing that is called research. But, in spite of the fact they are all research, they do have many differences. You cannot learn to do great research in astrophysics, for example, and then use that research expertise alone to become a good nursing researcher or archaeologist.

THE APPLIED VERSUS BASIC RESEARCH DISTINCTION

There is also another major division in the world of research. It is between basic and applied research. Each of the three cultures of research in Figure 1.1 has a basic and an applied branch. That distinction is sometimes blurred, especially in the humanities, but it is still an important point to discuss in an introduction to action research. That is because one of the points of disagreement among proponents of action research is whether AR is a purely applied and practical form of research or a flexible and adaptable form that can be used for both basic research and applied research goals.

The applied versus basic division was the focus of *Pasteur's Quadrant,* a book by Donald Stokes (1997). Stokes rejected the simple idea that research could be organized into one of two categories (Basic or Applied). He developed a four quadrant diagram that represented the relative importance a researcher puts on the development of basic or "foundational" versus applied knowledge (see Figure 1.2).

The work of the Danish physicist Niels Bohr was Stokes' example of a research program that had a high interest in Foundational Knowledge and little or no interest in Applied Use. When he developed a description of the atomic structure of the universe, Bohr was searching for basic, foundational knowledge, but he had little or no interest in how that knowledge might be applied. Thomas Edison's research, on the other hand, is Stokes' example of work with a very high interest in Applied Use and no interest in Foundational Knowledge. When he developed the light bulb, the phonograph, and the film projector, Edison's interest was in developing a useful product. And, while he was quite willing to use foundational knowledge discovered by others, he had little or no interest in developing basic or foundational knowledge in his own work. He was a *consumer,* not a producer, of foundational knowledge.

Stokes (1997) commented that it would be appropriate to call his bottom right quadrant *Edison's quadrant* "in view of how strictly this brilliant inventor kept his coworkers at Menlo Park, in the first industrial research laboratory in America, from pursuing the deeper scientific implications of what they were discovering in their headlong rush toward commercially profitable electric lighting. A great deal of modern research that belongs in this category is extremely sophisticated, although narrowly targeted on immediate applied goals" (p. 74).

Stokes suggests calling the upper right quadrant *Pasteur's Quadrant* "in view of how clearly Pasteur's drive toward understanding and use illustrates

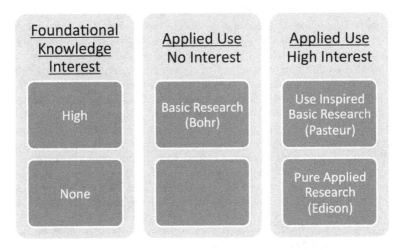

Figure 1.2 Stokes' four quadrants of basic and applied research.

this combination of [basic and applied] goals" (p. 74). Pasteur worked from the context of practice; he looked for problems in practice and then tried to understand the origins and causes of the problem. For example, he became concerned with the practical problem of stopping milk and wine from going sour. His research led to an understanding that living micro-organisms entered nutrient broths such as milk or wine when they were open to the air. (An earlier and widely accepted explanation of spoiling was the *spontaneous generation* of living organisms from non-living matter such as milk or wine.) He showed that these microorganisms were in the air and that when they polluted milk or wine, they multiplied rapidly, and were the cause of spoilage. That was basic knowledge not known before Pasteur's research. To prevent the problem, he also developed the process now called pasteurization, based on his discovery that even microscopic organisms would die if exposed to enough heat. That was his applied contribution to solving a real world problem.

Stokes' wrote his book, *Pasteur's Quadrant,* to encourage researchers to avoid both the extreme of basic research in the tradition of Neils Bohr and applied research in the tradition of Thomas Edison. He argued that Pasteur was correct—we should do research that addresses *both* basic and applied questions. In the field of education, that would mean we do research that makes a difference in the practice of education *as well as* contributes to basic knowledge about, for example, human learning.

Working in Pasteur's Quadrant has been proposed by scholars in many disciplines, including the general field of educational research. Burkhardt and Schoenfelt (2003), for example, mentioned the "awful reputation of educational research" and used *Pasteur's Quadrant* to advocate design research based on an engineering model:

> In the educational research community the engineering approach is often undervalued. At major universities only "insight" research in the humanities or science tradition tends to be regarded as true research currency for publication, tenure, and promotion. Yet engineering research has a key role to play in making educational research as a whole more useful. In *Pasteur's Quadrant,* Stokes (1997) argues that better insights come from situating inquiry in arenas of practice where engineering is a major concern. Stokes's motivating example is Pasteur, whose work on solving real world issues contributed fundamentally to theory while addressing pressing problems such as anthrax, cholera, and food spoilage....Analogous arguments have been made regarding the potential for such work in education...and serve as a justification for design experiments. Our point is that the same profitable dialectic between theory and practice can and should occur (with differing emphases on the R & D components) from the initial stages of design all the way through robust implementation on a large scale. We also argue that success will breed success: Once this approach is shown to produce improved materials that work on a large scale, more funding will become available for it. Such has been the history in other applied fields, such as medicine and consumer electronics. (p. 5)

Burkhardt and Schoenfelt used *Pasteur's Quadrant* to advocate a particular type of applied research that has several names, including engineering research and design-based research or DBR. This is either a "fellow traveler" of action research or a form of action research, depending on your point of view. DBR typically involves designing something—instructional materials, a curriculum, a training manual, a teaching procedure—and demonstrating that it works. The goal of DBR can also be an AR goal, but AR is broader and more diverse than DBR. There are AR approaches that serve other types of goals, and for that reason, in this book we will treat DBR as a type of AR. We recognize, however, that many DBR proponents would disagree with that typology and we acknowledge that a very good case can be made for considering DBR as a separate approach to research that is sympathetic to AR but not a type of AR.

PASTEUR OR EDISON: WHAT MODEL SHOULD ACTION RESEARCH USE?

Are proponents of Pasteur's Quadrant correct? Should good research address both basic and applied questions? Or, did Thomas Edison have a point? Are there times when it is more effective and more sensible to focus on finding a solution to a significant local problem without trying to address fundamental or basic questions as well? We think the answer to this question is not either/or. Instead, the answer is to consider both Pasteur's and Edison's approaches viable and make the decision about what types of questions your AR will be asking (Applied, or Applied and Basic) in context. There will be times when it makes sense to do action research that addresses both applied and basic questions, and times when you are more likely to answer the applied questions successfully if you do not invest much effort, if any, in dealing with basic research questions. In fact, there will be times when introducing basic questions will actually interfere with solving applied problems.

For example, in the social sciences, doing basic research generally means you will be collecting and analyzing research data in order to provide support for or against a particular theoretical position. In reading and literacy research, for instance, there are theories that support the use of whole language instructional approaches and theories that emphasize the need to include systematic phonics instruction in early reading instruction. There are fierce proponents of each approach and debates between them can be entertaining to disinterested observers. However, a group of educators trying to improve the reading instruction of a school or district might decide that there are elements of both whole language theory and systematic phonics theory that should be included in a reformed reading instruction curriculum for the district. Combining methods and procedures based on the two theories would present no problem in an AR project that had an applied goal of improving the district's reading instruction. There would, however, be a problem if a basic research question such as "Do the results support whole language theory?" was added to the AR project. This is because content and teaching methods from opposing theories have been mixed. There would be no way to use the results to "test" either whole language or systematic phonics theory because the instructional methods and curriculum do not purely follow either theory.

The same point could be made when a leadership training group in a corporation decides to do an AR project to revise the leadership training for the company's middle managers. Transactional leadership theory and transformational leadership theory are two popular theories that sometimes offer conflicting directions on how a leader should be trained. There are quite a few research studies that have addressed the basic question of whether, say, transformational leadership is better than transactional leadership models. However, a corporate training group trying to build an effective leadership development program might decide to use elements from both leadership theories. As with the reading research example, an AR project with purely applied goals would have no problem with this poly-theoretical approach. This approach can be characterized as doing research that is "theory informed" rather than "theory directed." However, if an AR team wanted to add a basic question such as, "Is transformational leadership the best approach in this company?" to their research agenda, the mingling of methods from the two theories would be a problem.

In such situations, we suggest you focus on applied goals and use ideas, concepts, and procedures from *any* theory the AR participants agree may be useful. On the other hand, if the AR project is one where applied and basic questions support each other, and may even be mutually facilitative, then by all means use AR methodologies to address both applied and basic goals. As you will see when you read about different approaches to AR in the chapters that follow this one, some types of AR are much more suited to local, personal, and applied research problems, while others are quite capable of generating research data that helps us answer local applied *and* basic questions that have the potential to be generalizable beyond the local context where the AR was conducted.

A SHORT HISTORY OF ACTION RESEARCH

The term action research was made popular in the late 1940s to describe systematic work in the field to solve a problem or answer an important question about professional practice. Kurt Lewin, the founder of social psychology, and one of the European Jewish intellectuals who came to America after the rise of Hitler in Germany, was concerned about authoritarianism and power relationships in a society. (In German the letter W is pronounced like a V, thus Lewin is pronounced LeVEEN.) He developed the idea of action research as a more democratic way of improving professional practice than traditional research methods. Lewin also made major contributions to a branch of sociopsychological research called field theory. Lewin, and field theory, propose that you cannot fully understand human behavior without also understanding the context in which the behavior occurs. He developed a procedure called *force field analysis* that graphically depicts the forces that impede or facilitate progress toward a particular goal or objective. Several types of graphics are used to represent force fields, but Figure 1.3 illustrates one type. It depicts *forces for* and *forces against* a proposed change as well as the strength of those forces. Force field analysis helps practicing professionals make judgments about how to facilitate and support efforts to bring about change in organizations and communities. Lewin was an early proponent of the need to consider local context and local history when trying to support change, and his development of action research methods is another illustration of that aspect of his work. Action research is a way of supporting local, context-sensitive change.

Lewin (1948) described his idea of action research this way:

> The research needed for social practice can best be characterized as research for social management or social engineering. It is a type of action-research, a comparative research on the conditions and effects of various forms of social action, and research leading to social action. Research that produces nothing but books will not suffice. (p. 202–203)

The quote highlights two of Lewin's basic assumptions about action research. The first is that changing "social practice" is a sociocultural process, not an individual process. If you focus on individuals you are less likely to be successful. The second is that the focus must be on "action." He drives this point home by saying that if the research produces "nothing but books" that will not be enough.

Lewin wanted a research model that emphasized making an immediate difference in the real world. Action research would involve either:

- Developing and implementing an action that would be studied to see if it made an important difference, or
- The study of a particular context or setting to develop knowledge that leads directly to action.

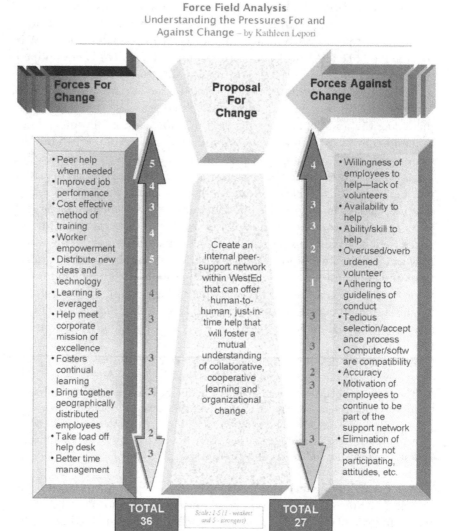

Figure 1.3 Example of a force field analysis developed by Kathleen Lepori, a graduate student at Pepperdine University in the educational technology graduate program. *Source:* http://cadres.pepperdine.edu/ar/c11/lepori/ForceField.html

Figure 1.4 summarizes the general model of action research proposed by Lewin. As you can see, it involves seven recursive or iterative steps. Lewin (1946) called the process a "spiral of steps, each of which is composed of a circle of planning, action, and fact finding about the results of the action" (p. 266). Figure 1.4 depicts one full circle, but a complete AR project may

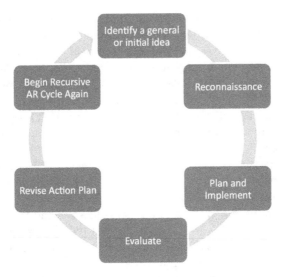

Figure 1.4 Kurt Lewin's original plan for action research.

include many such circles, each based on the results and reflections from the previous circle.

A circle begins with the collaborative development of an idea or plan. Then it progresses through a series of stages that include studying the problem and solutions, creating and implementing an action plan for the particular context or setting, evaluating the results of implementing the plan, revising the action plan based on the results, and conducting another cycle of action research.

Lewin's first paper on his action research concept was titled "Action Research and Minority Problems" (1946) and it was published in the *Journal of Social Issues.* Even before coming to America, Lewin's work had focused on the treatment of disenfranchised groups in society. "His particular concerns appear to have been the combating of anti-Semitism, the democratization of society, and the need to improve the position of women" (Smith, 2001, p. 1). His 1946 paper addressed the difficulties of minorities in America with an emphasis on how to improve "intergroup relations." Lewin did not try to provide "the answer" to this problem. Instead, he noted that at the moment there did not seem to be any universal answers. What he did suggest was a framework for developing and trying out practical solutions to the problem. He called this "action research" and he described AR as "research that will help the practitioner" (p. 34). Lewin then described some work he and his colleagues were doing in Connecticut. It involved interviewing workers involved in dealing with minority issues. The questions he asked them were about their perceptions of minority relations. He said "we wanted to know their line of thinking, their line of action, and the major barriers which they encounter" (p. 34). His conclusion was that "Not a few of those whose very job is the improvement of intergroup relations state that perhaps the greatest obstacle to their work is their own lack of clarity of what ought to be done. How is economic and social discrimination to be attacked if we think not in terms of generalities but in terms of the inhabitants of that particular main street and those side and end streets which make up that small or large town in which the individual group worker is supposed to do his job?" (p. 34).

Another characteristic of Lewin's action research is that it is not a way of getting people to accept an existing solution. He did not develop AR to help implement an easily identified and well established solution that only required a simple implementation process to solve the problem the AR group identified. Lewin's AR is a process that helps a group in a particular situation or setting—a village, company, institution, school, classroom, or culture—identify a problem and then try to find a tentative solution. Some approaches to supporting change assume the change agent enters the situation with a known and validated solution. In such cases, the job of the leader is to convince members of the organization to buy into the solution and implement it. That is not the job of the leader in AR. Lewin's AR model assumes the group will not have a great deal of difficulty identifying the problem that concerns them, but the solution to that problem will be more difficult to identify. It is more difficult for two major reasons. First, the problem may be one for which no universal or generally accepted solution exists. For example, the high dropout rate of poor minority students in American urban schools is a problem that has resisted decades of solutions proposed and implemented. The second reason why finding a workable solution is so difficult is that the solution for a particular context may require considerable customization. Even if there is a well accepted "universal solution," its success may depend on extensive customization to make it "fit" the local context. Lewin's AR was designed to facilitate that process of creating, and then trying out, a unique solution that has been specially designed for a particular local situation by people who know that local situation well.

This approach—expecting a team of local stakeholders to create and try out customized, contextualized solutions—is a core concept of action research. However, it is precisely the opposite of a movement from the 1970s that critics, and some proponents, called "teacher proofing." In his paper on disciplined improvisation, which we consider one promising model for action research, Keith Sawyer (2004) traced the history of attempts to teacher proof the curriculum and the classroom over the last 50 years.

> Although the teacher-proof movement of the post-Sputnik 1960s has long been considered a failure, new versions of teacher proofing have gained adherents

in the 1990s as increasing numbers of schools continue to implement scripted curricula that turn teachers into script readers. These curricula often provide word-for-word scripts that teachers are strongly encouraged to follow.... Scripted teacher-proof curricula do not rely either on teachers' creative potential or their subject matter expertise; the message of these programs seems to be, if you can perform well from a script, you can teach. (p. 12)

While Sawyer's focus is on education, his point is equally applicable to other fields such as business, health care, and social services. He makes many arguments against scripting and other forms of teacher proofing the curriculum and he suggests that this unsatisfactory form of educational reform is often used in failing urban schools where creative and customized, not scripted and predesigned, solutions are sorely needed. He concludes that:

Underperforming schools are faced with two very different visions for reform. Scripted approaches attempt to teacher proof the curriculum by rigidly specifying teacher actions, and essentially removing all creativity and professional judgment from the classroom. (p. 12)

Creative teaching suggests a very different vision—teachers are knowledgeable and expert professionals and are granted creative autonomy to improvise in their classrooms. (p. 12)

Sawyer uses the metaphor of *teaching as improvisation,* which he supports by asserting that "creative teaching is disciplined improvisation because it always occurs within broad structures and frameworks. Expert teachers use routines and activity structures more than novice teachers, but they are able to invoke and apply these routines in a creative, improvisational fashion" (p. 13). Sawyer's teaching as improvisation is a specific instance of Lewin's insistence that solutions to the problems may need to be developed by people with local knowledge because those solutions require considerable customization to work in that context. This assumption, advocated by both Sawyer and Lewin, is the opposite of the assumption made to justify a scripted curriculum. That approach, which eliminates as much variation from teacher to teacher as possible, is based on the assumption that there is One Right Way to do something and that the general experts are the most likely to know what that Right Way is.

Another element of Sawyer's *teaching as improvisation* is the idea of social collaboration. Sawyer invokes constructivist models of learning, including Vygotskian and Piagetian theories, to justify an emphasis on discourse, discussion, and group communication in the classroom. In AR, Lewin emphasizes the importance of communication within the AR group, and the development of shared understandings of the problem (and a possible solution) through effective communication. Sawyer refers to this as "collaborative discussion." Lewin refers to AR as a form of "social engineering" and emphasizes that the goal of action research is "social action," which means that, in most situations, to be successful AR must involve one or more groups rather than one or more individuals.

Lewin's original explanation of action research included another element that opposed the then-dominant views of how research in the social sciences should be conducted. He argued that social and organizational issues are complex and multifaceted. No single social science discipline, such as psychology, sociology, or anthropology, has the breadth of understanding required. He proposed instead an "integrated" approach that would draw from the knowledge base of many different disciplines. And, in his paper, Sawyer (2004) applied that approach to teaching by integrating knowledge and perspectives from many different fields including constructivist child development, performance theater, contemporary pedagogical theories, and sociocultural communication research.

ACTION RESEARCH IN THE 1950S AND 60S

Kurt Lewin was a social thinker who fled Nazi Germany when both his religion and his way of thinking, which included paying attention to the needs of minorities and the oppressed, put his life at risk. His idea of action research was a continuation in America of the work he had been doing in Germany, and while that did not put his life at risk, the American culture of that period was not as hospitable to his aims and methods as he might have liked. The nation was steeped in religious and racial prejudice—the state of Connecticut where Lewin worked still had property deeds with restrictive covenants that forbade new owners from ever selling to Jewish or African American buyers. One such restrictive covenant from 1940 was part of the deeds to a housing development in West Hartford:

> No persons of any race other than the Caucasian race shall use or occupy any building or any lot, except that this covenant shall not prevent occupancy by domestic servants of a different race domiciled with an owner or tenant. (Quoted from http://magic.lib.uconn.edu/otl/doclink_covenant.html)

Kurt Lewin died in 1947 and it was not until 1948 that the Supreme Court finally outlawed the enforcement of race restrictive covenants in deeds. Lewin's focus on improving "intergroup relations" was sorely needed in 1940s America, and his action research model was one way of involving people other than academic researchers and government officials in leading the effort. Unfortunately for action research, America in the 1950s may have been an even worse environment than the 1940s for action research in the tradition of Kurt Lewin. A major reason was the "red scare" after World War II, which was also called McCarthyism, after Senator Joseph McCarthy who pursued and persecuted many American citizens who were active in efforts to improve the conditions of workers or to secure civil rights for minorities. Anything extreme right wing leaders and activists considered unacceptable was tarred with the very broad brush of Communism. Ellen Schrecker (2002) noted a few of the many thousands of examples:

> Mississippi Senator James Eastland ... personified this. He repeatedly used his [Senate] committee as a forum to present the segregationist case that integration was a Communist plot. J. Edgar Hoover, who secretly harassed Martin Luther King Jr. for years, also sought to expose the connection between the civil rights movement and the Communist party.... At the state level, anti-Communist investigators, promoted similar charges. (p. 85)

The mood of the country, and the widespread efforts to root out "Communists" in government, Hollywood, and academia, had a chilling effect on virtually all movements with an avowed aim of bringing more equity into the American culture.

> The main academic purges occurred from 1952 to 1954 when the congressional committees had run out of more glamorous targets and turned to the nation's colleges and universities.... Although the faculty committees that mounted the investigations did not normally demand that their colleagues name names, they did expect them to cooperate and discuss their past political activities. People who refused ... were invariably fired, as were most of the others, especially at schools where conservative or politically insecure administrators and trustees refused to accept the favorable recommendations of faculty committees.
>
> Once fired, the politically tainted professors could rarely find other academic jobs.... The university blacklist began to subside by the early 1960s. Most of the banned professors returned to the academic world, but their careers had suffered in the interim.
>
> Hundreds of elementary and high school teachers also lost their jobs, sometimes after an appearance before HUAC [House UnAmerican Activities Committee) and sometimes as the result of a local loyalty probe. Social workers were similarly affected, especially in the welfare agencies of cities like New York and Philadelphia where they had formed unions and agitated on behalf of their clients. (Schrecker, 2002, p. 94–95)

The *zeitgeist* of America in the 1950s was very unfavorable toward both the method of action research (involving ordinary people and local practitioners in searching for solutions to problems they identified) and many of the goals of AR projects (expanding civil and legal rights, reducing racism and discrimination). Even in education, where the work of Stephen Corey (the Dean of Teachers College at Columbia University in the late 1940s), was very influential, the 1950s were a period when action research was redefined to mean something much more tame and controllable by authorities. Corey's 1949 book, *Action Research to Improve School Practices,* emphasized action research as a way of empowering teachers to find solutions to the problems of education. Hinchey (2008) noted that Corey also offered a strong defense against the growing criticisms that action research was not "scientific" and that teachers were not competent to do research on education.

> Corey offered a vigorous defense, arguing that it [AR] is an important and legitimate tool for educators to improve their practice: 'The action researcher is interested in the improvement of the educational practices in which he is engaging. He undertakes research in order to find out how to do his job better—action research means research that affects actions (Corey, 1949, p. 509) ... Corey's emphasis on collaboration and on teachers researching elements of their own practice are characteristic of many contemporary action research approaches. (Hinchey, 2008, p. 13)

Action research in the tradition of Lewin and Corey faded in the 1950s and was replaced by models that were more expert-based, more focused on relatively simple or technical issues of professional practice (and less focused on social equity), and less participatory. Quite a few of the action research studies in that era were ways for an outside expert to gain access to practitioners in a particular setting and train them to implement a solution that was developed by experts working elsewhere. We will devote little time in this book to this type of AR because it seems to embody only two common characteristics of AR—that the research is done in the field rather than in a laboratory and that the purpose of the research is at least in part practical and action oriented.

In the 40 plus years since the decade of the fifties, many models of AR have emerged, and a great many of them exemplify many more of the characteristics of Lewin's original AR model. One reason for that was the changes in the social sciences that occurred in the last 30 years of the twentieth century. Positivism, the dominant paradigm or "worldview" in both the basic and applied social sciences, was challenged by alternative paradigms that took dramatically different positions on fundamental questions. The two most important and influential alternative paradigms were, and are, interpretive and critical theory, and some refer to the last decades of the twentieth century as the era of the *paradigm wars* because of the intensity of the debates between proponents of the three broad conceptual frameworks—positivism, interpretive theory, and critical theory—that offered very different perspectives on how to do both basic and applied research in the social sciences. For anyone interested in AR, the important result of the paradigm wars was that versions of AR in the tradition of Lewin and other pioneers became popular again. In fact, most of the popular AR models in use today are based on either the interpretive or critical paradigm. Chapter 2 will focus on the three paradigms and explore the implications they have for how AR is practiced.

SUMMARY

Action research is a form of systematic investigation that typically involves attempts to solve practical problems in real world settings through the involvement of stakeholders who work or live in those settings. AR is one of many forms of research practiced in the social sciences, broadly defined to include both "basic" disciplines such as sociology, psychology, and economics as well as professional fields such as education, psychology, business, and social work. Whether AR should address both basic and applied research questions is still open to debate, but there is a growing consensus that practical and applied questions should receive priority while basic and theoretical questions may also be addressed if they do not interfere with accomplishing the practical and applied goals of the research.

Over its short history of less than 80 years, AR has been heavily influenced by the major ideological shifts and cultural trends that American, British, and Australian cultures experienced. For example, during the "Red Scare" era in America, AR that advocated goals such as civil rights and worker rights fell into disfavor. However, as both mainstream culture and the foundational paradigms of the social sciences changed in the past 40 years, AR has become a very strong influence on the way practitioners and applied researchers work in the field.

REFERENCES

Burkhardt, H., & Schoenfeld, A. (2003). Improving educational research: Toward a more useful, more influential, and better-funded enterprise. *Educational Researcher, 32*(9), 3–14.

Corey, S. (1949). *Action research to improve school practices.* New York: Wiley.

Hinchey, P. (2008). *Action research primer.* New York: Peter Lang.

Lewin, K. (1948). *Resolving social conflicts: Selected papers on group dynamics.* In G. W. Lewin (Ed.). New York: Harper & Row.

Lewin, K. (1946). Action research and minority problems. *Journal of Social Issues, 2*(4), 34–46.

Sawyer, K. (2004). Creative teaching: Improvisation in the constructivist classroom. *Educational Researcher, 33*(2), 12–20.

Schrecker, E. (2002). *The age of McCarthyism.* New York: Bedford/St. Martins Press.

Smith, M. (2001). Kurt Lewin, groups, experimental learning and action research. *The encyclopedia of informational education.* Retrieved January 12, 2012 from http://www.infed.org/thinkers/et-lewin.htm

Snow, C. P. (1968). *The two cultures: And a second look.* Cambridge, UK: Cambridge University Press.

Snow, C. P. (1959). *The two cultures.* Cambridge, UK: Cambridge University Press.

Stokes, D. (1997). *Pasteur's quadrant: Basic science and technological innovation .* Washington, DC: Brookings Institution Press.

CHAPTER 2

THEORETICAL FOUNDATIONS FOR THE PRACTICE OF ACTION RESEARCH

Jerry Willis and Claudia L. Edwards
St. John Fisher College

ABSTRACT

Three major paradigms serve as the theoretical foundation for different types of action research. They are positivism, interpretive theory, and critical theory. These three paradigms are all in use today but they offer different and sometimes conflicting answers to basic questions relevant to applied research. Their influence has also varied considerably over the modern history of action research. While positivism was a popular foundation for American action research in the 1950s, it is not as popular in action research today. Currently, interpretive theory and critical theory are more popular with many different models and approaches to action research based on these two paradigms.

The history of action research, perhaps more than most research methods, has been heavily influenced by the broader cultural and political movements of the time. In the 50s and early 60s there was regular repression of

Action Research, pages 21–43
Copyright © 2014 by Information Age Publishing

traditional liberal causes such as the civil rights movement, labor organization, antiracist projects, freedom of religion, separation of church and state, and equitable treatment of the poor. However, as the worst excesses of McCarthyism were repudiated, the 60s became a time of flower power, campus sit-ins, massive opposition to the war in Vietnam, and an increasingly active civil rights movement. The Montgomery to Selma marches happened in 1965, and Bloody Sunday, when local and state police attacked the marchers on Edmund Pettus Bridge outside Selma, happened on March 7 of that same year. And, on March 12, 1967, a three page ad in the *New York Times* was published. Over the signatures of 6,766 teachers and professors, the ad made the case against continuing the Vietnam War. These two events exemplify a shift in the American culture that is still with us today. Opposition to the war and advocacy for civil rights were both still criticized by the right wing as being Communist or Communist inspired, but the official support to convert those condemnations into arrests, firings, and isolation was no longer widely available. It is true that some did wish to continue to penalize what they believed to be Communist-inspired thoughts; however, the mainstream of American thought had shifted. Drastic actions by law enforcement officials, such as turning the fire hoses on children in Birmingham, or a gang including law enforcement officers murdering three civil rights workers in Mississippi, did not intimidate ordinary citizens into quiet submission. Instead, these types of actions roused more and more of them and also made it much more difficult to get away with such outrageous violations of both the law and morality.

The most long lasting impact on action research that emerged from the 1960s was probably the loss of faith in official sources of truth. By the 1960s, citizens of the Soviet Union had long ago learned to distrust the official truths published in government controlled newspapers and presented on government controlled radio and TV. (Note from JW: When I checked with my wife, who grew up in Russia, to verify this she said, "Jerry, not by the 1960s. By that time the Soviet people had a "PhD" in not trusting the government!"). In America, massive media coverage of the war and live TV coverage of thousands of civil rights actions and political protests (such as the antiwar protests outside the Democratic National Convention in 1968 where protestors shouted "the whole world is watching" while police beat them) literally forced Americans to face the fact that what the government told them and what was really happening were not always in synch. Today, most people accept the idea that there will be different truths, different viewpoints, and different perspectives on any significant issue. That perspective began to take hold of the American psyche in the 1960s, and President Nixon's Watergate Scandal in the 1970s helped make it a relatively permanent American character trait.

Kurt Lewin's and Stephen Corey's versions of action research began to grow again in the fertile soil of the 1960s and 1970s, along with a wide range of activist methods that depended on the participation of many different "stakeholder" groups. Grass roots research and activism became popular again and with it the original goals and methods of action research.

The American culture of the last half of the twentieth century may also have influenced even broader significant changes in the American social sciences. Up to that point, many of the social sciences, but especially psychology at the basic research level and the applied research work of education, had tried to emulate the natural and physical sciences by adopting a relatively strict version of the scientific method as the sole valid source of new knowledge. The result was a research enterprise in both psychology and education that tended to look for universal answers to broad questions through the testing of theories. However, in the last forty years of the twentieth century the social sciences entered a period sometimes referred to as the era of *the paradigm wars*. Alternative "worldviews," or paradigms, were proposed and then gradually gained acceptance within the social sciences. These alternatives to traditional positivist, empiricist, objectivist foundations influenced our thinking about virtually every aspect of the research enterprise—from what questions were important to ask to who should interpret research results and how. The various editions of the *Handbook of Qualitative Research*, first published in 1993 by Sage and edited by Norman Denzin and Yvonna Lincoln, are probably the best known publication outlets for social science research methodologies that are alternatives to positivist methods. The latest edition of that huge book, now called the *Sage Handbook of Qualitative Research*, was published in 2011. In the 2011 edition of the handbook, Brydon-Miller, Kral, Maguire, Noffke, and Sabhlok's chapter on participatory action research summarized the essential characteristics of what we are calling critical action research:

> It is the belief in collaboration and respect for local knowledge, the commitment to social justice, and trust in the ability of democratic processes to lead to positive personal, organizational, and community transformation that provide the common set of principles that guide [participatory action research]. (p. 398)

Space is not available here to review the paradigm wars in detail, but there are a number of useful resources, including Bent Flyvbjerg's (2001) *Making Social Sciences Matter: Why Social Science Fails and How it Can Succeed Again*, Willis' (2007) *Foundations of Qualitative Research: Interpretive and Critical Approaches*, and *Postpositivism and Educational Research* (Phillips & Barbules, 2000). The books by Flyvbjerg and Willis are justifications for adopting one of the alternative paradigms for research, while Phillips and Barbules take the position that the traditional positivist/postpositivist paradigm is the best alternative. A fourth book, the second edition of Norman Blaikie's (2007) *Approaches to Social Inquiry: Advancing Knowledge* is a detailed but very readable analysis of the history and current status of the debate over the guiding frameworks for research in the social sciences.

The paradigm wars were about three very different paradigms that social scientists proposed as foundations for research—*postpositivism,* which is a modern version of positivism, *critical theory,* which is a modern version of traditional Marxist/neoMarxist theory, and *interpretive theory,* which has roots in several different ways of knowing including pragmatism, progressivism, and constructivism. Several scholars have used critical theory as a foundation for action research models, and there are also a number of models based on the interpretive paradigm. While there are very important differences between the interpretive and critical worldviews, they do share a strong opposition to positivism as a foundation for social science research and professional practice. Both also emphasize the importance of context in interpreting research results and they are both strongly inclined toward field research and the importance of doing research *with* rather than *on* participants. However, despite the popularity of the critical and interpretive paradigms in the action research community, there are also a number of models that are compatible with, and based upon, a positivist paradigm. The three sections below explore how AR has been practiced from each of the three major paradigm alternatives.

AR FROM A POSITIVIST PERSPECTIVE

Positivism is not widely accepted today by philosophers. However, as a framework for guiding research in the natural and physical sciences it is, nevertheless, alive and well. It is more important for this discussion that positivism is the philosophical foundation for the traditional version of the scientific method, which is still widely practiced and taught in the social sciences. It is no exaggeration to say that in many of the main branches of social science research the positivist paradigm, which emphasizes experimental research and seeks universal answers to questions about human behavior, is so dominant that other approaches must be explained and justified in ways that positivist research does not. That is certainly true of AR, which is one of those "other approaches" that has been regularly and routinely criticized by positivists because it violates many of the principles of positivist research (e.g., objectivity, separation of practice from research, the search for universal knowledge). As DeLuca and Kock (2007) noted, "AR is typically viewed from an interpretive perspective" (p. 10). They also commented that "AR can be conducted with positivist, interpretive, and critical epistemologies" (p. 10). Earlier,

Kock had written a paper titled, "Can action research be made more rigorous in a positivist sense? The contributions of an iterative approach?" (Kock, McQueen, & Scott, 1997). In that paper, the authors discussed the common criticisms positivists make of interpretive models of action research and proposed ways of meeting some of the positivist criteria for "good" research.

Trying to make action research more positivist in nature is a minority view within the field of AR. Most scholars of AR methods seem to be trying to get beyond the restrictions of positivism and build action research methods on other foundations. Cassell and Johnson (2006), for example, noted that a long line of scholars have "proposed that action research is incompatible with the scientific norms established by positivist epistemology" (p. 785). As long ago as 1978, Susman and Evered were highlighting the "deficiencies of positivist science for generating knowledge for use in solving problems" (p. 532) and made the case for action research being a "method for correcting these deficiencies." However, despite the declining influence of positivism in social science research over the past 50 years, it remains the dominant model. And, as you might expect, there are models of AR based on a positivist foundation.

The AR model proposed by Hult and Lennung (1980) is one of many AR models based on the positivist paradigm:

> Action research simultaneously assists in practical problem-solving and expands scientific knowledge, as well as enhances the competencies of the respective actors, being performed collaboratively in an immediate situation using data feedback in a cyclical process. . . . (p. 247)

The most obvious positivist element of Hult and Lennung's definition of AR is the emphasis on expanding "scientific knowledge," which is not a universal component of AR based on other perspectives. In their paper, Hult and Lennung are critical of other scholars who have not included the search for new scientific knowledge in the requirements for AR. They justify their viewpoint in two ways:

- The "emphasis on practice bears a danger that the scientific interest may be reduced to a mere means toward improved problem solving." (p. 242)
- "The use of scientific method solely as a problem-solving procedure is not in accordance with our proposed definition. Action research must aim at action *and* research." (p. 242)

Of course, you already know that in Lewin's original development of AR the interest in finding "scientific knowledge" (which means general or relatively universal knowledge that can be generalized to other settings) in AR was not as high as developing solutions that would work in a particular context. Lewin recognized that there was less "universal" knowledge to be found in the social sciences than there might be in the physical sciences. Lewin's belief that the local context in which AR was conducted was a major factor in whether a particular solution worked or not pushed action researchers to seek and use local knowledge. His force field analysis method was an effort to help researchers and practitioners identify the local factors that would need to be considered in any effort to bring about change. It is an over simplification, but if you divide what we know about how to work with people into *universal knowledge* and *local knowledge,* then Hult and Lennung's positivist model of AR is based on the assumption that a great deal—the vast majority—of knowledge about human behavior is universal. If that assumption is true, then it makes sense to search for that type of knowledge when doing AR. If, on the other hand, Lewin was correct and a great deal, perhaps the majority, of our knowledge about how to solve problems that involve humans and groups is local knowledge (context dependent), then the positivist model of AR is less viable. An approach that involves knowledgeable locals in the search for a solution is more viable because a successful solution will likely require adaptation and customization to the local context.

Hult and Lennung's insistence on including the search for scientific knowledge in any reasonable definition of action research is an expression of their positivist ideology. Positivism as a framework for research insists that the major goal of research is the pursuit of generalizable knowledge. In a positivist paradigm, such a goal is usually accomplished through theory testing, and the authors support that idea in their view of AR. "The assumption is that [AR] projects can be simultaneously beneficial for problem-solving, theory expansion and competence enhancement" (p. 243).

Positivism also tends to separate the researcher role from the practitioner role and to consider the researcher to be the "expert" who is in charge. There are elements of that viewpoint in Hult and Lennung's paper. For example, they talk about the action researcher and the client as if they were different people with different responsibilities. They are particularly concerned that any research reports be written by the "action researcher," who is assumed to have the expertise while other participants do not. "It is only rational...that the task of editing research reports to the scientific community is left with the action researcher—unless the mastery of such skills are deemed to be of importance for the client" (p. 243). In another section of the paper, the authors discuss the roles of the action researcher (the expert) and the client. The action researcher has expertise in research "methods, a preunderstanding of the problem as well as intervention skills"

(p. 244). The client, on the other hand, "contributes his understanding of the specific situation and its idiosyncracies." This is not a the type of equal partnership and mutual respect that is expected in other models of AR, but it is in keeping with the positivist paradigm that tends to privilege the position of the researcher as an expert.

Other AR models assume the action researcher can also be the "client"—that is, a member of the staff in the setting where the AR is being conducted. Other AR models also assume that every participant in a project is an action researcher and that the decision making and leadership responsibilities are shared.

In addition, Hult and Lennung argued that no decisions should interfere with the multiple goals of the AR project. This requirement means the search for scientific knowledge cannot be compromised, and that imposes a limitation on what types of interventions can be tried. This can limit AR projects to interventions that are theoretically compatible, which is not a serious problem for positivists who are most comfortable with research that tests a theory. However, interpretive and critical theorists are far less concerned with theoretical purity and often seek to develop and test the best possible solution to a problem they can devise, even if it means drawing from a wide range of theoretical, applied research, and professional practice knowledge bases.

Other aspects of Hult and Lennung's definition—the iterative nature of the research, the focus on work in context, the focus on practical problem solving, and even building the competencies of the participants—are all characteristics of AR included in models and definitions based on other paradigms.

A more recent description of AR from a positivist perspective was published by DeLuca and Kock (2007). They use the term "canonical action research" to identify their model of AR and the approach is compatible with what we are calling positivist AR.

THE PURPOSE OF AR FROM A POSITIVIST PERSPECTIVE

To this point in the discussion, several aspects of positivist perspectives on AR stand out. Positivist AR:

- Expects the research to contribute to both basic and applied goals.
- Tends to start with a particular theory as an a priori beginning point and to work toward solving problems with solutions based on that guiding theory.

- Tends to separate researcher roles from practitioner roles and to treat the researcher as the expert who leads and directs the research project.
- Prefers use of the traditional scientific method but makes adaptations because the research is being conducted in the field rather than in a controlled laboratory setting, and
- Because of the emphasis on using the scientific method puts considerable emphasis on the technical aspects of "good" research, such as establishing validity and reliability of instruments used in the research and obtaining objective data on outcomes.

Before moving on to a discussion of interpretive AR, the purposes of AR from a positivist perspective deserve a bit more attention. Figure 2.1 summarizes the differences between the purposes of AR from a positivist perspective versus interpretive and critical AR.

Figure 2.1 reflects Carr and Kemmis' (1986; based on Habermas' 1972) explanation of the three types of interests or concerns humans in general, and action researchers in particular, may have: "technical control" which is the goal of positivist AR, "practical knowledge" which is the goal of interpretive AR, and "emancipatory interest" which is the goal of critical AR. Positivist AR thus tends to be narrowly focused on a specific, well-defined problem of practice that is amenable to what might be called a "technical" solution.

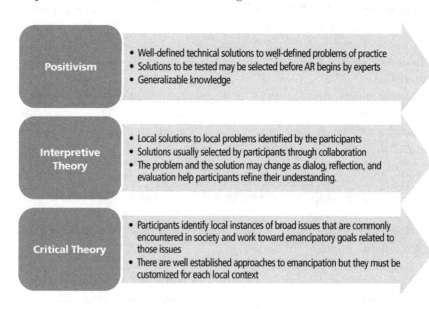

Figure 2.1 Types of problems and solutions preferred in AR projects based on different paradigms.

These technical solutions are often predetermined, and the AR project is often organized around successful implementation of the solution. For example, a company might institute a new procedure for keeping track of inventory in its regional warehouses and retail stores. An AR project at one of its stores or warehouses could involve training and supporting staff as they learn and begin using the new procedures. The project might also collect data on methods of staff development or inventory management and related logistical issues. One outcome of the action research might be a paper discussing the findings in terms of whether the results support one of the major theories about inventory management (or staff development).

Some scholars have attributed the positivist approach to solving problems through AR to Lewin himself. For example, Masters (1995) discussed AR in a tradition with several names: technical, technical-collaborative, scientific-technical, technical action research, and positivist.

"Early advocates of action research...put forward a scientific method of problem solving.... The underlying goal of the researcher in this approach is to test a particular intervention based on a prespecified theoretical framework; the nature of the collaboration between the researcher and the practitioner is technical and faciliatory. The researcher identifies the problem and a specific intervention, then the practitioner is involved and they agree to facilitate with the implementation of the intervention" (p. 1). Masters used the term *technical action research* to describe this form of AR, and, using Grundy's (1987) framework, described the characteristics of a technical action research project:

- It is "instigated by a particular person or group of people who because of their greater experience or qualifications would be regarded as experts or authority figures."
- "Technical action research promotes more efficient and effective practice. It is product directed but promotes personal participation by practitioners in the process of improvement."
- "It fosters the disposition characteristic of the artisan within the participating practitioners (Grundy, 1987, p. 154).
- The result is "the accumulation of predictive knowledge, the major thrust is on validation and refinement of existing theories and is essentially deductive" (p. 154).

These are also characteristics of what we are calling positivist AR, and the approach is sometimes attributed to Lewin. This does not seem to be supported by what we know about Lewin's early work in America. He emphasized the importance of involving the practitioners in the process of developing as well as implementing solutions, and he was also concerned that a potential solution fit the local context. Several of the early AR studies done by Lewin's students exhibited both these characteristics. Passmore (2001) describes one such study:

Lewin's contributions to change in the workplace began shortly after the war. Alex Bevalas, one of Lewin's students at Iowa, worked with Alfred Marrow's Harwood manufacturing company to explore ways to enhance productivity by using action research methods in which workers participated in experimental changes in methods. The conditions they created resulted in what we would call a learning organization today; workers were encouraged to experiment with different methods, to discuss them among themselves and to choose the methods which they agreed were most effective. Groups of workers increased their own quotas after discovering and employing new methods. (p. 39)

The approach used by Lewin's student is not that of positivist AR. There was no predefined technical solution selected by experts and then taught to workers who were expected to implement it. Instead, the workers were intensively involved in making decisions across the entire AR process. Passmore also described a project Lewin did with Margaret Mead during World War II that reinforces the point that Lewin did not develop AR within the positivist tradition:

During the Second World War, Lewin collaborated with Margaret Mead in their now famous studies designed to reduce the civilian consumption of rationed foods. The researchers experimented with different methods of influencing behavior: first, experts were used to explain why behavior change was important and to exhort a group of housewives to change their cooking habits. Next, a second group of housewives was given the pertinent information and asked to discuss the problem of curtailing consumption among them in order to decide what could be done. The results of the participative approach to change were much more impressive, confirming Lewin's strong beliefs in democracy and more specifically in action research as a tool that could advance science while dealing with practical social concerns. (p. 39)

Thus, even when the goal was predetermined, Lewin's belief that involving the participants in decisions about how to achieve the goal was confirmed and reinforced. Lewin's early work is therefore the foundation for practices common to both interpretive and critical AR models, which will be discussed next. Note, however, that Lewin did believe that AR could solve both local problems as well as "advance science," but that viewpoint is also held by some intepretivist and critical theory practitioners of AR.

AR FROM AN INTERPRETIVE PERSPECTIVE

DeLuca and Kock (2007) described several aspects of the positivist paradigm that influences positivist models of AR:

- Using theory as a guide (e.g., use of a priori knowledge to make decisions in the AR process)
- Seeking generalizations (e.g., doing research to test theories and hypotheses)
- Using quantifiable measures
- Generalizing from a sample to a population

The authors also contrasted the implications of the interpretive paradigm for action research:

- Theory de-emphasized (e.g., avoiding the use of a priori knowledge to limit options or possibilities)
- Seeking local knowledge (e.g., creating subjective meaning and "not generalizing")

Generalizing from sample to population is an element of virtually all positivist research. It is an expression of the overall goal of positivist research that the results, derived from the study of a sample, should contribute to our knowledge and understanding about the population from which the sample was derived. Interpretive researchers tend to focus on developing a better understanding of the local context where the study is being conducted. That understanding may be useful to others who work in different settings, but the task of generalizing to other settings is the responsibility of the reader, not the researcher.

Deluca and Kock's paper is an attempt to get AR researchers to conduct and write up their studies in ways that will appeal to positivist readers because they are likely to be a majority of the potential audience. Their focus is on aspects of research that are linked to the core values of positivism, such as stating hypotheses before conducting research, including a literature review that sets the a priori context for the study including the theoretical base, and including a section in any AR report about what from the study can be generalized to other settings. They also suggest gathering at least some quantitative data because "a primarily positivist audience is generally looking for some numbers" (p. 20). The advice and suggestions of DeLuca and Kock are interesting, but they are essentially an effort to get those who conduct AR from an interpretive perspective to modify their approach so that it is more acceptable to positivist readers. Many interpretive action researchers would consider this bad advice and insist, instead, that AR be conducted from an interpretive perspective. Interpretivists also suggest that, when researchers write up their work for publication, they should make an extra effort to justify and explain their approach because some readers (and some journal reviewers) may not be familiar with the

approach and the differences in foundational assumptions that characterize interpretive AR. That is the advice we would give as well.

Foundational assumptions were the focus of a paper by Cassell and Johnson (2006). The authors began their paper with the comment that "For
nearly 70 years scholars have been discussing the characteristics of action
research and it is apparent that there is an increasingly wide range of forms
that action research takes in practice" (p. 783). The bulk of their paper
is an exploration of the relationship between the "different philosophical
stances, which usually remain tacit in published accounts thereby fueling
ambiguity and controversy about what action research should entail in
practice and as to its 'scientific' status" (p. 783). These authors contend
the diversity that typifies action research today is due in no small part to the
use of different philosophical foundations. For example, positivist action
researchers tend to view the task of AR as completing cycles of "deductive
causal analysis: a process of hypothesis building, testing and modification
within organizational contexts so as to solve problems with reference to
clearly defined goals and observable outcomes" (p. 784). This they refer
to as the positive preference for *erklaren* (causal explanation). It contrasts
with interpretive action researchers' preference for *verstehen* (interpretive
understanding), which is more a search for local understanding than it is
the discovery of universal truths that dominates the positivist tradition. The
use of one of these two epistemological perspectives (instead of the other)
as a foundation for designing an AR model has a huge impact on the resulting model. A positivist AR model seeking *erklaren* will look very different
from an interpretive AR model seeking *verstehen*. The two epistemologies
also have implications for how the AR team interacts, who decides what the
implications of the research results are, and how changes and revisions are
made as an AR project progresses from one cycle to the next.

Positivism and interpretive theory support different types of AR because
their assumptions on several fundamental issues are different (Willis, 2007).
Table 2.1 summarizes some of those differences.

The differences in foundational assumptions lead to major differences
between interpretive AR models and positivist AR models. Many of the differences in procedures and practices involve greater involvement and participation on the part of stakeholders, and a preference for developing the "solution" through discussion and reflection within the participating group rather
than starting with a solution experts have already selected. Interpretive AR
thus involves more deliberative interaction within the group conducting the
action research. Interpretive AR is much more of a collaborative activity based
on the assumption that all participants have something to contribute to the
discussion, and that a collaboratively developed solution is likely to be better
than one developed by a one or a few people, even if they are "experts." This
difference is in part based on the interpretive theorists' doubts about our

TABLE 2.1 Differences in Foundational Assumptions Between Positivism and Interpretive Theory

Issue	Positivist Perspective	Interpretive Perspective
The nature of reality	*Naïve reality*—humans can come to know what reality is through observation and experimentation. Universal knowledge is highly valued.	*Socially constructed reality*—humans construct their versions of reality through social interaction and communication. Universal knowledge is not possible because history and context influence knowing. Local, contextual knowledge is sought and valued.
The purposes for doing research	Solve problems in ways that are generalizable to other settings Discover universal knowledge and apply that knowledge to practice	Construct local knowledge and develop solutions to local problems
Preferred ways of knowing	Systematic, controlled, and objective experimentation and assessment of objectively defined and measured outcomes	Subjective knowing is the only possibility. Humans cannot be objective; they are always influenced by prior experience, perceptions, and beliefs. Many ways of knowing are accepted, with an emphasis on the social nature of knowledge construction
Relationship of research to practice	Tends to favor the researcher as an expert with the practitioner playing a secondary and follower role	Tends to favor broad participation of stakeholders in the research process because they have extensive local knowledge. The role of researcher and practitioner is blurred, often the distinctions are completely erased.

ability to find generalizable truths. Like Lewin (1946), Flyvbjerg (2001), and many other interpretivists, question the ability of the social sciences to uncover laws of human behavior that apply across many settings and circumstances. Instead, interpretive theorists believe our understanding of the world is often local and contextual. Thus, involving knowledgeable people from the local context of a particular AR project is important because that local knowledge helps the group develop good solutions to local problems.

Grundy (1982) described this type of AR as "practical action research" that "seeks to improve practice through the application of the personal wisdom of participants" (p. 33). Stringer's (2007) model of action research is one of the more popular interpretive AR models practiced today and it will be explored in Chapter 3. Here, the interpretive AR models of Swedish action researchers Johansson and Lindhult (2008) and the interpretive perspective of Manfra (2009) at North Carolina State University will complete the overview of interpretive AR. Johansson and Lindhult's paper is a discussion of whether the goal of emancipation is more or less appropriate for AR than the goal of "workability." Emancipation is the focus of critical AR while the authors propose "workability" as the goal of "pragmatic scientific" action research. Manfra's paper is similar in that it explores "the theoretical divide between practical and critical approaches" to AR.

Manfra's practical action research is similar to the concept of interpretive action research as presented here. Her contrasting approach is critical action research. She identifies many differences between the two approaches (see Table 2.2).

Interpretive AR tends to emphasize reflection and practical research conducted by professionals such as teachers who are interested in solving a local problem of practice. That local problem may also be a regional, national, or even worldwide problem, but a particular AR project will often focus on getting local results. Interpretive action researchers generally emphasize the stakeholders who are impacted by the problem and by any effort to deal with it. Interpretive AR often also tries to "empower" professionals such as teachers by helping them develop stronger and more powerful ways of dealing with the problems of practice. They do not, however, routinely focus exclusively on emancipatory goals, which are often the focus of critical AR.

TABLE 2.2 Differences Between Practical (Interpretive) and Critical Approaches to AR, According to Megan Mcglinn Manfra (2009)

Issue	Practical AR Position	Critical AR Position
Area of Action	Focus on solving problems in the setting where the participants work or live	Broader focus on practice that includes the social, political and cultural contexts that impact both practice and the striving for equity
National Origins	Developed and matured more in the United States	Developed and matured more in the UK and Australia
Focus	Empowering practitioners by helping them become researchers in their setting and to learn and change through collaboration with other participants	Emancipation of both practitioners and the disempowered. The goal is freedom from oppression and control, and the creation of a more democratic and equitable society
Type of Knowledge Sought	Practical or craft knowledge, including conceptual and theoretical understanding, that emerges from research and reflection in the local context	Understanding of local instances of universal conditions such as oppression and control, and ways to support emancipation in the local context
Typical Participants	Professionals such as teachers seeking to develop their skills and expertise, and to solve local problems of professional practice	Ethnic and racial minorities, women, and members of any disenfranchised, disempowered, or oppressed group, including professionals such as teachers, social workers, and the working poor

AR FROM A CRITICAL PERSPECTIVE

Critical action researchers do not seem to have difficulty describing what they do. They also seem to be comfortable explaining why their type of AR is superior to the models interpretive and positivist researchers use. For example, Oliver (1992) treated both interpretive and positive forms of social science research as inferior to research based on critical theory. He criticized positivist research as being too dependent on experts who both set the agenda of research and develop the implications for practice without much involvement on the part of those who are the target of study. In his field, disability research, he asserted that "research should not be seen as a set of technical, objective procedures carried out by experts" (p. 102). He criticized interpretive research as moving in the right direction but not going far enough. Specifically, he felt interpretive researchers did not typically make the subjects of research full partners and decision makers in the research enterprise—something he thought was essential. Further, like many critical researchers, he believed that both positivist and interpretive researchers tend to focus on technical solutions for day-to-day problems of practice and to ignore the need for radical reformations of cultures, organizations, and individual perspectives. Critical theorists often refer to this as "emancipation" and to research with this goal as "emancipatory research." This is, perhaps, the most important and most contested concept that is espoused by critical AR proponents, and it will be discussed in some detail in this section.

Oliver called both positivist and interpretive research "fundamentally flawed," and said it was "the product of a society which has a positivistic consciousness and a hierarchical social structure which accords experts an elite role" (p. 102). That is a view Oliver shares with many, if not the vast majority, of critical action researchers.

Despite the central role emancipation plays in critical action research, describing how critical theory influences the practice of AR is more difficult than explaining how positivism or interpretive theory impact AR. That is because both positivism and interpretive theory are at their base, epistemologies. That is, they address the philosophical question of how we can learn about the world we live in (ways of knowing). Both are complex, convoluted, and not always consistent from one part of the paradigm to another, but their core assumptions are mostly about how we can come to know something. Positivism favors controlled experimentation and the scientific method, which emphasizes objectivity, quantitative data, the search for generalizable truths, and the evaluation of predetermined hypotheses through testing the implications of theories.

An easy way to describe interpretive theory might be to take everything said in the previous sentence about positivism, and reverse it. Interpretive researchers accept many methods of research and often rely on qualitative rather than quantitative data. They typically seek local knowledge rather than universal truths, and interpretive research often begins with no hypotheses, null or otherwise. Instead, the research journey is often guided by questions and the hope that the result of the research will be a better understanding of those questions. In addition, interpretive research often begins without a guiding theory and may not even try to develop one at the end that others can apply in their own setting. Instead, the reader is given most of the responsibility to decide what he or she can generalize from the local knowledge developed in the interpretive research study.

Critical theory is not so easily categorized and compared to positivism and interpretive frameworks. In fact, it sometimes combines aspects of both, but in unique ways that reflect critical theory's assumptions about the social, economic, and political world we live in. Critical theory is not so much an epistemology as it is an ideology. It takes the position that human societies are rife with power struggles that generally result in some groups gaining power and some groups losing power. This leads to oppression. Traditional Marxist theory considered control of the means of production to be the seat of power, and thus framed the power struggles in human societies as capitalist versus worker. Modern versions of this theory are no longer focused solely on the struggle between capitalists and workers for control of the economic and social systems of a country. Control of channels of communication, of education, of health care, and of legal and political structures are a few of many types of power struggles that are the focus of critical theory research today. It is thus the purposes of critical theory that are different, rather than the methodologies of research. AR based on critical theory may well use the same methods of research as interpretive or positivist action research, but critical theorists will have different purposes for doing AR and they are very likely to interpret the results of their AR quite differently. Critical research tends to look for the oppression, disempowerment, and inequality in local contexts, and then to develop ways of redressing those inequities. Often, this first goal of critical AR—learning about oppression in a particular context—also includes "raising critical consciousness," which means it is important to help participants become aware of how society has disenfranchised and disempowered them. Once that goal has been accomplished, the second goal of critical AR is often designing and implementing plans that eliminate or reduce oppression, help build a more democratic society, and move us toward a more equitable and fair culture. This description of critical research may remind you of Lewin's original 1946 paper on action research where he talked about the need to develop ways of dealing with the racism and prejudice in American society. Modern AR based on critical theory is probably the closest, in terms of goals, to Lewin's original vision for AR. He saw possibilities for AR to help us deal with many types of problems in organizations and society, but his interests were often focused on the same issues that contemporary critical theorists emphasize.[1] The implication that Lewin focused on business and industrial applications of AR is not quite true. He was interested in those fields but he was also interested in the areas that are commonly studied by critical AR today.

One term that is used almost exclusively to describe AR based on critical theory is emancipation. That term encompasses the goals of raising critical consciousness in both individuals and groups, as well as implementing actions that empower the oppressed. The ultimate goal of critical action research is emancipation. "Emancipatory action research must not be seen as an optional extra, but an integral component of any approach to participatory practice, offering an evolving dynamic between theory, policy and practice in an engagement with the ever-changing political context of our lives. It is an ongoing process of generating knowledge in action, going deeper into knowing in order to act more relevantly.... Emancipatory action research offers us the scope to develop a more critical praxis, a form of practice that is symbiotically creating knowledge in action and action as knowledge.... In this way, different ways of knowing that have been effectively silenced in the positivist search for one truth are given voice" (Ledwith & Springett, 2009, p. 199).

The term Emancipatory Action Research is often used to indicate AR based on critical theory. Other terms used to describe critical AR include empowerment and participatory action research. However, all these terms refer, more or less, to the emancipatory focus that is a core concern of critical AR. Boog's 2003 paper takes the position that emancipatory goals have been there from the beginning of AR, and will continue to be at the heart of what it means to do action research.

Boog even defines three types of emancipation. The first involves participants becoming more competent in "the local situation" (p. 246). A second, and related, type involves "general enhanced action competencies" that may be used "in other comparable problematic situations in the future, sometimes even in broader contexts" (p. 242). A third type of emancipation involves "aims to enhance the theory and methodology of action research as a distinct social science approach, as well as the professional skills of action researchers" (p. 427). Taken together, Boog's three types of emancipation are all involved in efforts "to achieve freedom from the power exercised by the dominant groups and classes, and to obtain the power to be free to exert influence and give direction to one's own life" (p. 428).

Boog also ties three popular critical concepts together in his vision of critical action research: emancipation, empowerment, and participatory democracy. He often uses emancipation to mean freedom from unjust external restraints. Empowerment is a complimentary term Boog sometimes uses to refer to changes in the mental perspective, understanding, or view-point of individuals (and groups) that lead to and support emancipation. In that sense, empowerment is similar to the term "critical consciousness raising" that was mentioned earlier. The third term, participatory democracy, is the method Boog and many other critical theorists believe is essential to the creation of a more equitable society.

> The concepts of emancipation and empowerment are closely connected with the concept of participatory democracy. The values of equal rights, social justice, and solidarity with the socially deprived can only be realized within a community that is organized along the principles of participatory democracy. Participatory here means communication and participation in decision-making. Participatory democracy is not only seen as a goal inherent to emancipation or empowerment, but must also be experienced in the practice of action research: in the relationship between researcher and researched subjects. Thus learning by reflection and self-research in small 'direct democratic' groups...became one of the core activities of action research. (p. 428)

Because many critical theorists consider the democratic participation of participants in the entire process to be an essential element of AR, the term participatory action research is often used by critical researchers who practice AR to describe what they do. This insistence on broad and equitable participation is crucial to critical theorists because of their view of how change must be facilitated in social systems. However, when the term participatory action research is used by either positivist action researchers or interpretive action researchers, the meaning may be quite different. It may, for example, mean that some stakeholders from the setting where the action research project occurred were involved to one degree or another. It does not necessarily mean full and equal participation on the part of all the major stakeholders. It is, therefore, very important to determine exactly what someone means when they say the model of AR they used was Participatory Action Research (PAR).

Emancipation, empowerment, and participatory processes are all crucial elements of critical AR, but another difference between AR based on the three paradigms is purpose. The three paradigms used to guide AR typically encourage researchers to select different types of goals.

Positivist AR tends to be narrowly focused on a specific, well defined problem of practice that is amenable to what might be called a "technical" solution. This type of purpose is a direct result of the positivist epistemology, which tends to view all problems as well defined (if they are not, it means you need to do a better job of defining the problem) and all effective solutions as needing to be well defined, specific, and technical so they can be exported to other settings without any confusion. In his many books on reflective practice, Schön (1995) often criticized this approach, which he called "technical-rational." His famous statement about the high hard ground and the swamp succinctly and vividly expresses his opposition to technical-rationalism:

> In the varied topography of professional practice, there is a high, hard ground overlooking the swamp. On the high ground, manageable problems lend themselves to solution through the use of research-based theory and technique. In the swampy lowlands, problems are messy and confusing and incapable of technical solution. The irony of this situation is that the problems of the high ground tend to be relatively unimportant... however great their technical interest may be, while in the swamp lie the problems of greatest human concern. (Schön , 1983, p. 42)

Schön's model for strong professional practice, which is typically referred to as "reflective practice," rejected three assumptions of positivism—that all problems can be well-defined, that all problems have a universal solution, and that the local and professional knowledge of the practitioner is subservient to the knowledge developed through formal, objective research. Schön's approach, and the work of Argyris (1995) on "action science," have both become part of many contemporary models of AR based on both interpretive and critical foundations.

For slightly different reasons, both interpretive and critical AR emphasize the importance of reflective practice as a core concept of AR. Interpretive action researchers see reflection as important because participants develop and refine critical local knowledge through the processes of reflection and discourse with other participants. Critical action researchers emphasize reflection because it is a way for individuals and groups to develop the critical consciousness that will be the foundation for creating and acting on plans for emancipation.

Another concept shared by interpretive and critical theorists is participation. Both types of theorists emphasize the need for people to work in groups to bring about change. Interpretive researchers emphasize participation because they are constructivists who view the creation of knowledge as a group activity. Critical theorists emphasize it because the goal of emancipation is best accomplished by groups working together rather than by individuals working alone.

Any effort to identify the heart and soul of critical AR would probably focus on the emancipatory goals that are the justification of why anyone would do critical AR. The emancipatory goals are a reflection of the assumptions of critical theory about human cultures, and they are the reason why much critical AR is participatory; you cannot impose emancipation on individuals—the best you can do is help them on their journey towards emancipation. In this, critical AR shares the values of critical pedagogy and the methods of the international pioneer in emancipatory approaches,

Paulo Freire, the author of *Pedagogy of the Oppressed* (1970), *Pedagogy of Hope* (2004), and *Education for Critical Consciousness* (2005).

SUMMARY

There are many types of AR, but quite a few of the differences between them are due to differences in the foundational paradigms that guide the development and practice of the different types of AR. Thus, the tremendous variety in AR practices generally comes from the assumptions and values expressed in the three most commonly used foundational paradigms—positivism, interpretive theory, and critical theory. Each of these three foundations have experienced periods of dominance in the history of AR development. In the 1940s, Lewin's original version of AR owed much to what became critical theory (though aspects of his AR model have been described as positivist by some scholars). We agree with Boog (2003) who reviewed the historical development of AR and began with the comment that "the historical development of action research reveals that it had emancipatory intentions from the very beginning, and that this basis has become increasingly sophisticated with the refinement of action research into different approaches" (p. 426).

In the 1950s and early 60s, the conservative and authoritarian tone of American national life, along with widespread acceptance of the scientific method as the major if not sole source of new knowledge, encouraged positivist visions of AR. Then, in the last quarter of the twentieth century, interpretive epistemologies began to compete with positivism as the preferred foundation for research in the social sciences. The era of the paradigm wars generally pitted forms of established positivism against emerging versions of interpretive theory. In that context, many models of AR emerged that were more flexible, more focused on constructing local knowledge and testing local solutions, and less interested in developing and testing universal facts (theories) or universal solutions.

Today, with more than a decade of the twenty-first century behind us, action research has become a very popular way of addressing problems of professional practice as well as a common methodology for dissertations in applied doctoral programs created for practicing professionals rather than for students seeking careers as researchers. The three paradigms—positivism, interpretive theory, and critical theory—continue to influence the development of AR models and the procedures for practicing AR. However, the balance of power between these three foundations is different today. While various forms of positivism still dominate many mainstream segments of applied and basic social science research, the graphical representation of trends (which is the subjective judgment of the authors) in

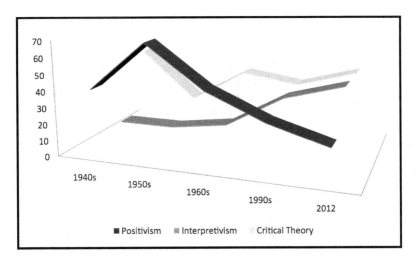

Figure 2.2 The influence of the three widely adopted paradigms on AR from the 1940s to 2012.

Figure 2.2 of paradigm influence depicts positivism as losing influence. Except for the spike during the 50s with McCarthyism, positivism's influence on AR has decreased over the past 70 years. On the other hand, the influence of critical theory was initially strong, dipped in the 50s and has since steadily risen. In contrast, interpretive theory was not very influential in the 1940s but has steadily increased in influence in the intervening years. Today, interpretive and critical theory are the dominant paradigms in the field of action research, while positivism retains some influence. Had the graphic represented our impression of the impact of these three paradigms on the broad mainstream of social science research, the position of positivism would have been much stronger. It was strong in the 40s, and while it no longer has a hegemonic dominance in the social sciences, it remains the strongest influence on social science research. And, as noted in this chapter, the continuing strength of positivism means that writing about AR sometimes calls for more explanation and more justification because some aspects of AR go against the historically dominant positivist model of what constitutes "good" research.

    In the next chapter, the question of just what the term AR means will be explored in more detail. Chapter 3 also presents two additional models of AR in some detail. They will complement Lewin's original model that was explored in this chapter. One of the models of AR explored in Chapter 3 is an interpretive model of AR and the other is a recently revised model based on critical theory.

NOTE

1. Lewin's contribution to critical AR is sometimes missed in papers about the history of AR. For example, Manfra (2009) described the origin of AR this way: "Action research originated from industrialist Kurt Lewin's work about 'how participation in decision making could lead to enhanced productivity' (McNiff & Whitehead, 2002), p. 40). While Lewin's original model applied to factories, its core premises appealed to educators."

REFERENCES

Argyris, C. (1995). Action science and organizational learning. *Journal of Managerial Psychology, 10*(6), 20–26.

Blaikie, N. (2007). *Approaches to social inquiry: Advancing knowledge* (2nd ed.). Cambridge, UK: Polity Press.

Boog, B. (2003). The emancipator character of action research, its history and the present state of the art. *Journal of Community and Applied Social Psychology, 13,* 426–438).

Brydon-Miller, M., Kral, M., Maguire, P., Noffke, S., & Sabhlok, A. (2011). Jazz and the banyan tree: Roots and riffs on participatory action research. In N. Denzin & Y. Lincoln (Eds.), *Sage Handbook of Qualitative Research* (4th ed., pp. 387–399). Thousand Oaks, CA: Sage.

Cassell, C., & Johnson, P. (2006). Action research: Explaining the diversity. *Human Relations, 59*(6), 783–814.

Carr, W., & Kemmis, S. (1986). *Becoming critical: Education, knowledge, and action research.* London: Falmer Press.

DeLuca, D., & Kock, N. (2007). Publishing Information Systems: Action research for a positivist audience. *Communications of the AIS, 19*(10), 1–30.

Denzin, N., & Lincoln, Y. (Eds.). (2011). *Sage Handbook of Qualitative Research* (4th ed.). Thousand Oaks, CA: Sage.

Denzin, N., & Lincoln, Y. (Eds.) (1993). *Handbook of qualitative research.* Thousand Oaks, CA: Sage.

Flyvbjerg, B. (2001). *Making social sciences matter: Why social science fails and how it can succeed again.* Cambridge, UK: Cambridge University Press.

Freire, P. (2005). *Education for critical consciousness.* New York: Continuum.

Freire, P. (2004). *Pedagogy of hope.* New York: Continuum.

Freire, P. (1970). *Pedagogy of the oppressed.* New York: Continuum.

Grundy, D. (1995). Knowing-in-action: The new scholarship requires a new epistemology. *Change, 27,* 26–34.

Grundy, S. (1987). *Curriculum: Product or Praxis* London: The Falmer Press

Habermas, J. (1972). *Knowledge and human interest.* London: Heinemann.

Hult, M., & Lennung, S. (1980). Towards a definition of action research: A note and bibliography. *Journal of Management Studies, 17*(2), 241–250.

Johansson, A. W., & Lindhult, E. (2008). Emancipation or workability? Critical versus pragmatic scientific orientation in action research. *Action Research. 6,* 95–115.

Kock, N. N, McQueen, R., & Scott, J. (1997). Can action research be made more rigorous in a positivist sense? The contribution of an iterative approach. *Journal of Systems and Information Technology, 1*(1), 1–23.

Ledwith, M., & Springett, J. (2009). *Participatory practice: Community-based action for transformative change.* Bristol, UK: The Policy Press, University of Bristol.

Lewin, K. (1946). Action research and minority problems. *Journal of Social Issues, 2*(4), 34–46.

Manfra, M. M. (2009). The middle ground in action research: Integrating practical and critical inquiry. *Journal of Curriculum & Instruction, 3*(1), 32–46.

Masters, J. (1995). The history of action research. In I. Hughes (Ed), *Action research electronic reader.* Sydney, Australia: The University of Sydney. Available: http://www.behs.ccs.usyd.edu/au/arrow/Reader/rmasters.htm)

McNiff, J., & Whitehead, J. (2002) *Action research: Principles and practice* (2nd. ed.) London: RoutledgeFalmer.

Oliver, M. (1992). Changing the social relations of social disability. *Disability, Handicap & Society, 7*(2), 101–115.

Passmore, W. (2001). Action research in the workplace: The socio-technical perspective. In P. Reason & H. Bradbury (Eds.), Handbook of action research: Participative inquiry and practice (pp. 38–47). Thousand Oaks, CA: Sage.

Phillips, D. C., & Barbules, N. (2000). *Postpositivism and educational research.* Lanham, MD: Rowman and Littlefield.

Schön, D. (1983). *The reflective practitioner: How professionals think in action.* New York: Basic Books.

Schön, D. (1995). The reflective practitioner. Burlington, VT: Ashgate Publishing.

Stringer, E. (2007). *Action research* (3rd ed.). Thousand Oaks, CA: Sage.

Susman, G., & Evred, R. (1978). An assessment of the scientific merits of action research. *Administrative Science Quarterly, 23*(4), 582–603.

Willis, J. (2007). *Foundations of qualitative research: Interpretive and critical approaches.* Thousand Oaks, CA: Sage.

CHAPTER 3

VARIETIES OF ACTION RESEARCH

Jerry Willis and Claudia L. Edwards
St. John Fisher College

ABSTRACT

In this chapter fourteen "family resemblances" of action research are presented along with a discussion of how these resemblances are valued by action research models based on three different theoretical perspectives: positivism, interpretive theory, and critical theory.

Chapter 1 provided some basic information and perspectives about the historical and contemporary context in which action research operates. Chapter 2 continued the search for historical context and also focused on the major theoretical foundations for AR. As illustrated in those chapters, the history of AR has been unstable and marked by major, sometimes sudden, changes in purpose, procedure, and process. This introductory chapter will focus more on the current context—what is happening now in the field of action research and the common characteristics of AR. The final introductory chapter will explore the options and alternatives that are still being

Action Research, pages 45–84
Copyright © 2014 by Information Age Publishing
45

debated and discussed. We will start with an exploration of a basic question: what do most forms of AR have in common?

THE FAMILY RESEMBLANCES OF AR

In his reinterpretation of how humans develop meaning, the philosopher Ludwig Wittgenstein proposed that we do not define meaning by referring to concrete, fixed definitions such as those found in the dictionary. Instead, we construct meaning by looking for family resemblances. For example, we decide whether something is action research or not based on whether the activity in question shares some family resemblances with other members of the action research family. This is an interpretive way of developing meaning that is quite different from a positivist approach. Positivists might come up with a set of criteria that must be met if the activity in question is to be called action research, and they might also have a list of characteristics that would prohibit calling something action research (such as conducting the research in a laboratory setting instead of in the field). We prefer the broader and more flexible approach of Wittgenstein's family resemblance theory of meaning. This section will present a set of "family resemblances" that, while not exhibited in every instance of action research, tend to be more commonly found in action research than in other forms of research. However, as you will see in Figure 3.1 and in the discussion that follows, some of the family resemblances are more

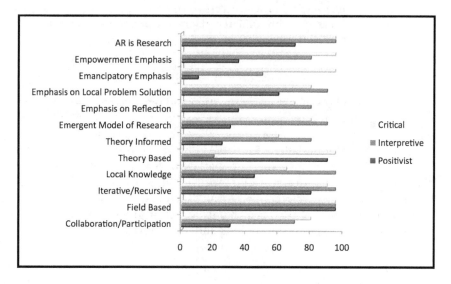

Figure 3.1 Family resemblances of AR and the emphasis each of the major theoretical foundations puts on each of them.

characteristic of AR based on one or the other of the three commonly used paradigmatic foundations. Despite that, we have tried to emphasize those family characteristics that are shared across the entire family of research models called action research.

Family Characteristics Emphasized in All Three Types of AR

Field Based
AR is research
Emphasis on local problem solution
Iterative/Recursive

Figure 3.1 depicts the relative emphasis positivist, interpretive, and critical AR puts on ten different family characteristics. The scale of 0 to 100 is subjective and for comparative purposes only. A rating near 0 indicates virtually no interest or emphasis on that family characteristic in models of AR based on the particular paradigm. A score near 100 indicates that particular type of AR puts a high emphasis on the characteristic, and action researchers from that family might not even consider a study to be action research if it does not have that characteristic. For example, all three types of AR put a very high emphasis on doing research in the field. Regardless of the theoretical foundation used, AR is conducted in the field where the problem or issue exists. AR does not simplify and control the study by conducting research in a controlled environment such as a laboratory. The bars for the "field based" characteristic are high for AR based on positivist, interpretive, and critical foundations.

A second family characteristic valued by all three theoretical strands of AR is the proposition that AR is research. Both critical and interpretive strands have taken the position that AR is a very desirable and useful form of field-based, applied research that is generally conducted by stakeholder groups that have a significant investment in the outcome of the research. Positivist AR, on the other hand, still struggles for acceptance even from other positivists, and most of the literature written which says that this or that form of AR is not "really" research is written by positivists. Nevertheless, positivists who advocate AR (in the positivist tradition) still make a case for research in the field and propose AR as one highly desirable form of applied research.

A third family characteristic that is valued by all three theoretical strands of AR is the emphasis on local problem solution. However, there are differences across the three theories. Interpretive AR puts the highest emphasis on local problem solution because it rejects the search for laws of human behavior or generalizable truths that many positivists insist should be an additional goal of AR. Stringer's (2007) view is typical of intepretivists who tend to be very skeptical about universal solutions advocated by experts. They prefer, instead, locally developed solutions based on the local knowledge and experience of participants:

> Long-term, entrenched problems frequently defy the remedial efforts of professional practitioners.... They exist as part of a complex system of interwoven events and circumstances that are deeply embedded in the social fabric of the community.
>
> ...
>
> Quick-fix, "spray on" solutions rarely work. (Stringer, 2007, p. 112)

> Complex or highly abstract theories, when applied to small, localized issues, are likely to drain people's energy and inhibit action. Explanations and interpretations produced in action research processes should be framed in terms that participants use in their everyday lives, rather than in terms derived from the academic disciplines or professional practices.

> Restricted or cursory analyses that produce superficial solutions to deep-seated and complex problems are unlikely to be effective. (Stringer, 2007, p. 97)

> Too often we have come to accept the impersonal, mechanistic, and allegedly objective procedures common to many contexts as a necessary evil. We endure hierarchical and authoritarian modes of organization and control despite the sense of frustration, powerlessness, and stress frequently felt by practitioners, client groups, students, or others affected by underlying issues in the situation.

> Professional practitioners often feel compelled to implement programs and services according to formally sanctioned practices and procedures, despite their ineffectiveness in achieving the goals they were designed to accomplish. (Stringer, 2007, p. 22)

> This research stance [interpretive AR] acknowledges the limitations of the knowledge and understanding of the "expert" researcher and takes account of the experience and understanding of those who are centrally involved in the issues explored—the stakeholders. (Stringer, 2007, p. 20)

> Action research... is based on the proposition that generalized solutions may not fit particular contexts or groups of people and that the purpose of inquiry is to find an appropriate solution for the particular dynamics at work in a local situation.... Generalized solutions must be modified and adapted in order to fit the context in which they are used. (Stringer, 2007, p. 5)

The emphasis on local problem solution is not as strong in critical AR because the broader and more encompassing goal of emancipation is always there as an imperative for critical action researchers. Critical researchers reject as inappropriate the focus on technical solutions sought by positivists as well as what they see as the narrow local goals of interpretive action researchers. Critical AR sees the local issues that are most important to them as examples of the oppression and disenfranchisement that is endemic in the culture. Critical AR, even when it is working on a "local" problem, is working on broad, national, and even global problems. Similarly, positivist AR, because it is based on the belief that generalizable solutions can be discovered and then transferred to other settings, does not put as much emphasis on local knowledge and understanding as interpretive AR. Positivists still hold to the belief that careful research will yield solutions and knowledge that is broadly applicable and useful as well as locally applicable.

It is also important, however, to note that even interpretive AR does not receive a 100 for emphasis on solving local problems. One reason is that there is considerable emphasis on developing the capabilities of participants to deal with new problems and issues after a particular AR project ends. Interpretive AR shares with critical AR a concern for helping the participants become stronger and more effective at dealing with a range of issues and problems, not just the specific "presenting problem" that is the beginning of an AR project. Interpretive action researchers often use the term *empowerment* to talk about this aspect of AR, while critical action researchers often use the term *emancipation.* Such goals go beyond simply solving the problem in front of us, and there are typically additional reasons for doing interpretive or critical AR even when the main focus is on solving a particular local problem.

The last characteristic emphasized by all three theoretical strands of AR is iteration. This is sometimes called recursion, but the basic idea is the same. Almost all AR models are a series of cycles. The AR team uses a single cycle to study the problem, develop and implement a solution, and evaluate that solution. AR is iterative because the method does not anticipate that an effective solution to a significant issue or problem will be found, developed, tested, and celebrated within a single cycle. Solving any significant problem will probably take a number of cycles, each based on the results of the previous cycle. Interpretive AR tends to emphasize iteration more than either of the alternatives, in part because it assumes that even if a general and already developed solution is adopted, it will need to be customized and adapted for that particular local context. Critical AR also emphasizes iteration but perhaps with slightly less vigor because the solutions used in a particular local context are often adaptations of solutions that have already been developed and used in many other places. The local adaptations of critical action researchers tend to be less comprehensive than those of interpretive action researchers. That is because interpretive AR puts the most emphasis on participants developing solutions and evaluating them, and that emphasis tends to encourage several iterative cycles in an AR project. Positivist AR tends to be the least iterative because it is more likely to select a well-defined general solution and apply it in the local context with fewer revisions and adaptations.

Family Characteristics Emphasized by Interpretive AR

Empowerment Emphasis
Emphasis on Reflection
Emergent Model of Research
Local Knowledge
Theory Informed
Collaboration Emphasis

There are several characteristics that interpretive AR highly values. One of them is empowerment, which is not easy to distinguish from emancipation, the ultimate goal of critical AR. When used by interpretive action researchers, empowerment often means that someone has developed better life or professional skills. They have learned basic skills such as how to study, how to plan a budget, or how to communicate more effectively in groups. Empowerment often emphasizes a change in the perceptions of an individual about her or his ability to handle the demands of personal or work life. Empowerment does not necessarily, however, mean the individual has adopted a new ideological base. For example, a teacher who develops better skills for teaching literacy skills to students in a particular school is professionally empowered. On the other hand, a teacher who becomes critically conscious of how the culture of her Hispanic students is ignored in the literature courses she teaches is emancipated when she understands that and adds classic and contemporary Hispanic literature to the reading list for her course. And, at the same time, she is using critical pedagogy that contributes to the empowerment and emancipation of her Hispanic students.

Interpretive AR tends to put more emphasis on what we have referred to as empowerment, while critical AR emphasizes ideological change, which is part of emancipation. In contrast, positivist AR rarely emphasizes emancipation and does not put a great deal of emphasis on individual empowerment. Positivist AR virtually never has a goal of emancipation.

A second family characteristic particularly emphasized by interpretive action researchers is reflection. As Stringer (2007) put it, "action research envisages processes of inquiry that are based on a practitioner's reflections on his or her professional practices" (p. xv). More than any other form of AR, interpretive AR has incorporated the ideas of Donald Schön (1995a, b), who developed the concept of reflective practice. The central idea of reflection is that thoughtful reflection on day-to-day practice can lead to insights and perspectives that become the foundation for improvement in professional practice. The goal, improvement in professional practice, is much more important to interpretive action researchers than to positive or critical action researchers. One reason is that they share with Schön a deep suspicion of general solutions and doubts about the idea that good professional practice involves "correctly" applying those solutions in your professional practice. They reject this technical-rational model and propose that effective solutions must be constructed to fit the local context and history. The participants of interpretive AR projects are often professionals—teachers, managers, nurses, social workers—and the focus of the project is typically the improvement of the professional practice of those participants. In positivist AR, the critical connection is between a well-defined problem and a well-defined solution. Reflection on the part of participants is not as important. What is important is correct application of the solution. In critical AR, reflection can be very important but it often plays a different role; it is part of the development of a critical consciousness that helps participants better understand the hidden oppression in their work, home, or community environments.

A third difference between interpretive AR and other forms is acceptance of an emergent model of research. In this context, the term emergent means that all aspects of the AR project are subject to change. Action research is:

> a living, emergent process that cannot be predetermined but changes and develops as those engaged deepen their understanding of the issues to be addressed and develop their capacity as co-enquirers both individually and collectively. (Reason & Bradbury, 2008, p. 4)

> It is our experience that no matter how well we prepare ourselves, we can never know what will emerge in the process. To us action research is about giving up the power of knowing in advance, albeit resting on many years of scholarship, inquiry and engagement with the questions of organization change, and instead being prepared to meet what is unexpected. . . . Originally, we understood this as our naiveté, now we call it "productive not-knowing." We consider this to be a central part of emergent, mutual involvement more in line with a dialogic tendency within organizational development than with a strategic or instrumental one. (Johns, 2008, p. 465)

> It is more important to respond to the real and emergent needs of participants than it is to implement a pre-determined design, no matter how good. (Mead, 2008, p. 641)

Positivist AR tends to focus on intensive planning and then on following that planning rather strictly as different aspects of the AR cycle are implemented. Change will come between the cycles when the data analysis tells participants what worked and what did not. The next cycle then begins with a revision of the intervention to make it more effective. This formal and structured approach is not required in interpretive AR projects. In fact, interpretive action researchers may even see them as inhibiting innovation and creativity. In an interpretive AR project, the subjective experiences and perceptions of the participatory team may lead to immediate changes in the project. This can be as simple as a small change in the way the solution is being implemented, or as comprehensive as total abandonment of that solution and the development of another. This flexible, emergent, on-the-fly method of doing AR would be anathema to many positivist action researchers and at the same time standard practice for many interpretive action researchers. Critical researchers are not as structured as positivists, but they are devoted to a particular ideology and thus are not as comfortable making changes on the fly, especially if the changes seem to contradict the foundational ideology of critical AR. Nevertheless, critical AR can involve considerable flexibility and adaptability as the team works toward developing ways of dealing with problems they have identified.

Another important difference between interpretive AR and other forms is the focus on local knowledge. Local knowledge has a privileged position because the constructivist epistemology of interpretive AR rejects the idea that robust, generalizable truths are routinely available in social science research. Individuals "construct" their knowledge and their truths through experience, interaction, and communication with other group members and stakeholders. Interpretive AR uses a number of procedures to encourage members of different stakeholder groups to work together and communicate with each other so that a consensus is reached. That consensus is "local truth" and it is the basis for decisions the stakeholders make in an AR project. Positivists consider "local truths" to be subjective and therefore suspect, and they believe expert-based and research-based truths are more objective and more dependable. They thus put less emphasis on local truth. Critical theorists, in contrast, have adopted an ideological framework that says the local truths uncovered in AR are an expression of universal truths defined by their ideology. This is a limit on what "local truth" can be, which is why the rating in Figure 3.1 is less for critical AR on this characteristic than it is for interpretive AR.

The next family characteristic that interpretive AR emphasizes differently is the role of theory in the AR process. Interpretive AR tends to be "theory informed," which means participants are encouraged to consider and use any theories that seem helpful. In a very real sense, a social science theory, whether it be a basic or an applied theory, is a presentation of the "truth" as seen by proponents of that theory. It is their "perspective" of the truth. Interpretive and constructive theories of truth are nonfoundational—proponents believe there is no foundation for truth or theory so solid that the truth derived cannot be questioned. Therefore, interpretive research tends to emphasize the need to consider "multiple perspectives," which is another way of saying you must consider the theories and truths of all the stakeholder groups participating in an AR project instead of determining which perspective is the correct one and using it alone. In contrast, positivist AR tends to push for the selection of one particular theory, or family of theories, to guide an AR project. And, in some ways, critical AR is even more theory based rather than theory informed because the foundational theory has already been selected when the AR project starts. However, unlike positivist AR, critical AR puts a heavy emphasis on understanding the local context and on the participation of local stakeholders in the AR process. For that reason, critical AR often leaves considerable room for participants to develop their own truths—their own theories—about what is happening in their setting.

The final family characteristic emphasized by interpretive AR is collaboration. In Figure 3.1, the characteristic is listed as collaboration/participation. Positivist AR does not put a very high emphasis on either collaboration or participatory forms of AR. Positivist AR tends to be expert-based, which means there is someone designated as the "researcher" who has a special position of power. This person is often based outside the setting where the AR project will be conducted. This approach often leads to a director/worker division of labor that involves the expert making important decisions and the other participants playing the roles of workers who implement the decision. Action research from the interpretive perspective can also involve someone who has the title of researcher. The researcher may be an outsider who works as a consultant or an insider who has special expertise or enthusiasm for the project. However, the job of the interpretive researcher is to facilitate in a way that supports a team of stakeholders that is involved heavily in every aspect of the project. A few quotes illustrate the perspective of interpretive action researchers:

There is no functional distinction between the researcher and the researched "subjects" (in conventional parlance). They are all defined as participants, and they all have equal footing in determining what questions will be asked, what information will be analyzed, and how conclusions and courses of action will be determined. These participants, sometimes called *stakeholders* or *local members,* may include some with special training in inquiry, but if so, these specialists have no privilege in determining how the study will go; *all* participants share the perquisites of privilege. I insist on this joint approach both because local stakeholders are the only extant experts on local culture, beliefs, and practices and because moral considerations require that local perspectives be honored. (Guba, 2007, p. xii)

The task of the practitioner researcher is to provide leadership and direction to other participants or stakeholders in the research process. I therefore speak...to those who coordinate or facilitate the research as *research facilita-tors*....I often shorten this to *researchers* or *facilitators*....Ultimately, however, all participants in the research process should rightfully be called *researchers*. (Stringer, 2007, p. xvi)

In many situations, the demands of professional or community life prevent practitioners from taking such an active leadership role, and these practitio-ners may call on the services of outside consultants to perform coordinating, facilitating functions. (Stringer, 2007, p. xvi)

While Stringer creates room for an outsider to provide leadership, it is not the leadership of an expert who makes major decisions that others follow. Instead, it is the leadership of a facilitator who helps stakeholders make the major decisions:

By sharing their diverse knowledge and experience—expert, professional, and lay—stakeholders can create solutions to their problems and, in the pro-cess, improve the quality of their professional life.

The role of the research facilitator, in this context, becomes more facilitative and less directive. Knowledge acquisition/production proceeds as a collective process, engaging people who have previously been the "subjects" of research in the process of defining and redefining the corpus of understanding on which their community or organizational life is based. As they collectively investigate their own situation, stakeholders build a consensual vision of their lifeworld. Community-based action research results not only in a collective vision but also in a sense of community. It operates at the intellectual level as well as the social, cultural, political, and emotional levels. (Stringer, 2007, p. 13)

The collaborative approach described by Stringer is typical of interpretive action research, and it is sometimes referred to as participatory action research because the stakeholders make the decisions about what is to be done. Critical action researchers also use the term participatory and may mean essentially the same thing as interpretive theorists. However, they can also mean that the par-ticipants are involved in the decision-making process much more intensely and with more emphasis on the ideological levels of decision making that require participants to think seriously about their place in the structure of the society and cultures in which they live. A further complication in understanding what participatory means in critical AR is that critical action research is often based on the concept of a "participatory democracy," which is like the historic town meetings of New England where everyone in the community could speak and vote. This approach to AR has a much "flatter" leadership structure.

Family Characteristics Emphasized by Critical AR

Theory Based
Emancipatory Emphasis
Participatory Emphasis

Interestingly enough, there are no family characteristics in Figure 3.1 that positivist AR emphasizes more than interpretive or critical AR. That is perhaps because of the way the family characteristics were phrased. Positivist AR does put a very low emphasis on some family characteristics that are very important to both interpretive and critical AR. The reverse is not true, however, perhaps because mainstream AR is a reaction against positivism. There is, though, one family characteristic that positivist AR shares with only one of the other two alternatives. That is the tendency to be theory based, which involves selecting a particular theory to guide decision making in AR. Positivist AR puts a heavy emphasis on positivist principles and positivist foundational assumptions about research. The influence of positivism is apparent in most aspects of positivist AR. The same is true of critical AR—theory guides much of the work in critical AR. However, the theoretical foundation for critical AR is critical theory, not positivist theory.

These two foundations—positivism and critical theory—are not the same type of foundation. Positivism is a philosophical theory that advocates certain assumptions about ontology (e.g., the material or physical world is all there is) and epistemology (e.g., systematic, objective, empirical research is the best source of new, generalizable knowledge). Positivist theory has direct implications for how social science research should be conducted. Critical theory is more of an economic or political theory than it is a framework for making decisions about research design. And, when critical theory does have something to say about research design, it is usually a criticism of positivist methods or a proposal to do research in ways that are contradictory to positivist perspectives.

A second emphasis of critical AR is not shared with positivist AR. That is emancipation. As you would expect after reading Chapter 1, the characteristic most emphasized by critical AR is the purpose of emancipation. It is so important that some authors use the term Emancipatory Action Research for critical AR. The ideological focus of critical theory on broad, deeply embedded, societal and cultural problems that involve oppression and use of power to privilege one group over another makes emancipation a core purpose for critical AR. That is also somewhat important to interpretive AR, but some interpretive practitioners believe emancipation is confrontational and combative, and therefore likely to be ineffective. Instead of the revolutionary tone and confrontational methods of some types of critical AR, they prefer, instead, to work toward solutions through collaborative and cooperative approaches that encourage dialog and interaction between groups that may have distinctively different perceptions of the local context.

> In the 1960s, change processes were often driven by campaigns in which groups achieved their objectives by engaging in overtly social and political action. Community action research is not oriented toward this social action approach. Its purposes and objectives are to formulate links with and among parties who might be seen to be in conflict and to negotiate settlements of interest that allow all stakeholders to enhance their work, community, and/ or personal life.

> When researchers engage in political processes based on polarities of interest, they are likely to engage in conflictual interactions that generate antagonism. Although the potential for short-term gains is enticing, long term enmities, in my experience, have a habit of coming back to bite you. (Stringer, 2007, p. 154)

Stringer's negative views of emancipatory methods that involve conflict with established power structures are typical of interpretive action researchers who tend to prefer collaboration, communication, and negotiation instead of confrontation and "social action." Stringer, like many interpretive theorists, does make room for confrontation, but only as a last resort after collaborative efforts have been exhausted. Interpretive researchers do not, however, object to emancipatory AR on philosophical grounds. The goal of emancipation is generally accepted; they simply do not believe that some of the methods used to achieve emancipation will work as well as the collaborative and cooperative approaches they prefer to use in AR.

A third family characteristic emphasized by critical AR is participation. The second most common term to designate critical AR is Participatory Action Research or PAR. However, as noted earlier, there can be differences in the meaning of PAR, depending on whether critical or interpretive action researchers are using it. When used by interpretive action researchers, it may reflect the constructivist emphasis on real change occurring when those most directly involved in and impacted by the change take the lead in the process. Often, interpretive action research is concerned about making the change process local, contextual, and focused on the stakeholders. "To the extent that people can participate in the process of exploring the nature and context of the problems that concern them, they have the opportunity to develop immediate and deeply relevant understandings of their situation and to be involved actively in the process of dealing with those problems" (Stringer, 2007, p. 32). Stringer contrasted this interpretive participatory approach with what he considers the more common but undesirable approach: "Today, the large and centralized social systems that are characteristic of modern societies alienate people from those who provide for their well-being and from the decisions that affect their lives" (Stringer,

207, p. 32). Participation on the part of stakeholders is thus an essential aspect of bringing change to a particular context as well as an antidote to bureaucratized, mechanized, and alienating systems that are officially supposed to serve the needs of local participants.

When used by critical theorists, the term PAR often reflects a fundamental perspective of critical theory:

> The philosophical root of PAR thinking is traceable to the philosophy of Marx and Engels calling the working class to create their own history, a vision they cannot logically realize without the "means of mental production," and not only the "means of material production," under their control.

> In recent times the concept of *conscientizaton* of Paulo Freire, also with a radical vision of social change, has inspired microlevel grassroots work with oppressed groups in many parts of the world with the aim of advancing their collective self-reflected awareness and action, independently of the formal left. Other quarters have also been working independently of allegiance to Marxism or Freirianism, to promote *conscientization* and self-development initiatives of oppressed groups guided by their own thinking, from a general social concern for promoting popular participation, grassroots self-reliance and broad-based development with a better balance in the distribution of social power and product. (Rahman, 2007, p. 49)

In summarizing this discussion of participation in AR, we should note that the distinctions drawn here between interpretive and critical forms of PAR are real, but the actual differences in day-to-day practice are rarely so sharply defined. Papers on PAR based on interpretive foundations often describe participatory activities that are remarkably similar to those described in papers based on critical theory. One way to describe the relationship between critical and interpretive AR involves paraphrasing and managing what Irish writer and critical theorist George Bernard Shaw said about America and England: Interpretive and critical AR are two approaches separated by conflicting theories but united by many common values, perspectives, goals, and methods. Perhaps in the near future someone will develop a conceptual model of AR that integrates the interpretive and critical foundations and practices of AR in a way that eliminates some of the theoretical conflicts and builds upon the professional practice knowledge that has developed over the last half century in these two traditions of AR.

A Summary of the Family Characteristics of AR

The 11 family resemblances of AR in Figure 3.1 are not all present in every instance of AR. You cannot, for example, use the resemblances as a checklist and decide that a project that has eight or more of the resemblances is

AR while those with less are not. Calling something AR is subjective, and in most cases the same project could be labeled as some other type of research, or even some other type of work such as "social action." A further complication is that AR based on different foundations puts different levels of emphasis on the 11 resemblances. Nevertheless, the family resemblances do help us understand what AR is about and how it works. In the next section some of the more popular models of AR will be explored.

MODELS OF AR

Although action research has existed at least since the late 1940s, for most of its history it has been an alternative to the regular forms of research that were routinely taught in university classes. Students often learned about "action research" after they learned the rules of doing traditional research. And, because AR tends to violate many of the rules of traditional research, students had to unlearn some of those rules before they could accept AR as a legitimate way of studying the world around them. For example, the dominant forms of action research do not focus on answering broad theoretical questions, and they do not emphasize the discovery of universal truths. Instead, action research identifies real world, practical problems or issues and tries to develop and validate solutions or answers to them.

Also, action research tends to emphasize working in the real world over meeting technical requirements for research. A well designed and executed laboratory study is not valued as highly as a messier study done in the real world. Action research methods tend to emphasize collaboration and research within the workplace, school, or community. Action researchers also tend to put what they learn to immediate use. If they are in the middle of a study of preparing platoon leaders for deployment to combat zones and they realize there are problems with the training on logistics, they do not stop the study and start again from the beginning. Instead, they make the needed changes and proceed with the study. This, like many other things about AR, violates the rules detailed in many guides to doing traditional social science research.

Still another variation from the rules of traditional research is iteration. Many action research projects go through the AR cycle several times as the group tries something out, realizes it needs improvement, makes the revisions, and then continues to evaluate the revised procedure or approach. Action research thus tends to be subjective, flexible, iterative, emergent and very context bound. The goal is to figure out how to bring about change *in a particular context*. Few, if any, of these characteristics are presented as desirable in traditional presentations of the right way to do social science research. Readers new to AR thus often have to overcome prior learning when they begin to explore AR.

Doing Action Research

Most models for action research have four to six phases or "moments" that are organized into an iterative spiral. A complete action research project may progress through several spirals of the four to six moments. The four-moment model of action research depicted in Figure 3.2 is based on the models proposed by two well-known Australian action research pioneers, Kemmis & McTaggart (1988), and on the work of Seymour-Rolls & Hughes (1995).

Reflection. Action research begins with reflection on the issues of interest. In this phase, discussions with colleagues and collaborators as well as thoughtful reflection brings the group that is doing the action research study to a consensus on what the issues/problems are and what the goal of the action research should be. All this is tentative and may change many times over the course of the project, but it is the beginning point for thinking about other steps in the action research project. Although some forms of action research make one person the sole initiator and researcher, most models emphasize the need for collaboration and cooperation in doing action research. While there is value to action research as a model for individual professional development, in many situations it will be much more

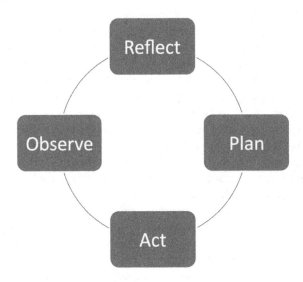

Figure 3.2   A conceptual framework for Action Research.

effective as a collaborative process. Thus, even an individual computer co-ordinator who has decided to do an action research study of ways to enhance the support provided technology-using teachers will want to involve others in the action research process.

Plan. Once there is at least an initial and tentative understanding of the goal of the action research (AR) project, the next step involves exploring ways to address the problem that is the reason for doing the study. This step may involve many forms of information gathering—from literature reviews and conference attendance to consulting with colleagues and experts as well as visiting other sites that appear to have successfully dealt with problems and issues similar to those the AR project is addressing. In the end, however, the AR project group will discuss the options and develop a plan for addressing the problem. This plan is not likely to be the simple adoption of a plan developed and used elsewhere. It may reflect the team's awareness and appreciation of plans and solutions developed elsewhere, but it will probably be different in many ways, which is a reflection of the fact that each professional situation is different—be it a school, a community health care center, or a neighborhood cooperative.

Act. A third moment is action. The plan is implemented with the resources, support, and collaborative group structure needed to both successfully implement and evaluate the plan.

Observe. The change is carefully observed and evaluated. The data gathered, which may include a wide range of qualitative and quantitative information, is used to decide whether the change was effective or not. Most forms of AR do not include the systematic collection of outcome data that is often the hallmark of positivist research. Often, the evaluation of the change is informal, qualitative, and based on reflection and dialog between the participants. The likely outcome of a particular cycle is information that leads participants to reformulate the plan to make it more effective. AR rarely ends with one round through the Reflect-Plan-Act-Observe cycle. A change worth trying is rarely done well the first time; it requires adjustments, improvements, and enhancements. Several iterations of the AR cycle may be needed before the AR team is pleased with the results.

Note that there are no arrows in Figure 3.2. There is no arrow pointing, for example, from Reflect to Plan. Moving sequentially from Reflect to Plan to Act to Observe makes sense, but there will be times when work on a plan results in a return to reflection. The process is thus not a rigid, linear cycle; it is flexible and allows for movements backward and forward as well as diagonally. In fact, in actual practice an AR team may be working on several moments at once. AR is a nonlinear process even though diagrams like Figure 3.2 give the impression of linearity.

As presented here, the Reflect, Plan, Act, Observe model of AR is relatively generic. It is similar to hundreds of other AR models that have been proposed over the last 60 years. There are, however, two strands of mainstream AR in use today—critical AR and interpretive AR. The next two sections introduce popular models of critical and interpretive AR.

Models of Critical Action Research

Critical action research typically has, as discussed in Chapter 2, the goal of emancipation. Boog (2003), who teaches at the University of Groningen in the Netherlands, is a proponent of that view. "Right from the start, action research was intended to be emancipatory research, and it still is" (p. 426). He believes that all forms of action research are "supported by a participatory worldview and are meant to be a double-sided process of research, self research and education directed at individual empowerment and collective empowerment and/or emancipation" (p. 426). Boog's paper is an exploration of the history of action research as an emancipatory practice and it includes a number of recommendations about how to make AR a more effective method of empowerment and/or emancipation. Boog believes all approaches to AR tend to share six characteristics:

- The research process involves *cycles* or iterations. AR is not a one-shot process of identifying a problem, searching for a solution, implementing the solution, and then evaluating the impact of the solution. It is, instead, an ongoing series of such cycles.
- The purpose of AR is individual and group *emancipation,* empowerment, a more equitable society, and greater participatory democracy.
- "The theoretical and methodological stance of action [research] theory is inherently *critical* and grounded in an emancipatory worldview. Active experiential learning is fundamental to the notion of the human being as the active creator of his or her world" (p. 432).
- An important assumption underlying AR is that new "knowledge in social research is basically gained through a process of mutual understanding, a so-called *double hermeneutic* process. Researchers interpret an already interpreted world; researched subjects comment on that interpretation, and so on. In the process of mutual understanding, the research partners try to get to know and trust each other as equals in self-knowledge about their other-ness" (p. 433).
- The resulting relationship between participants in an AR project is more *subject–subject* than the typical subject–object relationship that often characterizes positivist research in the social sciences.
- All forms of AR "share a cogenerative research assessment procedure" (p. 434). That is, both intended and unintended *outcomes* of the research are *assessed collaboratively by the participants.* Further, at

both the individual and the group or social level, the ultimate goals of emancipation and empowerment must be kept in mind.

Boog's six characteristics of AR are based on critical theory, and some of those characteristics would not be accepted as essential, or even desirable, characteristics of AR by proponents of interpretive or positivist AR. Even some critical action researchers might debate the emphasis Boog puts on some of the characteristics. For example, he emphasizes the collaborative construction of meaning by all participants much more than some critical theorists do. On this point his position bridges the interpretive and critical approaches to AR. Despite his insistence that AR is predominantly a critical form of research, his approach might best be considered a blend of interpretive and critical paradigms. However, the importance of the collaborative construction of meaning is at the heart of an important issue—how authoritative a researcher should be and how far AR leaders and facilitators should go in imposing their own ideologies and interpretations on other participants in the AR process. That Oliver (2002) manages to come down on both sides of this issue in a relatively short article highlights the difficult and complicated nature of this question.

Boog is one of many AR specialists who view action research as an expression of a particular paradigm. However, as used in the field today, action research is the general term used for systematic efforts to enhance practice through careful study in the context of practice. Further, while he operates from a critical perspective, some of his conceptual underpinnings are certainly compatible with interpretive approaches to AR. His use of the idea of a collaboratively developed and agreed upon statement about reality is more interpretive than critical, yet it has become a core belief of many, if not most, forms of participatory action research. The term *participatory action research,* or PAR, signifies action research conducted by the practitioner working collaboratively within a group that supports and contributes to the research effort. For example, Ditrano and Silverstein (2006) described a participatory action research project with a group of parents of children classified as having emotional disabilities. They describe PAR as "a process in which researchers and participants operate as full collaborators in creating action projects that are designed to meet specific needs of the participants. PAR provides opportunities for researchers and participants to coconstruct knowledge, unsettling the power dynamics between outside experts and local community insiders. . . . The goal of PAR is transformation—transformation of the field of psychology to accept collaborative inquiry as a legitimate form of research and pedagogy and transformation in terms of social action (i.e., empowering citizens and communities)" (p. 360). Ditrano and Silverstein base their approach to PAR on critical theory, particularly the work of Brazilian educator Paulo Freire. They emphasize the need for teachers, psychologists, and other traditional "experts" to abandon their expert role and to develop a dialogue that allows participants to "ask critical questions about their place in society." And as the participants become aware of the social injustice built into the culture in which they live, they begin to think about how to redress the injustice. That phase of enlightened understanding or *critical consciousness* is followed by a phase of action. They see themselves "as empowered actors creating their own destiny" and they initiate actions designed to improve their situation. In their case study report, Ditrano and Silverstein tell how parents of children needing special education services developed an understanding of both the details of the way the education and mental health bureaucracies operate and also became aware of the reasons why "schools and mental health agencies have frequently failed to establish meaningful partnerships with families." The reasons revolved around the fact that "the professional staff and the families come from different socioeconomic, ethnic, and racial backgrounds."

Ditrano and Silverstein divide PAR into three overlapping and iterative phases—developing a collaborative relationship, education, and action. Their paper tells the story of a group of parents who progress through these three phases as they work with schools and other agencies to develop better services for their children.

In the AR and PAR literature a surprisingly large number of terms are sometimes used interchangeably with AR and PAR. They include action learning, action science, applied research, classroom action research, collaborative inquiry, emancipatory research, participatory inquiry, participatory research, PIM or participatory intervention model, and many more. There are real differences between the core meanings of some of these terms, and the meanings also vary from one part of the literature to another. However, a common characteristic is that the research occurs in the real world of practice, addresses a real-world problem of practice, and attempts to develop a working solution. PAR always includes the practitioner and other stakeholders in the research process.

Kemmis and McTaggart: Doing Participatory Action Research From a Critical Perspective

Several models of critical AR have been presented in previous sections but they have not been covered in detail. One conceptual framework for doing PAR from a critical perspective will be explored in some detail in this section. It is a recently revised version of the AR model developed by Stephen Kemmis and colleagues in Australia. Kemmis and McTaggart (2005) recently revised their critical AR model in some very important ways that have implications for the practice of AR as well as how we link theoretical underpinnings to day-to-day AR decision making. This critical AR model was proposed by Stephen Kemmis and Robin McTaggart (2005) in the third edition of the *Handbook for Qualitative Research*. Kemmis and McTaggart are Australian scholars with a long history of work both as developers of the concept of PAR and as researchers who use the PAR framework. We will use the term PAR to characterize their AR model, but it is PAR that emerged from the critical tradition of action research and is, from an international perspective, one of the most widely used models of critical AR. Here we treat it as an example of how critical AR has evolved over the past 60 years.

Kemmis and McTaggart's chapter on PAR is an attempt to reconceptualize this approach to research and also to correct some misconceptions that have developed over the years. These authors take some of the responsibility for some misconceptions and misapplications because the view they hold today is not always congruent with their prior scholarship on PAR. The chapter is thus a good overview of how the thinking of two critical theorists changed over the years.

In a section of the history of AR, Kemmis and McTaggart trace the development of action research through four generations. The first was an American effort in the fifties to define AR within the then dominant framework of positivism. In their view, "this led to a temporary decline in its development there" (p. 560). Another reason for the decline of AR in America during the mid-twentieth century was the widespread view that AR was leftist, even "Communist." That was the McCarthy era when many careers and lives were ruined in the right wing efforts to suppress virtually any opinion or action that was not approved by the ideological right. Action research that attempted to empower people to take more control over their lives was branded as subversive, or worse. Fortunately, one of the major influences during that period and later on the practice of AR was the Tavistock Institute, and today there are still web sites and publications about the Tavistock Institute in London that describe it as part of a vast left wing conspiracy.

The Tavistock Institute helped a second generation of AR emerge in the U.K. Second generation AR put a strong emphasis on practical problem solutions, often at the organizational level rather than at the level of individual practitioners. The idea of changing institutions, organizations, and political/social systems through AR is one reason the institute is still accused of being part of a world-wide system of power and thought control.

Kemmis and McTaggart believe the third generation of AR began in Australia with efforts to base AR more explicitly on critical and emancipatory foundations. That goal and the increasing use of critical theory as a foundation for AR spread to Europe and, to a lesser extent, America during this phase.

According to Kemmis and McTaggart, the current or fourth generation of AR "emerged in the connection between critical emancipatory action research and participatory action research that had developed in the context of social movements in the developing world, championed by people such as Paulo Freire, Orlando Fals Borda, ... as well as by North American and British workers in adult education and literacy, community development, and development studies ... Two key themes were (a) the development of theoretical arguments for more "actionist" approaches to action research; and (b) the need for participatory action researchers to make links with broad social movements" (p. 560). Kemmis and McTaggart related what they now refer to as Critical Participatory Action Research to movements such as liberation theology among the Catholic clergy in South America, neo-Marxist community development projects, and the human rights movement. In making those associations Kemmis and McTaggart are also making it clear that there is an important political component to their form of AR. They also put an emphasis on Aristotle's "sense of practical reasoning [e.g., phronesis] about how to act rightly and properly in a situation with which one is confronted" (p. 561).

Kemmis and McTaggart have their own model of PAR. It is a spiral of six recursive stages:

Planning a change
Acting and observing the process and consequences of the change
Reflecting on these processes and consequences
Replanning
Acting and observing again
Reflecting again, and so on ... (p. 563)

While the six stages are important, the core of this model of PAR is actually in some of the assumptions the developers use as their foundation for the model. In fact, the six stages are almost a fiction when it comes to actual practice. Despite their use of stages and diagrams to represent PAR, Kemmis and McTaggart consider PAR "only poorly described in terms of a mechanical sequence of steps" (p. 563). They are not even sure PAR should be represented as an orderly sequence of planned steps that lead, hopefully, to a solution. In practice, PAR is much more chaotic than the diagrams and steps represent. "The stages overlap and initial plans quickly become obsolete in the light of learning from experience. In reality, the process is likely to be more fluid, open, and responsive. The criterion of success is not whether participants have followed the steps faithfully but rather whether they have a strong and authentic sense of development and evolution in their practices, their understanding of their practices, and the situations in which they practice" (p. 563). Kemmis and McTaggart propose a set of guiding principles that, in their view, are more central to PAR than a set of sequential steps:

> PAR is a social process. It "explores the relationship between the realms of the individual and the social" and it acknowledges that, quoting Habermas [1972], "no individuation is possible without socialization, and no socialization is possible without individuation" (p. 566). Further. "the object of PAR is social,... directed toward studying, reframing, and reconstructing social practices. If practices are constituted in social interaction between people, changing practices is a social process". (p. 563)

> Kemmis and McTaggart put a great deal of emphasis on the social. Existing practices, which are not working, were developed socially, they are practiced in a social context, and they will be examined by a collaborating group that uses the PAR process as a forum to explore current practices through communication within what Habermas called *open communicative space*. That is, the participants join the discussion voluntarily, and collaboratively develop their view of current practices as well as ideas for new practices. This happens through communication both among members of the PAR project and with others who are not participants but who have an interest in solving the problem. Collaborative learning leads to both an agreement about what practices need to be changed and ideas about what should replace current practices. Implementing the changes is best accomplished by a group that has collectively come to the conclusion that these changes should be made. Such a group will be committed to implementing and evaluating them. Often, the changes needed will not be within the power of the PAR group. That group must influence others, often policy makers, to agree to and create the conditions for making the changes. This is a political aspect of PAR that was not always recognized as vitally important in the early PAR literature.

> PAR is participatory. "Each of the steps...in the spiral of self-reflection is best undertaken collaboratively by coparticipants" (p. 563). "All individuals in a group try to get a handle on the ways in which their knowledge shapes their sense of identity and agency and to reflect critically on how their current knowledge frames and constrains their action ..." (p. 567). PAR is also participatory in the sense that "people can only do action research 'on' themselves, either individually or collectively. It is *not* research done 'on' others" (p. 567). Kemmis and McTaggart also argue that participation should be broad. For example, in education PAR, "it is not only teachers who have the task of improving the social practices of schooling but also students and many others (e.g., parents, school communities, employers of graduates)" (p. 579).

> PAR is practical and collaborative. Kemmis and McTaggart believe a major difference between PAR and other forms of social science research is the tenacity with which it emphasizes the particular instance and situation over the general idea or theory. Participatory action researchers "may be interested in practices in general or in the abstract, but their principal concern is in changing practices in 'the here and now'" (p. 564). PAR "involves the investigation

of actual practices and not abstract practices" (p. 563–564). "Focusing on practices in a concrete and specific way makes them accessible for reflection, discussion, and reconstruction as products of past circumstances that are capable of being modified in and for present and future circumstances. . . . Participatory action researchers aim to understand their own particular practices as they emerge in their own particular circumstances without reducing them to the ghostly status of the general, the abstract, or the ideal—or, perhaps one should say, the unreal" (p. 565).

Another part of this guiding principle is that PAR is collaborative. Kemmis and McTaggart also use the term *collective* to refer to the necessity of working as a group to bring about lasting change. They believe AR should be collective rather than individualistic, in part because it generates better decisions through group communication and decision making, and also because the implementation of plans for change is easier if a group is committed to making change happen. Kemmis and McTaggart even recommend that PAR groups or *collectives* "include 'critical friends,' . . . build alliances with broader social movements, and . . . extend membership across institutional hierarchies . . . as a way of enhancing the understanding and political efficacy of individuals and groups" (p. 571).

PAR is emancipatory. It "aims to help people recover, and release themselves from, the constraints of irrational, unproductive, unjust, and unsatisfying social structures that limit their self-development and self-determination. It is a process in which people explore the ways in which their practices are shaped and constrained by wider social (cultural, economic, and political) structures and consider whether they can intervene to release themselves from these constraints—or, if they cannot, how best to work within and around them" (p. 567).

The traditional concepts of emancipation and empowerment focus on individuals or groups, and the struggle to free themselves from unhealthy controls. However, Kemmis and McTaggart have recently modified their view of emancipation or empowerment. They do not see it as a process that leads to individuals and groups that are completely autonomous, self-regulating, and self-controlled. "It turns out that neither individual actors nor states can be entirely and coherently autonomous and self-regulating. Their parts do not form unified and coherent wholes but rather must be understood in terms of notions such as difference, contradiction, and conflict as much as unity, coherence, and independence" (p. 594). Within this perspective, it is difficult to create a believable myth in which PAR is a process for empowering the mistreated group by wresting power from the powerful but misguided. Instead, the best that empowerment can achieve is to enhance the "capacity for individuals, groups, and states to interact more coherently with one another in the ceaseless process of social reproduction and transformation. At its best, it names a process in which people, groups, and stages engage one another more authentically and with greater recognition and respect for difference, in making decisions that they will regard as legitimate because they have participated in them openly and freely, more genuinely committed to mutual understanding, intersubjective agreement, and consensus about what to do" (p. 594). "We came to understand empowerment not only as a lifeworld process of cultural, social, and personal development and trans-formation but also as implying that protagonists experienced themselves as working both in and against system structures and functions" (p. 593). In formulating this new version of empowerment, they use Habermas' ideas of *lifeworld* and *system*. A major purpose of Habermas' theory building was to explain what is happening in late capitalist societies of the West. Essentially, he argues the normal integrative roles of communication in society no lon-ger work. In earlier times the communicative processes of a society helped citizens to both understand the structures and functions of society and, more importantly, to believe they were desirable and necessary to a smoothly func-tioning society which was beneficial to them. However, in late capitalism, the channels of communication have been high jacked or "colonized" for other purposes. Consider, for example, the now widespread view that different na-tional news services, such as CBS, NBC, CNN, and Fox, are not "fair and balanced" purveyors of the news. Instead, they select, produce, and present the news in ways that support particular political and social ideologies. The colonization of communications channels, such as television news networks, means the function of communication to help citizens reach a consensus of belief in the goodness of society's regulating systems has been lost. We do not always believe government operates in our interests; that corporations gener-ally have the best interests of consumers in mind, or that schools are run in ways that maximize the benefits to students. The result is a "crisis of legiti-mation." People no longer have a strong faith in "the system." The concept of *system* in Habermas' thinking means the organized and structured proce-dures that have been developed to achieve economic and bureaucratic goals (e.g., "money and power"). *Lifeworld* refers to the set of shared assumptions, beliefs, and values that citizens of a society develop through "communica-tive action." However, in late capitalist societies, Habermas believes too many channels of communication have been co-opted by those who seek money and power rather than the development of a society based on a shared set of beliefs and values. He thus proposes creating environments (*public spheres*) in which communication for that purpose is unhindered by forces focused on money and power. Kemmis and McTaggart see the PAR group as an example of that type of public sphere. In this view of PAR, empowerment is more than changing the lifeworld. That is certainly necessary because the way we view the world, and our place in it, is part of the oppression that disempowers us. For example, it is not uncommon for a battered woman to believe that she may "deserve" to be treated that way. That belief, which can be supported and encouraged by cultural and social practices, is part of the web of op-pression that keeps her from acting to improve her lot. Thus, changing the lifeworld is crucial in change efforts. However, PAR, and other efforts to make desirable changes, must also make changes in the *system*. Sometimes that may involve opposing or fighting the system, but at other times the most effective approach is to use the system to bring about changes in it and the lifeworld.

Kemmis and McTaggert thus view empowerment as a process of changing both the lifeworld and systems. Further, the process of becoming empowered or emancipated is not one great effort that happens in the last reel of the movie, followed by a lifetime of happiness and contentment. Instead, it is an ongoing and continuous process of communicative action and exploratory action. These two terms will be discussed in more detail a little later.

PAR is "reflexive (e.g., recursive, dialectical)." PAR "aims to help people investigate reality in order to change it...and...to change reality in order to investigate it. In particular, it is a deliberate process through which people aim to transform their practices through a spiral of cycles of critical and self-critical action and reflection.... It is a deliberate social process designed to help collaborating groups of people to transform their world" (p. 567).

PAR "aims to transform both theory and practice." Unlike some models of PAR, Kemmis and McTaggart's view emphasizes the role of both theory and practice in the process of action research. They do not see theory or practice as the dominant component in the theory-practice relationship. Instead, they see both as standing on the same level and they consider both as important, actually essential, to the other. Their form of PAR "does not aim to develop forms of theory that can stand above and beyond practice"..."nor does it aim to develop forms of practice that might be regarded as self-justifying, as if practice could be judged in the absence of theoretical frameworks" (p. 568). They use the terms "reaching out" and "reaching in" to emphasize the need to go from "specific practices in specific contexts" to broader viewpoints such as theories, and also to go from "standpoints provided by different perspectives, theories, and discourse to explore the extent to which they provide practitioners themselves with a critical grasp of the problems and issues they actually confront in specific local situations" (p. 568). Kemmis and McTaggart are more hopeful of broad theories and frameworks than I (JW) am, but that probably reflects the difference in their foundation—critical theory—and mine—interpretivism. Critical theory has always had a set of core beliefs about how the world really is that guides both practice and research, while interpretive approaches often urge us to give up on foundational truths and accept that whatever reality we have is a socially constructed reality.

The critical perspective of Kemmis and McTaggart is also obvious in what they see as their mistakes, and in the path their thinking has taken after more experience, and maturity. Today they have less faith in basic AR procedures yielding the personal empowerment they hoped for in the beginning. They believe "it was a mistake not to emphasize sufficiently that power comes from collective commitment and a methodology that invites the democratization of the objectification of experience and the disciplining of subjectivity" (p. 569). That is, they do not see AR freeing individuals from the restrictions of current practices and social restrictions without the influence of the collective mind—the shared exploration of practice that limits the influence of individual, subjective decision-making while enhancing the influence of the group on interpreting experience.

They also have more concerns today about the "facilitator," consultant, or outside expert (particularly university professors) in the PAR process. Such a role is prone to be misunderstood and perhaps misused. Outsiders who come into a practical professional setting such as a hospital or social service agency cannot and should not try to play a role as neutral arbitrator of what is right or correct, nor should they present themselves as technical experts in the process of PAR. Both roles tend to put the outsider in a superior position to the practitioners in that context, which is undesirable. They also tend to limit the ability of the group to democratically explore and understand the influence and control of local practice by wider social movements and frameworks, by history, and by traditions. Finally, they can also blind you "to the way in which practice is constituted as a 'multiple reality' that is perceived differently by different participants in and observers of practice (e.g., professionals, clients, clients' families and friends, interested observers" (p. 570).

Other issues that are clearer to Kemmis and McTaggart today include the need to accept that PAR involves both research and activism. Activism has always been a part of PAR, but Kemmis and McTaggart "find significant understatement of the role of theory and theory building in the literature of action research.... Our experience suggests that there should be both more theory and more action in action research. Political activism should be theoretically informed just like any other social practice" (p. 570). On the research side of PAR, they advocate using a range of research methods and approaches because different research methods tend to lead us naturally to certain types of conclusions and perceptions. Using multiple methods helps us keep that in mind and highlights the subjective nature of all research methods.

Kemmis and McTaggart's newest PAR theories move away from a confrontational "us versus them" mentality that often portrayed PAR participants as the revolutionaries fighting the entrenched power of "the establishment" and its bureaucratic functionaries. Instead, following Habermas, they argue that there is no monolithic establishment that makes uniform policy and practice decisions that are then routinely and rigorously implemented. There are "not unified systems but rather complex sets of subsystems having transactions of various kinds with one another economically... and administratively" (p. 579). From this perspective they urge participatory action researchers to make an effort to both influence and work with different "subsystems" in efforts to bring about change. However, when making the point that there is no monolithic "system" that opposes change, they also note that PAR groups are also not monolithic. All members do not hold the same viewpoints or advocate the same actions. PAR groups are "internally diverse, they generally have no unified 'core' from which their power and authority can emanate, and they frequently have little capacity to achieve their own ends if they must contend with the will of other powers and orders" (p. 580).

This view of both PAR groups, and the relevant systems, individuals, and organizations outside the PAR groups, leads Kemmis and McTaggart to propose a revised view of how PAR works. Using Habermas' theories of communication and social structure, they propose that "the most morally, practically, and politically compelling view of participatory action research is one that sees participatory action research as a practice through which people can create networks of communication, that is, sites for the practice of communicative action. It offers the prospect of opening communicative space in public spheres of the kind Habermas described. Based on such a view, participatory action research aims to engender practical critiques of existing states of affairs, the development of critical perspectives, and the shared formation of emancipatory commitments, that is, commitments to overcome distorted ways of understanding the world, distorted practices, and distorted social arrangements and situations" (p. 580).

This new perspective of PAR is summarized in Figure 3.3. PAR provides participants with a public sphere. For Habermas, public spheres are contexts where people come together to discuss social problems. They are a form of participatory democracy and Habermas sees them as a powerful way of giving people back some control over the society in which they live. In PAR the public sphere for communicative action allows participants to develop a shared understanding of the social problems they face and the reasons for them. A clearer understanding of social problems and their causes is often hampered or even prevented by established rules, structures, traditions, influence groups, and power structures. Thus, a primary goal of

Figure 3.3   A diagram of Kemmis and McTaggart's 2006 framework for PAR.

PAR is to help participants recognize those barriers, reduce or eliminate their influence, and develop a clearer, shared view of the problems and their causes. The emergence of this shared view is part of the second outcome of communications work in the public sphere—the development of a shared, critical perspective that links cause and effect, power and oppression, and so on. The third outcome is the development of a commitment on the part of the PAR community to a plan for emancipatory action.

The top half of Figure 3.3 focuses on the process of communication that occurs in PAR. People discuss, debate, explore, exhort, and share through an open, democratic process. The goal is educational rather than to initiate action. Participants should come to view their world differently. PAR thus "aims to change the researchers themselves as well as the social world they inhabit" (p. 578). In this process each participant's viewpoint and experience is respected, and input from outside the PAR group may often be sought and used. However, in the end the goal is a group that has both a desire to do something different and an idea of what that difference should be.

The bottom half of Figure 3.3 focuses on action. Once the PAR group has both the will to act and a shared view of what action should be taken, efforts to implement that action are undertaken. Kemmis and McTaggart call this *Exploratory Action* because it is considered only a tentative and potentially useful change. It must be implemented in an exploratory manner that involves careful observation of the impact of the action—both in terms of expected and unexpected effects, including unanticipated negative effects. If the action proposed is within the power of the PAR group, it may implement the exploratory action, carefully evaluate it, and complete one cycle of the PAR process by revising the action before beginning another cycle. Keep in mind, however, that this exploratory action is undertaken by a group that has already developed a more sophisticated and shared view of one or more social practices. Exploratory action is an attempt to change that practice for the better.

If the exploratory action is not within the power of the PAR group, there may be an extended period of work to influence decision makers and policy groups to make the exploratory action possible. Only then can it be implemented and evaluated. This involves a third type of change. In addition to changing "practitioner understanding," PAR must change "social practices," and "the situations and circumstances in which [the PAR participants] practice" (p. 586). This third type of change may emerge from exploratory action. On the other hand, changing the situations and circumstances of practice may be necessary before practice can change. Kemmis and McTaggart seem to feel that many needed changes will not be within the control of a PAR group and that political action in the sense of building coalitions and influencing decision-making and policy groups will be necessary more often than some AR proponents seem to realize.

Of course a diagram like Figure 3.3 oversimplifies the PAR process. The two processes—communicative action and exploratory action—overlap considerably and the processes of each interact and intertwine.

To summarize the discussion of PAR in the Kemmis and McTaggart tradition, it is probably best not thought of as a particular methodology of research with a set of prescribed procedures for doing valid research, but rather as a way of thinking about applied research that emphasizes several important concepts such as the critical nature of participation, the importance of emancipation as a goal, and the privileging of practical outcomes in a particular setting over broad, abstract theorizing.

Another Model of AR: Stringer's Version of Interpretive AR

Earnest Stringer, an Australian academic and action research practitioner/scholar at Curtin University, has worked in both Australia and North America as an action research consultant. He has written three editions of his book, *Action Research*. The third edition was published in 2007 and it is a popular text in AR courses as well as one of the clearest and comprehensive statements of the basic principles of AR from an interpretive perspective. This model of AR thus provides an interesting contrast to the Kemmis and McTaggart model for PAR that is based on critical theory.

Stringer's action research experience is extensive and includes work with aboriginal groups in Australia, teachers and parents as well as government officials in the newly formed nation of East Timor, and organizations, especially schools and school districts, in North America. His methods of practice are decidedly interpretive, but the goals and aims he states for AR often have a critical theory ring to them. The same is true of his criticisms of bureaucracies and social systems. In the tradition of Rousseau, he blames many modern problems on social and cultural dysfunction. "The pressures experienced in professional practice reflect tensions that exist in modern society. The complex influences that impinge on people's everyday social lives provide a fertile seedbed for proliferating a host of family, community, and institutional problems" (p. 2).

Unlike critical action research that often focuses on oppressed groups and individuals as participants in an AR project, Stringer tends to focus on the work of professionals such as teachers or social workers who are charged with helping and supporting members of society. He tends to view problems and solutions through the lens of practicing professionals instead of the oppressed and disempowered, though this is not always the case. His foundational causes—"tensions that exist in modern society"—have

generated a very diverse range of problems that professionals are supposed
to address and solve, but they have not been able to do so:

> Although adequately prepared to deal with the technical requirements of
> their daily work, practitioners often face recurrent crises that are outside
> the scope of their professional expertise. Teachers face children disturbed
> by conflict in their homes and communities, youth workers encounter re-
> sentful and alienated teenagers, health workers confront people apparently
> unconcerned about life-threatening lifestyles and social habits, and social and
> welfare workers are strained past their capacity to deal with the impossible
> caseloads spawned by increasing poverty and alienation. (Stringer, 2007, p. 2)

Stringer's general explanation of why professional practitioners are
failing to solve the problems of modern life like "drug abuse, crime, violence, school absenteeism" is the use of outdated modes of practice based
on positivism. "There is an expectation in social life that trained professionals, applying scientifically derived expertise, will provide answers to the
proliferating problems that confront people in their personal and public
lives. . . . These responses have failed to diminish the growing social problems that have multiplied much faster than the human and financial resources available to deal with them. Moreover, evidence suggests that centralized policies and programs generated by 'experts' have limited success
in resolving these problems. The billions of dollars invested in social programs have failed to stem the tide of alienation and disaffection that characterize social life in modern industrial nations" (p. 2). This is a theme he
repeats throughout his book on AR. "Unlike positivistic science, however,
its [community-based research] goal is not the production of an objective
body of knowledge that can be generalized to large populations. Instead,
its purpose is to build collaboratively constructed descriptions and interpretations of events that enable groups of people to formulate mutually
acceptable solutions to their problems" (pp. 189–190). Stringer's animos-
ity toward positivist models has been reciprocated by advocates of those
models. In his book, he reprints the comment of one anonymous reviewer
who rejected his proposal for a paper on action research to be presented at
the American Educational Research Association. "There may be a place for
this nonsense in AERA but not, hopefully, in this division" (p. 191). There
are clearly deep differences between positivist and interpretive researchers
in both the meaning of the term research and the guidelines for how it
should be conducted. Stringer spends most of the last chapter in the book
presenting his interpretive view of what research is and how that conception is expressed in action research. In that chapter he even attempts to be
a bit kinder and gentler to positivism. "My intent has not been to show that
scientific method is wrong or incorrect" and "Even within action research,
there is a place for some of the methods, procedures, and concepts usually

associated with traditional science" (p. 203). By this point, however, he has already made his case against positivist research practice and these olive branches stand out as being incongruous with what he has said in the previous 200 pages.

In Stringer's model of AR, the solution to the myriad of social problems starts with a rejection of the positivist approach that seeks universal solutions that can be applied with little or no adaptation in local settings. In a positivist model, the role of professionals such as teachers, social workers, and mental health professionals is to select those evidence-based methods that show the greatest promise of solving the problem and then to implement those solutions accurately and correctly. Stringer feels this approach has failed miserably and must be replaced. Bent Flyvbjerg (2001), in his book, *Making Social Science Matter: Why Social Inquiry Fails and How It Can Succeed Again,* makes a very similar point in the broader context of the applied and basic social sciences. Flyvbjerg suggests solutions that are compatible with the model of AR Stringer proposes. On the other hand, Bartoo (2004) was highly critical of Stringer's critique of positivism, commenting that "Stringer's descriptions of positivism are wrong at nearly every point" and cites the work of D. C. Phillips at Stanford University to back up his conclusions. Both Bartoo and Phillips (Phillips & Barbules, 2000) are positivists themselves and would probably have difficulty accepting any major criticism of the positivist research paradigm that comes from critical theorists or interpretivists.

Rejecting the positivist model of solving societal problems will clear the conceptual ground and allow another model to flourish. That, Stringer strongly believes, is the heart of his AR model—that social problems are local problems and that any effort to solve them must be based on local knowledge, local expertise, and local participation. Stringer rejects the distant expert as a source of direction and control over efforts to solve problems, but he does not view the local professional practitioners in the same way. They, he feels, must reject the positivist models of practice they were trained to follow, and embrace a different model that makes them partners and participants with local stakeholders—those who are being impacted by the problem and who will be impacted by any efforts to change the situation.

> This book has been written for those workers, both professional and nonprofessional, who provide services to people in community, organizational, or institutional contexts. It speaks, therefore, to teachers, health professionals, social workers, community and youth workers, businesspeople, planners, and a whole range of other people who function in teaching, service delivery, or managerial roles. Its purpose is to provide a set of research tools that will enable people to deal effectively with many of the problems that confront them as they perform their work. (p. xv)

Stringer goes on to specify the roles of professionals in his form of AR. They are supportive rather than directive, facilitative rather than expert-based, and collaborative rather than authoritative. For example, when discussing the role of a professional in writing documents about the AR study, he proposes a nontraditional model:

> The researcher-writer takes a different stance in the research and writing process. No longer "experts" capable of defining, describing, and interpreting the "facts" or "truth," researcher-writers position themselves toward writing processes that assist others in describing and interpreting their own experiences, sometimes acting as scribes for research participants or as coauthors or editors. The writer as scribe-for-the-other helps people give voice to their own interpretations of events, working with them to identify the key elements of their experience and shape them into a report. (p. 208)

The relationship is also deeply social in nature rather than individualistic:

> A common approach to action research envisages processes of inquiry that are based on a practitioner's reflection on his or her professional practices. It has been clear to me for many years that when practitioners remain locked into their own perceptions and interpretations of the situation, they fail to take into account the varied worldviews and life experiences of the people with whom they work. They fail to understand the fundamental dynamics that determine the way their clients, students, patients, or customers will behave in any given circumstances. (p. xv–xvi)

> Action research, however, is based on the proposition that generalized solutions may not fit particular contexts or groups of people and that the purpose of inquiry is to find an appropriate solution for the particular dynamics at work in a local situation. A lesson plan, a care plan, or a self-management plan that fits the lifeworld of a middle-class suburban client group may be only tangentially relevant in poor rural or urban environments or to people whose cultural lives differ significantly from the people who serve them. Generalized solutions must be modified and adapted in order to fit the context in which they are used. (p. 5)

Stringer thus questions the efficacy of AR models based completely or mostly on a professional's reflections on his or her practice. While he does not reject reflection as an effective tool, he does reject it as an individualistic and primary method of supporting change. He takes this view in part because of the constructivist/interpretive assumption that meaning making is a social process, not an individual cognitive process. The social nature of knowing should, therefore, come into play when thinking about how AR should proceed. The assumption that local knowledge is crucial to crafting workable and successful solutions impacts virtually all major aspects of

Stringer's interpretive AR. This is a local process that puts local stakeholders in the controlling and decision-making positions:

> We therefore need to change our vision of service professionals and administrators from mechanic/technician to facilitator and creative investigator. This new vision rejects the mindless application of standardized practices across all settings and contexts and instead advocates the use of contextually relevant procedures formulated by inquiring and resourceful practitioners. (p. 3)

And who should decide which "contextually relevant procedures" should be implemented? It is the group of stakeholders/participants:

> The primary purpose of action research is to provide the means for people to engage in systematic inquiry and investigation to "design" an appropriate way of accomplishing a desired goal and to evaluate its effectiveness. As will become evident, however, the practitioner does not engage this work in isolation. An assumption of action research is that those who have previously been designated as subjects should participate directly in the research. Community-based action research works on the assumption that all people who affect or are affected by the issue investigated should be included in the processes of inquiry. The "community" is not a neighborhood or a suburb, but a community of interest. Action research is a participatory process that involves all those who have a stake in the issue engaging in systematic inquiry into the issue to be investigated. Professional practitioners, as research facilitators, engage their communities of interest in careful and systematic explorations that provide them with knowledge and understanding that, in very direct ways, improve the quality of their lives. (p. 6)

Throughout his book, Stringer makes the point that the person taking on the role of "researcher" in an action research project is not a director, boss, or as George W. Bush put it in his defense of his Secretary of Defense, Donald Rumsfeldt, "the Decider." Stringer's researcher is a facilitator, a supporter, and an enabler. The researcher has no more privilege or power over decisions than other participants:

> As an evolving approach to inquiry, action research envisages a collaborative approach to investigation that seeks to engage "subjects" as equal and full participants in the research process. A fundamental premise of community-based action research is that it commences with an interest in the problems of a group, a community, or an organization. Its purpose is to assist people in extending their understanding of their situation and thus in resolving problems that confront them. Put another way, community-based action research provides a model for enacting local, action-oriented approaches to inquiry, applying small-scale theorizing to specific problems in specific situations. (p. 10)

Community-based action research works on the assumption, therefore, that all stakeholders—those whose lives are affected by the problem under study—should be engaged in the processes of investigation. Stakeholders participate in a process of rigorous inquiry, acquiring information (collecting data) and reflecting on that information (analyzing) to transform their understanding about the nature of the problem under investigation (theorizing). This new set of understandings is then applied to plans for resolution of the problem (action), which, in turn, provides the context for testing hypotheses derived from group theorizing (evaluation).

Collaborative exploration helps practitioners, agency workers, client groups, and other stakeholding parties to develop increasingly sophisticated understandings of the problems and issues that confront them. As they rigorously explore and reflect on their situation together, they can repudiate social myths, misconceptions, and misrepresentations and formulate more constructive analyses of their situation. By sharing their diverse knowledge and experience—expert, professional, and lay—stakeholders can create solutions to their problems and, in the process, improve the quality of their community life.

The role of the research facilitator, in this context, becomes more facilitative and less directive. Knowledge acquisition/production proceeds as a collective process, engaging people who have previously been the "subjects" of research in the process of defining and redefining the corpus of understanding on which their community or organizational life is based. As they collectively investigate their own situation, stakeholders build a consensual vision of their lifeworld. Community-based action research results not only in a collective vision but also in a sense of community. It operates at the intellectual level as well as at social, cultural, political, and emotional levels. (p. 11)

Stringer sometimes uses the term "community-based action research" as well as the term "participatory" when discussing the importance of full participation on the part of local stakeholders. The term *community-based* is probably preferable because it highlights the value of involving a diverse but invested group in the AR process. As noted earlier, some interpretive action researchers reject or criticize the emancipatory and participatory procedures of some critical AR models, which are based on confrontation rather than collaboration. Stringer is explicitly opposed to making confrontation a primary, first-line method of bringing about change. "Change is an intended outcome of action research: not the revolutionary changes envisioned by radical social theorists or political activists, but more subtle transformations brought about by the development of new programs or modifications to existing procedures" (p. 208). Community-based action research seeks to involve stakeholders and stakeholder groups in the process even though individuals and groups may actually be in conflict with each other. This has been an element of Stringer's approach from the beginning, but it is an important revision in the latest version of Kemmis and

McTaggart's (2005) model of critical action research that was described earlier. Although one is more influenced by critical theory and the other by interpretive theory, these two models, revised and published recently, are much closer to each other than were competing AR models developed 10 or 20 years ago.

Stringer's Basic AR Model

Stringer's version of interpretive AR is deceptively simple. It has three phases—Look, Think, Act. However, this model is not only simple, it is simplistic. Stringer uses Look, Think, Act to introduce his AR model, but there is so much more in the model that anyone who only knows these steps will have very little understanding of how this model really operates. Virtually all AR models are based on steps that involve identifying and investigating a problem, reflecting on and analyzing that problem, designing and implementing a plan to address the problem, and evaluating that plan so it can either be revised and improved or integrated into daily practice. These are virtually universal aspects of AR models.

Stringer does provide more detail in his book on each of the three phases, including dividing each of them into subphases:

- LOOK
  - "Gather relevant information"
  - Build an understanding of the context in which the AR will occur

- THINK
  - Explore and analyze the context to develop an understanding of "what is happening here"
  - Develop a local theory to "Interpret and explain" "how/why are things as they are"

- ACT
  - Make a plan for solving the problem
  - Implement that plan
  - Evaluate the implementation

Stringer also notes that while his description of his AR model appears to be linear, it is not:

Although the "look, think, act" routine is presented in a linear format throughout this book, it should be read as a continually recycling set of activities. . . . As participants work through each of the major stages, they will explore the details of their activities through a constant process of observation, reflection, and action. At the completion of each set of activities, they

will review (look again), reflect (reanalyze), and re-act (modify their actions).
As experience will show, action research is not a neat, orderly activity that allows participants to proceed step-by-step to the end of the process. People will
find themselves working backward through the routines, repeating processes,
revising procedures, rethinking interpretations, leapfrogging steps or stages,
and sometimes making radical changes in direction. (pp. 3–4)

This model of AR is less structured than many other models, but the
messiness is both expected and valued. It is part of a process that encourages thinking and rethinking about the fit between local needs/conditions
and the solutions being developed. Changes and adjustments may move
quickly from idea to adoption by the group of participants. Even this, however, is not very unique when compared to some of the other models for
AR currently in use.

The uniqueness of Stringer's AR model comes primarily from two areas:
the principles of practice discussed earlier and the details provided in the
chapters on how to actually implement those principles. Stringer's principles derive from three types of foundational assumptions:

1. The traditional positivist model of professional practice which is
    based on (a) privileging "experts;" (b) confidence in general and
    therefore universal solutions;" and (c) a technical-rational model of
    professional practice, has not, does not, and will not work.
2. The constructivists are correct. Local, contextual knowledge is cru-
    cial to successful solution of social problems and must be collected,
    analyzed, summarized, and used in the development of collabora-
    tively developed solutions.
3. The aggressive, confrontational, and divisive methods of critical ac-
    tion research are overused and tend to engender long-term animosi-
    ties that limit long-term solutions to social problems.

These three foundational assumptions result in perspectives on practice
that are very different from those of positivist, and some critical, action researchers. For example, in rejecting the positivist view, which makes theory
and generalizable knowledge the central focus of virtually all forms of research, Stringer proposes another role for theory. It is based on the constructivist assumption of multiple perspectives. Multiple perspectives is the
assumption that, when working with humans, research is not likely to end
in the discovery of one ultimate Truth. Instead, AR participants will become
aware of different, multiple, truths that are perceived by different groups.
Stringer argues that expecting different perceptions, which he treats as different theoretical attempts to explain why things are as they are, means
there is an important role for theories in his AR model. Local theories, developed by participants, are valuable and useful because "different theories

will focus on different aspects of the situation and interpret the information according to the assumptions and orientations of the theory. It is not that any theory is 'wrong' or 'right' but that it focuses on particular aspects of the situation and interprets them in particular ways" (p. 188).

He also emphasizes that the broad, abstract theories that are meant to be generalizable from one setting to another are not what he means when he uses the term theory. "One of the strengths of action research is that it accepts the diverse perspectives of different stakeholders—the 'theory' each will hold to explain how and why events occur as they do—and finds ways of incorporating them into mutually acceptable ways of understanding events that enable them to work toward a resolution of the problem investigated" (p. 188). And, just to be sure you know that theories created by outside experts are not very respected in his model of AR, he adds, "People from outside the research context who impose their own theories without having a deep understanding of the nature of events and the dynamics of the context are likely to either misrepresent or misinterpret the situation" (p. 188).

This model of AR puts a great deal of emphasis on the process of collecting data about the local context and then supporting the participants as they engage in a process of analysis and dialog that leads to both a mutually shared understanding of the situation and a shared view of what solutions to implement to deal with the problem. There is, in fact, much more emphasis on developing shared understanding and agreement about what is to be done than there is on implementation of the solution and evaluating it. Stringer tends to treat evaluation of the implementation as a matter of the participants discussing it and deciding what its strengths and weaknesses are. He does discuss the need for "formal reports" but tends to see them as necessary evils that may be required by outside agencies that fund or approve. Even here, he tends to focus on the perspectives of the participants rather than what positivists would call empirical data. "Sometimes there is considerable pressure to provide a 'definitive' evaluation, especially from people who wish to use numbers to justify expenditure or their personal involvement. Numbers, however, are illusory and usually reflect a distorted vision of the research process. Nevertheless, there are occasions when some quantitative information is useful and may be properly included in the evaluation process. We may provide numbers of students enrolled in a course, youth attending a program, mothers attending a child care clinic, and so on. Numbers by themselves are misleading, however, and often oversimplify the state of affairs. They also risk reifying—creating an illusory preeminence about—certain aspects of a project or program. People may focus on tables that quantify relatively trivial features or disregard significant features of the project. Research participants should be wary, therefore, of engaging in forms of evaluation that are contrary to the principles of community-based action research" (p. 141).

Stringer's second unique contribution to AR methodology is the detail he provides in chapters on how to turn assumptions and principles into day-to-day action research practices. For example, when discussing the process of planning, he covers how that might be done at many levels—from a small group developing an implementation plan to address a relatively circumscribed and specific problem, to community planning and strategic planning that involves many organizations and agencies as well as a large number of stakeholder groups. Another example of Stringer's comprehensiveness is a discussion of the need to celebrate the AR project as well as suggestions about how such celebrations should be organized. "A good action research project often has no well-defined ending. . . . Still, there is usually a time when it is possible to stand back, metaphorically speaking, and recognize significant accomplishments. The time for celebrating has arrived. Celebration is an important part of community-based work" (p. 164).

Still another example of his comprehensive approach is a chapter on "Strategic Planning for Sustainable Change and Development" that focuses primarily on larger organizations and institutions that require systemic changes if the successes of an action research project are to become institutionalized and the AR process itself is to become routine practice.

A Summary and Comparison

The two AR models that were used as contemporary exemplars for critical and interpretive AR are based on different theoretical frameworks. There is still a significant emphasis in the critical model on working directly with oppressed individuals and groups with a goal of emancipation and empowerment. In contrast, the interpretive AR model focuses on the work of local professional practitioners who have the job of helping oppressed groups. However, Stringer's emphasis on the roles of those local professionals concentrates on their need to be facilitative and supportive of the same oppressed groups that Kemmis and McTaggart emphasize. For Stringer, that means the perceptions, needs, and perspectives of the stakeholders are the focus, which is also the focus of the critical AR model. Further, both emphasize the need to solve local problems through a participative approach. Critical theorists tend to see the experts who control organizations and systems as part of the oppressive elements of society, while interpretive AR practitioners like Stringer tend to see them as barriers to successfully dealing with real world problems. In either case, the idea of imposing externally selected solutions developed by distant experts is not acceptable.

The interpretive and critical AR models highlighted here thus seem to have some common approaches to solving problems. They also share similar goals—emancipation and empowerment, developing and implementing successful solutions to local problems, and helping change existing social, cultural, and bureaucratic structures so they are more responsive and more successful. In his book, Stringer consistently emphasizes needs and issues that have always been dear to critical theorists, and he is adamantly opposed to shallow technical solutions which he refers to as "spray on" solutions. He sees the need for deeper, more intense changes, and his AR model is designed to support that type of change.

In addition, Stringer's skepticism about the "revolutionary changes envisioned by radical social theorists or political activists" (p. 208) is shared by Kemmis and McTaggart. Stringer is critical of such change methods because he believes they are less effective than other, more collaborative methods. This is close to contemporary views of Kemmis and McTaggart. Earlier versions of their critical model for AR did not shy away from confrontation, which is compatible with the Marxist maxim that power will not be shared without force. However, Kemmis and McTaggart, in their latest critical AR model, argue that for change to be long-term and deep, the process of change must engage those who control and represent the power groups that traditional Marxist ideology has considered the enemy. Thus, the most recent versions of both the interpretivist AR model of Stringer and the critical AR model of Kemmis and McTaggart suggest that Marxist theory was wrong—that collaboration and negotiation may be more effective. It will be interesting to see how the two major traditions of AR interact and develop over the next decade. Will AR models of practice based on the two paradigms increasingly share methods, goals, and procedures? Or will hybrid models of AR, based on a theoretical framework that bridges the narrowing gap between interpretive and critical paradigms, emerge and compete for the attention of action researchers?

REFERENCES

Bartoo, E. (2004). Review of E. Stringer, Action research in education. *Education Review.* Available: http://www.edrev.info/reviews/rev304.htm

Boog, B. (2003). The emancipator character of action research, its history and the present state of the art. *Journal of Community and Applied Social Psychology, 13,* 426–438).

Ditrano, C., & Silverstein, L. (2006). Listening to parents' voices: Participatory action research in the schools. *Professional Psychology: Research and Practice, 37*(4), 359–366.

Flyvbjerg, B. (2001). *Making social sciences matter: Why social science fails and how it can succeed again.* Cambridge, UK: Cambridge University Press.

Guba, E. (2007). Forward. In E. Stringer, *Action research* (pp. xi–xiv). Thousand Oaks, CA: Sage.

Habermas, J. (1972). *Knowledge and human interest.* London: Heinemann.

Johns, T. (2008). Learning to love our Black selves: Healing from internalized oppressions. In P. Reason & H. Bradbury, (Eds.), *Sage handbook of action research* (pp. 473–486). Thousand Oaks, CA: Sage.

Kemmis, S., & McTaggart, R. (2005). Participatory action research: Communicative action and the public sphere (pp. 559–603). In N . Denzin & Y. Lincoln (Eds.), *Sage Handbook of Qualitative Research*, (3rd ed.). Thousand Oaks, California: Sage.

Kemmis, S., & McTaggart, R. (1988). *The action research planner*. Geelong, Victoria: Deakin University Press.

Mead, G. (2008). Muddling through: Facing the challenges of managing a large-scale action research project. In P. Reason & H. Bradbury, (Eds.), *Sage handbook of action research* (pp. 629–642). Thousand Oaks, CA: Sage.

Oliver, M. (2002). Emancipatory research: A methodology for social transformation. Paper presented at the 1st Annual Disability Research Seminar, Dublin, December 3rd. Available: http://www.leeds.ac.uk/disability-studies/archiveuk/Oliver/Mike'spaper.pdf

Phillips, D. C., & Barbules, N. (2000). *Postpositivism and educational research*. Lanham, MD: Rowman and Littlefield.

Rahman, M. A. (2007). Some trends in the praxis of participatory action research. In P. Reason & H. Bradbury, (Eds.), *Handbook of action research* (pp. 49–61). Thousand Oaks, CA: Sage.

Reason, P., & Bradbury, H. (2008). *The Sage handbook of action research*. Thousand Oaks, CA: Sage.

Schön, D. (1995a). *The reflective practitioner: How professionals think in action*. New York: Basic Books.

Schön, D. (1995b). Knowing-in-action: The new scholarship requires a new epistemology. *Change, 27*, 26–34.

Seymour-Rolls, K., & Hughes, I. (1995). Participatory action research: Getting the job done. *Action Research Reader*. Available: http://www.scu.edu.au/schools/gcm/ar/arr/arow/rseymour.html

Stringer, E. (2007). *Action research*. Thousand Oaks, CA: Sage.

SECTION II

ACTION RESEARCH MODELS AND APPROACHES

The history of action research (AR) is a history of the varying influence of three worldviews or paradigms on this unique way of doing applied and practical research. In the second decade of the twenty-first century, two popular foundational paradigms, interpretive theory and critical theory, dominate the field of action research. There are many models of AR based on each of these two paradigms. Less popular, but still influential, is positivism, which is the paradigm that still dominates the American social sciences and is the most common foundation for research in education—even though its influence has decreased over the past thirty years.

Over the past 15 years, interpretive and critical models of AR seem to be moving closer together, particularly at the level of practice, and the influence of positivism on AR continues to weaken. In such a context, a novice learning about AR for the first time might rightly expect that the examples of AR in the current literature would be very similar. That is, you should be able to read published descriptions of an AR project and see many of the same activities, procedures, and processes in the next AR paper you read. At a very broad level that is true. Widely accepted characteristics such as conducting AR in the field rather than in the laboratory are virtually universal. However, at a more detailed level, there are many, many differences between one AR project and another. A cursory reading of recently published AR papers may even suggest that virtually every report describes an almost

Action Research, pages 85–94
Copyright © 2014 by Information Age Publishing
All rights of reproduction in any form reserved.

unique application of the basic AR concept. That conclusion also has a kernel of truth in it, but it is also untrue. After reviewing the current AR literature we believe most of the published AR research can be organized into fifteen loosely defined types. However, we do not present these categories as definitive or final. They are offered as "useful fictions" that may be helpful when thinking about AR. Those fifteen types of AR will be introduced here. The chapters that follow are examples of these types of AR.

The typology of AR types or categories proposed here is not based on a single criterion such as theoretical foundation. The typology includes a mixed bag with some types representing the level of application of AR while others reflect an emphasis on a particular purpose or process (see Table SII.1). Some also represent traditions of AR, such as Torbert's Developmental Action Inquiry, Heron & Reason's Cooperative Inquiry, or Design-Based Research, that have developed and matured somewhat separately from the mainstream (if there is such a thing as "mainstream" when it comes to the development of AR). AR types such as Developmental Action Inquiry and Cooperative Inquiry are part of the third group. The approaches to AR in that group are distinguishable primarily by the processes they favor.

As shown in Figure SII.1, we have organized the 15 types of AR into three clusters or groups—those distinguished by the level of *focus*, those that emphasize a particular *purpose*, and those that emphasize a particular *process*.

It is important to note that the types of AR shown in Figure SII.1 are "leaky" in the sense that an example of AR done with a small, collegial group (one of several possible Levels) might also be an example of interpretive

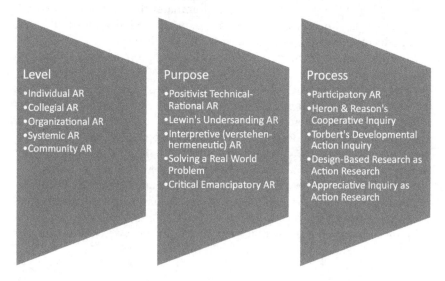

Figure SII.1   A typology for organizing types of AR according to their level, purpose, and process focus.

research (under Purpose) and of Torbert's Developmental Action Inquiry (under Process). Because one example may illustrate several different types of AR, the 10 chapters that follow this introduction to Section II of the book actually illustrate virtually all of the types of AR listed in Figure SII.1.

AR TYPES THAT FOCUS ON LEVEL

AR projects vary according to the size of the group that is involved in the AR project. The group can be as small as one individual and as large as a complex geopolitical system. Chapters in this book cover levels that range from one individual to small, collegial groups to organizations and systems. One type of AR that focuses on level requires a bit more explanation. That is community AR. Ernest Stringer's (2007) book is one of several guides to conducting community action research. Stringer summarized community AR this way: "A fundamental premise of community-based action research is that it commences with an interest in the problems of a group, a community, or an organization. Its purpose is to assist people in extending their understanding of their situation and thus in resolving problems that confront them.... Community-based action research provides a model for enacting local, action-oriented approaches to inquiry, applying small-scale theorizing to specific problems in specific situations" (p. 10). Stringer goes on to say that this type of AR is based on four core social values: It is democratic, equitable, liberating, and life enhancing. Several of the chapters that follow are examples of community AR.

AR TYPES THAT FOCUS ON PURPOSE

Purpose tends to be associated with the foundational paradigm for the research. AR based on a positivist paradigm tends to focus on what are called "technical-rational" solutions. Interpretive AR often emphasizes, more than other types, the need to develop a shared understanding of the local context among participants, and critical AR champions emancipatory purposes. Different purposes also lead to different approaches. For example, technical-rational AR tends to emphasize the careful and precise definition of the problem, detailed specification of a potential solution to the problem, and careful analysis of the impact of the solution using empirical, objective data. Often in technical-rational AR based on a positivist foundation the solution selected is one that already exists and the task of the AR group is to implement it correctly in a particular setting. In contrast, Stringer's community AR is based on an interpretive/critical foundation and if an existing "solution" is used in a new context, it will likely be heavily modified by the participants so that it fits the local context.

Technical-rational AR tends to emphasize well structured problems and well-structured solutions. Other types or AR do not. Instead, some emphasize the construction of *verstehen*, which is the German word for "understanding." In his original paper on action research, Kurt Lewin (1946) described three general purposes for doing action research. One was to develop and evaluate a local solution to a local problem. A second was to develop "scientific" knowledge that could be generalized from the research setting to other settings. The third was what we are calling Lewin's "other" purpose, that of developing a better understanding (e.g., *verstehen*) of both the context of a problem and the problem as it exists in that context. Lewin argued that this improved understanding was a critical foundation for working on solutions to the problem. The chapter in this book authored by Dr. Wenying Shi, is an example of this type of AR. Her research was a project to develop a better understanding of the process immigrant doctoral students go through to integrate into Canadian academia.

Lewin's three purposes for doing AR, including his third or "other" purpose, were framed and expressed in the language of 1940s social science, which was securely in the grip of positivism. Later in the twentieth century several intellectual movements led to the development of alternative paradigms for social science research that challenged positivism. There was also the "linguistic turn" in philosophy that emphasized the lack of objective foundations for meaning. The rise of these postmodern perspectives in both philosophy and the history of science also challenged cherished assumptions about whether scientific and technical advances were always good and positive. In addition, Ludwig Wittgenstein and Richard Rorty both questioned whether humans should put their faith in universal truths based on this or that foundation. Rorty and Wittgenstein were both "antifoundationalists" who argued there were no "facts of the matter" that everyone could agree on if they just looked at the relevant evidence properly and carefully. These philosophical positions led to serious questions about whether the social sciences could discover, no matter what research methods they used, anything resembling the universal and generalizable truths that were the stock and trade of the natural and physical sciences.

One type of research that became more appropriate and accepted as support for general truths or "laws of human behavior" waned, was phenomenology—which is the study of the perspectives and beliefs of individuals and groups. Another development was social science research that emphasized "local truths" or, perhaps more accurately, "local knowledge" or even "local understanding," which is anchored in local context and history. Social scientists who advocate this type of research are often described as following interpretive theory or as being "constructivists." There are a number of AR models based on interpretive theory. While interpretive AR, like most forms of AR, does emphasize developing solutions to local problems, it also considers the search for local knowledge and understanding to be a crucial foundation for that search. This is very much in the tradition of Lewin's "other" reason for doing AR, but interpretive theorists tend to put even more emphasis on the contextual and situated aspect of the knowledge constructed in AR projects. Interpretive action researchers do not share Lewin's hope that AR will also yield generalizable or universal knowledge that can be directly transferred to other settings. Instead, they believe the job of deciding what to take from an AR study is not so much the responsibility of the authors of the report. It is their job to provide enough detail and context for the readers to thoughtfully decide what they can use, adapt, or revise for their own context.

Having discussed several reasons for doing AR, we come to the most common purpose of this form of research. It is "AR to solve a problem" and there are many examples of this type of AR in the chapters that follow. In fact, virtually all the examples in this book illustrate an approach to solving a real world problem. However, many AR projects that have this as a goal also have one or more additional purposes. There are also many ways for AR to approach the task of developing a solution to a problem, and the following chapters illustrate a diverse range of approaches.

Finally, several chapters illustrate a purpose of AR that is not as universal as solving a real world problem. Emancipatory action research is typically based on critical theory and it has the goal of helping individuals and groups overcome oppression as well as develop ways of bringing more freedom and equity to both their own lives and the society they live in. Several chapters illustrate this form of AR which has several names including "Critical AR", "Emancipatory Action Research," and "Participatory Emancipatory Action Research." Several chapters, including some from international settings, are examples of emancipatory action research.

TYPES OF AR THAT FOCUS ON PROCESS

The final cluster of AR approaches are differentiated by the processes they advocate. As noted in Chapter 3 the general characteristics of AR are more like "family resemblances" than absolute criteria for deciding whether a particular study was based AR methods or not. AR studies "tend" to share certain characteristics but few have all the characteristics included in any particular list, including the one we presented in a previous chapter. In addition, there are approaches to AR that are distinguished primarily by the particular process they emphasize. For example, Participatory Action Research (PAR) is characterized by the involvement and participation of local stakeholders in all aspects of AR. In PAR the local stakeholders decide what to study, the data to be collected, and the solution to be tried. They also decide whether the solution worked and what changes should be made in the next AR cycle. PAR is often based on the principles of democratic participation that emphasize the need for those who will be impacted by change to be the ones who make the decisions about that change. PAR is also supported by aspects of constructivist theory that emphasize the importance of local knowledge and the need to develop custom solutions to problems that take local history and context into consideration. This does not mean outside experts have no role in participatory AR. They do, but they are participants like everyone else instead of automatically becoming the leaders or the sources of pre-packaged solutions.

Several other types of AR that are distinguished by the processes they emphasize were developed by groups working more independently and less in the mainstream of AR development. The result is three types of AR that differ significantly from most of the other AR models. Cooperative inquiry is one such model. It was originally developed by John Heron (1995) with significant contributions by Peter Reason and Hillary Bradbury (Reason & Bradbury, 2007). Cooperative inquiry is often associated with the University of Bath in the UK where Heron and Reason both worked. It is an approach to AR that focuses on groups of professional practitioners working on meaningful issues with the help and support of a researcher who uses the principles of cooperative inquiry.

Another type of AR that is distinguished by the process employed was developed by William Torbert, who taught in the School of Management at Boston College for many years. Torbert's model for change is called Developmental Action Inquiry (DAI) and it is an attempt to combine actions with focused research. DAI includes procedures to help individuals focus their attention on their perceptions and experiences as well as steps for building "mini-communities of inquiry" made up of friends, family, or colleagues. Torbert (1999) calls the activities that focus on individual reflection and analysis "first person research/practice." The second level of DAI, working with "mini-communities of inquiry" are "second person research/practice." Torbert's third level of DAI is "the third person dynamics of the larger institutions within which one's action is situated" (Torbert, 1999, p. 189). The word "developmental" in DAI refers to Torbert's assumption that a great deal of individual growth and self development must occur if actions are to be effective and successful. Torbert's DAI has a much more individualistic focus than most forms of AR, even though it incorporates activities carried out in small groups. The approach and structure tends to appeal primarily to managers and leaders. However, it offers a number of unique perspectives on how change should be conceptualized and how it can be supported.

Still another type of AR deviates considerably from the more common forms of AR. Design-based research or DBR has a unique focus as well as a unique process. The goal of DBR is generally to design and develop a resource, usually a learning resource. The most popular forms of DBR use a positivist paradigm that also expects the research to produce generalizable knowledge that can be used in settings beyond the one where the research was conducted. However, some forms of DBR are based on interpretive theory and focus much more on creating resources for a particular context. DBR and DAI are probably the two most distinctive forms of AR discussed in this book. They are not really odd or unusual, but they do stand out because they do not "fit" into the most common conceptual frameworks for AR. Dunning's (2012) book is a recent exploration of DBR from a moderately positivist perspective. In addition, special issues of both *Educational Technology* (2005, volume 45, issue 1) and the *Journal of Learning Sciences* (2004, volume 13, issue 1) have been about DBR. In addition, the edited book by Willis (2007) contains examples of constructivist instructional design models that illustrate how a constructivist/interpretive paradigm can be used to do design-based research.

The last type of AR that emphasizes a particular process is appreciative inquiry. It is sometimes abbreviated as AI but not often because most people think of AI as the abbreviation for artificial intelligence. Appreciative inquiry is also referred to as AIM which is short for appreciative inquiry method. One interesting aspect of AIM is its emphasis on focusing on strengths rather than weaknesses. For example, a corporation interested in improvement could start with a "gap analysis" which looks for weaknesses or mismatches between the mission of the organization and current practices. There are many approaches to change that begin with an identification of weaknesses in an organization. AIM does the opposite; it looks for strengths that can be the foundation for additional improvements. The "positive" approach of AIM has been applied to individual as well as organizational development and it is based on a movement called positive psychology. In a special issue *Time* magazine referred to positive psychology and AIM as "The New Science of Happiness" (Wallis, 2004).

LINKING CHAPTERS TO TYPES OF AR

Table SII.1 lists each of the remaining chapters in the book and indicates what types of AR they represent. The types printed in bold are heavily emphasized in that chapter, but few of the chapters are examples of only one type of AR. Taken together the ten chapters listed in the table illustrate how diverse AR is across the dimensions of level, purpose, and process.

With this overview, we now turn to an exploration of action research as described by practitioners of the art of AR. Please see Table SII.1 for information on each chapter's focus points.

TABLE SII.1 Chapters Relevant to Different Types of Action Research

Chapter	Relevant Level	Relevant Purposes	Relevant Processes
4. Dr. La-Kicia K. Walker-Floyd *Individual Action Research: The PARf and Self-Study*	**Individual Level AR**	Lewin's Understanding AR Interpretive AR **Solving a Real World Problem**	Reflective Journaling as a Component of Action Research
5. Dr. Carol Ann St. George *An Action Research Study: How Can Elementary Teachers Collaborate More Effectively with Parents to Support Student Literacy Learning?*	**Collegial AR** Organizational AR	**Solving a Real World Problem** Critical Emancipatory AR	Collegial Circles Participatory AR
6. Dr. Shankar Shankaran *Implementing Organizational Change Using Action Learning and Action Research in an Asian Setting*	Collegial AR **Organizational AR** Systemic AR	Positivist Technical-Rational AR Solving a Real World Problem	Action Learning Learning Sets Action Science Search Conferences
7. Dr. Wenying Shi *Immigrant Ph.D. Students Using Action Research as a Tool in Career Preparation*	Individual AR **Collegial AR** Organizational AR	Lewin's Understanding AR Interpretive (verstehen-hermeneutic) AR **Solving a Real World Problem** **Critical Emancipatory AR**	Participatory AR Auto-ethnography
8. Dr. Maria Casamassa *Situated Literacies in the Homes and Communities of Three Children*	Collegial AR **Organizational AR**	**Lewin's Understanding AR** Interpretive (verstehen-hermeneutic) AR Solving a Real World Problem	Participant Observation Participatory AR Collaborative Inquiry Critical teacher research Teacher Study Groups
9. Dr. Dan Cernuska & Dr. Ioan Ionas *Design-Based Research as a Form of Action Research*	Collegial AR	Solving a Real World Problem	Design-Based Research Instructional Design

(continued)

TABLE SII.1 Chapters Relevant to Different Types of Action Research (continued)

Chapter	Relevant Level	Relevant Purposes	Relevant Processes
10. Dr. Caleb J Othieno, Dr. Anne A Obondo, & Dr. Mathai Muthoni *Improving Adherence to Ante-Retroviral Treatment for People With Harmful Alcohol Use in Kariobangi, Kenya Through Participatory Research and Action*	**Community AR** Collegial AR Systemic AR	Solving a Real World Problem	Participatory AR
11. Dr. Kingsley Chikaphupha, Dr. Patnice Nkhonjera, Dr. Ireen Namakhoma, & Dr. Rene Loewenson *Access to Hiv Treatment and Care Amongst Commercial Sex Workers in Malawi: A Participatory Reflection and Action (Pra) Project Report*	Community AR Organizational AR Systemic AR	**Solving a Real World Problem** Lewin's Understanding AR Interpretive AR **Critical Emancipatory AR**	Participatory AR
12. Dr. Mona Leigh Guha, Dr. Allison Druin, & Dr. Jerry Alan Fails *Cooperative Inquiry Revisited: Reflections of The Past and Guidelines for the Future of Intergenerational Co-Design*	Collegial AR	Interpretive AR	**Cooperative Inquiry** (which is not based on Heron and Reason's version of Cooperative Inquiry) **Design Based AR** **Instructional Design**
13. Dr. Kathleen Thompson *Transitions in Well-Being and Recovery: Cooperative Inquiry Involving Older Adults with Lived Experience of a Mental Illness*	Individual AR Collegial AR Organizational AR Systemic AR	Interpretive AR **Solving a Real World Problem**	Cooperative Inquiry

REFERENCES

Dunning, T. (2012). *Natural experiments in the social sciences: A design-based approach.* New York: Cambridge University Press.

Heron, J. (1995). *Co-operative inquiry: Research into the human condition.* Thousand Oaks, CA: Sage.

Lewin, K. (1946). Action research and minority problems. *Journal of Social Issues, 2*(4), 34–46.

Reason, P., & Bradbury, H. (2007). *The Sage handbook of action research: Participative inquiry and practice.* Thousand Oaks, CA: Sage.

Stringer, E. (2007). *Action research* (3rd ed.). Thousand Oaks, CA: Sage.

Torbert, W. (1999). The distinctive questions developmental action inquiry asks. *Management Learning, 30*(2), 189–206.

Wallis, C. (2004). The New Science of Happiness. Available at http://www.authentichappiness.sas.upenn.edu/images/TimeMagazine/Time-Happiness.pdf

CHAPTER 4

INDIVIDUAL ACTION RESEARCH

The PARJ and Self Study

La-Kicia K. Walker-Floyd
Independent Consultant

ABSTRACT

Chapter 4 examines the action research process undertaken in my doctoral dissertation, "A Narrative Study of How an Online Practitioner Used a Personal Action Research Journal as a Form of Professional Development." In response to asynchronous online classroom challenges, I created a personal action research journal (PARJ) in 2006 and used it to (a) record experiences and/or classroom challenges; (b) explore ideas and/or methods to address the challenges; (c) try the new practice; (d) monitor students; and (e) reflect upon the experience and new practice.

This paper also analyzes the interpretive paradigm of action research, the setting and problem, description of my action research project, personal insights, and variables I would change in my dissertation. It is hoped that readers will learn how to use a personal action research journal as a tool for self-study.

Action Research, pages 95–109

Tell me and I'll forget. Show me, and I may not remember.
Involve me, and I'll understand.

—Native American Proverb

Scientists are simply individuals who ask questions and seek answers. Teachers are scientists of nature. They diligently engage in a form of science when they ask questions such as, how will using this technique assist the students in my classrooms? Is Student Y beginning to show signs of comprehending and incorporating the study strategies learned in Week 4? Although these examples are simply that, examples, they do point us to the conclusion that we, no matter our occupation, are all scientists. However, as an educator, this paper addresses the analysis of action research from the perspective of a teaching professional.

Henson (1996) and Schmuck (1997) suggest that action research (teacher action research) is a process, and one type of research methodology which allows practitioners an opportunity to study real classroom or school-related issues to understand and improve the quality of actions or instruction. Essentially, action research is a systematic orderly way for educators to observe practice and find solutions. Action research is also a type of inquiry that is planned, organized and can be shared with others (Johnson, 2008). Finally, action research can also serve as a tool in professional development.

As an online practitioner, I am an action researcher. I extract a great deal of information while studying my practice and have experienced moments of frustration. Nonetheless, action research has served and continues to provide me a methodological tool with which I study my classrooms and professional practice. Chapter 2 (of this text) highlighted three paradigms of action research: positivism, interpretive, and critical. My doctoral dissertation embraced the interpretive action research paradigm. O'Brien (2001) describes the interpretive action research paradigm as:

> [Interpretive action research] has emerged in the social sciences to break out of the constraints imposed by positivism. With its emphasis on the relationship between socially-engendered concept formation and language, it can be referred to as the Interpretive paradigm. Containing such qualitative methodological approaches as phenomenology, ethnography, and hermeneutics, it is characterized by a belief in a socially constructed, subjectively-based reality, one that is influenced by culture and history. Nonetheless it still retains the ideals of researcher objectivity, and researcher as passive collector and expert interpreter of data.

Unlike the positivist approach, the interpretive approach required me to seek local, contextual knowledge and to devise solutions to local problems (Willis, 2007). Interpretive action research is not primarily concerned with universal "truths." Instead it focuses on local understandings or *verstehen* (interpretive understanding) and does not profess to be generalizable in the traditional, positivist meaning of that term (Cassell & Johnson, 2006). Further, the interpretive approach, like the critical paradigm, required me to engage in reflective practice. My 2011 dissertation, "A Narrative Study of How an Online Practitioner Used a Personal Action Research Journal as a Form of Professional Development" was a narrative study, enmeshed in action research and dipped in the interpretive paradigm. The premise of the self-study was to articulate the benefits of adopting the use of a personal action research journal (PARJ) to examine professional practice as a form of professional development (Walker-Floyd, 2011).

Self-study is central to the focus of this chapter. It describes the setting and problem, offers a description of my action research project, personal insights, and discusses the limitations of my dissertation.

SETTING AND PROBLEM

Teachers hold significant knowledge which is accumulated as their teaching careers build (Dewey, 1938; Johnson, 1987; Polanyi, 1962; Schwab, 1971). Clandinin and Connelly (1999) saw that teachers are knowers themselves, of their situations, of students, of subject matter, of teaching, and of learning. Teachers' knowledge stems from circumstances, practices, and the questions of they ask. Therefore, practice is part of what the researchers meant by personal practical knowledge. Practice includes intellectual acts and self-exploration. When we see practice, we see personal practical knowledge in practice (Clandinin & Connelly, 2000).

As an online practitioner, I am well aware of the challenges associated with distance education. Further, the academic welfare of my students is important. It is my desire in each of my online, asynchronous classrooms that my students experience a smooth transition from brick-and-mortar instruction into online facilitation.

In my first semester of teaching (before committing to the creation of a teacher's journal to examine my practice) I had five virtual learners who were struggling with navigating the online classroom. Each student was diverse in terms of background (e.g., gender, stage in life, employment status, age group) and years absent from the classroom. I recall students assailing my office phone with messages related to "Where do I find the reading materials for Week 1? Please help because I am confused!" In my mind, navigating the online forums was a no brainer. This assertion was incorrect! After reviewing the frustrations relayed by my students, I started to question my ability as an online educator.

In 2006 I began keeping a learning journal detailing my professional experiences as an online educator. I felt the need to write down challenges encountered in my classrooms, to reflect on each problem, devise a solution, and again, reflect upon whether my solutions helped remedy the problems. My journal has been my safe haven for writing about my experiences as an online instructor. It has served as the one place that I could let out my frustrations, as well as triumph in my achievements. My ability to write and let go in each entry has contributed to finding solutions to dilemmas in my classrooms. My journal led me to a place where I could focus on improving my practice.

Reflective practice is focusing upon detailed stories of life and practice, and upon the thoughts and feelings associated with the actions in them (Bolton, 1999). If meaningfully engaged in, journal writing and reflective practice have the capacity to reveal how we learn best and they have the potential to reveal possible solutions to classroom issues (Walker-Floyd, 2011). Journal writing and reflective practice is a way for a teacher as an autonomous practitioner—who may or may not have access to professional development and/or close peer communication—to extract feedback on his or her practice (McAlpine & Weston, 2000).

Scholars have also noted that journaling and reflection is a responsible way to analyze practice. While journaling was the selected action research strategy for improving my performance as an online instructor, it also addressed the larger problem of the lack of transfer of professional development from becoming aware of different concepts, models and theories to actual classroom practice and improved student learning. Exposure to theory and methods through formal workshops does not guarantee effective implementation of a new practice, especially when teachers do not make meaning from what they have learned. In Dadds' (1997) view, "[teachers] have been taught to devalue their inner voice, their own experience, their own hard-earned insights about [learners] ... When the formal [staff development] course has ended, professional judgment in the classroom goes on, often without continuing support" (p. 34). The isolation that online educators face makes it even more challenging to follow through with new and better approaches in the absence of colleagues to dialogue with during the implementation phase.

The theories are there that support both formal staff development and more personal ways of supporting professional growth and development. There are, however, practical concerns that must be addressed. One is that many practitioners do not believe they have the time or cannot take the time to archive their experiences in a journal (Dadds, 1997). In addition, while there is considerable literature on the use of journaling by educators working in brick and mortar schools, very little has been published about the use of a journal by online educators. My intent in the dissertation research was to illustrate how keeping an action research journal can work for an online teacher.

The Transition to an Action Research Study

I transitioned from exploring how to write a traditional dissertation for which I would have been a mere observer, commenting on the situation and trying to make sense of it, to a process in which I was the participant, and researcher. Essentially, my learning was at the heart of my research. This transition changed the way I think about the world around me, which continues to recast my work as an educator, adult learner, and scholar-practitioner.

By incorporating phenomenology and narrative inquiry as a research strategy, I was equipped to analyze, question, and synthesize meanings and intentions of various situations—both professional and personal. This shift contributed to my authentic voice—my meaning-making of my experiences—for I was embracing my ability to understand my own experiences. The conversion from what was originally a mixed methods approach to a qualitative strategy of inquiry contributed to my understanding of the humanness of research in education. I came to understand that there is a great deal to be learned in the stories of others, as well as when we attentively listen to our own narrative.

Description of the Personal Action Research Journal

Western ways of thinking tend to prefer abstract and out-of-context views of the world, but Schön (1983) argued it is essential to incorporate practitioners' knowledge in explanatory models of their work. Kleinman (1983) pointed out that many educational problems require additional knowledge of the meaning systems of practitioners, as well as sociocultural factors shaping their communication with one another. Erickson (1988) further argued that to move forward toward such theories in teacher education, practitioners' knowledge and meaning systems must be tapped as part of the explanatory process. Isolated descriptions of classroom procedure, or measure of behavioral outcomes of those procedures, may miss the "very heart" of the process of conceptual change between teacher and student (Krathwohl, Bloom, & Masia, 1964).

In order to document and analyze these conceptual changes, Erickson (1982) recommended the crafting of stories of teaching and learning in which practitioners play key author roles. These stories have a number of advantages. First, primed by their personal research experiences, teachers can add richness and validity to accounts of their work by uncovering and sharing their own implicit theories about teaching and learning (Clark & Yinger, 1979). Second, stories are representations of knowledge that do not dodge moral consequences, and to the extent that teaching is a moral craft, as well as an array of technical skills, stories of teaching may represent that craft more adequately than monographs of formal research (Ryan, 1981; Tom, 1985). Third, teachers' stories are a critical source of information about teaching and an opportunity for teachers to communicate about their work.

My individual self-study was relevant across several dimensions of professional practice and efficacy that have direct implications for program quality and cost, student learning, and faculty/adjunct retention in higher education and distance learning. The term *Personal Action Research Journal (PARJ)* emerged from discussions with a member of my dissertation committee. Cochran-Smith and Lytle (1990) identified teachers' published and unpublished journals as one of four types of teacher inquiry research that is intentional and systematic and that contributes to the professional knowledge base when shared. The authors described journals as "accounts of classroom life in which teachers record observations, analyze their experiences, reflect on, and interpret their practices over time" (p. 44).

In my dissertation (Walker-Floyd, 2011), the PARJ was a written account of a practitioner's professional experiences using a blend of structure (action research) and richness throughout the journal. My PARJ was a series of hand-written texts entered in hardbound journals purchased at my local office supply store. During the course of a year, I would record between 125 and 210 entries. In the PARJ, my practice was analyzed, and possible solutions developed and noted. The PARJ also told the story of how those solutions were implemented in the classroom and how they were themselves analyzed for effectiveness or ineffectiveness. Intermittently I had to revisit and rework a solution—essentially the use of a PARJ requires educators to try new things in the hope of developing successful solutions. However, "developing solutions" does not mean a teacher creates a local solution out of thin air. Personal experience is a valuable course of insight and understanding but for most problems a professional faces, there is also a rich vein of research and professional practice literature, including other PARJ, that also offer guidance and insights. My personal online experiences were, therefore, not the only source of information. In conjunction with journal articles, textbooks, and workshops, experiences were contextualized within my web of experiences. The process of keeping a PARJ is often cyclical (see Figure 4.1).

The PARJ texts were either full action research cycles, partial cycles, or informal in nature. *Informal entries* were texts that detailed humor, quick

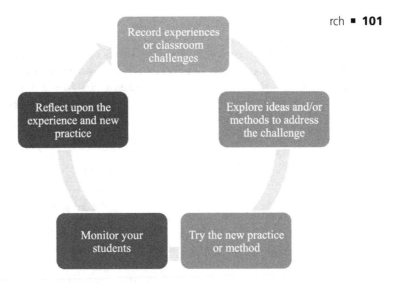

Figure 4.1 Personal Action Research Journal Cycle.

observations, notes about articles I had read and how they pertained to my online practice, and any notes about my feelings relative to my professional practice. *Full cycle* texts reflected archives that detailed the five-stage personal action research journal cycle in its entirety as illustrated in Figure 4.1. *Partial cycle* texts were those that partially covered the personal action research journal cycle.

Action research provides a structure enabling teachers to take charge of effectively implementing new practices to improve student learning. Rust (2009) described the benefit of this approach:

> We posit teacher action research as a bridge connecting research, practice, and education policy—as an important and practical way to engage teachers as consumers of research, as researchers of their own practice who use research to shape practice, as designers of their own professional development, and as informants to scholars and policy makers regarding critical issues in the field. (p. 1885)

My PARJ provided a means for me to work in my profession as a scholar-practitioner. I did not begin the process with a clearly articulated idea of what it mean to use a PARJ as a vehicle for doing action research as described by Rust (2009). However, while reading some of my journal entries, an sudden insight led me to begin shifting my research focus. I came to realize there were personal inquiries conducted every day that I wrote about in my PARJ. This was part of a process I came to rely on for analyzing, changing, and evaluating my pedagogy. One way of looking at the process is to say that I assumed the role of scholar and critical friend to the novice practitioner (my past self) who wrote those entries.

In my study, I explored how my asynchronous online experiences were shaped by the virtual context. The exploration of my experiences (as detailed in my PARJ) provided readers with insight into how I implemented action research to structure the analysis of my journal as a form of continuous professional development. In the dissertation I addressed several research questions but the one I will focus on in this chapter is:

> In what ways did the PARJ (used as a tool in professional development) assist me in becoming a better online practitioner?

I took my journal entries—analyzing those pertinent to my study—and surveyed them through my current lens of knowledge, skills, and insight. In that process I attempted to maintain intellectual humility and integrity. Intellectual humility postulates a lack of intellectual conceit, boastfulness, or pretentiousness. Intellectual integrity requires researchers to be consistent in the application of intellectual standards, as well as to admit discrepancies and inconsistencies in their thoughts and actions (Paul & Elder, 2006).

I used my PARJ entries as a source of data, which allowed me to make sense of the classroom situations. Those ongoing entries—some of which included dreadful moments in practice—lived in the field, are the texts out of which we can tell stories of our experiences. The process of sharing those stories facilitates what Clandinin & Connelley (2000) called reflective balance.

PARJ DATA COLLECTION PROCEDURES

Teachers' knowledge is inherently personal and organized in terms of stories or narratives (Clandinin & Connelly, 1988; Elbaz, 1988; Olson & Craig, 2001). Therefore, action research, narrative inquiry and phenomenology were used as the methods of my research. The data collected as a part of the study included: journal writing and teacher deliverables I created. However, I only reviewed entries dated from 2006 through April 2010.

PARJ Analysis and Interpretation Procedures

After collecting data, I transformed my journal text into research texts, whose meanings and social significance I explored. Before arriving to the question of, "What do I do with all this data?" I needed to know what data existed. I read and reread all of the journal texts and sorted them, so that I had an understanding of all data collected. This involved careful coding (Creswell, 2005) of journal entries, and my teacher creations, with a notation of dates, and contexts for the composition of the research texts. Juxtaposed with my narrative account and using van Manen's (1990) approach to conducting phenomenological research, I looked for patterns, narrative threads, tensions, and common themes either within or across my experiences and social settings, thereby composing a research text (Clandinin & Connelley, 2000).

My research required me to unearth catalyst entries. A *catalyst entry* is a primary text that sparked the writing of additional entries in response to a classroom problem. I examined all journal entries written thereafter and analyzed the text looking for common themes and/or a direct connection to a catalyst. Although some journal text had a direct connection to a catalyst, others did not. If the secondary entry was connected to the catalyst, it was included in my *inclusion list.* After examining the journal text/data on the inclusion list, I coded each entry (i.e., Stage 1, Stage 2, Stage 3, Stage 4, and Stage 5). Lastly, I synthesized the themes into a single storyline describing how I improved my practice. These research texts were not cross-sectional survey data but data I continuously revisited.

How did I arrive at this process of analyzing my journal text and data? While reviewing each text, I looked for action research patterns. For example, there were 11 entries written about plagiarism and online learners—two entries were focused on Student A, five journal texts were related to Student B, the remaining four had nothing to do with Student A or Student B and were clearly *independent entries* written about my students and/ or faculty scenarios. I eliminated any independent journal entries and only focused my attention on those entries that were classified as catalyst and *secondary* journal entries related to a catalyst. Both the catalyst and secondary text had to: (a) be directly connected; and (b) illustrate the personal action research journal process (as explained earlier in this chapter). After revisiting the journal text/data threads (the series of entries that were connected), I synthesized the threads looking for common themes, which led me to discover the storyline describing how I improved classroom practice. Figure 4.2 illustrates data analysis and representation steps that were undertaken during the completion of this dissertation.

Personal Insights

We start as fools and become wise through experience.
—Tanzanian Proverb

As a form of interpretive phenomenology, my narrative study described my experiences as an online instructor. In my study three pivotal issues were relevant: First, the focus was on the advantage of using action research for improving practice during the process of course administration, online

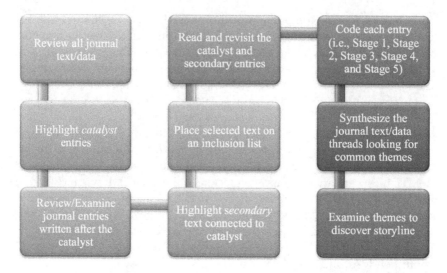

Figure 4.2 Data analysis procedures for personal action research journal texts.

discussion, and interaction with students because it is based on the assumption that experienced teachers possess a certain kind of knowledge—knowledge that is practical, experiential, and shaped by the teacher's purposes and values (Elbaz, 1988; Clandinin, 1985). The second inquiry was centered on the journal texts and their analysis in order to determine if they were a full action research cycle, partial cycle, or informal, as well the contributions of each style of text. Third, I explored ways the personal action research journal (PARJ; used as a tool in professional development) assisted me in becoming a better online practitioner.

Although the PARJ contained formal full and partial cycle journal texts, there were other dimensions to the journal as well (i.e., humor, informal practice, analysis of literature, and new information learned). However, my personal online experiences documented in the PARJ were not the only data resource. They were analyzed in conjunction with analysis of journal articles, textbooks, and workshops.

While completing my dissertation study I became aware that there was a need to be less formal because practitioners need to establish space to let words flow in order to be better equipped to dig deeper (Gibbs, 1988). Without restriction, I encouraged myself to dig deeper, to question everything that I learned up to that point, and work toward "truths" discovered in my experiences. Respectively, the formal, full cycle allowed me to still let the words flow, to dig deeper, to question, and to discover some of the hidden truths in the data I had available. The full cycle entries were embedded in narrative and revealed that I was in action research mode. Both the formal and informal elements of the journal entries were valuable and no one method was better than the other. I felt free and uninhibited while writing.

I had an "aha" moment while managing the analysis of the PARJ: I had a broader understanding of its value. I restructured a method (not consciously doing so). In 2006 I was unaware of action research and its use in education. A research method in which educators could collect their own data and use it to the benefit of students and classroom practices was certainly not in my mental database in 2006. I was formally introduced to action research in the summer of 2009. In a deeper sense, I realized action research was a learned process which provided me a lens through which to examine self and practice.

The examination of the journal data led me to a place where I discovered the purpose of my PARJ in the action research cycle. The journal, however, was enhanced by informal, natural entries along the way. If the journal were not a place for informality, then what is the point? Informal entries as a form of professional development present practitioners with an opportunity to write with authenticity (Hiemstra, 2001). Full action research cycle transcriptions still allowed me to write authentically, but I was cognizant that I would need to observe specific behaviors or check results. Essentially, the examination of my journal data revealed that journal writing should be fluid and natural or else it can become no more than another chore in an already busy day. I value journals written in the narrative form and realize going into the formal action research mode benefited my online practice. One reason for that may be that the PARJ was filled with informal, almost spontaneous "thinking aloud" segments as well as more formal material.

The journal texts shared in the study illustrated how I learned to personalize the online experience, learned about the importance of posting a student bio thread, and creating/supporting student–teacher relationships. Other material helped me understand the PARJ content and its purpose. For example, while keeping the journal I created various deliverables relative to how students might improve participation and substantive responses. I also created a deliverable to help students understand the content that was the focus during each academic week. As I read the journal material I also saw how keeping the journal led to improvements in my teaching that also benefitted student outcomes.

WOULD I DO THINGS DIFFERENTLY?

Professional development for educators requires teachers to focus on changing their own practice. Those who engage in professional development share a common purpose of enhancing their ability to do their work. Jasper (2006) contended that at the heart of professional develop-ment is the individual's interest in lifelong learning and increasing his or her own skills and knowledge. Without this core commitment to the process I am not sure the effort will be worth the result. That core com-mitment may thus be a prerequisite to effective use of action research methods such as PARJ.

Other than the question of necessary prerequisite attitudes and inclina-tions, I also considered other responses to the question, "What would I do differently?" I was forced to revisit my dissertation research. The findings of, "A Narrative Study of How an Online Practitioner Used a Personal Ac-tion Research Journal as a Form of Professional Development," were not generalizable in the traditional sense of that term, nor was it my intent to dispute theory or create a new ideology. Simply, my narrative, action research self-study unearthed the richness and authenticity of the journal text and illustrated how using action research documented in a journal is advantageous to myself, a higher education online practitioner, as a con-tinuous form of professional development. For me, the process was a very beneficial one, but I do not present it as a "proven" tool for the professional development of online college instructors. Deciding whether this approach would be helpful to another online educator rests with that online educator rather than me.

One of the limitations of my study was that I did not have access to the shared stories of other online practitioners. While that was not possible in my situation, collaboration and sharing among small groups of online educators, or even pairs of autonomous online educators sharing journals, seems to have considerable potential.

If humans are social creatures who learn through social interaction, a small "community" seeking to develop their professional skills might find it easier to embrace the examination of common problems found in their personal action research journals and through dialogue and collaboration develop interesting solutions to those common problems. In addition, while my own research was based on an interpretive rather than a critical para-digm, it would be interesting to read about the efforts of other individuals, and groups that based their efforts on a critical/emancipatory paradigm. As Ledwith & Springett (2009) suggested, "Emancipatory action research offers us the scope to develop a more critical praxis, a form of practice that is symbiotically creating knowledge in action and action as knowledge. In this way, different ways of knowing that have been effectively silenced in the positivist search for one truth are given voice" (p. 199).

CLOSING REMARKS

As I have noted already, I do not view the research described in this chapter as establishing or proving anything. I have described a process I hoped would improve my personal and professional skills, expertise, and understanding. I believe it accomplished that goal and was well worth the time and effort I invested. Whether this approach would be helpful to someone else is a decision that must, I believe, be made individually. It requires considerable effort over an extended time, and it is based on certain professional beliefs, and needs, that not all professionals share. Even in my own experience, which has been documented here, I did not begin the journey with the understanding of action research and the usefulness of PARJ that I ended the dissertation work with. I suggest that if you decide to this approach, or if you support its use with a group of colleagues, that you and your group freely, adopt, adapt, revise, omit, and adjust the process at will. Traditional research methods have often made teachers at all levels the objects of research. They were also expected to consume the research of others and practice as the research told them to practice. Action research breaks down the barrier between researcher and practitioner, and makes each of us a contributing force in research that brings a wealth of resources, knowledge, expertise, and personal practical knowledge to the table (Clandinin & Connelly, 2000). Action research takes teachers from the margins of scholarship, and puts them in the middle of the process. I believe that opens us to many new possibilities, new perspectives, and new understandings.

REFERENCES

Bolton, G. (1999). *The therapeutic potential of creative writing—Writing myself.* London, UK: Jessica Kingsley.

Cassell, C., & Johnson, P. (2006). Action research: explaining the diversity. *Human Relations, 59*(6), 783–814.

Clandinin, D. J. (1985, Winter). Personal practical knowledge: A study of teachers' classroom images. *Curriculum Inquiry. 15,* 361–385.

Clandinin, D. J., & Connelly, F. M. (1988). *Teachers as a curriculum planner: Narratives of experience.* New York, NY: Teachers College.

Clandinin, D. J., & Connelly, F. M. (1999). *Shaping a professional identity.* New York, NY: Teachers College, Columbia University.

Clandinin, D. J., & Connelly, F. M. (2000). *Narrative inquiry: Experience and story in qualitative research.* San Francisco, CA: Jossey-Bass.

Cochran-Smith, M., & Lytle, S. L. (1990). Teacher research and research on teaching: The issues that divide. *Educational Researcher, 19*(2), 2–11.

Clark, C. M., & Yinger, R. J. (1979). Teacher thinking. In P. Peterson & H. Wahlberg (Eds.), *Research on teaching: Concepts, findings, and implications* (pp. 231–263). Berkeley, CA: McCutchan.

Creswell, J. (2005). *Educational research: Planning, conducting, and evaluating quantitative and qualitative research* (2nd ed.). Upper Saddle River, NJ: Pearson Education.

Dadds, M. (1997). Continuing professional development: Nurturing the expert within. *Professional Development in Education, 23*(1), 31–38.

Dewey, J. (1938). *Experience and education.* New York, NY: McMillan Company.

Elbaz, F. (1988). *Teacher thinking: A study of practical knowledge.* New York, NY: Nichols.

Erickson, F. (1982). Taught cognitive learning in its immediate environments: A neglected topic in the anthropology of education. *Anthropology and Education Quarterly, 13,* 149–180.

Erickson, F. (1988). School reasoning, literacy, and civility. In E. Kintgen, B. Kroll, & M. Rose (Eds.), *Perspectives and literacy* (pp. 205–226). Carbondale, IL: Southern Illinois University Press.

Gibbs, G. (1988). *Learning by doing.* London: FEU

Henson, K. T. (1996). Teachers as researchers. In J. Sikula (Ed), *Handbook of research on teacher education* (2nd ed., pp. 53–66). New York: Macmillan.

Hiemstra, R. (2001). Uses and benefits of journal writing. *New Directions for Adult and Continuing Education, 90,* 19–26.

Jasper, M. (2006). *Professional development, reflection, and decision making.* Oxford UK: Blackwell Publishing.

Johnson, A. (2008). *A short guide to action research (3rd ed.).* Upper Saddle River, NJ: Pearson.

Kleinman, D. (1983). The cultural meanings and social uses of illness. *Journal of Family Practice, 16,* 539–545.

Krathwohl, D. R., Bloom, B. S., & Masia, B. B. (1964). *Taxonomy of educational objectives: The affective domain.* New York, NY: McCay.

Ledwith, M., & Springett, J. (2009). *Participatory practice: Community-based action for transformative change.* Bristol, UK: The Policy Press, University of Bristol.

McAlpine, L., & Weston C. (2000). Reflection: Issues related to improving professors' teaching and students' learning. *Instructional Science, 28*(5–6), 363–385.

O'Brien, R. (2001). Um exame da abordagem metodológica da pesquisa ação [An Overview of the Methodological Approach of Action Research]. In R. Richardson (Ed.), *Teoria e Prática da Pesquisa Ação [Theory and Practice of Action Research].* João Pessoa, Brazil: Universidade Federal da Paraíba. (English version) retrieved from: http://www.web.ca/~robrien/papers/arfinal.html

Olson, M., & Craig, C. J. (2001). Opportunities and challenges in the development of teachers' knowledge: The development of narrative authority through knowledge communities. *Teaching and Teacher Education, 17*(6), 669–670.

Paul, R., & Elder, L. (2006). *The miniature guide to critical thinking: Concepts & tools.* Dillon Beach, CA: Foundation for Critical Thinking.

Polanyi, M. (1962). *Personal knowledge: Towards a post-critical philosophy.* Chicago: University of Chicago Press.

Rust, F. O. (2009). Teacher research and the problem of practice [Part of a special issue: Teacher Research]. *Teachers College Record, 111*(8), 1882–1893.

Ryan, K. (1981). *The teacher's story: The oldest and newest form of educational research.* Paper presented at the annual meeting of the American Educational Research Association, Los Angeles, CA. Retrieved from http://www.aera.net/publications/Default.aspx?menu_id=30&id=52

Schmuck, R. A. (1997). *Practical action research for change.* Arlington Heights, IL: IRI Skylight Training and Publishing.

Schön, D. (1983). *The reflective practitioner.* San Francisco, CA: Jossey-Bass.

Tom, A. (1985). Rethinking the relation between research and practice in teaching. *Teaching and Teacher Education, 1,* 139–153.

Van Manen, M. (1990). *Researching lived experience: Human science for an action sensitive pedagogy.* London, Ontario: University of Western Ontario.

Walker-Floyd, L. K. (2011). A narrative study of how an online practitioner used a personal action research journal as a form of professional development. (The School of Educational Leadership and Change). ProQuest Dissertations and Theses.

Willis, J. (2007). Foundations *of qualitative research: Interpretive and critical approaches.* Thousand Oaks, CA: Sage.

CHAPTER 5

AN ACTION RESEARCH STUDY

How Can Elementary Teachers Collaborate More Effectively With Parents to Support Student Literacy Learning?

Carol Anne St. George
University of Rochester

ABSTRACT

Parental involvement (broadly defined as including both natural parents and other significant adults) has been consistently shown to produce positive results in students' literacy achievement, and there is widespread agreement among parents and school personnel about the value of parental involvement in education. However, educators do not routinely include parents in literacy learning programs. I developed this participatory action research study with the ultimate goal of initiating better home-school partnerships to support elementary students' literacy learning in my district, capitalizing on the findings of the rich literature on parental involvement.

Action Research, pages 111–130
Copyright © 2014 by Information Age Publishing
All rights of reproduction in any form reserved.

I engaged a mixed group of elementary teachers and parents in my district in a Collegial Circle (a type of professional development) designed to explore effective ways to collaborate with parents to support literacy learning. The Collegial Circle involved the participants in readings and discussions to make them aware of relevant literature findings, personal perceptions and biases, and alternative viewpoints, with the ultimate goal of producing a list of concrete recommendations about how to establish productive home-school collaborations to support literacy learning in our district.

Assuming participatory action research as the methodology, this intervention along with the accompanying data collection and analysis was designed to address the following research questions: What are some of the perceived challenges to building effective partnerships between parents (broadly defined) and teachers in our district? How can the challenges thus identified be overcome? How has participation in the Collegial Circle changed the thinking of the participating parents and teachers concerning the concepts of parent–teacher partnerships and literacy? In the spirit of action research, teachers and parents participating in the Collegial Circle were not "passive participants" but rather were involved in on-going reflection about the Collegial Circle activities and provided input that changed some of the original plan and activities, as well as coconstructed with the researcher, a list of recommendations constituting the end product of the Collegial Circle.

Research documents the importance of active and meaningful involvement by parents in their children's education. Educators who value parental involvement, and actively seek to include parents, create better school environments for students (Epstein et al., 2002). This is especially true in the case of literacy. Strong literacy skills are crucial to student achievement in all academic areas. Elementary school (i.e., grades pre-K–5) is a key time for students to develop basic learning and attitudes towards literacy that will affect their future academic success. Research indicates that literacy programs involving home and school partnerships can provide essential support for students that eventually strengthen their literacy performance (Epstein, 2001). While it seems clear that parent–teacher collaborations can support student literacy learning, not many educators organize partnerships that include bridging home school connections (Dearing, McCartney, Weiss, Kreider & Simpkins, 2004).

The situation can be explained by the many issues and challenges associated with building parent–teacher collaborations. The literature suggests these challenges may include lack of teacher time, teachers' misconceptions of parents' abilities, limited family resources such as transportation and child care, limited understanding of parents' communication style, parents' lack of comfort in the school setting, tensions between families and school staff, and many other reasons (Baker, 2000; Caplan, 2000).

There can also be a disconnect between what parents and teachers consider as effective parental involvement (Lawson, 2003). In addition, some teachers appear unaware of the value and benefits of family involvement for their students and themselves, or resent adding one more element to the mix (parents) when there are enormous district and state requirements and demands. Other teachers may be well aware of the benefits of including families, but are unfamiliar with how to engage parents. As a result, many teachers view parents as trespassers in schools, unwanted and excluded, and at best, as invited guests but not as full partners in their children's education.

As a parent, educator and researcher, I had the advantage of multiple perspectives for approaching the educational problem of establishing more productive home-school partnerships in support of elementary students' literacy learning. As a widowed, working mother of three school-aged children, I know the desire as well as the challenges of being involved in my own children's education. As a veteran classroom teacher, I know that parents can make a significant contribution to their children's education and yet it is not easy to orchestrate their participation within the already complex context of learning experiences. From my experience, and as supported in the literature, parents care about their children's school success and want to be included in the educational process (Caplan, 2000), and they can do so even without having to be physically present in school.

A personal experience that also motivated this study was my involvement with a school-wide sponsored reading program. This was a read-at-home supplement to the school curriculum, with the main purpose of increasing actual time reading at home, and promoting enthusiasm for reading. Teachers planned and promoted the program with speakers, prizes, and incentives. An evaluation of the program revealed interesting findings, as it showed that the levels of participation varied considerably among the classrooms (from 0% to 100%, with average of 67%), and that parents identified the lack of time as a major factor in choosing whether to participate. Further surveys of the participants indicated that the reading programs did succeed in making the teachers feel good about their efforts, but it was not really successful in motivating future reading at home (independent reading), improving student literacy achievement or including parents in their children's literacy learning. These findings made me wonder about what caused the failure to meet the program goals; was failure due to challenges faced by parents (thereby decreasing the likelihood of their participation), problems with the program design, conflicts with philosophies of classroom teachers to involve parents, lack of communication, or other reasons?

As I began investigating the issue of parental involvement beyond my school building and into the wider arena of the 13 elementary schools within my school district, I found similar constraints to parental involvement and made some alarming discoveries. There appeared to be no consistent district policy or procedure for including parents in their children's education among the various schools and, in actuality, practices varied widely from classroom to classroom. This discovery along with my previously mentioned personal experience with parental involvement was the final impetus for this study.

The study called for using participatory action research as the methodological approach. Participatory action research is especially appropriate for research done by practitioners using their own site as the focus of their study, as I did in my dual role of teacher and professional development provider in my district. Of paramount importance, and what separates participatory action research from other methodologies, is that it is research done with the participants (Herr & Anderson, 2005). Furthermore, Anderson, Herr and Nihlen, (2007) emphasize the role of "insider" as the main goal of action research is to generate knowledge. It (action research) is different from academic research in that it represents insider or local knowledge about a setting. There is no way an outsider, even an ethnographer who spends years as an observer, can acquire the tactic knowledge of a setting that those who must daily act within possess (p. 4).

As described in chapter 2 of this book, action research is an on-going series of actions that involve planning, acting on the plan, observing the effects, and reflecting on one's observations. As Anderson, Herr and Nihlen (2007) state, "These cycles form a spiral that results in refinement of research question, resolution of the problem, and a transformation in the perspectives of researchers and participants" (p. 3). As such, participatory action research methodology seemed to me an especially appropriate methodology for involving a group of teachers and parents in my district to coconstruct a working understanding of parental involvement, and examine and explore different strategies and approaches to building partnerships of parents and educators to support literacy learning as a first step towards improving school-home partnership to support literacy learning in my district.

What separates action research from other methodologies is that action research is done with the participants' intense involvement (Herr & Anderson, 2005). My study included two groups of stakeholders, parents and teachers, in collegial workshops to explore collaborations. This allowed for equal participation and the development of shared values and perspectives among both of these stakeholder groups. One of the results was respect for both parents and teachers as valuable coparticipants and knowledge coconstructors.

My role in this action research study was twofold. I was both the researcher and the facilitator of the Collegial Circle. I positioned myself as an insider in the study. Herr and Anderson (2005) state that positionality is important because, "... the degree to which researchers position themselves as insiders and outsiders will determine how they frame epistemologically, methodological, and ethical issues in the dissertation" (p. 30). However, they also caution that, "It is often no simple matter to define one's position" (p. 32). As I determined my role, I saw that I brought to the group my experience as an educator who embraces collaborative relationships with families. I also brought to the study my experience as a mother of three children. The dual role of researcher and participant required me to be facilitator and collaborator, as well as observer and participant (Herr & Anderson, 2005).

Participatory action research is also a model for collaboration. Herr and Anderson (2005) state that "collaboration can be a crucial component of action research which not only might have a greater impact on the setting, but can also be more democratic" (p. 36). In the spirit of an action research approach, the teachers and parents in this study were not "passive participants" but rather were involved in on-going reflection about the professional development activities developed for the Collegial Circle they participated in. As they provided input into the design of these activities; they also actively participated in the compilation of a recommended list of parental involvement strategies and activities that constituted the end product of their Collegial Circle. Action research provided a mechanism for a transformation in participant's thinking and understanding of the concepts of literacy and parental involvement and also provided each participant, whether parent or teacher, a better understanding and appreciation of the other group member's role and responsibilities within the educational process.

Maas (1997) identified several key features to the process of action research. These include that action research is self-directed, is about building professional relationships, is systematic and it is ongoing. These salient features of action research were integral components of my study design. The action portion of the research followed the planning stage in Kemmis's (1982) spiral. In this study, that consisted first in implementing my original plans for the Collegial Circle and conducting the related data collection and analysis.

It was my hope that the Collegial Circle discussions would yield a plan of action for new initiatives to partner parents and teachers in ways that support literacy development for elementary students in the district, thus starting a new action research cycle—although completion of that cycle would be beyond this study. Indeed, this did happen.

It was my expectation that there would need to be many revisions, changes and adaptations of the original plan. This was consistent with action research as, "Typically, we do not get a plan absolutely 'right,' and in fact, as we implement a plan; the very implementation raises new issues or things we hadn't expected or anticipated" (Anderson, Herr, & Nihlen, 2007, p. 146). Therefore, I was open to these changes.

THE SETTING

The study took place in the school district where I worked for over three decades as a classroom teacher of grades K–5 and where I served as a teacher on special assignment (TOSA) in the role of district instructional mentor teacher. In this position, my responsibilities included serving as a mentor to new teachers in the district and delivering a variety of professional development offerings around various topics including Parents as Partners, and Basic Literacy In-service Courses (BLIC).

The school district in which the study was conducted is situated in a suburb of a large upstate city in New York and is comprised of approximately 1,200 educators and 13,000 students. There are 13 elementary schools in the district, with seven of these schools designated as Title 1 (i.e., having 53% or greater student populations of free and reduced lunch buyers, an indication of economic disadvantage). The teacher gender distribution for the district is 78% female and 22% male, with a race/ethnicity of 98% White, .9% Black, 1% Hispanic. The ethnic breakdown of the school district's student population is 85% White, 8% Black, 5% Hispanic, 2% Asian or Pacific Islander, with each individual school building demographics having a wide range. Student socioeconomic status in the district also has a wide range among the different buildings. For example, one school has 8% of the students receiving free and reduced lunch, (a typical measure of economic status) while another has over 85% of their students in the same category. Similarly, the number of students attending each elementary school varies with one school having 278 students and another with over 800. Teachers' years of experience varies greatly within the district from first year teachers to veteran teachers like myself, with over thirty years of classroom practice. Consequently, each of the district pre-k through grade 5 schools has a very different population and culture, with different needs and goals.

THE PROBLEM

Although there were many differences among elementary schools in my district, there were also similarities that specifically related to the goals of this study. The goal of improving literacy achievement is an on-going identified priority by each school's management team. Increasing parental involvement was another major district goal for the school year in which this study was conducted.

As stated previously, past attempts at parent involvement were inconsistent in my school district. An evaluation of past programs revealed that many parents were reluctant to become involved in literacy projects designed to support literacy learning for a variety of reasons. Also, teachers often did not know the value of including parents or ways to encourage involvement. As a result, they underused parents as a resource and did not appreciated them as a powerful force in improving student achievement. Research demonstrates that there is a lack of training for teachers and administrators in ways to collaborate with parents. Prior to this study, my district offered only one 45 minute session to new teachers to the district about working with parents in general and no other professional development related to including parents. These findings are consistent with the literature and motivated my desire to design an action research study that would move my district toward implementing more effective home-school partnerships to support literacy learning for students.

The research study plans followed the identified steps or stages of action research. Specifically, the initial work involved identifying the academic problem. Quality action research demands that the study begin with a research question that is significant, manageable, contextual, clearly stated, open-ended and self-reflective (Youngman, 1995; Caro-Bruce, 2002). What arose from my review of the literature was the following essential question: how can teachers collaborate more effectively with parents to support literacy learning in my district? To address this question, I designed and implemented a semester-long Collegial Circle for a group of teachers and parents in my district committed to improving literacy learning.

The Collegial Learning Circle (Collegial Circle hereafter) format used for the study was a regular feature in the district's professional development offerings. Collegial Circles are small groups of learners (usually teachers) who engage in their own professional development, meeting regularly to support each other's learning. Collegial Circles are a familiar, nonthreatening format in my district and, as such, offered a comfortable nonintimidating, nonjudgmental arena for the teacher participants to dialogue and reflect on how elementary teachers can more effectively collaborate with parents to support literacy learning. Although the parent participants were not as familiar with Collegial Circles, the format allowed for a democratic approach to research where all participants, parents and teachers had an equal voice. Thus, the Collegial Circle format provided a forum for a meaningful, authentic and respectful experience for both groups of participants. I selected this format for all of these reasons and benefits.

The Collegial Circle was offered as part of the district's professional development program and met in four monthly two-hour sessions during the Fall 2008 semester. The implementation of the Collegial Circle provided the context to collect and analyze data to address the following, more specific, research subquestions:

1. What are the perceived challenges to building effective partnerships between parents (broadly defined) and teachers in this district?

2. How can the challenges thus identified be overcome?
3. How has participation in the Collegial Circle changed the thinking of the participating parents and teachers concerning parent–teacher partnerships and literacy?

The focus of the Collegial Circle sessions was to develop a better understanding of the concept of parental involvement and what it meant specifically to this group of parents and teachers, and how parental involvement could be encouraged in our district to support literacy. Additionally, one of my goals was to foster among the participants a better understanding, recognition and appreciation of each other's role in the educational process, as well as the value and need for overlapping their efforts to better support students. Embracing the idea that parents must be partners with teachers in the education of their children, the study was designed to be authentic, respectful of both participant groups of parents and teachers, and included an opportunity for a variety of parents to have a voice beyond the traditional, easily accessible in-school parent volunteers program.

Creating a list of suggested strategies, approaches and parental involvement program design elements was explicitly articulated as the end product of the Collegial Circle. In addition, the work from the Collegial Circle also had some unexpected outcomes, as it helped establish the need and desire in our district for a Parent University and helped to begin initial investigations about making a Parent University a formal offering within our district professional development offerings.

As a result of this study, major changes in perception and practice regarding parent involvement in student learning were established. The study also generated additional unexpected insights about parents and teachers' views of each other and their potential roles in home-school partnerships, as well as the value of engaging in the kind of dialogue and professional development offered by the Collegial Circle format—where teachers and parents were given the opportunity to work together as equals, and together explore how they could best collaborate to support student learning.

A Narrative Description of the Research

The Collegial Circle sessions occurred in the district's Professional Learning Center, where meetings and professional development workshops commonly take place. The Collegial Circle sessions took place on four Mondays, one each during September through December, from 4:00 to 6:00 p.m. Because I anticipated that the time could be problematic for the parent participants who have elementary school-aged children, I arranged for childcare services in an adjacent room. A number of parents utilized the provided childcare services while participating in the Collegial Circle sessions. Dinner was also provided.

Participant Recruitment and Selection

I advertised this professional development offering in various and multiple ways including using the district web site, flyers, and newsletters. In addition, word of mouth and networking helped promote participation in the Collegial Circle. For example, one parent made copies and handed them out at her son's soccer games. As a result of these combined recruiting efforts, along with the interest in both improving student literacy learning and increasing parent–teacher collaborations, initial interest in the Collegial Circle was strong. Indeed, many more potential participants registered than was possible to accommodate which necessitated a selection process for the twenty participants (10 teachers and 10 parents) who eventually became subjects for the study. I based selection on a number of factors in order to have a nonbiased representation from a wide variety of district school buildings and grade levels, teaching experience and other factors. As a result, participants represented all of the district schools.

Initial Plans and Unanticipated Events

I originally organized the Collegial Circle sessions with the following topics:
Session 1: (a) How has reading/literacy instruction changed over the years and what are the implications of the changes? (b) How is a commitment to parental involvement consistent with an expanded view of literacy in a sociocultural historical theoretical framework? Session 2: What research has been done in the area of literacy and parental involvement and how does this inform our practice? And Sessions 3 & 4: How can teachers of grades K–5 more effectively collaborate with parents to support student literacy learning?

This structure and these topics remained intact; however, over time the Collegial Circle accepted additional responsibilities requiring a broadening of the scope and focus of most sessions. As mentioned previously, the College Circle was the first professional development of its kind offered in our district and, as such, accounted for much interest and curiosity from both parent and district personnel. This was the first local Collegial Circle to provide an opportunity for both parent and teacher participants to work and learn together in a workshop setting, as opposed to previous efforts contained within specific school buildings that had teachers holding workshops *for* parents, not *with* them.

Also, since participants for the Collegial Circle represented a varied and diverse segment of the district parent and teacher population, this unique group offered a valuable base of information and support of parental involvement for the district. As a result, the Collegial Circle sessions and the participants' ideas and opinions provided an unanticipated influence on district issues revolving around parental involvement and future district plans.

The district recognized that the Collegial Circle participants represented all schools in our district and therefore could provide valuable input into concurrent new district efforts to improve parental involvement. Just prior to the first session of the Collegial Circle, district administrators contacted me about serving in the newly created role of Title 1 Parent Involvement Coordinator, in addition to my other district roles. They also sought to include the Collegial Circle participants' ideas and recommendations for increasing parent involvement specifically from the Title 1 schools in our district (research demonstrates Title 1 parents are often the hardest to include). The Collegial Circle participants enthusiastically took on the added responsibility of becoming advisors to the district about initiatives to include parents.

Although our original plans remained intact, the action research spiral changed to accommodate our new focus and authentic task of pursuing concrete recommendations for the district. This paralleled our original work and was consistent with our interest in seeking ways that teachers could more effectively collaborate with parents in our district. Thus, true to the original study design, the participants dialogued and reflected on their personal experiences with literacy and parent–teacher partnerships and collectively explored strategies, activities and programs designed to encourage parent–teacher partnerships and literacy achievement producing a list of recommendations for our district on strategies and approaches for building effective partnerships of parents and teachers to support student literacy that was the end product of the Collegial Circle. Now we also had district attention to bring about the changes we suggested.

The work of the Collegial Circle expanded to explore other professional development offerings, including developing and implementing a Parent University for our district to support student learning and parent–teacher partnerships. Parent University is a concept suggested in the federal Title 1 Parent Involvement Document to provide parents with resources and training to assist parents in working with students at home. The goal of a Parent University is "to help parents to work with their children to improve their children's achievement, such as literacy training" (p. 5). In suggesting potential offerings for the Parent University, respondents recommended classes on how to help children deal with stress, positive discipline, cyber-safety and how to advocate for your child. A district survey to evaluate interest in Parent University classes incorporated these suggestions from the Collegial

Circle. It became apparent that the Collegial Circle reflected the larger population of elementary school parents because results from the survey found that the most popular Parent University classes on the survey were the same ones suggested by the Collegial Circle participants.

Collegial Circle Sessions

Participants represented all of the district schools, and as the demographics demonstrated, each of the district pre-K through grade 5 schools had a very different population and culture, with different needs and goals. While all participants shared the same goal of increasing student literacy learning through more effective parent–teacher partnerships, most participants did not know each other and had never previously worked together. At first, participants were polite and formal with each other.

> **Terry (teacher):** This is the most well-behaved workshop I have ever been in; usually people are talking, not listening to each other. Maybe it's the seating arrangement, or maybe people are just respectful in this group (collegial circle transcript, session one, 9/22/08).

Grounding the group with some introductory activities and developing a shared definition of literacy as well as a conceptual understanding for parental involvement (as these concepts affected later decisions and recommendations about literacy instruction and the role of both parents and educators in literacy learning) helped ease initial discomfort or anxiety. It also helped keep the group focused to ensure our meetings did not become "complaint sessions."

Within an hour of the first session, participants were engaged in a discussion about how they learned to read. This topic provided an opportunity for a meaningful discussion about their experiences with school and literacy, and participants felt comfortable enough to share personal challenges related to literacy and parenting as illustrated in these excerpts from the Collegial Circle transcript from session one:

> **Kinley (parent):** My own parents were not involved in my schooling. That is why I try to take an active role in my own children's education. My son is having trouble with reading and I want to be able to help him (Collegial Circle transcript, session one, 9/22/08).
>
> **Terry (teacher):** I had problems in reading when I was in school, but I never knew it then. I asked my mother recently

> about a teacher I had and she told me she was the remedial reading teacher. I had no idea that I was behind or that reading was hard for me when I was younger, but now I know it was (Collegial Circle transcript, session one, 9/22/08).

Daily (parent): I still get confused with all the (school) acronyms and I get embarrassed that I don't know them and have to ask someone what they all mean (Collegial Circle transcript, session one, 9/22/08).

Kayden (parent): My child is having a lot of difficulty learning to read. I don't know how to help him; I'm not trained in reading. Homework becomes a nightmare and it's very, very frustrating (Collegial Circle transcript, session one, 9/22/08).

Similarly, within the first hour, participants laughed together, became friendly, supportive and appeared very comfortable with each other:

> Everyone is huddled over their work, engaged, laughing and talking. It took me a number of times to regroup the participants because their conversations were so well established and lively (Researcher Journal, 10/20/08).

Participants were highly engaged in the work during each Collegial Circle session and enthusiastic about the group's potential contribution to our district. Participants made a great effort to attend every session. Many participants commented on their enjoyment of being part of the Collegial Circle throughout the intervention. For example:

Kinley (parent): I couldn't wait for this month's session (Collegial Circle transcript, session 2, 10/20/08).

Lee (parent): I thought about our issues all the time since our last meeting, I found a great article to share with the group (Journal #2, 10/20/08).

During the four-month period of the Collegial Circle, there were regular e-mail correspondences, and sharing of research articles and ideas among the participants.

By the last session, there was general agreement that the Collegial Circle was a valuable and successful experience. Participants were able to have open, honest discussions in an atmosphere of trust and mutual respect. Cameron articulates this clearly in the following journal response:

Cameron (teacher): I think we were able to be very honest and very candid about taboo subjects with our discussions. I think we have a common investment. (Journal #4, 12/15/08).

Indeed, the fact that the vast majority (17 of 20) teacher and parent participants expressed a desire to continue working together to promote parent involvement by serving on the advisory board of the planned district Parent University is further evidence of how well the group worked together.

It is of interest to note that after the study was done, this advisory group used the knowledge gained from their Collegial Circle work to organize a highly successful first Parent University event for the district called "A Night of Fun and Learning." Focusing on literacy, over 600 people attended. A second event soon followed focusing on math, and brought over 800 participants from just the Title 1 schools. As a result of this study, every school in the district now has multiple procedures in place to encourage and sustain parental involvement in their child's learning.

Data Analysis in This Action Research Study

Data for this study was collected from a variety of sources, including participants' reflective journals, and other written assignments and activities from the collegial circle sessions, audiotapes and artifacts, and my researcher's journal. A grounded theory approach was used to code data to uncover emerging themes that could shed light on each of the research questions (Charmaz, 2006). The analysis of my data was continual and ongoing and in the spirit of action research, the data gathering and analysis informed each other because the analysis guided the next steps of my data gathering and action (Anderson, Herr, & Nihlen, 2007). For example, the ongoing analysis of the data helped me decide which research studies to share with the Collegial Circle participants and which workshop topics should be included in our district parent survey design. Ongoing reflection was essential, and my focus was on addressing the research questions of the study. I followed the advice of Anderson, Herr, and Nihlen (2007), and stopped periodically to see if anything needed changing in the inquiry process so that there were no gaps in the data. Additionally, I trusted my instincts as Anderson, Herr, and Nihlen (2007) urge researchers to follow their hunches and intuition, as "these are very important and usually extremely significant in the process of analysis and should not be ignored" (p. 215).

It was very important for me to have safeguards in place to assure the validity and trustworthiness of my study. My researcher's journal was one method included in the research design. It was useful for tracing my thinking, reorienting and refocusing as the study evolved. Similarly, I employed member checking as I brought data analysis, interpretations and conclusions back to the entire Collegial Circle for verification and input. I asked participants for clarification of their ideas, and verification that I captured their thoughts accurately in compiled group work. I shared the draft of the end product for approval that it accurately reflected the thinking and intention of the group during the third and final Collegial Circle sessions. Participants affirmed, clarified, corrected, and directed what was important to include or exclude for the final draft. After the 4th and final Collegial Circle session, I organized and typed the complied list and shared it with two parent and two teacher participants who had agreed to serve in the member checking capacity, assuring the accuracy of the groups' efforts and intent was in the final version of the end product (Anderson, Herr, & Nihlen, 2007).

DISCOVERIES

Participants in the Collegial Circle identified a number of challenges to partnering parents and teachers to support literacy. Findings show that the challenges are interrelated and this interrelationship with various obstacles intensifies each contributing challenge. As suggested in the literature, lack of resources, particularly the limited availability of time for both parents and teachers, appeared consistently as the greatest challenge to parental involvement in our district. What emerged as a theme in the findings, in addition, was that time constraints affect all obstacles to parent involvement. For example, lack of time creates difficulty in organizing schedules and results in the associated stress from having a limited amount of time. Time constraints also exacerbate difficulty with communication, the second most widely identified challenge to involving families in education. Difficulties with communication, in turn, affect building relationships, which the participants believe is a necessary component of effective parent–teacher partnerships. Complicating the process is stress. The study found that stress arises from all the other challenges and acts as a thread that connects each obstacle to another, making partnerships of teachers and parents more difficult. There was also consensus that the lack of time affects stress levels for both families and teachers.

The second main challenge identified by the participants, effective communication, is also essential for building relationships. However, along with time constraints, the challenges are again interrelated. For example, classroom newsletters are a valuable tool for communication, but training and skill may affect the teacher's desire and ability to create effective newsletters. In addition, newsletters require time commitments, both from teachers to produce them and from parents to read them. Since time is an issue, it affects the usefulness of newsletters as communication tools. Phone calls, web pages, and 'back and forth note books' were all discussed as other valuable communication tools, although all are often hindered by time constraints. Another obstacle to effective communication identified in this study is that it requires specific skills. Consistent with the literature, this study found that not all educators are effective in communicating with families, especially when discussing student literacy growth.

A third challenge to parent–teacher partnerships that may not be as apparent is the confusion and insecurity that often exists about the parents' and teachers' roles and responsibilities in the partnerships. Consequently, perceived intrusions into the others' role or confusion about their own responsibility in the educational process are more subtle challenges to collaborating. This is sometimes what is behind teachers questioning the ability of and skill of parents to help their children academically. In addition, teachers are not sure how to include parents and still maintain their authority or role as teacher. Parents, too, are not certain about how to help their child at home, fear that they do not have the necessary skills to help and worry that the teacher will think they are interfering.

Finally, the data revealed that there may be specific, systemic challenges to parental involvement within a district. The structure of elementary, middle and high schools, and the many changes in administration may contribute to difficulties in building relationships.

The study also identified a number of strategies to enable teachers to overcome the challenges and more effectively collaborate with parents to support student literacy learning. These were included in the end product. The list of recommendations included three sections: home activities that support literary learning, classroom practices that encourage parental involvement, and programs to support and encourage partnerships of parents and teachers. Within these three sections were specific suggestions for improving communication, reconceptualizing homework and specific programs to support parent–teacher partnerships in our district.

Changes in Participants' Thinking as a Result of Participation in the Collegial Circle

Data from journal entries and Collegial Circle sessions indicates that participants' thoughts indeed changed in three distinct ways. First, there was a new appreciation or a stronger commitment to building partnerships of teachers and parents to support student literacy learning. Second, there was a new awareness about the role of the other in the parent–teacher partnership as well as self-insights. Third, participants reported changes in practice or anticipate changes in practice that indicate participants acquired a new perception of the concepts of both literacy and parental involvement. Data from the final journal entries explicitly indicate a strengthened commitment and determination to find ways to build strong bonds between home and school, as well as a positive attitude about the success of efforts to partner parents and teachers to support literacy learning. The following quotes are representative of these findings:

> **Pat (parent):** The circle confirmed what I knew all along; that many teachers are parents as well as parents are teachers. The responsibilities of both roles can be overwhelming, but they can be supported successfully. Communication, planning and unified desire to foster literacy in our children is not only necessary, it is increasingly possible (Journal #4, 12/15/08).
>
> **Tracy (teacher):** It was great to sit with parents and teachers and gather different perspectives about home-school connections. It is important to understand the challenges that occur at home and school so we can all work as a team. The richer our conversations and communication, the stronger collaboration (Journal #4, 12/15/08).

Changes in Thinking About the Role of the Other in the Parent–Teacher Partnerships

Both parent and teacher participants voiced an awareness of the demands and responsibilities of the others' role in the partnership. Participants' showed a new view and deeper understanding of the others' role, as illustrated by the following journal entries:

> **Bailey (parent):** It is interesting to listen to teachers. They seem a little afraid of parents (Journal #4, 12/15/08).
>
> **Cameron (teacher):** I learned how eager many parents are to help and how much expertise they have to share! Finding the right Method of communication seems key! (Journal #4, 12/15/08).
>
> **Amari (teacher):** I found that we learn so much more about our children (students) by listening to their parents (Journal #4, 12/15/08).

Terry (teacher): Not being a parent myself, I now realize all of the constraints that families might have. Not being there does not mean they aren't being supportive. [I learned] that some parents might be afraid to approach you (Journal #4, 12/15/08).

Participants were thoughtful and insightful in seeing how they personally contribute to or detract from successful partnerships of parents and teachers. The responses demonstrated that as with all relationships, many factors are involved. Feelings of resentment, competition or the need for control can compete with the desire to collaborate as indicated in the following responses:

Kendall (parent): I learned that I have some feelings about teachers telling me how to parent (Journal #4, 12/15/08).
Cameron (teacher): The main thing that I've done and I feel like it has made such a difference is I decided to do a book group with parents and use the format from the Collegial Circle. I learned I don't always need to be in charge of picking the topic and controlling the discussion. I think I will have more involved (Journal #4, 12/15/08).

Changes in Practice or Anticipated Changes in Practice

The majority of participants explicitly stated they had already changed or intended to change, refine or enhance their teaching or home practices around literacy in some way as a result of their participation in the Collegial Circle, as indicated in the following responses.

Shay (teacher): I will get parents more involved. I think how I communicate with parents regarding literacy will be different and more often.
Kasey (teacher): Mostly, I need to connect to students' experiences and prior knowledge during literacy activities (Journal #4, 12/15/08).
Lee (parent): I will continue to read to my children every day and encourage love for reading. I have some different strategies I can apply (Journal #4, 12/15/08).
Kayden (parent): I will have increased dialogue w/teachers and make the teacher aware of what is happening at home and

that the load of homework is stressful for all (Journal #4, 12/15/08).

In summary, responses reflected both parent and teacher participants' intention to change their practices. The teacher participants' intended to change their practices of how they communicate with parents, how they involve parents, and how they deliver literacy instruction. Parent participant responses reflected their intention to encourage their child to spend increased time reading at home, utilize new strategies and focus while reading with their child, and communicate more information to their child's teachers.

GROUP AND PERSONAL INSIGHTS

I found that having parent and teacher participants explore their own literacy instruction along with current literacy practices, exposed biases and beliefs that contradicted and interfered with current literacy theory and instruction, and the role that parents can and should take in their children's literacy learning, thus hindering the acceptance of parents as partners in their children's education. Coconstructing a conceptual understanding of literacy among the parent and teacher participants was important foundational work for this study and resulted in changing individual perceptions from each participant group, both teachers and parents, about the concepts of literacy and parent involvement.

I found it interesting also, that although the Collegial Circle format per se was not part of the research investigation, it was a noteworthy discovery that an interactive gathering of stakeholders, focused on a topic of mutual interest within a professional setting, facilitated an open exchange of ideas between teachers and parents. In this study, the Collegial Circle format helped participants to work and learn together by focusing on their mutual goal of supporting student literacy learning. Designing professional development in ways that combine parents and teachers as equal participants fosters the focus on students' success as the common goal, and allows participants to collaborate effectively in the educational process, and develop an understanding and appreciation for the role of the other in the partnership.

Another insight was that parents wanted another avenue to voice their concerns, outside of the traditional PTA meetings, which they viewed as socially focused, and exclusionary. Both teachers and parents who registered for the Collegial Circle felt that participation would offer them personal growth. They felt empowered and successful through the group's success. The majority of the participants, both teachers and parents, have moved into leadership positions within the district as a direct result of their involvement in this study.

WHAT I WOULD DO DIFFERENTLY

Prior to undertaking this participatory action research study, I had no idea of the potential power or long term benefits that could occur. The idea of combining two groups of stakeholders, parents and teachers, to discuss ways of working together more collaboratively to support student learning seemed benign. I was naïve in how radical an idea it actually was.

Teachers and parents in my district had specific roles and for decades they did not cross their "boundaries." However, collegial participatory action research, by its very design, allowed the collegial circle sessions to be more than just "complaint sessions" and actually lead to long term, positive change in the ways teachers and parents partner within our district.

REFERENCES

Anderson, G., Herr, K., & Nihlen, A. S. (2007). *Studying your own school: An educator's guide to practitioner action research* (2nd ed.). Thousand Oaks, CA: Corwin Press.

Baker. L. (1999). Opportunities at home and in the community that foster reading engagement. In J. T. Guthrie & D. Alvermann (Eds.), *Engagement in reading: Processes and practices, and policy implications* (pp. 105–133). New York: Teachers College Press.

Caplan, J. G. (2000). Building strong family–school partnerships to support high student achievement. *The Informed Educator Series.* Arlington, VA: Educational Research Service.

Caro-Bruce, C. (2000). *Action research facilitator's handbook.* Wichita Falls, TX: National Staff Development Council.

Caspe, M., Lopez, M. E., & Wolos, C. (2006). *Family involvement in elementary children's education: Family involvement makes a difference* Number 2, Winter 2006/2007. Cambridge, MA: Harvard Family Research Project. (ERIC Document Reproduction Service No. 495467).

Charmaz, K. (2006). *Constructing grounded theory: A practical guide through qualitative analysis.* London, UK: Sage.

Dearing, E., Kreider, H., Simpkins, S., & Weiss, H. B. (2004). Family involvement in school and low-income children's literacy performance: Longitudinal associations between and within families. *Journal of Educational Psychology, 98,* 653–664.

Dearing, E., McCartney, K., Weiss, H. B., Kreider, H., & Simpkins, S. (2004). The promotive effects of family educational involvement for low-income children's literacy: How and for whom does involvement matter? *Journal of School Psychology, 42,* 445–460.

Epstein, J. (2001). *School, family, and community partnerships.* Boulder, CO: Westview Press.

Epstein, J. L., Sanders, M. G., Simon, B. S., Salinas, K. C., Jansorn, N. R., & Van Voorhis, F. L. (2002). *School, family, and community partnerships: Your handbook for action* (2nd ed.). Thousand Oaks, CA: Corwin Press.

Glanz, J. (2003). Action research: An educational leader's guide to school improvement (2nd ed.). Lanham, MD: Rowman & Littlefield.

Herr, K., & Anderson, G, (2005). *The action research dissertation: A guide for students and faculty.* London: Sage.

Kemmis, S. (Ed.). (1982). *The action research planner.* Greelong, Victoria, Australia: Deakin University Press.

Maas, J. (1997). Action research: What do we mean? *Action Research of Wisconsin Network, 3*(1), 261–268.

Springett, J. (2003). Issues in participatory evaluation. In M. Minkler, & N. Wallerstein (Eds.), *Community based participatory research for health* (pp. 263–288). San Franciso:Jossey-Bass.

Youngman, N. (1995). Focusing a research question with support from colleagues. *Action Research of Wisconsin Network, 1*(1), 18–24..

CHAPTER 6

IMPLEMENTING ORGANIZATION CHANGE USING ACTION LEARNING AND ACTION RESEARCH IN AN ASIAN SETTING

Shankar Sankaran
University of Technology Sydney, Australia

ABSTRACT

In this chapter I will describe an action research (AR) study that I used to develop local managers in a multinational company where I was a senior manager and had taken over responsibility for managing a newly set up global engineering operation. My study also contributed to completing a PhD thesis with the University of South Australia. I have structured the chapter as follows: I have started with a description of the context for my study and the reasons why the problem addressed in the study was important to the organisation where it was carried out, to me, and to the six managers reporting to me who became my coresearchers in the study. I will explain why I selected the action research model that I used it in my study. I will then introduce my Australian doctoral supervisors, the Singaporean managers who were involved as coresearchers as well as three other Singapor-

Action Research, pages 131–152

ean managers, who were also doctoral candidates and who were being supervised by the same supervisors, with whom I formed an action learning set during the study. The role played by a virtual action learning set that I formed with an international group of action researchers will also be explained. I will then describe the setting which was a Japanese company, where the study took place. This will be followed by a description of the research carried out. I will follow this up with insights from my study. I will close the chapter with a reflection on how my study could have been done differently as I have now gained experience as an academic and supervisor of doctoral students who are using action research.

The AR study described in this chapter was carried out in a large engineering centre of a Japanese multinational company in Singapore, which wanted to reduce its cost of operations significantly for the organisation to stay profitable (in fact, survive) while at the same time not sacrificing the quality of its products and services. I was appointed as the head of this centre and wanted to use innovative approaches to achieve the goals of the organisation with the help of young managers who were reporting to me. I also saw this as an opportunity to help these managers develop by solving real challenging problems at the workplace. The Japanese culture did not believe in sending managers to MBA programs but in developing their capabilities in-house. I had also recently enrolled in a PhD program started in Singapore by an Australian university aimed at practicing managers. We were the first cohort of PhD students enrolled in this program.

Having a degree in science and engineering and having worked as an engineer all my professional life I was used to scientific ways of solving problems using predominantly positivist approaches. Therefore action research was a new challenge for me when the University of South Australia announced that we had to use AR as our dissertation methodology. However, I also found the concept of "action learning" (Revans, 1998, p. 4) appealing. The action learning framework proposed by Revans is similar to the *Planning-Doing-Reflecting-Consolidating* learning cycle proposed for action learning by Weinstein (2002, p. 11). In addition, both these models of action learning are similar to the cyclic nature of action research. I also realised that the *Plan-Do-Check-Act* or *Deming cycle* (Deming, 2000, p. 8) used in my company for *kaizen* or continuous improvement resonated with the principles of action learning and action research. After studying the process of conducting action research, I found a model for action research proposed by Perry and Zuber-Skerritt (1992) recommended for postgraduate doctoral programs that seemed to fit my study. Using this model, I set up my study as a combination of an "action research thesis" that was a reflection on data collected from "core action research" projects conducted at my company. My core action research project, which was used as a vehicle to conduct action research, was designed as an action learning project to render it

politically acceptable in a Japanese company that firmly believed in the usefulness of quality control circles. The model will be explained in more detail.

While attending the courses conducted by the University to help us learn
about conducting research, I was inspired by Professor Alan Davies from Southern Cross University who facilitated a search conference (Emery & Purser, 1996)
to help us formulate a vision for our study. I requested Alan to be my supervisor,
which he readily agreed to. He then suggested that Bob Dick, a prominent action researcher from Australia, be a cosupervisor as Alan was not an expert in
action research. Bob Dick also taught us a course about action research, which
was very practical and useful for managers like me to make sense of action research and it's potential. Four more students were allocated to Alan and Bob
for supervision. The four of us set up an "action learning set" to learn from and
support each other during our journey. The term "action learning set" refers to
groups that meet to study, plan, and implement actions that address the issue
at hand. One organization that regularly uses this method defined it this way:
"A typical Action Learning Set will consist of 5 or 6 people who commit to work
together over a period of at least six months" (quoted from http://www.bond.
org.uk/data/files/resources/463/No-5.1-Action-Learning-Sets.pdf).

As part of the organisational change we were introducing in my engineering operation we decided to use "outsourcing" as a strategy to reduce
our costs. The work model we were using had to be changed to suit our new
way of doing projects. Changing our work model became the focus of my
study as it contributed to both management and research outcomes. I then
recruited six young managers from my operation who became interested in
working with me as a second "action learning set" to help change our work
model. The development of these managers through addressing a common
concern at work became the focus of my doctoral research.

THE SETTING

The organization where this study was conducted (which is called YES in
this chapter) was established in Singapore as a customer service company
to support Japanese contractors who bought the parent company's (YHQ)
products for use in South East Asian countries. As YHQ's market was satu-
rating in Japan the company decided to expand its business overseas and
established a regional headquarters in Singapore. As part of this strategy
more than a hundred engineers were recruited in Singapore over two years
and sent to Japan for training to learn the company's ways of working. These
engineers were mostly new graduates from local universities or polytechnics
(technical colleges that offer diplomas and not degrees).

The Japanese method of engineering was Tayloristic (i.e., the work was
carefully divided and designed for efficiency and increased productivity

through repetition). The total engineering required for a project was divided into precise tasks, and engineers were trained to do their job over many years so that efficiency, quality, and productivity were assured. Thus the engineers who were employed by YES were first trained as project engineers (dealing with administrative tasks associated with project handling and hardware engineering) or as system engineers. To support these project and system engineers, specialist engineers such as computer engineers and start-up engineers were also recruited. The system engineers configured standard software packages developed by the company to suit customer requirements. When additional customised software was required to meet customer needs that could not be satisfied by using the standard software packages, computer engineers wrote programs to meet those needs. Start-up engineers worked at the customer's site to install and assist in commissioning the systems that were delivered to the customer.

Initially, YHQ subcontracted the jobs it secured from South East Asia to YES. These jobs were typically executed by the engineering division in YHQ. The job at YHQ was broken down into its constituent parts, such as project engineering, system engineering, and software engineering, and given to the respective departments in the engineering division at YES. This helped reduce the cost of engineering by using the less expensive engineers from Singapore to do more routine tasks.

As the cost of engineering in Singapore also started to rise, a new strategy was required. A project called "global engineering" was conceptualised at YHQ, and YES was asked to test the concept by outsourcing work to India and the Philippines. YES also proposed that it would now take total responsibility for major projects. Orders were now placed directly by the sales division in Japan with the engineering division in Singapore. Thus major responsibilities were thrust into the hands of the younger managers in Singapore. An organization called Asean Technical Centre (ATC) was formed to symbolise the metamorphosis of the engineering division at YES from a subcontractor for the YHQ's engineering division to a main operation responsible for total project execution. YES then set up companies/operations to outsource software work to India and the Philippines. The goal was to reduce project cost.

Because I was about to introduce a large-scale change in my operation, I wanted to build consensus for this change among the people who would be affected by it. The change being contemplated had not been attempted, even in YHQ, although they were exploring outsourcing. The plan was risky and there was considerable uncertainty about how to go about implementing it. I knew the change we were planning would have long-term implications on how we would work in the future. I felt this could be achieved only if the younger managers took ownership of this change. I also felt that if the young managers were fully involved in the change process they would also "learn by doing." This was a revolutionary idea for a Japanese company accustomed to providing direction from the top. There were some initial misgivings about the "bottom-up" approach I was proposing.

In all, six managers participated in my study as my coresearchers. All six were local Singaporeans of Chinese origin who belonged to the majority ethnic community in Singapore. The Japanese management of the company wanted local Singaporeans, whom they employed fresh from university, to take over major responsibilities in the company in the future. Although I had lived in Singapore for many years and had been a manager at YES for a few years before I took on the responsibility to manage the Asean Technical Centre (ATC). I was of Indian origin.

THE PROBLEM

I will use the term "thematic concern" to explain the problem I was addressing during my research. According to Kemmis and McTaggart (1988, p. 9), "The thematic concern defines the substantive area in which the (AR) group decides to focus its improvement strategies." Our thematic concern was derived from the concerns of YES and my own concerns.

The Concerns of YES

YES had several concerns when I started this study. One of these concerns was that it was facing a price war for market share in the fast-growing South East Asian region. Although customers valued the quality and reliability of YHQ's products and services, the corresponding higher cost could often not be justified by the customers.

The number of Japanese personnel assigned to work in YES had increased due to its rapid expansion and this was not looked upon kindly by the locals. Although they accepted the necessity of the Japanese presence to help them communicate with the parent company, they resented the accompanying costs of stationing these employees in Singapore which added to the cost of the operations. The management of YES also wanted to reduce the number of Japanese expatriates, with a view to handing over key responsibilities to local staff.

My Concerns

I was set a big challenge by the management when ATC was set up. I needed capable managers to help me meet this. However, I did not want to recruit experienced managers from outside, since this could create resentment among the local staff. Hence I had to find a way to accelerate the development of local managers to fill this gap.

Common Thematic Concerns

Taking these concerns into consideration I felt that addressing the rapid development of local managers in YES would be of great value to both YES and ATC. Therefore, I took up local manager development as the thematic concern for my research based on a reading of the literature. (Mumford, 1993).

Research Questions

From the common thematic concern, I developed the following research questions.

My primary research question was:

Will developing "conscious learning" among managers make them more effective?

I felt that broadening the horizons of my managers would help them to become better managers. I wanted to pass on whatever knowledge I had gained through my international exposure to my managers without appearing to act like the "expert."

My secondary research question then became:

Can a senior manager of my background, with international exposure and experience, channel such knowledge to his younger managers using participatory AR?

DESCRIPTION OF THE RESEARCH

The purpose of my study was to enhance the learning ability of my managers through the actions they took to solve real problems in YES. This was necessary as the company was not interested in academic research that had no direct relevance to its objectives. For top management, even the term "action research" sounded too academic and, at the time, I had to use the term "action learning" to make it more palatable.

When I started out on this research I had a very fuzzy idea about what I was planning to achieve. I also could not delay beginning the research as operational problems needed urgent attention. I was not sure what results my actions would have, but I felt it necessary to continue with the

Plan-Do-Check-Act (PDCA) cycle used by quality control circles in Japanese companies. However, while this model was adequate for ensuring continuous improvement in the organisation, it lacked the "reflection" that would support innovative approaches.

Learning in YES was usually associated with technical aspects of our work. Non-technical training was limited to skills training by attending workshops. We also used on-the-job training, but this was related to specific tasks and was not broad enough. Workplace collaboration was limited to quality control circles, which were heavily influenced by our manufacturing division and did not appeal to the sales or engineering divisions. This gave me an opportunity to investigate new ways to promote management learning at my workplace.

Why AR?

There were three reasons why I chose AR as my research methodology. As noted earlier, the university where I was completing my doctorate expected me to complete an AR dissertation. However, as I learned more about AR I saw reasons why AR was very desirable way to approach the research questions. First, the phenomenon I was studying did not seem to fit traditional research methods as I was studying my managers in their natural settings. Second, I was wanted to do something I had not done before both for my personal knowledge development as well as for professional development. The constraints I faced would have violated the assumptions of traditional positivist research methods but were not such serious issues from the perspective of AR:

1. I had to use a small sample of engineering managers within my operation for the study.
2. It was difficult to isolate the sample in a controlled setting, as we could not afford to take the managers away from their work environment due to the workload.
3. I had to actively participate in the processes and could not be isolated from the managers while the research was being conducted as it was carried out along with the normal work.
4. It was difficult to set up quantitative measures to check the learning of the managers, and conclusions could only be made about this indirectly.

My research was thus an AR study that spanned two years and consisted of five large AR cycles. However, the study also had many small cycles, each driving the next.

My definition of action research was based on (Dick, 2001, p. 21) "AR is a change methodology and research methodology within a single process.

It seeks to bring about change—the action—in such a way that more understanding is developed as a parallel outcome. It pursues understanding—the research—in ways which allow the action to be based on a better understanding of the situation."

Initial AR Model

Initially, I adopted Perry and Zuber-Skerrit's (1992, p. 204) model shown in Figure 6.1 for a proposed postgraduate AR study. In my model, management learning was my "thesis AR" and the problem that we tackled during this research about new work model implementation was our common "core AR" project. Together, these formed the AR approach to my research.

Final AR Model

During this study, I also participated in two other "learning sets" that had a significant impact on my research questions:

1. The PhD set, formed by candidates doing their doctoral research through the University of South Australia and supervised by Alan and Bob. This set met regularly face-to-face in Singapore as an action learning set. Participating in this set helped me to answer my primary as well as my secondary research question partially.
2. Elogue, a virtual action learning set that communicated mainly through email, was formed while attending a course called AREOL (Action Research and Evaluation On-line) facilitated by my supervisor Bob Dick. Participating in this set helped me to answer my secondary research question.

My final AR model, including the interaction between my research set and the two external sets, is shown in Figure 6.2.

The planning phase of the individual cycle drove the action phase of the "participatory cycle." The reflection phase of the individual cycle was carried out with members of the PhD set and Elogue. This led to changes in the planning phase of the individual cycle that then acted on in the action phase of the participatory cycle. The symbols in my model have been combined to show this.

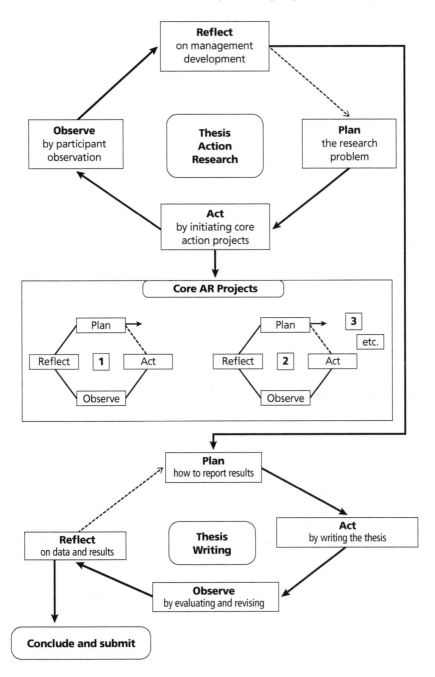

Figure 6.1 Initial action research model.

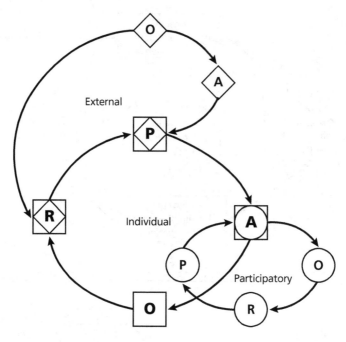

Figure 6.2   Final action research Model 1.

Action Learning

I used action learning, which is closely related to AR, as the technique for involving my coresearchers in management learning activities in the workplace.

Action Learning was developed by Reg Revans after the World War II to help managers learn from each other while solving real problems that were affecting them and for which there were no obvious solutions. He used the formula $L = P + Q$ (Revans, 1998, p. 4) to describe a social learning process, where L is learning, P is programmed knowledge (i.e., knowledge that we learn from books, courses etc.) and Q as insightful questioning. According to Revans, 90% of the learning in action comes from questioning, as yesterday's knowledge is often not sufficient to solve today's problems. Action learning needs the support of a group called a "set" of peers working on a real problem of significance to them. Most action learning programs have the following elements (Weinstein, 2002, p. 10; McGill & Broadbank, 2004; Pedler, 2008):

1. A "set" of 5 to 8 participants who meet regularly over a period of time voluntarily.

2. They work on a real-time work project of concern that defies solution (i.e., these are not puzzles that can be solved by an individual or solved quickly by a group).

3. The action learning set usually has a sponsor or a client who champions the set, is interested in the problem being resolved, and who clears away any barriers. Usually the sponsor has a lot of authority or influence in the organisation.

4. An emphasis on questioning that is helpful and exploratory but does not aim to provide answers. The process of questioning is often compared to "peeling the onion" to uncover the real problem through questioning and not acting just on symptoms.

5. A focus on reflection to become aware of insights and to learn.

6. The sets are initially supported by a facilitator often called a "set adviser" who helps the set with the process of action learning. Often the set adviser becomes unnecessary as the set progresses and learns to manage itself.

7. The learning takes place in a cycle by continuously planning —doing— reflecting—consolidating. When one cycle is completed another begins.

My coresearchers and I formed an "action learning set" that worked in parallel with the work model implementation committee, meeting separately to help improve the process by which this committee performed its task. This provided a valuable opportunity for the managers involved in this research, who were also members of the new work model implementation committee, to enhance their learning. Their actions were planned in our action learning meetings, and reflections were also carried out in the meetings to take the next step.

In all, we conducted 12 action learning meetings. Data collected during this phase of the study were mainly minutes of meetings, action learning guides used to record our reflections, and a video of the workshop we conducted.

Action Science

The basic goal of action science as developed by Chris Argyris is "increasing professional effectiveness by helping individuals in small groups to shift from using Model 1 to using Model 2 in resolving difficult problems" (Action Science, 2012, p. 1). Model 1 involves single loop learning, which is often defensive and reduces the possibility of learning. Model 2 encourages double loop learning, which results in a productive learning process. By moving from Model 1 to Model 2 behaviour managers can close the gap between their "espoused theories" and "theories in use."

As I approached the end of my study, I became an internal consultant to YES. During this time I had occasions to evaluate my own performance as the previous director of the organisation, based on my study of "action science." Like the famous Pogo (Kelly, 1996) I was surprised to realise that "We have met the enemy and he is us."

On reflection, I became excited about the prospect of adding action science to my management learning model. To help me understand the usefulness of action science I carried out a detailed analysis of the dilemma of the power relationship I faced in my research as a personal case study.

I used the "left-hand:" and "right-hand" column process advocated by Argyris and Schön (1974, p. 41) to analyse my power relationship with my managers by recording "what I said" at a meeting in the right-hand column against "what I was thinking" in the left-hand column and reflecting on the differences.

Action Learning, Action Research, and Action Science

While action learning, action research, and action science have many similarities and can be used in conjunction with each other in an action research intervention, they also have some differences as detailed in Table 6.1.

Search Conferences

As per Frank, Angus, and Rehm (1992, p. 141) "Search conferences have been linked with AR as the 'generative side' of AR to introduce social innovation and recognise system level themes and trends." Search conferences are also recommended by Greenwood and Levin (2006) while conducting AR.

Bunker and Alban (1997, p. 34) describe a search conference (created by Fred Emery and Eric Trist in 1959) as "a participatory planning method that enable communities, institutions and organizations to identify, plan and implement their most desired future." The search conference process includes environmental scanning to understand changes happening in the environment, reflect on the group's history (where we came from), analyse where we are now, discuss a desirable future to cope with the changes in the environment and develop action plans to achieve the desired future.

I understood the value of search conferences from Alan Davies (who worked closely with Fred and Merrelyn Emery) and who taught us the process as part of our PhD program. I used search conferences to build a

TABLE 6.1 Comparing Action Research With Action Learning and Action Science

Criteria	Action Research	Action Learning	Action Science
Philosophical basis	Gestalt psychology, pragmatism, democracy	Learning from experience, action research and other eclectic views	Lewinian action research, Dewey's theory of inquiry
Purpose	Social change through involvement and improvement	Understanding and changing of self and or system through action and reflection-on-action	Change in reasoning and behaviour leading to increased competence, justice, and capacity of learning and human development
Epistemology	Knowing through doing; making and applying discoveries	Problem solving, and also problem framing	Reflecting-in-action, making explicit tacit theories-in-use
Ideology	Focus on participation, involvement and empowerment of organizational members affected by the problem	Arising from natural learning processes and influenced by beliefs or participants and staff	Subscribing to a Model II action model, which engages people in transforming and improving their world
Methodology	Interactive cycles of problem defining, data collection, taking action or implementing a solution, followed by further testing	Cycles of framing, action, reflection, concluding, reframing	Reflection on there-and-then and here-and-now reasoning, with an emphasis on online interactions

shared vision for my new operation. This was followed by two search conferences for one of the divisions that was managed by one of my coresearchers.

Sample

I used a purposeful or criterion-based sampling for this study. I was introducing Western methods in a traditional Japanese company. So when I started my AR and set up a learning set, I used managers who had either completed or were in the process of completing MBA programs offered through Western universities. I needed these managers to initiate and reduce resistance to the program. As the research progressed, we added three more managers to the set who had not enrolled in MBA programs but were core members of the new work model implementation committee. In the end, the learning set was evenly balanced between the two categories of managers.

Data Collection

I collected data in various ways:

1. Minutes of action learning set meetings, including reflections
2. Reflective memos written by me during the research
3. Company records of the work model implementation committee's work
4. Company documents relevant to the research
5. Videotape of an action learning workshop conducted by my core-searchers and myself at a public conference
6. Reports of search conferences that were held during the study
7. Review of work done by the new work model implementation committee by an operation manager who was not part of our learning set and who later took over my job in the operation for which this study was mainly conducted
8. Convergent interviews of the coresearchers by independent action researchers from outside my organisation
9. Feedback from the research set on what they had learnt
10. Notes taken during PhD set meetings
11. Review of management outcomes of the PhD set and emails with them about their work
12. Feedback from workshops conducted during the study with both my coresearchers and the PhD set
13. Emails exchanged with Elogue
14. Feedback on my conclusions from my participants
15. Personal case study of my "power relationship" dilemma

All the data collected were systematically coded under specific headings using techniques applied to build grounded theory.

Data Analysis

For quite some time I was puzzled about how to analyse my data. I did not have a large amount of data and I had worked mainly with one group of managers on a single core AR project. While thinking about this dilemma I came across a book edited by Peter Frost and Ralph Stablein titled *Doing Exemplary Research* (Frost & Stablein, 1992).

In this book, Professor Richard Hackman, commenting on the exemplary research conducted by his doctoral student Connie Gersick, stated that "one lesson we learn from this research is about the value of staying very close to the phenomenon one is studying, rather than do scholarly work at arm's length.... The research question should drive the methodology...Connie invented a unique research methodology specifically tailored to her particular research question" (Hackman, 1992, p. 75).

I decided that I would look at my data in different ways to make sense of them. Therefore, my data analysis uses multiple methods of analysis, but in each instance I carried out the analysis to a sufficient depth to bring to the surface the answers relevant to my research questions. Thus, like Gersick, I stayed close to my phenomenon and designed a data analysis process tailored to answer my particular research questions.

My idea was to analyse the data from a "helicopter view" and go deeper and deeper into them to uncover more findings through iterations. Each of the iterations drove the next like an AR spiral. My data analysis is based on the methods detailed by Chenitz and Swanson (1986), Miles and Huberman (1994), and Dick (1990a, 1990b, 1993).

Initially, I divided my AR into three major cycles. However, when I did my data analysis using an event listing, I found that I actually had five distinct cycles. I then rewrote my data analysis using five cycles. Next, using a helicopter view, I drew an "event network" (Miles & Huberman, 1994) that broke down the management learning into several phases.

I then coded the minutes of meetings, and wrote theoretical notes and reflective memos on the key variables of my study (Miles & Huberman, 1994, pp. 55–72, Corbin, 1986, pp. 102–121). I followed this with an "event listing" (Miles & Huberman, 1994) to study the effects of external events on my research. I then prepared a "role-ordered matrix" (Miles & Huberman, 1994) to study the background of each researcher—where they were in the organisation when the study started and where they moved to at the end of the study—to trace their growth in the organisation. The matrix also summarises their learning from the research, which was obtained through their feedback one year after the research was conducted. I then carried out a comparison between what I found with similar cases reported in the literature, to confirm/disconfirm my findings. This helped strengthen my findings by triangulating it with the literature.

Rigour

I attempted to address the question of rigour by checking the validity of my findings from the following perspectives:

- Qualitative research
- AR
- Action inquiry

In addition to this, I carried out the following checks on my research:

- Quality assurance checks
- Ethical issues considerations

Outcomes

The study contributed to both management and research outcomes. The organisation expected management outcomes and the university wanted to see research outcomes. Table 6.2 shows an effect matrix that summarises the three types of outcomes from this research—management, research and personal. The columns summarize three types of effects: direct, indirect, and surprises that were not anticipated.

Management Outcomes

The direct management outcome of the research was the effective establishment of the new work model in the ATC.

An opinion poll of the new work model's success confirmed that the members of the work model committee rated the success of the new work model as being nearly 60% and decided to continue using it with improvements. The new head of the ATC also confirmed the impressive business results attained by the operation since the implementation of the new work model. The minutes of a meeting that was held after the new work model was successfully implemented recorded that:

> The impressive results in the past two years can be attributed to a large extent to the implementation of the new work model.

The managers who participated as coresearchers credited the "management learning model" with the successful implementation of the new work model. The managers who participated in the research also took up higher responsibilities in the organisation.

Research Outcomes

The direct research outcome of this study was the establishment of a management learning model at the workplace.

The answer to my primary research question contributed directly to the research outcome that managerial learning can result in management development both individually and as a team. The management outcomes

TABLE 6.2   Outcomes From Research Effects Matrix—Outcomes

Outcomes	Direct	Indirect	Surprise
Management	1. New Work Model well established. 2. Promotion to higher positions.	ATC met its goals by increasing its income by 2.5 fold, while halving the cost and maintaining the same number of staff	1. Learning set faded. 2. Did not think of using the PhD set for verifying my hypothesis.
Research	1. Established criteria for management learning in the workplace. 2. Management learning leads to more effective managers. 3. Surprise is a trigger for managerial learning. 4. The action learning guide that was requested by many practitioners over the world for their own use. 5. Action learning and AR led to the researchers of the PhD set to develop as more effective managers.	1. AL/AR can be applied in Asian cultures with local adjustments. 2. Camouflaging action research to be politically acceptable to the organisation where it is carried out is effective in introducing change management processes. 3. Transfer of learning is possible through participatory AR.	
Personal	1. Smooth transition into a consultant. 2. Became a reflective practitioner.	1. Learnt new skills for own business. 2. Won recognition in the international community as an action researcher. 3. Learnt electronic facilitation skills. 4. A vignette about my action learning process was published in a book written by Professor Mike Marquardt.	My own weaknesses as a manager were exposed. Learnt how to analyse dilemmas using "action science"

achieved by the PhD set using action learning/research added further cred-ibility to my claim.

I also learnt the value of "surprise" as a trigger for management learning, which matches Schön's (1983, p. 68) concept about learning from surprises when reflecting-in-action and Foote-Whyte, Greenwood, and Lazes' (1991, p. 97) notion of learning from "creative surprises" in participatory AR. Some of these key "surprises" that led me to learn are listed in Table 6.2.

The indirect outcomes of my research provided the answer to my two secondary research questions. I think that my experience with the research set and the PhD set as well as the feedback received locally suggests that action learning/research can be adapted to an Asian environment with ad-justments to suit local conditions.

Personal Outcomes

My research has also personally transformed me as a manager, an obser-vation that was echoed by the other members of the PhD set.

Through this study I was able to change my role from that of a senior manager to that of a consultant with very little impact felt by the organisa-tion, as managers rose in the organisation to take over my functions. I also became a reflective practitioner in the true sense.

INSIGHTS

The study demonstrated to me that action research, as an approach for orga-nizational change, would find acceptance in societies that are systemic in their understanding of the world. It is therefore suited to Asian beliefs embedded in the Buddhist and Hindu philosophies. In countries where a systemic approach is valued, action research will likely be an acceptable form of learning by doing.

In conducting action research in an Asian setting, I believe there is a need to understand that "communication in the East is often indirect, sug-gestive and symbolic rather than descriptive and precise" (Abe, 1990, quot-ed in Chia, 2003, p. 957). Action in the West is seen as having a purpose, driven by anticipation, incentives and desires (March, 1996). However, the East gives more importance to perfecting action as the real basis for know-ing for its own sake and not for its consequences (Chia, 2003, p. 978).

Another insight I had during this study was how to write an action research thesis or dissertation. Initially I studied the five-chapter model suggested by Chad Perry (Perry, 1998), which was developed to help practitioners struc-ture their thesis to meet academic requirements. As I started following this model I began to improvise. First, I chose the first person to write my thesis, arguing that there was no other way to tell my story. I also used three chapters to describe my action research cycles instead of using one conventional data analysis chapter. I added a "personal learning" chapter as I learnt a great deal about myself as a manager and how to be a better one. The literature also supports the use of more creative ways of crafting an action research thesis. (Dick, 1993; Fisher & Phelps, 2006; Willis, Inman, & Valenti, 2010).

I also learned through the dissertation experience that there are both advantages and disadvantages to doing research in your own work setting. One advantage is that as an "insider" researcher you have much more knowledge of the history and context of the organization than an "outsider" researcher typically would. There were, however, disadvantages as well. Coghlan and Brannick (2001, pp. 48–57) caution action researchers conducting research in their own organizations to be wary of some critical issues that managers need to pay attention to: There will be role ambiguity when you are an agent of change that affects you as well. The organizational role may expect total commitment from you while the research role may expect you to be neutral and objective.

While you may have access to certain parts of your organization, you may be denied access to other parts due to the political situation in the organization. The advantage of being an insider researcher is the valuable knowledge you possess about the culture, power blocks, politics, traditions, and informal structure of your organization. However, this may inhibit you from standing back to be able to be critical of the situations in the organization. As long as managers are able to realize the strengths and weaknesses of being an insider action researcher it is a practical and effective way of managing organizational change.

WHAT I WOULD HAVE DONE DIFFERENTLY

I feel that that if I were to start over, I would be unlikely to make any significant changes to my original approach, as both action research and action learning are learned best by doing. However, I learned about action science late in the process and, had I been aware of it earlier, I would have used action science right from the start to support the action research initiative. Action science helps you to reflect and inquire more about your own strengths and weaknesses and develops your capacity to conduct action research. In addition, action science developed in and is appropriate for the problems of business. It, in my opinion, is a good fit the types of problems managers face in many types of business organizations.

While the change implemented using action research worked well for the new project managers and system integrators, it did not work well with the specialists who felt they lost their importance in the organisation. Perhaps having a representative of the specialists in the action learning set could have improved the situation. One of the broad principles emphasized in many models of action research is "stakeholder participation." The specialists were an important stakeholder group but they were not participants in the learning sets that led to the changes. Had they been involved their "buy in" might have been stronger and the change itself might have been different given the benefit of their input.

As a practitioner unfamiliar with academic research I also did not conduct an academic literature review at the start of my doctoral research. I feel that practitioners should also be guided to do their literature review at the start even though action research starts with a thematic concern felt by the action researcher or his/her client and coresearchers. The literature review need not be very extensive as is often the case of conventional research to identify a gap to do research and make a contribution. However, action researchers should do sufficient background reading before starting their research and be informed by previously developed knowledge. I also started keeping a journal late in my research. I would have benefited by starting to write a professional journal early. There are some good guides to write a reflective journal (e.g., Holly, 1997). This has been made even easier with hand held-devices that can record your reflections supported by software such as the Dragon speech recognition software to convert voice into text. Starting my data analysis early and starting to write early would also have helped to avoid the last-minute scramble and would have minimised the stress involved to complete the thesis.

NOTES

1. I would like to acknowledge that the action research study presented in this chapter was presented as one of the case studies in a paper presented at the Project Management Academic and Research Conference held at Washington in 2010 (Sankaran & Kumar, 2010).
2. The spelling in this chapter reflects international and British conventions rather than American spelling and the editors made no attempt to "Americanize" spelling.

REFERENCES

Abe, M. (1990). *An inquiry into the good.* New Haven: Yale University Press.
Action Science. (2012). What is Action Science? [online]. Available at http://www. actionscience.com/actinq.htm
Argyris, C., & Schön, D. A. (1974). *Theory in practice: Increasing professional effectiveness.* San Francisco: Jossey Bass.
Bunker, B. B., & Alban, B. T. (1997). *Large group interventions: Engaging the whole system for rapid change,* San Francisco, CA: Jossey Bass.

Chia, R. (2003). From knowledge-creation to the perfecting of action: Tao, Basho and pure experience as the ultimate ground of knowing. *Human Relations, 56*(8), 953–981.

Chenitz, W. C., & Swanson, J. M. (Eds.). (1986). *From practice to grounded theory: Qualitative research in nursing.* Reading, MA: Addison-Wesley.

Coghlan, D., & Brannick, T. (2001). *Doing action research in your own organization.* London: Sage.

Corbin, J. (1986). Coding, writing memos and diagramming, In W. C. Chenitz & J. M. Swanson (Eds.), *From practice to grounded theory: Qualitative research in nursing.* Reading, MA: Addison-Wesley.

Dick, B. (1990a). *Convergent interviewing,* (3rd ed.), Brisbane, Australia: Interchange.

Dick, B. (1990b). *Rigour without numbers: The potential of dialectical processes as qualitative research tools.* Brisbane, Australia: Interchange.

Dick, B. (1993). *So you want to do an action research thesis? How to conduct and report action research,* (Vol. 2, No. 6). Brisbane, Australia: Interchange.

Dick, B. (2001). Action research: Action and research. In S. Sankaran, B. Dick, R. Passfield, & P. Swepson, (Eds), *Effective change management using action learning and action research: Concepts, frameworks, processes and applications,* Lismore, NSW, Australia: Southern Cross University Press.

Deming, W. E. (2000). *Out of the crisis,* Boston: MIT Press

Emery, M., & Purser, R. E. (1996). *The Search Conference: A powerful method for planning organizational change and community action.* San Francisco: Jossey-Bass.

Fisher, K., & Phelps, R. (2006). Recipe or a performing art? Challenging conversations for writing action research theses, *Action Research, 4*(2), 143–164.

Frank, G., Angus, D., & Rehm, B. (1992). Theory into practice: Prelude to chapters 14 and 15. In M. R. Weisbord, (Ed.), *Discovering common ground* (pp. 141–142). San Francisco: Berrett-Koehler.

Foote-Whyte, W., Greenwood, D. J., & Lazes, P. (1991). Participatory Action Research: Through practice to science in social research. In W. Foote-Whyte (Ed.), *Participatory action research* (pp. 19–55). Thousand Oaks, CA: Sage.

Frost, P., & Stablein, R. (Eds). (1992). *Doing exemplary research.* Thousand Oaks, CA: Sage.

Greenwood, D. J., & Levin, M. (2006). *Introduction to action research: Social research for social change* (2nd ed.). Thousand Oaks, CA: Sage.

Hackman, J. R. (1992), Time and transitions. In B. Frost & P. Stabelin, (Eds), *Doing exemplary research* (pp. 73–78). Thousand Oaks, CA: Sage.

Holly, M. L. (Ed.) (1997). *Keeping a personal-professional journal* (2nd ed.). Geelong, Victoria, Deakin University:

Kelly, W. (1996). *We have met the enemy and he is us.* [online] Accessed Aug 27 2012. Available at http://en.wikipedia.org/wiki/Pogo_(comic_strip)

Kemmis, S., & McTaggart, R. (Eds). (1988). *The action research planner* (3rd ed.). Geelong, Victoria, Australia: Deakin University.

March, J. (1996). *A scholar's quest.* Retrieved 10-Apr-2010, from http://www.gsb.stanford.edu/community/bmag/sbsm0696/Ascholar.

McGill, I., & Broadbank, A. (2004). *The action learning handbook: Powerful techniques for education, professional development and training.* New York: Routledge-Farmer.

Miles, M. B., & Huberman, A. M. (1994). *An expanded sourcebook: Qualitative data analysis* (2nd ed.). Thousand Oaks, CA: Sage.

Mumford, A. (1993). *How managers can develop managers.* Aldershot, UK: Gower.

Pedler, M. (2008). *Action learning for managers,* Aldershot, UK: Gower.

Perry, C., & Zuber-Skerritt, O. (1992). Action research in graduate management research programs. *Higher Education 23,* 195–208.

Perry, C. (1998,). A structured approach for presenting research theses, *Australasian Marketing Journal, 6*(1), 63–86.

Revans, R. (1998). *ABC of action learning: Empowering managers to act and learn from action.* London: Lemos & Crane.

Schön, D. (1983). *The reflective practitioner: How professionals think in action.* New York: Basic Books.

Sankaran, S., & Kumar, M., (2010). *Implementing organizational change using action research in two Asian cultures.* Proceedings of the Project Management Institute's Education and Research Conference, Washington, July 7–10, 8 pages.

Weinstein, K. (2002). Action learning: The classic approach. In Boshyk, Y. (Ed.), *Action learning worldwide: Experiences of leadership and organizational development,* Basingstoke, UK, Palgrave MacMillan.

Willis, J., Inman, D., & Valenti, R. (2010). *Completing a professional practice dissertation: A guide for doctoral students and faculty.* Charlotte, NC: Information Age.

CHAPTER 7

IMMIGRANT PHD STUDENTS USING ACTION RESEARCH AS A TOOL IN CAREER PREPARATION

Wenying Shi
University of Alberta

ABSTRACT

This chapter describes an action research study that had as its main goals: (a) a better understanding of the difficulties and barriers immigrant PhD students faced when entering the Canadian academic culture; and (b) helping the participants develop ways of addressing the problems they faced as they prepared for and became members of the Canadian academic community.

My dissertation was about the experiences of immigrant PhD students who are pursuing academic careers in Canada. That was not, however, why I came to Canada from China. I had planned to continue my work in English as a second language (ESL) education in which I had been exclusively engaged during the past 25 years. That is what I planned to study when I be-

Action Research, pages 153–178
Copyright © 2014 by Information Age Publishing
All rights of reproduction in any form reserved.

gan my doctoral study in Canada in 2005 as an immigrant from the People's Republic of China. My goal was to obtain a doctoral degree in ESL teacher education so that I could continue an academic career in Canada.

Soon this goal seemed to be wishful thinking. Somehow, I realized that I had turned into a student of ignorance (what I knew was of no importance; what I was learning did not make sense to me), a member of Canadian society who was of little or no use (an immigrant support staff member at my university suggested that, due to a lack of experience, I was not even qualified to work as a waitress which is a very low-end position in Chinese culture), and a professional with no hope of continuing to work in my chosen field of ESL (I was forced to resign from my first ESL teaching job in Canada when, after my director had warned me not to "rock the boat," I did it anyway perhaps due to an entrepreneur spirit carried over from thirteen years as a business owner).

Like other newcomers to Canada, I was offered a variety of support services. However, most of the services were not what I needed. They offered help to someone who needed the basic knowledge and skills to survive in the new and different culture. However, I did not come to Canada only to *survive*. I wanted to thrive and to join a particular community in Canadian culture—that of higher education. Instead of thriving and being accepted into the academic culture of higher education I felt I had been transformed from a contributing member of society into a dependent receiver of services. That was a severe challenge to my self-identity and my self-esteem. I was very confused and disoriented.

I asked myself questions. "What is wrong with me?" "Am I the only one who has been through all this?" More importantly, "Will my pursuit of an academic career be in vain after earning a Canadian doctoral degree?" To seek an answer, I turned my attention from self-blaming to examining the similar experiences of other immigrant doctoral students. Soon I became aware of external barriers that existed in the culture and then I began a personal journey of career exploration. Two years after I began that personal journey I took doctoral courses on action research and understood that my personal journey had much in common with the concepts and ideas of action research. That link between topic and method became the foundation for my dissertation research—an action research study of the barriers, issues, and problems immigrant doctoral students face when they attempt to become members of the academic community of another culture.

ACTION RESEARCH AS A RESCUE

Emancipatory action research caught my attention and became my focus while taking a course called Action Research in Theory. Carr and Kemmis (1986) defined it as "a self-reflective, self-critical and critical enquiry undertaken by professionals to improve the rationality and justice of their own practices, their understanding of these practices, and the wider context of their practice" (p. 122). In this version of emancipatory action research, the emphasis is on individual professionals who are situated in a particular social and political context. Critique, which is an important aspect of emancipatory action research, is at both a personal and a wider system level. Achieving emancipation may involve changes in personal attitudes, beliefs, and understanding but it may also involve identifying and understanding problems and issues in the broader context as well as working toward changing them. The end result should be emancipation for both the individual and for society in general. And, while the meaning of the term emancipation will vary from person to person and situation to situation, the overall goal of emancipatory action research is to facilitate a more participative and democratic society that strives for greater social equity.

Emancipatory action research is personally oriented action research, which meant to me that my study could also be part of my effort to solve my own career problems. However, there was a dilemma. If I used action research to study immigrant students, would it place me in a disadvantageous position when I applied for work in the field of ESL teacher education and my research was not directly related to a core ESL topic? I posed this question to several scholars, including guest speakers in graduate classes who gave talks on how doctoral students should develop their research topics. When I asked whether I should choose a research topic in the field I wanted to teach in which was ESL teacher education (a predetermined research area of mine) or academic career preparation (a pathway towards it)—I received a vague but unmistakable message: a researcher should not be so selfish as to focus on a dissertation topic that would serve her own personal needs.

My problem was that I was living in the then and there world of uncertainty about my future as an academic in Canada. I was simply incapable of skipping over living in the present, a reality I had to change. No matter how much respect I held for the professors who advised me to pick a dissertation topic in the field of ESL teacher education, I eventually elected to follow my heart and deal through my dissertation with an issue that seemed to be to be so serious that it stood between my present which seemed bleak and unpromising, and a possible future that included a career as a Canadian academic. The need of changing my current reality surpassed all other considerations.

WHY ALSO AUTO-ETHNOGRAPHY?

For most doctoral students there are identifiable points where different aspects of the dissertation research begin. However, my research had actually started before I realized it had begun. When I looked back, I realized there had already been a year of self-exploration that was the first part of an action research process. It was a period when I investigated the contradictory messages between a university publication and the immigrants' stories disclosed through a literature review and personal communications. At the time, neither I nor my advisors had considered this the beginning of my dissertation. There had been no Institutional Review Board proposal and approval because the only "subject" or "participant" in that part of the dissertation research was myself. Yet, this was the beginning of the dissertation and the primary methodology was autoethnography.

One reason that autoethnography was chosen as a complementary method can be illustrated through the analogy of training psychotherapists who are generally expected to undergo therapy themselves by exploring every angle of their own minds in order to support future clients who will be exploring theirs. Likewise, self-awareness and attention to one's own feelings, thoughts, and experiences can contribute to the therapeutic use of self as an effective strategy of teaching ESL and encouraging the development of immigrant students with whom my academic career is involved. This purposeful use of self, inherent in the role of an ESL instructor, may also be seen as synchronous to the role of the qualitative researcher who seeks to uncover the meaning of others' experiences.

The other reason relates to the unique characteristic of autoethnography. By allowing the researcher to write herself into her own work as a major character, the accepted views of silent authorship are challenged —the idea that the researcher's voice is not included in the presentation of findings is rejected. This approach may liberate some researchers from the constraints of the dominant ideological representations of empirical ethnography because *how* researchers write influences *what* they can write about (Charmaz & Mitchell, 1997). However, since my work also explores the voices of my peers, autoethnography was used in conjunction with survey data, interviews, and the journal responses of others. Incorporating the strengths of both approaches—an exploration of my own personal journey and helping others analyze and reflect on their journeys—provided a more comprehensive view of the phenomena being studied. I still remember how excited I was when the idea of integrating autoethnography into the action research framework was first mentioned by my dissertation supervisor. One question I asked myself was: "Are my stories really so valuable that they can stand alone?" In the end I was convinced that my stories were valuable and that they were enhanced and deepened by the perceptions, experiences, and interpretations of other immigrant doctoral students who participated in this study.

AN OVERVIEW OF THE ACTION RESEARCH PROJECT

As noted above this action research (AR) project combined autoethnographic methods (both as a way of accomplishing the goals of AR and as a data collection method) with more traditional AR approaches. In this section I will describe the three phases or cycles of the AR project and also describe in more detail what happened in each of the phases.

The 3-Cycle Action Research Design

The following diagram (Figure 7.1) shows the three-cycle action research components and procedure I used in the dissertation research, including goals, types of work, theoretical lenses, and action outcomes.

Action research is normally considered a recursive cycle but in this study the process was more like a series of phases in which the same issues were addressed but with a different focus. In the first phase the focus was on my own personal understanding of the process of career preparation. A useful theoretical framework for this phase was critical pedagogy and the actions called for involved personal liberation or emancipation. My own beliefs were severely limiting my ability to make important decisions about my professional career. The second phase included a broader exploration of the knowledge, concepts, and strategies that could be used to address the problems immigrants have when they try to become members of another culture's academic community. This phase was less personal and involved both a review of the existing literature and an exploration of the issues with other immigrants in graduate programs. A particularly useful theoretical framework in this phase was social constructivism because it emphasizes the "socially constructed" nature of knowing and focuses on the need to contextualize and localize knowledge. The action called for in this phase was integration—the development of a holistic and integrated understanding of the problems and barriers immigrants face when they wish to join

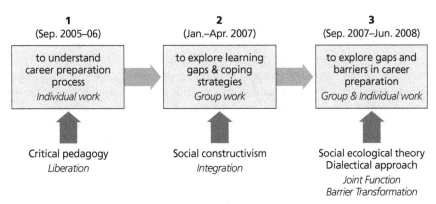

Theoretical Franework & *Action Outcome*

Figure 7.1   The 3-cycle action research model used in this research.

the academic community of another culture. In my research this involved both group and individual work and it was guided both by socio ecological theory and a dialectical approach. The two major goals of actions in this phase were to collaboratively develop solutions with the other immigrants who participated in the action research and to identify and implement ways of reducing, eliminating, or bypassing barriers that stand in the way of immigrants who want to pursue an academic career path.

A NARRATIVE DESCRIPTION OF THE RESEARCH

The narration that follows is organized by phases of the AR project and stays close to the chronology of what actually happened throughout my quest. The three cycles to be presented collectively offer both a picture of the complexity facing immigrant doctoral students in their professional career transition and raise awareness of the responsibilities of action researchers in facilitating sensitivity, responsiveness, and flexibility throughout the course of change.

Cycle One: Conceptualizing a Cross-Cultural Academic Career Preparation Process

The incident of my forced resignation from my first teaching job and later a failure in applying for a teaching certificate due to three grammatical errors in an interview made me wonder if it was just me having such experiences in my effort to become an ESL teacher in Canada. Wondering if I would continue to fail in gaining entry to an academic career even after earning a doctoral degree, I shifted my attention to examining similar experiences of other immigrant doctoral students.

I began by searching information provided by the university. I found a report on graduate student employment released by the university's career service center. It revealed the results of an employment survey in 2000. The report stated that "since graduating in 2000, the majority of respondents have enjoyed steady employment and rising salaries. The vast majority of respondents indicated that their university studies were critical both in securing employment and performing effectively in the workplace" (Kennedy & Snicer, 2006, p. 2).

Did this study include immigrant and international students? If so, then why did the results contradict my own experiences and those of immigrants around me? Which findings should I believe—the university's report or the immigrants' stories? I began to read eagerly about the employment situation of professional immigrants.

A number of studies have shown that many highly educated professional immigrants experience formidable barriers when they seek to have their foreign credentials and work experience recognized (Basran & Zong, 1998; Henry et al., 2000; Krahn et al., 2000; Li, 2001; Reitz, 2001). Several other studies use census data to demonstrate the difficulties faced especially by visible minority immigrants in translating educational achievements into professional advantage (Grindstaff, 1986; Trovato & Grindstaff, 1986). In a study of 404 Indo- and Chinese-Canadian immigrant professionals in Vancouver, Basran and Zong (1998) reported that only 18.8% of their respondents worked as professionals (doctors, engineers, school/university teachers, and other professionals) after immigrating to Canada.

This general pattern of barriers and difficulties was also noted by Zong (2004) who pointed out that professional immigrants are generally challenged by individual and structural barriers that prevent them from attaining a level of career success that their credentials and experience would justify. Instead of gaining social sympathy and support, Zong (2004) concluded that when individuals and the society in general, do not recognize that many barriers are inherent in the social conditions and structural arrangements of the culture. When this is not understood there is, according to Zong, a tendency to "assign blame to immigrant professionals themselves for failing to acquire professional jobs in Canada" (p. 2).

Whether failure to thrive professionally is at its core a problem of individual immigrants or a problem with the host culture is a critical issue. My own experience suggested that Zong was correct—the host culture must take considerable responsibility for what appears to be a systematic problem. Gowricharn (2001) also came to the same conclusion—"the causal root of the problem is the host countries' opportunity structure—the external barriers rather than internal ones. The opportunity structure in the host country is essential for a proper understanding of the mobility process" (p. 157).

How about the professional employment situation of those having Canadian formal education? Could it be that those who chose to invest time and money in receiving a Canadian graduate education would have better employment opportunities? With these questions in mind, I began to examine Canadian doctoral programs to evaluate their effectiveness in assisting graduate students with their career preparation and planning. Golde and Dore's (2001) claim unfortunately confirmed my assumption about career-related problems in graduate programs. It also reflects a general consensus in the literature: "The training doctoral students receive is not what they want, nor does it prepare them for the jobs they take" (p. 5). Golde and Dore's concern is about all graduate students, not just immigrants and it suggests the problems immigrant students face in establishing an academic career may not be unique but instead a special instance of a much broader issue—whether graduate programs effectively prepare students for the careers they hope to pursue. This point was further reinforced by Nagle, Suldo, Christenson, and Hansen (2004) who emphasized that "job stress was the number one concern of graduate students considering entry into academia" (p. 321). The literature reviewed also indicated that there was little offering of constructive suggestions, coping strategies and success stories by immigrant students themselves on what might be done to improve their situations, how to adapt themselves to the established systems, and how to foster changes in the systems.

Another important discovery from a self-exploration standpoint is that North American higher education has been heavily influenced by Boyer's (1997) book, *Scholarship Reconsidered: Priorities for the Professoriate,* which proposes that the idea of scholarship be redefined and broadened considerably. Boyer's proposals are being adopted by more and more colleges and universities in North America and that leads to the recommendation that doctoral students' academic career preparation should include Boyer's four types of academic scholarship: discovery, integration, application, and teaching (Boyer, 1997). Having experienced a different educational system, and having worked in different academic-cultural environments, I realized that immigrant students need to be aware of the great differences between the academic and professional systems of their home countries' and those of their host country. Boyer's broad model of what should count as scholarship is one of many critical areas where an immigrant graduate student's preexisting professional knowledge and orientation may not be fully applicable in the new systems. Boyer's (1997) scholarships identified academic gaps for mainstream students who already understand the basic premises of living, thinking, and functioning in Western society; whereas immigrant students are expected to "adapt" to a new society *and* learn a new way of academic functioning. This need to unlearn and relearn in such a drastic way may be unrecognized or underestimated by both immigrant students and graduate programs of studies.

This potential learning gap and the contradiction between the university survey results and the literature review led me to believe that there was something wrong in the system, and that my personal problem could only be resolved through addressing those systemic problems. However, that consciousness of deficiency in graduate programs actually enhanced rather than reduced my fear that I might permanently lose the possibility of a teaching career in Canada.

As I worked to change that reality Freire's (1970) critical pedagogy was a helpful framework because it looks at the world from the perspective of someone who is being oppressed by the organizational and structural aspects of society and proposes that while it is not the individual's "fault" that they are not as successful as they could be, there is some responsibility to try and understand why that is the case and develop ways of overcoming the barriers they face. At that point I still hoped to make individual break-throughs by utilizing the university's resources. However, I also wondered whether I, as an individual, was capable of identifying the major gaps in my academic career preparation and working out coping strategies. I concluded that, if possible, this was not something that should be attempted individually. Collective effort seemed to be the only promising approach for accomplishing such a daunting task.

Cycle Two: Exploring Career Preparation Gaps With Others

Through self-study, I learned that there were three stages in career exploration: (a) building knowledge and information about oneself and the environment (Blustein, 1997; Jordan, 1963; Stumpf et al., 1983); (b) the intent of choosing an alternative career path/occupation (Schein, 1978); and (c) the determination to further one's career (Kanfer et al., 2001).

My personal need to make the 3-stage career exploration with others correlated with an assignment in a graduate course called, *Action Research in Practice.* That assignment had guided me through a complete process of planning an AR study: formulating research questions, designing the research, applying for ethics review to the Institutional Review Board, recruiting participants, collecting and analyzing data, reporting, and presenting, as well as conceptualizing, the previous cycle of the study. The research I planned became my dissertation study aimed at discovering gaps in immigrant PhD students' academic career preparation.

The recruitment of research participants was accomplished through advertising in the E-newsletter of the Graduate Student Association in the beginning of the 2007 winter term. Three immigrant doctoral students volunteered to join the research.

Recognizing how a career planning survey (*Graduate Student Survey of University of Colorado–Boulder, Academic Year 2003–2004*) had helped me understand the importance of early career planning in the first cycle, I revised the survey into an introductory questionnaire and asked the participants to complete it on the first day of our meeting. The participants were asked to self-assess the effectiveness of career-related professional training and to respond to questions on a Likert-like (5-point agree to disagree) scale. For example, "How useful have you found your training in basic teaching skills? (e.g., curriculum development, lecturing, leading discussions, writing examinations, creating and/or grading assignments)." Five answer options were provided to choose from: excellent, very good, good, fair, and poor.

The survey results and demographic data revealed that we were all Asian and working on doctorates in four different school faculties. Ages ranged from mid-30s to early 40s. In their home countries all of the participants were either researchers and/or university assistant professors.

The survey results also revealed that all the participants were taking graduate courses and none of us had taught as a primary course instructor in Canada. Little or no training had been received in basic teaching skills, curriculum development, lecturing, leading discussions, creating and/or grading assignments, or developing examinations. Most had not received faculty guidance in formulating a research topic or conducting research in collaboration with faculty members. Most had not received research funding from a faculty grant. None had assisted in writing a grant proposal. None had published as a sole author or coauthor. Most had received advice about employment opportunities inside and outside academia, looking for a job, and writing their CV with the aid of the university career service centre, friends, a department seminar, professors, a professional consultant, or government agencies. Most concluded that their career preparation was poor.

Next, we engaged in "self- reflective enquiry undertaken by participants in social situations in order to improve the rationality and justice ... in which ... practices are carried out" (Carr & Kemmis, 1983, p. 5). My task, as the leader of the AR project, was "to develop theories of practice which are rooted in the concrete experiences and situations of [participants] and then attempt to confront and resolve the problems to which these experiences give rise" (Carr & Kemmis, 1983, p. 118). We followed the same 3-stage career exploration processes noted earlier as a way to discover the gaps.

Between February and April of 2007, data were collected from several sources in addition to the initial survey questionnaire: detailed field notes which were completed after every related activity of the four-month research project; summary notes of each meeting which were circulated for member checks; and reflections that were written and submitted after every event that constituted the study. A variety of data sources offered opportunities for triangulation.

The organization of the data began by inputting every datum and by making sure that all was complete. Since this was my first time analyzing primary data, I was quite lost. The greatest challenge was finding themes. I had spent a huge amount of time in making sense of every single datum, and then put them together to look for overarching themes. When some themes emerged, they seemed vague and ambiguous. I had to go back again and again to my research questions in order to stick to the point.

After the themes emerged, I shared my findings with the participants during our last meeting. As we went through them, the participants often interrupted me for clarification or correction, or raised new questions. A scheduled meeting of 60–90 minutes often ended up lasting three or four hours. A lesson learned from this was that the selection and interpretation of data can be very subjective even when there are unquestioned agreements supported by more objective data.

The result of this collective effort was still not satisfactory. The themes seemed to be reporting answers to the research questions and summarizing discussions. My supervisor told me to read all the data and to take as much time as needed. After becoming very familiar with the data, I was eventually able to see recurring themes which allowed all the data to be categorized systematically. The challenge was to ensure that the categories were *internally homogeneous* and *externally heterogeneous,* which required that everything in one category be held together in a meaningful way and that the differences between categories be bold and clear (Guba & Lincoln, 1981). Naming the thematic categories was another challenge which took a couple of years of rereading, reinterpreting, recategorizing, and renaming.

To summarize the research experience of this cycle, the survey provided background information to be used as a starting point for action and discussion. The narration of our cross-cultural learning and initial professional experiences unveiled gaps in reconstructing professional identity and skills. The written reflections provided the participants with an opportunity for deep reflection on the beliefs we took for granted and the practices which might have partially constituted internal barriers in establishing and pursuing our career goals. The data analysis and interpretation were informed by social constructivism in alignment with critical pedagogy.

CYCLE THREE: EXPLORING GAPS AND BARRIERS

Preparing for Taking Action

Based on the findings of Cycle Two, my supervisor and I collaboratively made several presentations. The research need of moving from observation to action was addressed:

> From working on course assignments, researching and teaching assistant work, to adapting to Canadian graduate studies and life, international PhD students have very little time left to focus on anything else. For many of them, ... taking the next step into a career in the Canadian professional sector can be quite a challenging endeavour. The frustrations emerging most consistently... include: the tensions in adapting to the values embodied in higher education, the ambiguous messages received about priorities in the academy, a significant mismatch between the training received and what the jobs require, lack of confidence in one's expertise and developmental capacity, and disillusion in graduate studies, professional career, and societal recognition. (Bilash & Shi, 2007)

Inspired by the participants' strong desire to continue with career preparation, I was ready to take a leadership role in Cycle Three. Having already discovered the gaps in academic career preparation and some strategies for filling in the major gaps identified, I designed a year-long action plan for the next research group to follow. I named it "Dare to Thrive" in the hopes of inspiring participants.

The activities were developed based on five key components of academic career preparation: (a) asking why we are here; (b) joining a discipline or profession; (c) establishing expertise; (d) developing networks and relationships; and (e) becoming a professional. The types of activities designed included workshops, mentoring, hands-on experiences, working group discussions, and conferences to help the participants create and pursue professional development paths that were appropriate for our particular career aspirations, disciplinary contexts, cross-cultural experiences and stages in our graduate programs. The action plan emphasized individuals' initiatives and responsibilities in integrating career preparation into our graduate studies to complement our specialized training in our degree programs.

I took the action plan to the campus international student service centre and asked for permission to use its facilities for meetings. After several exchanges, including a meeting involving my supervisor, those in charge were very interested in my action plan and offered to join in. They even suggested a name for the research group—International Graduate Student Career Club (IGSCC)—which was later adopted. Soon, my expected outcomes were providing insight into the effectiveness of the graduate programs in preparing immigrant PhD students for an academic career, and helping us recognize and capitalize on the support resources for better career preparation.

The participants were recruited through the E-newsletters of the Graduate Student Association and the university's international student service centre. Very soon, nine immigrant PhD students joined, including the four from Cycle Two. To my happy surprise, the advertisement also attracted the attention of a graduate career advisor from the campus student career service centre, who offered to join our group.

To begin with, the student participants were asked to complete the survey 'piloted' in the previous cycle of the study. The findings revealed that the participants' ages ranged from early 20s to 40s, and they came from Iran, Japan, Korea, Peoples' Republic of China, and Russia. Their occupations in their home countries included a physiotherapist, some assistant professors, a researcher, an engineer, an engineer designer, and a technical manager. The driving force for pursuing a PhD program was unanimously to become an assistant professor in the Canadian or U.S. academia. In terms of education status, all were enrolled as full-time students and were in the mid- or late stage of PhD programs. The disciplines were diverse: business, chemistry, medicine, engineering, agriculture, arts, and education. All had completed course study. The participants were also asked to join in the semi-structured monthly peer-support professional development program activities, which were designed to introduce them to the wide range of academic career requirements and to support those who were engaging in activities to prepare for academic careers in the North American context. After every monthly activity, they were asked to fill in an activity evaluation form including a self-assessment on the progress they were making as a result of participating in the IGSCC activities. All forms were anonymous.

Between meetings, I communicated with the participants either in person or by email. In the meantime, I wrote and sent my reflections to the participants on the activities and progress in order to enhance the group's understanding of our preparation process. These were unplanned data sources but later generated some important themes.

At the end of each term, participants provided their perception of their professional change by completing an open ended reflection. When the research was completed, a postresearch interview questionnaire was sent and conducted online. Finally, I wrote field notes outlining my impressions of events throughout the year-long project.

TENSIONS IN IMPLEMENTING THE ACTION PLAN

Despite my passion and sufficient preparation, the IGSCC activities did not happen as I had scheduled. The two staffs' intensive involvement in addition to a larger-than-anticipated number of participants from more diverse linguistic, geographic and disciplinary backgrounds had changed the direction from taking action in advancing career preparation to a further exploration of gaps and barriers experienced on campus.

This shift began with a difference in opinion about the effectiveness of the university's career support. Although I had already prepared five activities to help the participants explore their career goals and identify their related strengths and weaknesses, none of the activities had a chance to be implemented because a simple warm-up question during the first meeting had become surprisingly complicated and completely changed the intended direction. I recorded the following after this meeting:

> When I asked "How supportive do you think your programs and the available supportive organizations are for your professional career preparation?" one participant said none. I could tell that it was difficult for the graduate career advisor to accept this statement. The international student advisor also seemed eager to understand why there was such an opinion. The career advisor cut into the students' discussion and spent a long time in introducing all the supports the career center has provided. I realized a great learning op-

portunity was emerging from both sides—the international graduate students and the institution. So I asked the following question: "I believe we all know about the career center and its services, why have we ignored it and haven't utilized it? What are the obstacles in taking advantage of these supports?" I guided the student participants to think from the perspectives of language difficulties, cultural barriers, social factors, personal reasons, and discriminations if there is any. (C. Shi, Field notes, October 13, 2007)

While the student participants were thinking and writing their answers to this question, the two staff participants were also eager to hear the students' thoughts. The day before the following month's meeting, I received an email from them asking me to direct the students to a discussion on "why they don't think the services are for them" so that the student career advisor could "have an opportunity to present how they might use the services." This email demonstrated that the staff were very concerned about the issues unique to those students and were striving to understand both whether the centers had taken all variables into consideration in providing needed services and also how any gaps might be addressed.

As a result, the next meeting focused on getting to know the services provided by the career center. The career advisor played a major role at the meeting which ended with a tour to the career center led by the advisor. Two weeks later, I received an email from Nick, who had participated in the research of Cycle Two but had been absent soon after Cycle Three began.

> What I am trying to do is becoming part of this society whatever the "society" I say is small, such as a student association. I may be becoming part of the "society" these days. Or maybe, I have not yet been recognized part of them. I am not sure about that. But, no matter what, I feel lonely doing it, or what it takes me to get involved in their society, I have to overcome this difficulty. It is a really tough situation. Sometimes, I feel I want to run away. In other times, I want to give it up. (Nick)

Nick's mood was not in complete harmony with the spirit of the IGSCC, which, guided by the caring staff, was busily exploring why we did not utilize the university's services. Nevertheless, my mood was affected and I began to feel that the career services did not meet the special needs of the student participants. I also felt that the staff attending the meetings had become a bit too self-defensive. Despite their good intentions, they did not seem to understand that the students' situation was far too complicated for simple encouragement of using the available services to solve the issue.

I was plagued by Nick's depression but struggled to stay resilient:

> I can't help thinking about the feelings revealed in your last letter such as "loneliness," "tough," "give up," and "run away." I feel painful actually because I have experienced the same or worse feelings than yours. That's why we

are working together...Just as you have been doing, I am also in the process of working towards my career goal. I don't know what the future will be. But I learned from my past experience that we have to construct our own pathway which is right beneath our feet. We need...strong willpower. (C. Shi, Email to Nick, November 28, 2007)

But just how could we begin to "construct our own pathway" with "strong willpower?" Two months had passed since this cycle had begun, and although I kept reminding the participants of the action plan to be implemented, I had received no response from either the students or the staff.

This was how I came to understand the change of the research direction. First of all, with the two staff members' active involvement, I felt intimidated and incompetent in continuing to act as a group leader or function as a "more capable peer" (Vygotsky, 1978) as I did in Cycle Two. Secondly, most new participants in this group had stronger personalities, more successful experiences, and more optimistic attitudes than those of Cycle Two. Further, many of the new participants were from disciplines such as science and engineering, which yield greater job opportunities than those in the social sciences and humanities (where Cycle Two participants mainly came from). It became evident that the action plan had been written based on the needs of Cycle Two.

The following month's meeting focused again on our experiences using the university services in addition to sharing our career preparation experiences. The learning need identified in this meeting was to develop social skills other than those used to gain professional knowledge and skills, so the following month's self-directed activity was suggested by a staff participant: "Could you double your current daily social conversational time with native speakers? For example, if your average talking time with native speakers is two minutes a day before, could you extend it to 4 minutes a day? Please also make a record on how hard it is for you? What are the obstacles? What are you going to do to overcome the obstacles?"

This task, honestly speaking, shocked me. I believed that it was intended to meet a general need of the student participants, but it definitely was not something I valued. I probably spoke English every minute of my day, for I had been living with my English-speaking fiancé and had also been teaching an undergraduate curriculum course.

At this point, I felt that this group had actually started to restrict me from advancing in my career preparation. Moreover, Nick's withdrawal from the club had made me feel guilty. I felt I had disappointed him when I had not been able to implement the action plan, as he, like me, could not afford waiting any longer; both he and I needed to experience a little success to stay resilient.

When the second term began, it became apparent that it would be impossible for the IGSCC to follow my predetermined action plan. I consulted with my supervisor, and she agreed that I change the research question from finding out effective coping strategies to the further exploration of barriers in career preparation.

The data analysis was a difficult task to perform with a changed research question, lengthy time requirements, and the richness of data from various sources. However, with an eagerness to find the themes, and equipped with the thematic coding skills learned in Cycle Two, after very hard work over a period of three months, a thematic classification system gradually emerged. The effort was aimed at achieving mutually exclusive, exhaustive, and meaningful *theme* coding (Krippendorff, 1980).

Another challenge came from my unstable mood caused by the ups and downs of my personal academic career preparation experience. While I was employed, my interpretations were overly-optimistic, which might overlook difficulties. When suffering from job loss or negative course evaluations, I became too depressed and pessimistic to work.

The analysis disclosed some significant external and internal barriers experienced by the nine immigrant doctoral students on campus. The analysis and interpretation of these data were informed mainly by social ecological theory. The four external barriers identified and analyzed were (a) adapting to doctoral programs of studies; (b) bridging gaps in professional knowledge and skills; (c) socializing to the academic profession; and (d) utilizing the university's career support services. The three identified internal barriers in maintaining career aspiration and persistence included (a) career immaturity; (b) conflicts in academic cultural values and norms; and (c) the stress of acculturation.

The barriers identified are often caused by a lack of understanding of immigrant students' career preparation needs from various levels (university, faculty, department and even the immigrants themselves). Although an individual's coping attitudes and strategies made a big difference either negatively or positively, the data showed that some barriers were impossible to be overcome by individual endeavours alone. Supports, such as clear expectations from programs of studies in students' career development, were identified as crucial. Long-term and procedural assistance was another needy area. Career-oriented supervising, courses, teaching, and research were also identified as essential. Finally, moral support such as understanding, patience, encouragement, and recognition were also identified as very important.

It is worth addressing that some of the barriers identified by each individual participant were not necessarily affected by cultural and discipline backgrounds, and that different individual coping strategies lead to significantly different results. Although confronting similar obstacles, some participants did not view them as obstacles (instead considering them merely challenges or inspirations), while others regarded them as huge or unconquerable.

Some were able to break through major barriers and make significant progress by adopting a proactive and more aggressive approach. This phenomenon indicated that other factors, such as attitude, self-esteem, personal initiatives, motivation, resilience, personality, social and cultural capital, previous professional experience, and an effective support network, may play important roles in influencing students' success during intercultural career transitions and in turbulent environments.

INSIGHTS

Group insights were obtained from the responses to the IGSCC; the participants generally regarded it as a much needed form of support. Three major benefits were identified:

Clearer Goals and Enhanced Confidence

IGSCC, recognized by all the participants, led them to contemplate tough questions: why did they invest time and money to pursue a doctoral degree? What would be their desired learning outcomes? How should they manage time between their career preparation priorities and academic requirements? Who had real power and control over their success? Searching for answers helped them envision their career goals more clearly.

> My career objective gets specified. Know some career goal options for PhD students, Identified my needs for my career. Get serious about my career, have confidence in my future. (Anonymous)

> I know what I want to do in the next two years. I know what fields I won't enter. I can envision my career in the next five years. (Mohsen)

> This project helps me in considering my objective, and what I can do in order to obtain my objective. (Anonymous)

> ...it provides me with an excellent opportunity to think over what I have done and what I have to do in order to obtain my objective. Reflection is a process involving pains and that's why sometimes many people just don't want to reflect. Consider my own experience in Canada. For the first one and a half years, I kept myself in studying and isolated in a small group of Chinese students. It seemed that I lived in a very small world in Canada with a very narrow focus. I attended the workshop by Cathy in 2007 when I realized that I couldn't live and study in this isolated world, where I have been asked again and again about my goals and the tools that I could use to achieve the goals... Through the processes of reflection, I have identified my career objectives... (Yun)

Yun's deep reflection helped her realize the importance of setting her career goal. This kind of awareness can lead to a systematic career planning approach, which can help her make an informed choice in integrating career preparation into her programs of studies.

Enlightened and Empowered by Faculty and Peer Support

Faculty support is more important according to Cain (1999): "...the support staff, administrators, politicians and students, might help draw up the route for the trip, but it is the faculty members who drive the bus" (p. 47). Some participants had listened to three lectures from the university on language and culture, international education, and career preparation in academia. The exposure to career-related interactive lectures proved to be very helpful.

> I think Dr. X understands the situation that faces the immigrant students. I read the part of the thesis of his student afterwards. I find myself also thinking of the difficulties that the immigrants confront, but not in depth. What I am going to do is to face the problems both in my study and in the daily life directly and try to overcome them in a positive attitude. (Ju-an)

> Dr. B's mentioning of "popular culture" and her identification that what affects the communication is background knowledge, not "words," is very insightful. It allows me to see that our focus on improving language itself doesn't help much if we do not integrate authentic cultural learning and experiences. (C. Shi, Reflection, March 23, 2007)

In my case, a few professors provided crucial support. My supervisor offered me a teaching position even though she was aware of the forced resignation incident, and this gesture had healing and motivational effects. Another professor was an excellent listener. I could tell that not just his mind but his heart and soul were with me whenever I shared the struggles experienced by others and me. As a close friend, a female professor personalized the image of "professor" and made the abstract concept of "Canadian professor" accessible and understandable. The only professor of Chinese origin in the faculty became my role model. His perceptions and approaches in dealing with issues were culturally translated, which helped me solve problems in a strategic manner.

Peers also played an irreplaceable role. Having set clearer goals, the participants then aspired to know how to prepare for an academic career. Some responses clearly indicate that ideas, experiences, and implications drawn from peers were much needed for participants' preparation.

I got information from peer graduate students, other people's opinions and positions. (Anonymous)

I got to know some new people at the same professional development stage. (Anonymous)

... aware of the competitiveness to apply for academic job as most of the students who participated liked to stay in academia. (Anonymous)

Communications with other graduates in our department make me realize that I should prepare beforehand. (Anonymous)

It provides an opportunity to listen to opinions and experiences of other students, especially those from other countries and with similar objectives. I used to focus on academic study only. I never paid much attention to job search. By participating this club's activities, I've changed a lot. I become more active, more open-minded, and begin to like living in Canada ... I hope that the club will continue in the future at the University. Although [the career centre] is there for career development, our club, serving as an informal organization where we can communicate and share experiences and look for emotional support, is a supplement to [the centre]. (Yun)

The benefits gained from peers went beyond obtaining factual information. Knowing that one is at the same professional development stage as others brings acknowledgement, recognition, inclusion, and acceptance. Even though participants may not have been able to obtain a sense of belonging from the mainstream society, the companionship of people in a similar situation helped alleviate some of the most difficult aspects of reestablishing a career in a foreign country and made the process a less lonely journey.

Enhanced Motivation

Accompanied and empowered by other members, the participants felt much more motivated to achieve their career goals.

I was encouraged to build up more knowledge about my field. (Anonymous)

I began to pay attention to people's way of interacting. For now, I am trying to speak out in every student's meeting. (Anonymous)

International students have more challenges: language problems, final difficulties, over-qualification ... Next we need to fix the problems we have identified ... We should be goal-oriented, committed, confident, and consciously looking for opportunities. (Mohamed)

The positive feedback indicates that the inspiration drawn from the career club would assist the participants with their career preparation to a greater extent; all hoped that the club could continue its run. However, in order for activities like the career club to achieve great success, financial support from the university is probably necessary. The appropriate financial support would allow club members to have access to some charged services and to pay guest speakers. Furthermore, some participants suggested that membership not be limited to international and PhD students.

In brief, action-oriented research was embraced and evidenced by the participants' changed attitudes and behaviours.

WHAT WE WOULD DO DIFFERENTLY

With regard to methodology, the use of a survey questionnaire can be problematic. It can be a useful tool in generating significant themes, but the prescribed questions may unduly frame the thinking and the responses of the participants. Another problem is that the questionnaire form was completed away from the researcher, so the respondents did not have a chance to ask about anything that was unclear. In addition, the researcher had no control over how the questionnaire was answered: the respondent might have answered questions incompletely or missed certain questions altogether. Finally, the questionnaire's format made it difficult to examine complex issues and opinions, although open-ended questions and other means of data collection were used. Consequently, the depth of answers in Cycle Three was limited in general. A proposed response to the challenges inherent to the nature of a questionnaire would be to conduct the survey at a meeting, providing participants with sufficient time and facilitation. Furthermore, more open-ended questions can be added, and interviews can be used to complement questionnaire data.

The other area I would approach differently is the development of the career club activities that were planned but failed to be implemented in Cycle Three. The tension caused by my and the participants' conflicting needs showed the nature of action research—the action plan should be based on participants' emerging needs and should be planned together as a group.

From a theoretical perspective, I would adopt an integrated theoretical framework throughout the course of action research. Of the four theories (critical pedagogy, social constructivism, social ecological theory, and dialectical theory) used in the study, all have their own strengths and are evidenced to be particularly insightful in offering an understanding of barrier breaking experiences of immigrant doctoral students in their academic career preparation. However, none of the theories fit all needs if adopted in an isolated way. Leong (1995) noticed that limitation—lack of a theoretical framework. He suggested an interdisciplinary theoretical framework. Informed by Leong's thinking, I would integrate the four theories to form a procedural, integral, and holistic conceptual framework for similar research cases.

One major weakness of critical pedagogy is its division and separation from O*thers* without the diligent examination of one's own gaps, which could be a barrier in assisting immigrant students in creating and maintaining a healthy academic and professional environment and relationships. Take me for example. I once developed a blaming attitude which had blinded me to the fact that some difficulties were caused by personal and professional limitations rather than by social prejudices. Regarding an individual as a changing agent in socio-cultural contexts is where social constructivism comes into full play.

Social constructivism does not center on *why* but instead *how* people make meaning of their taught, experienced or given knowledge, and how they coconstruct their identities and realities out of uncertainty and ambiguity. This understanding of the importance of the coexploring and changing processes in a social context gives immigrant students a tool to work with. However, social constructivism denies objective knowledge since "there are many ways to structure the world, and there are many meanings or perspectives for any event or concept." Thus, "there is not a correct meaning that we are striving for" (Duffy & Jonassen, 1992). This rejection of absolutism characterizes constructivist approaches to learning. Mayer (2004) argues that constructivist learning may not be effective for all learners, suggesting that learners may become behaviourally active rather than "cognitively active." Mayer proposes "guided practice" (Mayer, 2004, p. 15). The "guided practice" and universal decontextualised knowledge can very much be needed by new immigrant doctoral students who do not have the adequate attitude, knowledge, and skills to explore, to evaluate, and to transform themselves in a complex and new environment. Therefore, the necessary awareness of the environment, a joint functioning with *Others* rather than a solo effort in creating or changing a social reality, is overlooked. Social ecological theory provides this multilayered and interactive perspective.

Bronfenbrenner's (1995) ecological theory is appropriate for describing the complex systems of an internationalized university campus and its relationship to the broader society. Ecological theory considers aspects of doctoral education and experience as in part reflecting immigrant students' past academic practices, traditions and conventions, complex webs of relationships between people and the strategies they use, the social groups with whom they interact, norms guiding social interaction, and the structure of culturally organized environments. A social ecological approach views individuals' activities as operations on the lowest level and the margin of an organizational micro system. This theory "builds on the ideas of Charles Darwin about nature, of Adam Smith about economic life and of Herbert Spencer about the evolution of human societies" (Glaser, 2006, p. 134).

A biological perspective in perceiving economic movement within human society leads to an assumption that humanity, like other forms of life, is invariably driven by competition which pushes into the background other potential system drivers such as cooperation, self-sacrifice, community-orientation or love (Hosang et al., 2005). It also neglects the human capacity for reflection and value change (Glaser, 2006).

This weakness of social ecological theory in viewing humanity as "being driven" rather than "driving" implies that competition will invariably prevail; as a result, only the strongest and the fittest dominant members will grasp and occupy the most and the best social wealth, resources, and opportunities. In contrast, the insignificant, weak, and marginalized immigrants will hardly survive the competition. This biological angle of evaluating humanity not only neglects and discourages a human's reflective and changing power, but also entices immigrants to merely accept their reality. To address this unjust issue, critical pedagogy is a more relevant approach. It educates and empowers immigrant PhD students to function as active agents in influencing their environment in order to create a reality of equality and fairness.

Dialectical theory, like ecological theory, views the reality of professional immigrants as living multilayered, unknown, unpredictable, and in tension. However, a dialectical approach goes beyond that. It can enable immigrant doctoral students to envision their marginalized social status from a macro and changing perspective which indicates that no barriers are permanent—that, instead, there is a possibility of changing their situations. A dialectical approach can inspire them to take initiatives and responsibilities for their own future. In other words, a dialectical approach not only shows possibilities and opportunities, but also provides the tool to make changes happen; change starts from inside, and outside support can only become effective through inside cooperation. Understanding and dealing with contradictions and transformations embedded in a dialectical approach are what vulnerable groups need most.

Dialectical theory also has its limitations. It has been criticised by some philosophers such as Karl Popper (1992) for its willingness "to put up with contradictions" and encourage and justify irrationalism. My argument is that many vulnerable new professional immigrants may not have the strength not to "put up" with social control. They can be victimized and traumatized without even being noticed by others and even without themselves understanding what has happened. What they need initially is not to fight for what is "just"; instead, they need to survive by understanding that there is no final reality but a dynamic and changing reality based on subjective assumptions. A dialectical perspective encourages the development of a person's agency, motivation, and resilience in dealing with some of the oppositions present in their professional career establishment.

Despite the limitations of each theory, a combination of their strengths may produce a holistic framework for researchers to interpret immigrant students' barrier breaking experiences and a set of useful tools for the students in their career preparation.

CONCLUSION

Action research, especially emancipatory action research, acknowledges the need for a long-term exploration of issues. In this study I was able to proceed through three cycles of an action research over a four year period. That work was based on my own experiences as well as the experiences of several immigrant PhD students. Together we used action research methodologies as a tool to identify, explore and better understand gaps and barriers in our academic career preparation in a Canadian university. Huge amounts of data were produced and various external, internal and interaction barriers were identified. Over the three cycles or phases of the AR, critical pedagogy, social constructivism, social ecological theory, and dialectical philosophy became the lenses through which I interpreted the data. In addition, an understanding of these theories helped the group to break down some major barriers encountered while integrating into Canadian academia.

In terms of advice for researchers I note that while data from the survey I conducted was helpful, it is not a data collection method that should stand alone when topics like this one are the focus of research. Interviews, group work, reflection, and autoethnographic processes all contributed to a deeper and more meaningful understanding of both the problem and potential solutions. A second suggestion relates to the use of theory. While I used different theoretical frameworks at different points in the AR process, there may be merit in using one holistic and integrated theoretical framework for data interpretation and barrier breaking. Finally, it is important to be aware that immigrant doctoral students will be expected to behave differently in different environments, and the reinforcements which individuals, and groups, receive for a particular action may be quite different in different contexts.

The dissertation itself (Shi, 2011) provides a more detailed synthesis of the findings but those summarized in this chapter should be useful to both other researchers and to practitioners who provide services to graduate students or design and deliver graduate programs. It seems fairly clear that North American graduate programs do not yet pay enough attention to preparing students for their careers and that the situation is particularly serious when it comes to immigrant doctoral students who hope to join the academic community of the host country. When I reflect on the personal benefits I gained from this action research dissertation, I can say that it transformed me to such an extent that I felt like the phoenix rising from the pyre, so to speak, although upon graduation I was still a sessional instructor—which is on the edge of integration into Canadian academia.

REFERENCES

Basran, G., & Zong, L. (1998). Devaluation of foreign credentials as perceived by visible minority professional immigrants. *Canadian Ethnic Studies, 30*(3), 6–23.

Bilash, O., & Shi, W. (2007). *Leveling the playing field: Providing an infrastructure to help immigrant graduate students compete for academic opportunities.* Paper presented at The Society for Teaching and Learning in Higher Education (STLHE) Conference, Edmonton, AB.

Blustein, D. L. (1997). A context-rich perspective of career exploration across the life roles. *Career Development Quarterly, 45*, 260–274.

Boyer, E. L. (1997). *Scholarship reconsidered: Priorities of the professoriate.* Princeton, NJ: Carnegie Foundation for the Advancement of Teaching.

Bronfenbrenner, U. (1995). Developmental ecology through space and time: A future perspective. In P. Moen & G. H. Elder (Eds.), *Examining lives in context: Perspectives on the ecology of human development* (pp. 619–647). Washington, DC: American Psychological Association.

Cain, M. (1999). The community college in the twenty-first century: A systems approach. New York: University Press of America.

Carr, W., & Kemmis, S. (1983). *Becoming critical: Knowing through action research.* Geelong, Victoria: Deakin Press.

Carr, W., & Kemmis, S. (1986). *Becoming critical: Education, knowledge and action research.* London: Falmer Press.

Charmaz, K., & Mitchell, R. (1997). The myth of silent authorship: Self, substance, and style in ethnographic writing. In R. Hertz (Ed.), *Reflexivity and voice* (pp. 193–215). London: Sage.

Duffy, T. M., & Jonassen, D. H. (1992). Constructivism: New implications for instructional technology. In T. M. Duffy & D. H. Jonassen (Eds.), *Constructivism and the technology of instruction: A conversation* (pp. 1–16). Hillsdale, NJ: Lawrence Erlbaum.

Freire, P. (1970). *Pedagogy of the oppressed.* New York: Continuum.

Glaser, M. (2006). The social dimension in ecosystem management: Strengths and weaknesses of human-nature mind maps. *Human Ecology Review, 13*(2), 122–142.

Golde, C. M., & Dore, T. (2001). *At cross purposes: What the experiences of today's doctoral students reveal about doctoral education.* Philadelphia: Pew Charitable Trusts.

Gowricharn, R. (2001). Introduction: Ethic minorities and elite formation. *Journal of International Migration and Integration, 2*, 155–167.

Graduate student survey, Academic year 2003–2004, of University of Colorado-Boulder. Retrieved November, 1, 2006, from http://www.colorado.edu/pba/surveys/grad/03/questionnaire.pdf

Grindstaff, C. F. (1986). *A socio-demographic profile of immigrant woman in Canada, 1981, by age at immigration, for women age 30–44.* London, ON: University of Western Ontario Press.

Guba, E., & Lincoln, Y. S. (1981). *Effective evaluation.* San Francisco, CA: Jossey Bass.

Henry, F., Tator, C., Mattis, W., & Rees, T. (2000). *The colour of democracy.* Toronto: Harcourt Brace & Company.

Hosang, M., Fraenzle, S., & Markert, B. (2005). Die emotionale Matrix. Grundlagen für gesellschaftlichen Wandel und nachhaltige Innovation.

Jordan, J. P. (1963). Exploratory behavior: The formation of self and occupational concepts. In D. E. Super (Ed.), *Career development: Self-concept theory, College entrance examination* (pp. 42–78). New York, NY.

Kanfer, R., Wanberg, C. R., & Kantrowitz, T. M. (2001). Job search and employment: Personality-motivational analysis and meta-analytic review. *Journal of Applied Psychology, 86*(5), 837–855.

Kennedy, T., & Snicer, T. J. (2006). *The CaPS employment survey of University of Alberta graduates of 2000.* Retrieved September 10, 2007, from http://www.ualberta.ca/CAPS/

Krahn, H., Derwing, T., Mulder, M., & Wilkinson, L. (2000). Educated and under-employed: Refugee integration into the Canadian labour market. *Journal of International Migration and Integration, 1*(1), 59–84.

Krippendorff, K. (1980). *Content analysis: An introduction to its methodology.* London: Sage.

Leong, F. T. L., & Serafica, F. C. (1995). Career development of Asian Americans: A research area in need of a good theory. In F. T. L. Leong (Ed.), *Career development and vocational behavior of racial and ethnic minorities* (pp. 67–102). Mahwah, NJ: Lawrence Erlbaum.

Li, P. S. (2001). The market worth of immigrants' educational credentials. *Canadian Public Policy, 27*(1), 23–38.

Mayer, R. (2004). Should there be a three-strikes rule against pure discovery learning? The case for guided methods of instruction. *American Psychologist, 59*(1), 14–19.

Nagle, R. J., Suldo, S. M., Christenson, S. L., & Hansen, A. L. (2004). Graduates perceptions of academic positions in school psychology. *School Psychology Quarterly, 19*(4), 311–326.

Popper, K. (1992). What is Dialectic? In K. Popper. *Conjectures and refutations: The growth of scientific knowledge,* (pp. 312–35). New York: Routledge.

Reitz, J. G. (2001). Immigrant skill utilization in the Canadian labour market: Implications of human capital research. *Journal of International Migration and Integration, 2*(3), 347–78.

Schein, E. H. (1978). *Career dynamics: Matching individual and organizational needs.* Reading, MA: Addison-Wesley.

Shi, W. (2011). A journey towards professional integration—Experiences of immigrant PhD students in breaking down barriers to entering Canadian academia. Unpublished doctoral dissertation, University of Alberta.

Stumpf, S. A., Colarelli, S. M., & Hartman, K. (1983). Development of the career exploration survey. (CES). *Journal of Vocational Behaviour, 22,* 191–226.

Trovato, F., & Grindstaff, C. F. (1986). Economic status: A census analysis of immigrant women at age thirty in Canada. *Review of Sociology and Anthropology, 23*(4), 569–687.

Vygotsky, L. S. (1978). *Mind in society: Development of higher psychological processes.* In M. Cole, V. John-Steiner, S. Scribner, & E. Souberman (Eds.). Cambridge, MA: Harvard University.

Zong, L. (2004). International transference of human capital and occupational attainment of recent Chinese professional immigrants in Canada. *American Review of China Studies, 5*(1&2), 81–89.

CHAPTER 8

PRAGMATIC INTERPRETIVE ACTION RESEARCH

Addressing a Problem: Situated Literacies in the Homes and Communities of Three Children

Maria Casamassa
Teachers College

ABSTRACT

When the home and community literacies of students are not seen as resources in the school setting, children may experience difficulties in the classroom. The rejection of students' out of school literacies makes it difficult for children to acquire school literacies as they struggle to become literacy learners in the classroom. The purpose of this action research study was to (a) document the home and community literacies of three children; and (b) collaborate with teachers to explore ways of linking home and community literacies with school literacy practices. This study was grounded in a theoretical framework that conceptualized literacies as socially situated and culturally constructed. The research methodology was a version of participatory action research.

Action Research, pages 179–194
Copyright © 2014 by Information Age Publishing
All rights of reproduction in any form reserved.

Participatory action research focuses on "the construction of local knowl-edge and theory with a particular group of research participants" (Genat, 2009, p. 102). My action research project stemmed from questions about the out-of-school literacy practices of children. One of the goals was to examine the situated literacies of the children revealing how they used those literacies to interpret and understand their world. More specifically, the study exempli-fies interpretive action research in which the participants became research-ers, constructing knowledge and understanding about an issue in their own lives. All of the participants were also coresearchers as we sought to learn more about their interpretation of literacy practices (Genat, 2009).

ONTOLOGY AND EPISTEMOLOGY

As a postpositivist, my ontological stance is that there are multiple construct-ed realities and that reality is an interactive process between an individual, other individuals, and the environment. My ontological stance led to an epistemological belief that positioned the participants as knowers. Accord-ing to Denzin and Lincoln (1998), ontology and epistemology determine the method of inquiry, because how researchers ask and answer questions has its foundation in their conception of reality and the relationship be-tween knowledge and the knowledge seeker. Consequently, the approach of this study was to represent the experiences of the students as accurately as possible, and through that representation tell a collaborative story of three children's literacy practices in the home and community. The story was a shared construction incorporating the voices of the students, their guardians, and their teachers. I conceptualized my study as interpretive ac-tion research because I was involved in the process of "systemic, intentional inquiry" (p. 23) about an issue that emerged out of my own personal and professional experiences with children who struggled in the school setting (Cochran-Smith & Lytle, 1993). This issue was reiterated and discussed by some of my colleagues as we identified questions about children who were competent in their home and community literacies but were experiencing difficulty in acquiring school literacies. The idea of teachers reflecting on their practice is not a novel idea because as early as the beginning of the twentieth century Dewey "emphasized the importance of teachers' reflect-ing on their practices and integrating their observations into their emerg-ing theories of teaching and learning" (Cochran-Smith & Lytle, 1993, p. 9).

Goswami and Stillman (1987) characterized teacher research as a process of inquiry and reflection that leads to action. My own research questions echoed this process as I learned about the home and community literacies of children and then collaborated with teachers as we reflected on what these literacies meant to the children and how we could make room for these literacies in our classrooms. One of the goals of the research was to create change in the class-rooms through the study of home and community literacies.

Today many educators and researchers (Cochran-Smith & Lytle, 1993; Morrell, 2004) advocate for research that is written from the perspectives of teachers. Morrell (2004) acknowledged teacher research but went further and encouraged educators to "become critical researchers who engage in collaborative inquiry with students intended to challenge practices, discourses, and texts for the purpose of literacy learning and self- and social transformation' (p. 150). In my own research I emphasized this idea of a shared construction as I learned alongside the children in order to alter, and not just add to, what we know about home and community literacies. In this research I worked with all the participants to create a community of inquiry in which "teachers and others conjoin their efforts to construct knowledge" (Cochran-Smith & Lytle, 1993, p. 273).

SITUATED LITERACIES

Literacy has been defined as the ability to read and write, which is related to societal and school concepts that emphasize print literacy practices (Gee, 1996). Within the context of schooling, literacy has been conceived "as a 'set' of skills divorced from use" (Nespor, 1991, p. 177). When the definition of literacy is narrowed to only include print practices and when it is seen to be independent of context, the interests, intentions, and background knowledge of the learner is rarely taken into account. The way a society defines literacy has implications for all those who live in that society but especially for those who do not adhere to the narrow definition imposed by dominant institutions, such as schools (Gee, 1996).

When the home and community literacies of children are not seen as resources in schools, children may experience difficulties in the classroom. The rejection of students' out-of-school literacies makes it difficult for some children to acquire school literacies as they struggle to become literacy learners in the classroom. As educators and researchers we need to incorporate the literacy experiences that students bring to classrooms from the home and community settings. Research that extends beyond the classroom door, involves parents, and necessitates understandings of the lived experiences of students and their families has the potential to lead to the creation of spaces in which teachers can learn about their students, challenge their own assumptions, and ultimately construct learning experiences that reflect and build upon the literacy resources of students (Compton-Lilly, 2003). My research was designed to discover the literacies that children used in their homes by partnering with children and their parents and also connecting with their teachers to see how we could make room for those literacies in school.

DESCRIPTION OF THE RESEARCH

The methodological decisions involved consideration of ontological and epistemological principles regarding the nature of literacies. Since I view literacies as socially and culturally constructed, I used an interpretive action research approach to understand the situated nature of the home and community literacies. The goal of an interpretive approach is to understand the situated meanings of an experience from the perspective of those who are living it (Erickson, 1986). An interpretive approach to inquiry highlighted the research questions of this study and the conceptual framework because I believe children's literacies are historically, socially, and culturally situated (Graue & Walsh, 1998). Interpretive research "involves being unusually thorough and reflective in noticing and describing everyday events in the field setting, and in attempting to identify the significance of actions in the events from the various points of view of the actors themselves" (Erickson, 1986, p. 121).

Overview of the Study

In order to implement this interpretative approach, the study explored the home and community literacy practices of three children. It provided an in-depth description of an educational phenomenon within a specific context using an interpretive framework. Observations, interviews, study groups and artifacts were used to collect data. Research took place in natural settings and focused on process in an attempt to obtain a holistic picture of the phenomenon being studied. The case studies were framed in interpretive action research as I collaborated with the classroom teachers of the children to reflect on the children's home and community literacies and act to make room for these literacies in the school setting.

The focus of the study was on three children who were identified by their teachers as struggling in school literacy. The home and community settings of these students were examined in order to address the following questions:

1. What are some of the home and community literacy practices of the student?
2. How are the students positioned within these practices?
3. How can a staff developer/researcher collaborate with teachers to explore ways of linking home and community literacies with school literacy practices?
4. How do teachers use the resources of home and community literacies to build success in school literacy?

In order to document the literacies of the children as well as address the research questions, I observed them in their homes and also participated in study groups with the teachers. I presented the data using both narrative vignettes and discourse analysis (Gee, 1999). The vignettes provide a global understanding of the interrelationships of the literacies, funds of knowledge, and discourses in each family. Presenting the data as a narrative allowed the voices of the participants to be heard and situated the children's literacies in the stories that occurred in their homes. Figure 8.1 summarizes the phases of data collection and briefly describes the focus and tools used in the study.

Participants

When I led this research the selected school had four first grade classrooms and four second-grade classrooms. Of the eight teachers, I selected two first grade teachers and one second-grade teacher to participate in the study. Criteria for teacher selection included the following: willingness to

Phase and Time Period	Focus	Tools
Phase 1 October	Gaining entry and developing rapport; becoming familiar with the settings and the participants; documenting the literacy events and literacy practices in the homes and community settings	Initial interview with guardians Participant observation Fieldnotes Artifacts
Phase 2 November December	Documenting literacy events and literacy practices in the homes and community settings; meaning of the literacy events and literacy practices from the perspective of the children and their guardians	Participant observation Fieldnotes Artifacts
Phase 3 January February March April May	Documenting literacy events and literacy practices in the home and community settings; meaning of the literacy events and literacy practices from the perspectives of the children, their guardians and their teachers; collaborating with teachers to explore ways of linking home and community literacies to school literacy practices	Participant observation Fieldnotes Artifacts Audiotapes Informal interviews with the children Informal interviews with the guardians Study groups with the teachers

Figure 8.1   Phases of data collection.

participate in the after school study groups, openness to inquiry and learning, willingness to differentiate instruction, and commitment to learning more about children's literacies by initiating conversation in a collaborative setting with colleagues.

The criteria for selection of the children participants were (a) the guardians and the child agreed to the child's participation in the study, and (b) the child was identified as a struggling reader and writer. The children had been identified as struggling readers and writers on the basis of assessments, which include the Observation Survey (Clay, 2002) and literacy benchmarks developed by the school district in which the study took place.

Of the three children selected, two (Jaclyn and Lucas) were brother and sister. The Estrada family lived in a suburban area that is primarily residential with one and two story homes. It is here that seven-year old Jaclyn and six-year old Lucas lived with an older brother, Roberto and their parents, Rosa and Alex. Rosa, Alex, and Roberto were born in Mexico and both Jaclyn and Lucas were born in the United States.

In this predominantly middle-class, White suburban neighborhood the differences in the race, class and language of the family were apparent. The fact they rented a small apartment and the entire family slept in one bedroom was evidence of this class difference. Although Alex, Lucas and Jaclyn's father, ran his own landscaping business, the price of living in a middle-class neighborhood was high, leaving no money for anything beyond the basic needs such as food and housing. Race was also a significant social marker and their status as members of a migrant Mexican family positioned Jaclyn and Lucas as different in the school setting. In their neighborhood, Mexican migrant families experienced racial tensions and prejudice from White community members that affected their participation in the community. Linguistically, the bilingualism of the family was another marker that separated them from the mainstream community. For Jaclyn and Lucas, their language placed them in English as a Second Language (ESL) classes in school. It is significant to note the class, race, and linguistic differences when discussing the literacies and funds of knowledge in the setting where Jaclyn and Lucas lived.

The third child in this study was Tara, a six-year old female who lived with her family in a two-story home in a suburban, middle class neighborhood. Tara lived in this house with her mother, Debbie, her father, Frank, an older brother, Eric, and a baby sister, Grace. All of the Moore family members were born in the United States. The picture of Tara's home depicted a family that had many financial resources. In contrast to Jaclyn and Lucas' one bedroom home, each member of Tara's family had their own bedroom. Tara's playroom was filled with toys, games and dolls. It is important to note this family's middle-class socioeconomic status when discussing Tara's literacies and the family's funds of knowledge.

Data Collection

The first step in the data collection process was an interview with the guardians of each of the children in order to gather information about the children's activities and plan the observation sessions. Observations then took place in the home settings of the students three days a month for eight months. The purpose of the observations was to obtain holistic descriptions of the events and activities of the students, thereby providing a picture of what was occurring in the home and community settings.

Participant Observation

As a participant observer, I generated data from the perspective of the individuals being studied. In the homes I was able to watch "what people do, listen to what people say, and interact with participants" (LeCompte & Preissle, 1993, p. 196). Because I believe there are multiple realities I wanted to bring forth the participants' definitions of reality and determine what literacy meant to them within the context of their homes. My emphasis was on capturing the perspective of the participants as I observed literacy events in their homes.

As I entered the homes of the children I participated in events that uncovered the literacies of the students. On one of my first visits to the Estrada home, Jaclyn shared her Doodle Bear and the story she had constructed about the bear's life. She told me that she was able to write on the bear and that Doodle bear glowed in the dark. In this event Jaclyn's practice was connected to writing and speaking, however, the addition of her bear added a dimension that was not seen in the two-dimensional pencil and paper literacy activities that dominate the school context. During another visit to the Estrada home, Lucas introduced me to video games. Lucas was hooking up a video game to the television and he taught me about this practice. He was learning how to play the games as well as how to set up the games, which was a complex process that involved many skills. Tara shared her artistic talents during many of my visits to the Moore home. She participated in scrapbooking and while I was in her home Tara shared the intricacies of this practice. These literacies encapsulate the idea of children as multimodal meaning makers as they engaged both nonprint and print texts in their practices. In accessing these literacy practices, the children's meaning and knowledge was built through modalities that included images, texts, symbols and sounds, as well as words (Vasquez, 2003). Tara's mother articulated in one of our conversations that Tara has always been involved in art activities, "It's what she grew up knowing." As educators we should be aware of what our students "grow up knowing" and invite them to bring those "knowings" into their classrooms.

As we learn more about the lived experiences of our students it helps us understand how they make sense of the texts in their homes and how they make sense of the texts they encounter in the school setting. The conversations with the parents and children helped to situate the literacies within the funds of knowledge in each of the households. Observations in the homes provided opportunities for the participants to work as coresearchers in constructing the children's literacies.

Interviews

Interviewing provides access to the context of people's beliefs and actions and thereby provided a way for me to understand the meaning of the actions I observed in the homes. A basic assumption in the type of interviewing research I conducted is that the meaning people make of their experiences affects the way they carry out the experience (Seidman, 1998). The observations provided access to the literacies of the students and the interviews allowed me to put the literacies in context and provided an understanding of their actions. The interviews presented opportunities for the participants to embed the literacies of the children within the funds of knowledge in each household.

In one of the interviews with Rosa she spoke about her heritage, which was an important aspect of the Estrada household. Rosa was proud of her Mexican heritage and her desire was that her children "know it and the school understand it." In her wisdom she knew that it was important for her children to embrace their heritage and yet she realized their Mexican background might not be recognized in the school environment. Rosa was attempting to preserve her own culture while learning to navigate the culture of the country in which her family lived.

The interviews with Debbie helped me to understand Tara's out-of-school literacies and her struggles to be successful in school literacy. In one of my conversations with Debbie she said that Tara's "biggest interest is anything artistic." However she also articulated her concerns about Tara's guided reading level and her desire for Tara to "move to level E." As educators and parents we need to uncover children's home literacies and make room for them in the school setting so that students can be competent knowers in both environments.

The interviews were embedded in the participatory framework of the research because they were based on "an assumption fundamental to qualitative research: the participant's perspective on the phenomenon of interest should unfold as the participant views it, not as the researcher views it"

(Marshall & Rossman, 1999, p. 108). In this study the interviews provided another way to coconstruct the findings with the participants.

The Study Groups

A key component of this study was the participation of the children's teachers in a collaborative group. I met with the teachers in their school using a study group format, which provided the forum for discussing the home and community literacies of the children and talking about how to make room for these literacies in the classroom. One of the goals of this research was to create change through the study of home and community literacies, and this forum was influential in helping to achieve that objective by providing opportunities for the teachers to engage in a process of inquiry and reflection leading to action.

As a researcher, I shared the data from the homes and took field notes during the study groups. I introduced the teachers to outside readings that engaged "us with the broader group of people who were involved in similar work" (Brown et al., 1998, p. 121). As we engaged in inquiry, the teachers were informants and experts on what was happening in the classrooms. They brought artifacts from the classrooms (i.e., portfolios of the children's work), and these documents as well as the data I collected facilitated our discussions about the children and their literacies.

Together we worked as coresearchers as we explored ways to make room for the children's home and community literacies in the classroom. The intent of these groups was to engage in inquiry, which was not about a new method or set of instructional practices but involved a shift in viewing curriculum, students, learning, and teaching (Short & Burke, 1996). It was not about a deficit view that saw educators as needing to make changes because something was wrong with their teaching, but instead the emphasis was on inquiry that examines and transforms beliefs and actions that "fundamentally questions how schooling is done" (Short & Burke, 1996, p. 103).

The Children's Literacies

I entered the research with a concept of literacies as being "many, not singular" and as "socially created constitutive elements of larger human practices—discourses—that humans construct around their myriad purposes and values" (Lankshear & Knobel, 1997, p. 96). In this study literacies encompassed "cultural and material practices shaped by histories, localities, and the persons within them that give form and meaning to children's lives" (Hicks, 2002, p. 16). As I began my observations in the homes using this framework I realized that this view of literacies was complex and defied the making of any simplistic generalization about the out-of-school literacies of the children (Haneda, 2006). The collection and analysis of the data was as complex and diverse as the lives of the children. My goal was to understand the meaning that the students, their guardians, and teachers made of the children's literacy practices and the conversations with the participants provided opportunities to coconstruct the stories of their literacies. The literacies in the homes of the children included dramatic play, storytelling, art, music, gaming, reading and writing, and homework. In the sections below, the literacies of the children are situated within their family's funds of knowledge and embedded in particular discourses as they communicated and made sense of their worlds by interpreting and producing texts.

Participating in the Literacies of Play

In the literacies of play the children communicated and made meaning as they appropriated symbol systems from the funds of knowledge in their homes. As Jaclyn, Tara and Lucas participated in various activities during play, they were able to engage in diverse literacies, becoming creative and competent users of text. Oral and written language was evident in dramatic play events as the children took hold of specific material and symbolic resources. The children were grounding their literacies in their everyday lived experiences as they used their cultural and material practices to communicate and give meaning to their lives (Hicks, 2002).

Engaging in the Literacies of Storytelling

As the children engaged in the literacies of storytelling, they were using specific symbol systems (oral language, movement) to create complex cultural texts that were part of their lived experiences. Storytelling in the homes of Jaclyn, Lucas and Tara provided opportunities for the children to create and interpret texts using multiple sign systems that included oral and written language, images and movement. Their stories were not evaluated or measured against a standard and they freely chose what stories to tell and what sign systems to use in telling the story. They positioned themselves as competent storytellers who were able to use their literacies as resources to produce texts. As Jaclyn, Lucas and Tara shared their stories using both print and nonprint texts they were making their literacies visible (Bomer & Lamon, 2004).

Enacting the Literacies of Art

Art was another practice that Tara, Jaclyn and Lucas used to communicate meaning and shape their thoughts. As they participated in art activities, each used multiple sign systems to communicate and share meaning. They were making choices and decisions about how to interpret and produce texts as they learned the skills and knowledge associated with the particular literacies and the positions available within those practices (Bomer & Laman, 2004). Lucas, Tara and Jaclyn were doing this within a discourse that was not constantly evaluating them but was positioning them as knowledgeable (Dyson, 2003).

Literacies Mediated by Media and Popular Culture Texts

Many of the literacies that were enacted in Tara, Jaclyn, and Lucas' homes were embedded in activities introduced by media and popular culture texts. Television, music and gaming were an integral part of both households, and part of the cultural and material practices in the everyday lived experiences of the children. As Jaclyn, Tara, and Lucas interpreted media and popular culture texts, their meaning and knowledge was communicated by words as well as images and symbols. Lucas, Jaclyn and Tara "thrived as literate beings" (Vasquez, 2003, p. 125) in the world of media and popular culture texts. Although there was an "evaluative" aspect to learning the literate practice it was a learning that involved multiple opportunities to practice and improve. The literate learning was not dictated by a specific time frame developed by "others" but was customized by the children as they participated in the literacy practice (Vasquez, 2003). As they participated in these activities the children were able to engage in multiple ways of knowing using their literacies as meaning making and communicative tools (Dyson, 1999; Moje, 2000; Hicks, 2002). The children created and interpreted texts combining multiple symbol systems with their cultural and material resources (Dimitriadis, 2001; Hicks, 2002).

Literacies Embedded in Homework Practices

In their homes Lucas, Jaclyn, and Tara were also involved in homework practices. Dyson (1999) talks about the unofficial spaces represented by the discourses outside of school and the official spaces represented by the academic discourses of school. As the children participated in homework practices it was as if the official spaces of school overwhelmed the unofficial spaces outside of school. Rosa, Debbie and I became the "teachers" in the home as we enacted the literacies associated with the discourse of school. The words and phrases we used spoke to a discourse that valued looking, listening and remembering as a way of knowing. The decision about what was important was made for the children (you need to learn this). The way you displayed your work was significant... neatness counted. It was important to be sitting in a certain way while you did your homework. Finally, you were evaluated each time you did your homework and if you did it well you were positioned as smart. Oral and written language were privileged in this practice; images, artifacts, movement and other symbols the children used to communicate through art, media, and gaming were not present during homework time.

Although they did use oral and written language when communicating through art, music, gaming and other literacy practices they had more agency and control in those literate spaces in their homes. During homework practices, Tara, Jaclyn and Lucas were told what to learn, how to learn it and how to position their bodies while involved in the discourse of homework. The concept of multiple literacies was disrupted as literacy was defined as being able to read, write and speak to answer the comprehension questions, spell the words correctly, and solve the math problems.

Study Groups With the Teachers

Documenting the lived experiences of Jaclyn, Tara, and Lucas revealed the complexity of their lives and their literacies. During the study groups I shared my observations from the homes and the teachers discussed what was happening in the school setting so that we could explore ways of linking home literacies with school literacy practices. The experience was new for all of us and so we began our first meeting by reading and discussing a relevant article to help us develop a frame of reference. However despite this framework that focused on an expanded definition of literacy, which included both nonprint and print texts, it was difficult for us to "escape" the discourse of school.

The teachers and I discussed the children's literacies in the home and school settings and as we did, it became evident that school literacy was a dominant part of our lives as educators. In the study group, discussions focused on issues that included tests, spelling, vocabulary, comprehension, math, reading and writing workshop. The discussion of reading focused on "levels" and "benchmarks" that determined the path that children should take to achieve success in school literacy (Dyson, 2003). The teachers and I spoke about weekly spelling tests and comprehension that was "good." Then there was discussion about the importance of the ESL teachers "doing guided reading" with Jaclyn and Lucas. Writing was discussed and we spoke about spacing and grammar. It is not that these things are unimportant, but it seems as if they took on more importance than some of the literacies the children brought to the school setting.

However, as the teachers and I began to look at some of the transcripts from my observations in the homes, different pictures of Jaclyn, Lucas, and Tara emerged. In this setting the children were positioned as competent knowers as they participated in play, art, storytelling, and media practices. The use of multiple sign systems that included the use of language as well as images, sound, and movement to communicate and make meaning was evident in the home setting.

The teachers and I began to consciously position ourselves in a framework that looked at Jaclyn, Tara, and Lucas as being literate in the practices that were documented in their homes. In addition, the teachers began to recognize their resources in the school setting as they looked for the enactment of their literacies in the classroom. Ms. S spoke about Jaclyn's "amazing" oral vocabulary. She also recognized Jaclyn's position in a discourse of social activism as she discussed how Jaclyn commented that Martin Luther King Jr. "fought so that everyone could be treated equal and be treated fairly. It doesn't matter our skin color." Ms. S commented, "It was just amazing."

Ms. L spoke about Lucas' ability to speak two languages and that Lucas "could have success if given the opportunity." She was advocating for Lucas and concerned that "these kids are not being set up for success in school." Ms. L went on to discuss how children who are learning English are "just thrown under the rug, everything is blamed on them." Her questions and comments spoke to my constant wondering about why schools are always trying to make children struggle to "fit the system" instead of making the system "fit" their literacies.

The more we analyzed the transcripts from the children's homes the more we saw the children as being competent in literacies that were not enacted in the school setting. Ms. T spoke about Tara and the "scrapbooking and everything she does at home and how she's very creative and stuff like that, that really helped me to see her strengths." The teachers realized how we can narrow the definition of literacy and that even when we tried to work within a framework that reconceptualizes literacy we still needed to be aware of our focus on definitions that privilege reading and writing. Ms. L commented that we did focus on reading and writing in many of our conversations but we were growing in our awareness that "literacy is learning how to communicate." This newfound awareness was helping all of us to see the everyday lived experiences of Jaclyn, Tara and Lucas as ways they communicated and made sense of their world by producing and interpreting multiple texts. It was through this collaborative action research that we began to realize how literacies outside of the classroom impact a student's learning.

GROUP AND PERSONAL INSIGHTS

This research points to the significance of developing an awareness of our students' home and community literacy practices and their use of multiple sign systems. As the teachers and I looked at the children's literacies we realized the importance of developing relationships with the children and their families in order to learn about their literacies and to gain insights into how classroom instruction might be modified to include those literacies in the school setting (Gallego & Hollingsworth, 2000). The home visits pointed to the significance of knowing students and their funds of knowledge so that classrooms can become part of a social network that encompasses multiple bodies of knowledge (Gonzalez, Moll, & Amanti, 2005). Learning about the home and community literacies of Jaclyn, Tara, and Lucas, and working with parents and teachers to help the children negotiate the complex landscape of school is an important step in the process of linking home literacies and school literacy practices. As educators we can build upon students' complex out-of-school literacies, such as gaming, scrapbooking, basketball and art, and make authentic and powerful connections to classroom curriculum (Morrell, 2004).

Expanding our definition of literacy practices in the school setting to include both nonprint and print texts would position more children as competent knowers within school discourses. As educators, recognizing the social practices that children employ to communicate and make sense of their world "can establish the common ground necessary to help children differentiate and gain control over a wealth of symbolic tools and communicative practices" (Dyson, 2003, p. 107). Although we live in a time of mandated curriculums it is important to recognize the resources that children bring from home and make space for them in classrooms. Instead of children sitting in classrooms where their "literacies are threatened, rather than valued and expanded" teachers can "interrupt this process by embracing a sociocultural pedagogy that values all children's literacies" (Owocki & Goodman, 2002, p. 25).

CONCLUDING THOUGHTS

My initial interviews with parents were guided by earlier work in the area of literacies and funds of knowledge; therefore, in these interviews I used many questions that had been posed by researchers in similar work. However, it might have been more helpful to conduct observations in the home first and then speak to parents so that my initial questions would emerge from the observations.

Since children's literacy practices are complex the teachers and I struggled as we attempted to define and document their literacies. I did not want to narrow the observations to a list of what I observed in the homes and essentialize the complexity of their literacies. The idea of connecting their literacies and their funds of knowledge did help us as we discussed literacies within the context of their cultural and material practices. The process of documenting the literacies might have been strengthened if the teachers had spent time in the children's homes and I had spent time in their classrooms.

Another challenge was the conception of literacies as extending beyond reading and writing. The five months I spent with the teachers was not enough time to learn about the multiple literacies of the children and make room for those literacies in the classroom setting. What did happen was that the teachers and I used the data to recognize the literacies of the children and that awareness was the beginning of change as the teachers saw the children as competent knowers in those practices.

Our journey was both challenging and rewarding. It led us to question the "methods" we were using to teach literacy and to question our definition of literacy. There are still tensions as we work within an educational system that adheres to a narrow definition of literacy. However, hope endures as I continue to have professional conversations with other educators and parents and together we work to change our worlds to conceptualize a definition of literacies that includes practices such as storytelling, art, music, gaming, scrapbooking as well as reading and writing.

REFERENCES

Bomer, R., & Laman, T. (2004). Positioning in a primary writing workshop: Joint action in the discursive production of writing subjects. *Research in the Teaching of English, 38*(4), 420–466.

Brown, L., DeNino, E., Larson, K., McKenzie, M., Meyer, R., Ridder, K., & Zetterman, K., (1998). *Composing a teacher study group; Learning about inquiry in primary classrooms.* Mahwah, NJ: Lawrence Erlbaum Associates.

Clay, M. (2002). *An observation survey of early literacy achievement.* Portsmouth, NH: Heinemann.

Compton-Lilly, C. (2003). *Reading families: The literate lives of urban children.* New York: Teachers College Press.

Cochran-Smith, M., & Lytle, S. L. (1993). *Inside/outside: Teaching research and knowledge.* New York: Teachers College Press.

Denzin, N. K., & Lincoln, Y. S. (Ed.), (1998). *The landscape of qualitative research: Theories and issues.* Thousand Oaks, CA: Sage.

Dimitriadis, G. (2001). *Performing identity/performing culture: Hip hop as text, pedagogy, and lived practice.* New York: Peter Lang.

Dyson, A. H. (1993). *Social worlds of children learning to write in an urban primary school.* New York: Teachers College Press.

Dyson, A. H. (1999). Coach Bombay's students learn to write: Children's appropriation of media material for school literacy. *Research in the Teaching of English, 3*, 367–401.

Dyson, A. H. (2003). *The brothers and sisters learn to write: Popular literacies in childhood and school cultures.* New York: Teachers College Press.

Erickson, F. (1986). Qualitative methods in research on teaching. In M.Wittrock (Ed.), *Handbook of qualitative research on teaching* (pp. 119–161). Chicago, IL: MacMillan.

Gallego, M. A., & Hollingsworth, S. (2000). (Eds.). *What counts as literacy: Challenging the school standard.* New York: Teachers College Press.

Gee, J. P. (1996). *Social linguistics and literacies: Ideology in discourses.* London: Taylor & Francis.

Gee, J. P. (1999). *An introduction to discourse analysis.* New York: Routledge.

Genat, B. (2009). Building emergent situated knowledges in participatory action research. *Action Research, 7*(1), 101–115.

Gonzalez, N., Moll, L. C., & Amanti, C. (2005). Introduction: Theorizing practices. In N. Gonzalez, L.C. Moll, C. Amanti (Eds.) *Funds of knowledge* (pp. 1–28). Mahwah, NJ: Lawrence Erlbaum Associates.

Goswami, D., & Stillman, P. (Eds.). (1987). *Reclaiming the classroom: Teacher research as a agency for change.* Portsmouth, NH: Boyton/Cook Publishers.

Graue, M. E., & Walsh, D. J. (1998). *Studying children in context.* Thousand Oaks, CA: Sage Publications.

Haneda, M. (2006). Becoming literate in a second language: Connecting home, community, and school literacy practices. *Theory Into Practice, 45*(4), 337–345.

Hicks, D. (2002). *Reading lives: Working-class children and literacy learning.* New York: Teachers College Press.

Lankshear, C., & Knobel. M. (1997). *Changing literacies.* Buckingham, UK: Open University Press.

LeCompte, M., & Preissle, J. (1993). *Ethnography and qualitative design in educational research* (2nd ed). London: Academic Press.

Marshall, C., & Rossman, G. B. (1999). *Designing qualitative research* (3rd ed.). Thousand Oaks, CA: Sage Publications.

Moje, E. (2000). To be part of the story: The literacy practices of gangsta adolescents. *Teachers College Record, 102*, 652–690.

Morrell, E. (2004). *Linking literacy and popular culture.* Norwood, MA: Christopher-Gordon Publishers, Inc.

Nespor, J. (1991). The construction of school knowledge: A case study. In C. Mitchell & K. Weiler (Eds.), *Rewriting literacy: Culture and the discourse of the other* (pp. 169–188). Westpost, CT: Greenwood Publishing.

Owocki, G., & Goodman, Y. (2002). *Kidwatching: Documenting children's literacy development.* Portsmouth, NH: Heinemann.

Short, K., & Burke, C. (1996). Examining our beliefs and practices through inquiry. *Language Arts, 73*, 97–104.

Seidman, I. (1998). *Interviewing as qualitative research* (2nd ed). NY: Teachers College Press.

Vasquez, V. (2003). What Pokeman can teach us about learning and literacy. *Language Arts, 81*, 118–125.

CHAPTER 9

DESIGN-BASED RESEARCH AS A FORM OF ACTION RESEARCH

Dan Cernusca
Missouri University of Science and Technology

Ioan Gelu Ionas
University of Missouri Columbia

ABSTRACT

Design-Based Research or DBR is an approach to doing research that involves both the creative design and development of educational resources and the systematic study and evaluation of those resources. In this study DBR was used to develop and deploy several types of instructional resources in a course on biblical criticism. The project illustrates how DBR can be used to both develop effective and appropriate instructional resources and also evaluate them in order to improve their quality. In addition, DBR has the potential to contribute to the broader knowledge base that is the foundation for both instructional design and learning/teaching theory in general.

Action Research, pages 195–220
Copyright © 2014 by Information Age Publishing

It has been repeatedly noted that modern research in education is often "divorced from the problems and issues of everyday practice." (Collective, 2003). Nevertheless, as Creswell (2012) remarks, research is important because it suggests improvements for practice. The design-based research method (DBR) tries to mitigate this issue by merging research and practice together. DBR allows researchers and practitioners to interact while solving a real-life problem using a method borrowed from the practice of engineering design (Hjalmarson & Lesh, 2008). Similar to the mainstream forms of action research (AR), DBR occurs in naturalistic settings (e.g., Bannan-Ritland, 2003; Collective, 2003), involves practitioners in the design and research process, and is partially oriented towards solving a practical problem. Unlike some forms of AR, DBR is also designed to allow for the development of a "theoretical model . . . rooted in a firm empirical base" (Brown, 1992, p. 143).

While DBR shares many of the attributes of more traditional research approaches, it favors the fluid, future-oriented nature of design (Hjalmarson & Lesh, 2008). In many ways it embraces the traditional approach to instructional design that is referred to as the ADDIE (Analysis, Design, Development, Implementation, Evaluation) instructional design model. DBR, however, also moves beyond it to build an understanding of how and why the design works (Clements, 2008). In effect, the DBR process encourages design innovations, attempts to either use or generate local or proto-theories to explain their effectiveness or ineffectiveness, and to redesign and enhance these interventions while adding to the body of science (e.g., Bannan-Ritland, 2003; Barab, Baek, Schatz, Scheckler, & Moore, 2008; Cobb & Gravemeyjer, 2008).

Traditionally, the realization of a design requires multiple iterations of modeling and testing, and across those iterations the original conceptual idea is being altered based on empirical evidence about how each successive version performs in real-life use (Middleton, Gorard, Taylor, & Bannan-Ritland, 2008). Based on the same principle, design-based research is an iterative process, which takes place over several macrocycles, where the activities in each macrocycle are informed by the outcomes of the activities in the previous macrocycle(s). DBR, which emerged from the learning sciences, is a powerful way to move research out of the laboratory and into the field where the successive iterations of learning resources and procedures are evaluated, revised, and improved. All this happens in the contexts where learning takes place, and it allows teachers, learners, and researchers to carry out regular instructional tasks while also undertaking research activities. Thus, DBR increases the complexity of the research process by introducing a formalized feedback and adjustment process based on sound research methodologies (Jonassen, Cernusca, & Ionas, 2007).

CONCEPTUAL OVERVIEW

Design-based research can be viewed as a collaborative activity at the intersection of three domains or "spaces": Learning, Design, and Research (Figure 9.1), involving both researchers and practitioners in both the design and the research processes.

The *Learning Space* includes designed and natural activities that take place during the human learning process. While there are many definitions of learning, for our purposes, we consider learning as a "relatively permanent change in behavior due to experience" (King, 2010, p. 174). Learning can occur in many shapes or forms, either as a form of personal adaptation, under the direction and supervision of others, or a mixture of both.

The *Design Space* covers activities involved in designing things and experiences. While there is no generally accepted definition of what design is (Ralph & Wand, 2009), in this context design can be viewed as an organized way of defining the characteristics of a unique learning experience. As a verb, design is "the creative process by which designer(s), considering a problem in their field of expertise, generate a hypothetical solution to that problem," or "as a noun, design refers to that hypothetical solution, often embodied in a material form," such as a blueprint or physical model (Middleton et al., 2008). In the field of instructional design, the design space also includes the process of developing the solution to the point that it can be deployed as indicated by Gustafson and Branch's (2007) definition, "instructional design (ID) is a systematic process that is employed to develop education and training programs in a consistent and reliable manner" (p. 11).

The *Research Space* includes all activities that are involved in the study of objects, processes, or human activities. "In the broadest sense of the word, the definition of research includes any gathering of data, information and facts for the advancement of knowledge" (Shuttleworth, 2008) or it can

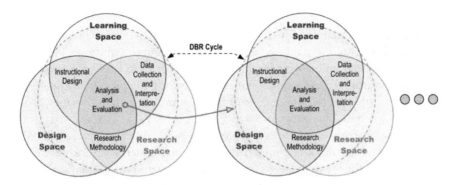

Figure 9.1 A conceptual view of design-based research.

be viewed as "a process of steps used to collect and analyze information to increase our understanding of a topic or issue" (Creswell, 2012).

In the field of education, fields of professional and research practice are defined by the intersections of the research space, design space, and learning space. For example, the field of Instructional Design, situated at the intersection of the Learning and Design spaces, aims to develop "instructional experiences which make the acquisition of knowledge and skills more efficient, effective, and appealing." (Merrill, Drake, Lacy, Pratt, & Group, 1996). Another important area of educational practice, Research Methodology, is situated at the intersection of the Design and Research spaces. In that field of practice, research methodology defines the logic behind the selection and implementation of "particular strategies researchers use to collect the evidence necessary for building and testing theories" (Frey, Botan, Friedman, & Kreps, 1991) as well as strategies for the assessment and evaluation of intervention and treatment efforts developed through the design process. Because of its iterative nature, at the core of the DBR model are the activities related to Analysis and Evaluation, which are aimed at evaluating the outcomes of the instructional process and at analyzing the research findings in context. In each macrocycle, these outcomes will be used to inform the design and research activities in the next DBR macrocycle.

THE DESIGN-BASED RESEARCH PROCESS

As a process, design-based research can be viewed as a sequence of microcycles covering specific tasks, such as the production of artifacts or teacher interaction with learners, grouped together in macrocycles associated with a given set of activities (Jonassen et al., 2007). The DBR process involves a number of steps, performed recursively over successive iterations (Figure 9.2).

Identify and Analyze a Practical Problem. The DBR process begins with the identification and analysis of a real-life problem practitioners encounter in their interaction with learners. In collaboration with practitioners, researchers work towards identifying and bounding the problem. The iterative nature of DBR requires constant analysis and refinement of the problem after each macrocycle.

Review Literature. Once the problem has been identified and analyzed, literature on instructional design principles and practice, as well as research literature on theory relevant to the problem is reviewed, summarized, and synthesized. This literature review serves two main purposes. One purpose is to look at relevant instructional design principles to inform the design of

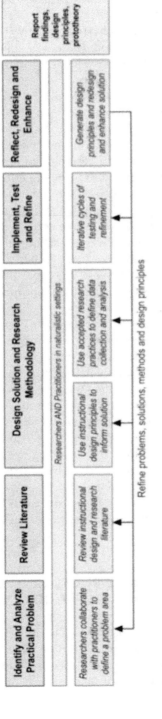

Figure 9.2 Steps in the design-based research process.

the solution, and the other is to review prior work to include existing findings and avoid potential pitfalls.

Design Solution and Research Methodology. This step is intended to help identify and design a solution to the problem, based on the reviewed literature and prior experience, as well as to design a research methodology and data collection and analysis procedure to capture the effects of the instructional design solution. Both the design solution and the research methodology make use of generally accepted principles and methods.

Implement, Test, and Refine. Once the design solution and the research methodology are defined, the team implements them in real-life settings, in a classroom for example, over a period of time, such as a week or semester, and collects and analyzes data to test the effectiveness of the chosen solution. Usually, the macrocycle is structured in a series of micro-cycles to allow the DBR team to make refinements as needed.

Reflect, Redesign, and Enhance. At the end of each macrocycle, the DBR team reflects on the findings and based on the outcomes of the retrospective analysis (Cobb & Gravemeijer, 2008). Depending on the results of this retrospective analysis, one or more of the previous steps might need to be revisited to generate a new design and the appropriate research methodology, typically as part of a new macrocycle.

Report Findings, Design Principles, and/or Prototheory. While findings can be reported (e.g., published) after each macrocycle, it is more customary to report on the findings, the design principles, and the eventual emergent prototheory, only after several macrocycles have been completed. Prototheory is broad implications suggested by the results of DBR that may have implications and applications to other settings.

To exemplify the proposed Design-Based Research (DBR) process, the remainder of this chapter will present a case study built around the development and implementation of a teaching resource that was based on Rand Spiro's concept of Cognitive Flexibility Hypertext (Spiro, Coulson, Feltovich & Anderson, 1988; Spiro, Feltovich, Jacobson & Coulson, 1991; Spiro et al., 1995). The resource was designed to support undergraduate student learning of biblical criticism methods. The associated DBR process follows two macrocycles.

BRINGING BIBLICAL CRITICISM TO UNDERGRADUATES—A DBR CASE STUDY

One of the major challenges instructors face is to find ways to expose their students to current topics and issues in their field of study and to engage them in the exploration of them. In modern biblical criticism, which is the context of this study, several independent but interrelated criticism methods complement the more traditional approach of historical interpretation (e.g., Miller, 1993). Methods adopted from fields such as literary criticism (redaction criticism) or social involvement (feminism) offer new perspectives on the meanings derived from the texts of the Scripture (e.g., Soulen & Soulen, 2001). Once these complex methods found their way into the graduate classroom, the debate moved toward the need to find ways to integrate these criticism methods into the undergraduate classrooms (McKenzie & Haynes, 1999). This effort becomes even more challenging when the undergraduate courses are large, and therefore the instructor has to address both the diversity of the student body and the need to engage each student in meaningful instructional tasks.

Instructors in this field also face an additional challenge, the competition between the students' own religious beliefs and the goal set forth by modern biblical criticism: to apply "neutral, i.e., scientific and nonsectarian, canons of judgment in its investigation of the biblical texts" (Soulen & Soulen, 2001, p.18). This beliefs-driven cognitive dissonance has the potential to create resistance, which can result in student disengagement and negative attitudes toward both the course and the instructor.

The opportunity to address these challenges came in 2002 when a group of faculty and graduate students from the Learning Sciences Institute at the University of Missouri in Columbia began collaborating with the instructor of the Introduction to the New Testament course. The goal of this collaboration was to devise novel ways to scaffold students' ability to apply various biblical criticism methods to the analysis of Gospel texts.

General Instructional Context

The instructor faced all three major challenges specific to the biblical criticism field: (a) complexity of the topic, (b) the diversity of a large undergraduate class, and (c) students' potential resistance to the topic. To address these major challenges in his classroom he decided to test the effects of introducing customized educational technology into his course. The DBR team decided to build an online learning environment to scaffold students' ability to apply biblical criticism methods to the analysis of Gospel texts.

Stakeholders

Three major groups of stakeholders were involved in this research study. The first group included the student body (about 150 students). The other two groups of stakeholders, the instructor, his teaching assistants and the host department was one group. The other was the research team from the Learning Sciences Institute at the University of Missouri in Columbia. They, respectively, formed the core design and research team. Despite the sequential introduction of the stakeholders presented below, due to frequent role overlap, their activity was complementary and synergistic throughout the DBR process.

Due to the service nature of the course, the student body was highly heterogeneous, ranging from sophomores to seniors and with departmental affiliations from schools across the university. Aside their primary role as participants in the research, the students also had a secondary role, that of providing feedback to the design and research team.

The second group of stakeholders included the instructor, his teaching assistants and the host department. Their primary role was to focus on the effectiveness of the instructional process, which included: (a) lectures augmented with PowerPoint presentations, (b) small-group activities to complement and reinforce major concepts, and (c) an online learning management system (WebCT) that served both as a repository for assignments and as a communication tool. They also played a secondary role in the design and development process by, for example, administering research instruments, evaluating and grading students' artifacts or participating in the instructional design group sessions.

Finally, the third stakeholder group was the team from the Learning Science Institute. The first author of this chapter joined the team in 2003 as a doctoral candidate to conduct research on the instructional design intervention in this course. His primary roles were both as instructional designer and as educational researcher. The second author had a support role and served as a "cognitive mirror" during the development and implementation of the study.

Design-Based Research Goals

Overall, for this study we considered two nested categories of research goals. At the design-based research process level, this study explored: (a) how the integration of a customized Cognitive Flexibility Hypertext (CFH) environment influenced students' learning, (b) what impact the implementation of a design-based research process had on the design of a CFH, and (c) how the progression of the CFH design and its implementation in the classroom informed the DBR process.

Nested within the overall DBR process we studied the following three areas related to the learning process: (a) the use of biblical criticism methods as contextual meaning-making tools in Religion Studies; (b) the ability of hypertexts to scaffold the use of biblical criticism methods in the context of Gospel texts; and (c) the differences in students' performance and conceptual understanding as they related to individual diversity measures such as entry-level skills, levels of epistemic beliefs, and major. Within each DBR macrocycle, for each of these areas, specific research questions were developed.

THE FIRST DBR MACROCYCLE

The first Design-Based Research (DBR) macrocycle followed the major steps of the DBR process: (a) the design of the instructional solution; (b) the design of the research methodology; (c) implementation of the environment and data collections; (d) analysis of findings, and, respectively, (e) reflections on the changes to the design and research solution for the next DBR macrocycle.

Solution Design: Cinema Hermeneutica

The starting point in the first DBR macrocycle was the design the Cognitive Flexibility Hypertext (CFH) environment. The goal behind the CFH was to create the operational grounds for the introduction of proposed biblical criticism methods through specific instructional tasks.

Theoretical Grounds

To address the three major challenges associated with the introduction of biblical criticism methods to undergraduate students, the design team chose Cognitive Flexibility Theory (CFT) as the theoretical foundation (e.g., Spiro, Coulson, Feltovich, & Anderson, 1988; Spiro, Feltovich, Jacobson, & Coulson, 1991; Spiro et al., 1995). From the many options CFT offers, Cognitive Flexibility Hypertexts was selected as the primary instructional tool, based on its ability to provide the appropriate scaffold (e.g., Spiro & Jeng, 1990) for the alternative interpretations used by the various methods of biblical criticism.

Empirical research on cognitive flexibility theory (CFT) suggests that: (a) knowledge can transfer to new tasks (Demetriadis & Pombortsis, 1999; Spiro et al., 1987), (b) the use of CFT in the learning process has a positive impact on students' epistemic beliefs (Demetriadis & Pombortsis, 1999; Jacobson et al., 1996; Jacobson & Spiro, 1995), and (c) CFT supports the effective use of students' prior knowledge (Jang, 2000). In addition, the impact of CFT on the transfer of knowledge to new tasks was reported to be significant for both advanced learners (Spiro et al., 1987) and novices (Demetriadis & Pombortsis, 1999).

Contemporary biblical criticism proposes more than 20 methods of criticism (Soulen & Soulen, 2001), but it would be difficult, if not impossible, to provide meaningful coverage of all 20 methods in a single undergraduate course. Therefore, the instructor selected only four methods (historical criticism, redaction criticism, narrative criticism, and feminist biblical interpretation) to be introduced in his course. These four methods cover the broad spectrum of the biblical criticism analysis, focusing on the sources of information, the text, the receiver, and the interpreter (Soulen & Soulen, 2001). The two major factors that informed the instructor's decision were: (a) the nature of the course and (b) the time budget for biblical criticism in the overall course time frame.

Learning Environment Design

To address the complexity of the texts and any potential resistance to new interpretation viewpoints, the cognitive flexibility hypertext environment that was developed incorporated two inquiry perspectives for each method. The students were introduced to each perspective through a modern-day activity, represented by a temporary job as movie reviewer working for one of the four specialized magazines hosted by Cinema Hermeneutica (Figure 9.3) followed by the traditional approach of a biblical critic, both using the same inquiry method, appropriate for that perspective.

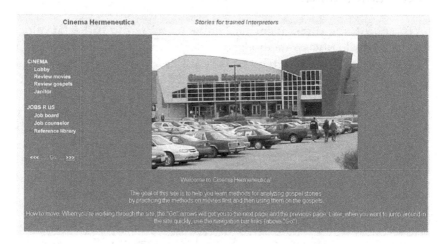

Figure 9.3 Cinema Hermeneutica—The cognitive hypertext used to introduce biblical criticism methods as modern-day activities.

TABLE 9.1 Biblical Criticism Methods and Their Embodiment

Biblical Criticism Method and Its Characteristics	Magazine
Historical Criticism "... seeks to understand the ancient text in light of its historical origins, the time and place in which it was written, its sources, if any, the events, dates, persons, places, things, customs, etc., mentioned or implied in the text (Soulen & Soulen, 2001, p. 79)." It is often praised for its objectivity, which ushered the use of scientific inquiry in the understanding of the Bible.	"Just the Facts" history magazine
Narrative Criticism The focus on the story in a given biblical text allows the analyst to reveal the events that occur, to identify spatial and temporal settings of these events, and to make informed assertions about the social location and values associated with them (e.g., Soulen & Soulen, 2001).	"Tales Told" literary magazine
Redaction Criticism "... seeks to lay bare the historical and theological perspectives of a biblical writer by analyzing the editorial (redactional) and compositional techniques and interpretations employed in shaping and framing the written and/or ORAL TRADITIONS (sic) at hand (Soulen & Soulen, 2001, p. 158)"	"One More Time" recycling magazine
Feminism Interpretation Expands the focus of analysis by including the interpreters and their social goals to expose the patriarchal character of biblical literature and then to reject the androcentric perspective that represents women as derivative.	"Wo/men" magazine

Table 9.1 summarizes the four tasks used to expose students to the nature and the basic structure of the four biblical criticism methods using the movie reviewer as activity metaphor.

The online learning environment was a plain html website which students accessed through a link posted in the learning management system, WebCT.

Impact

In previous years, face-to-face lectures and small-group discussions were used as scaffolding tools in the course. The major change in the instructional process was the nature of scaffolds used to support students' learning across the three major sections of the course. In the first section, the addition of Cinema Hermeneutica in the Gospel section provided a series of individual scaffolds to support students' learning. This change significantly differentiated the structure of learning activities in the first segment (Gospel section) from the structure of the remaining two segments of the instructional process.

The instructional sequence that used Cinema Hermeneutica included five major tasks. First, students had to visit the job board where, with the help of a job counselor, they reviewed worked examples that introduced the inquiry structure for each of the four methods. After the initial review students were required to rank their preference for each of the four jobs. Because a limited number of positions were available for each job, the "hiring" on one of the jobs was on a first-come-first-served basis, using students' ranked preferences.

Second, once they secured a job, students were asked to visit the Cinema Hermeneutica lobby to "train for the job." Students used the inquiry structure of their criticism method while reviewing several preselected movies. For example, for the feminist interpretation the instructor preselected *Titanic, My Big Fat Greek Wedding, Rocky I, Gone With the Wind, Star Wars IV,* and *The Godfather.* Figure 9.4 presents a screenshot of the practice environment for the *My Big Fat Greek Wedding,* which shows that, in addition to the scaffold for the inquiry framework, students also received instant, predefined expert feedback for each question.

Third, students had to the review a movie of their choice using the method practiced in the previous step. The assessment for this stage was an essay, which students had to submit through WebCT for grading.

The final two tasks replicated the previous two steps (2 and 3), this time using Gospel texts. The fourth instructional task required students to review, using the Cinema Hermeneutica environment, several Gospel texts, using the same sequence of questions coupled with predefined expert feedback as before. Finally, the fifth instructional task was to write a

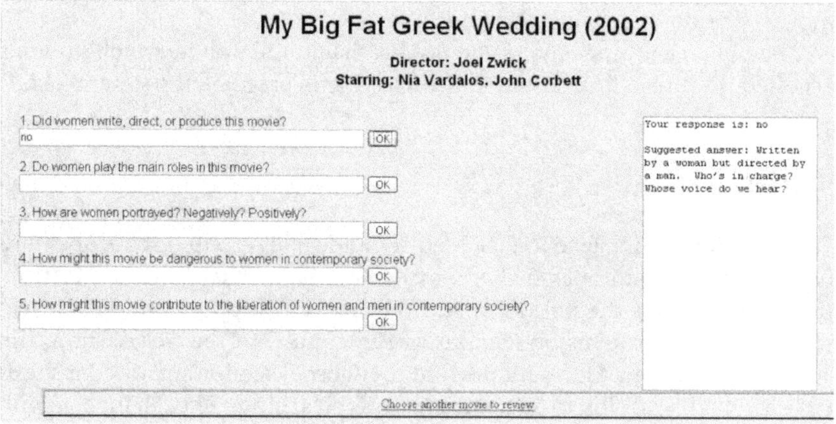

My Big Fat Greek Wedding (2002)

Director: Joel Zwick
Starring: Nia Vardalos, John Corbett

1. Did women write, direct, or produce this movie?
no   [OK]

2. Do women play the main roles in this movie?
                                                      [OK]

3. How are women portrayed? Negatively? Positively?
                                                      [OK]

4. How might this movie be dangerous to women in contemporary society?
                                                      [OK]

5. How might this movie contribute to the liberation of women and men in contemporary society?
                                                      [OK]

Your response is: no

Suggested answer: Written by a woman but directed by a man. Who's in charge? Whose voice do we hear?

Choose another movie to review

Figure 9.4 Cinema Hermeneutica—Practice environment for feminist interpretation.

full analysis of a Gospel text using the chosen method, and submit it for grading through WebCT.

The feedback provided by the instructors for the first essay was short and targeted the major weaknesses in interpretation, if any. The feedback for the Gospel essay was extensive, with a clear formative focus.

Research Design

Space is not available in this chapter to provide all the details of the research design used and the data generated at each stage of the DBR process. Instead, a brief summary and overview will illustrate how empirical research was integrated into the design process.

Traditional research studies on cognitive flexibility theory (CFT) tend to favor experiments that expose students to relatively short-term treatments, outside of the formal instructional process. While experiments explain contrasting treatments, they ignore the impact of CFT on the learning processes specific to long-term instruction. As a first step in addressing this gap, the major goal of our research during the first DBR macrocycle was to explore the impact of integrating a CFT-based learning environment, Cinema Hermeneutica, into the learning process associated with the Gospel interpretation section of the course. Because of the limitations of the CFT environment used in this first DBR macrocycle (static, website) the DBR team was not able to include the needed research measurement tools and strategies into the instructional flow built around Cinema Hermeneutica. Therefore, based on educational research literature on previous CFT implementations, we applied two research instruments, outside Cinema Hermeneutica, to measure: (a) effectiveness of transfer tasks associated with biblical criticism, in our case identifying the main ideas in a Gospel texts and (b) students' epistemic beliefs at the time of their engagement in the biblical criticism tasks.

The outcomes observed in this DBR macrocycle were used to inform the next design and research cycle. That cycle was conducted in the same course but in a different semester with a similar student population.

We evaluated essays written about the main idea of a gospel narrative passage. Three equivalent short gospel passages selected by the instructor were administered online as pretest, posttest, and delayed-posttest measures. The essays were scored for content and argumentation quality using specialized rubrics (Cernusca, 2007).

For each essay, the final score was calculated by adding the content and quality of argumentation scores together. The final score ranged from 2 = *low overall performance* to 11 = *high overall performance*. To measure

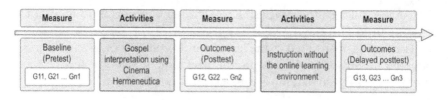

Figure 9.5 Single-group treatment design; Gij—the subgroups used as between-groups factors.

students' epistemic beliefs, we administered online, to all students, the Epistemic Beliefs Inventory (EBI) (Schraw, Bendixen, & Dunkle, 2002).

The basic sequence of instruction and measurement is shown in Figure 9.5. The data were analyzed using ANOVA procedures.

The main finding of this DBR macrocycle was strong support for the positive impact of Cinema Hermeneutica on students' ability to transfer contextual meaning-making skills to identification of the main point of gospel texts. The one-way ANOVA with time as a repeated-measure factor showed a significant within-subjects effect for time, $F(2, 202) = 9.95$, $p < .001$ (Table 9.2).

Contrasts of the mean differences using the Bonferroni adjustment for multiple comparisons showed that: (a) the mean score gains from pretest to posttest and from pretest to delayed-posttest respectively *were statistically significant* ($p < .05$) and (b) the mean score gain from posttest to delayed-posttest was not statistically significant ($p = .13$).

The analysis of the empirical data collected during the first DBR macrocycle suggested that while the Cognitive Flexibility Theory (CFT), as it was implemented in the designed learning environment, provided a solid scaffold for learning of biblical criticism methods, three main target areas for the CFT environment redesign needed to be addressed: (a) the consistency of metaphors, (b) the match between the structure of the instructional task and students' entry-level skills, and (c) the nature of the online environment.

TABLE 9.2   ANOVA Summary Table

Source	*df*	F	η^2	Observed Power
Between Subjects				
Error	101	(1.32)		
Within Subjects				
Time	2	9.95**	.09	.98
Error	202	(2.86)		

From a research design perspective, the major weakness we found during the first DBR macrocycle was the poor alignment between the nature of the research measures, the transfer task for the main point of a gospel text and the complexity of the learning process in the biblical criticism section. To address this weakness the DBR team decided to switch the focus of the research design to measures of conceptual understanding complexity as measured with specific tools, such as concept maps and think-aloud protocols.

SECOND DBR MACROCYCLE

Based on the findings from the first DBR macrocycle, the instructor proposed to redesign the online environment for his next course. For this process, eight graduate students from an advanced biblical criticism course joined the team. This activity offered an authentic learning experience for the graduate students while their perspectives on learning biblical criticism helped both to balance the instructor's expectations and shed light on the struggles of undergraduate students with the topic.

Solution Redesign: The Daily Intelligencer

The team used face-to-face and online brainstorming and analysis activities to define potential improvements to the cognitive flexibility hypertext used in the first DBR macrocycle. The focus was on finding a metaphor for students' activities aligned with the nature of the learning activities, analyzing Gospel texts. The final decision was to use a virtual newspaper metaphor for the entire activity. The newspaper offered a direct connection to text interpretation, the core element of the biblical criticism, while maintaining the ability to offer "jobs" similar to those in the previous environment. The virtual newspaper also provided a unified metaphor for student activities in the form of journalism careers, from intern to expert, within the various newspaper departments.

The new contextual metaphor became *The Daily Intelligencer* —a virtual newspaper that had openings for four virtual jobs tied to the four biblical criticism methods: (a) Editorials & Opinions (Op-Ed) for *feminist interpretation*, (b) Investigative Reporting for *historical criticism*, (c) Movie section for *narrative criticism*, and (d) Music section for *redaction criticism*. The DBR team made the instructional activities comparable and consistent across all four biblical criticism methods and developed detailed storyboards for the design of the new online environment. Table 9.3 exemplifies the structure of the learning tasks for two of the four biblical criticism methods in *The Daily Intelligencer*.

TABLE 9.3 Sample Structure of Learning Tasks in *The Daily Intelligencer*

	Intern Task	Staff Task	Expert (Gospel) Task
Feminist Interpretation: Editorials and Opinion (Op-Ed)			
Scaffolding	Worked example: five basic guiding questions developed by the expert and applied to a current newspaper article	Expert-guided reflection that introduces higher-level issues of hermeneutics of suspicion	Guided inquiry with built-in quick expert feedback for several gospel passages
Nature of task	Apply the basic questions to a similar newspaper article	Reflection on hermeneutics of suspicion applied to a news story	Apply the method-specific inquiry strategy to a gospel passage
Artifact	100–150 words essay	100–150 words essay	700–800 words essay
Historical Criticism: Investigative Reporting			
Scaffolding	Worked example: five basic guiding questions developed by the expert applied for two related newspaper articles	Expert-guided introduction of four certainty of knowledge criteria applied to intern worked example	Guided inquiry with built-in quick expert feedback for several gospel passages
Nature of task	Apply the basic questions to a specific issue in the two articles used in the worked example	Apply the four criteria of knowledge certainty to two new articles	Apply the method-specific inquiry strategy to a gospel passage
Artifact	100–150 words essay	100–150 words essay	700–800 words essay

Based on the storyboards, *The Daily Intelligencer* was developed as a modular, dynamic, and stand-alone online learning environment that required students to login and monitored their task completion. Students used this stand-alone online environment for all instructional tasks associated with biblical criticism. A basic administrator interface allowed the retrieval of students' artifacts and to make content adjustments, as needed. The redesigned learning environment also offered a private working space for students and provided them with real-time task completion information (Figure 9.6).

From a research perspective, the main strength of this new metaphor was its ability to allow for natural inclusion of research instruments into the instructional process. For example, the hiring process often requires applicants to complete knowledge, skills, and attitude surveys and/or tests for selection purposes, while the promotion process includes periodical reviews of one's knowledge and skills (Figure 9.7).

In addition, including the hiring application and survey as part of *The Daily Intelligencer* increased the authenticity of the job metaphor and, in turn, helped students take a logical first step in deciding which job (i.e., method) they would prefer to master as part of the online activity.

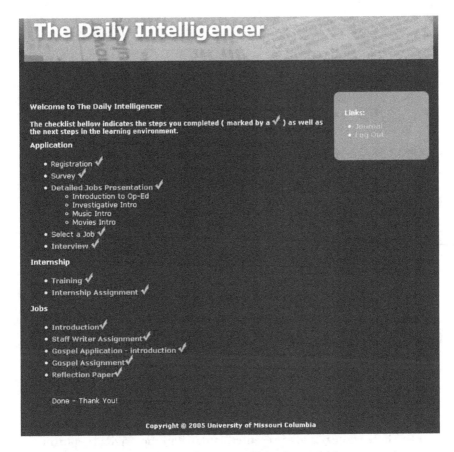

Figure 9.6 *The Daily Intelligencer.* Structure of learning activities.

The Daily Intelligencer offered several features that improved the quality of the research data collected during the second DBR macrocycle. The most important features were: (a) each student followed a predetermined sequence of instructional tasks defined by navigation constraints, (b) collection of demographic and entry-level knowledge data was part of the instructional process, and (c) inclusion of a reflection essay as an alternative assessment measure of students' performance.

Despite all the improvements in the learning and research trajectories (e.g., improved consistency and synchronicity), most of the students' learning activities in *The Daily Intelligencer* remained virtual. To understand in more depth how novices learn biblical criticism using *The Daily Intelligencer*, the students were invited to participate in a face-to-face exit interview at the end of the second DBR macrocycle. The interview allowed for assessing students' conceptual understanding using research strategies such as:

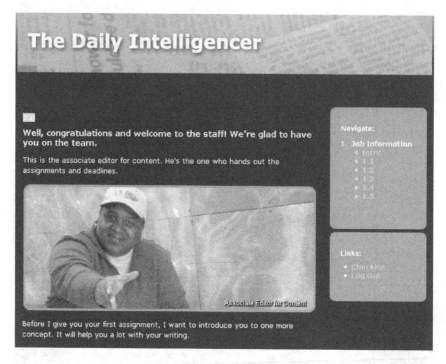

Figure 9.7 Promotion and welcome to the staff position in *The Daily Intelligencer*.

(a) free-association concept maps, (b) task-related concept maps, and (c) concept-in-use analyses using open-ended questions and think aloud protocols. These strategies are presented in detail in the original reporting of this study (Cernusca, 2007).

Research in This Cycle

Some of the same methods used in the previous cycle were also used in this cycle. However, additional measures were added, including asking students to create a concept map, using brainstorming software (either C-Mapper or Inspiration), and an exit interview at the end of the course. Finally, a think-aloud protocol was used to assess the dynamic aspects of concept use while students were performing a biblical criticism task and generating the associated concept map. The overall plan for this cycle of the DBR is presented in Figure 9.8. Aspects of the data were analyzed using structured equation modeling procedures and produced some interesting results. However, it is not presented here because the number of subjects was below the recommended level for valid results.

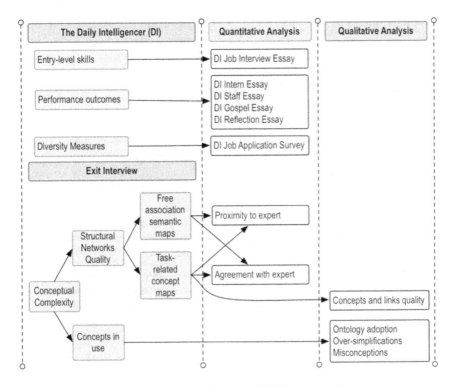

Figure 9.8 Research design process the second DBR macrocycle.

Some of the data were analyzed using qualitative methods and the main focus was on understanding the reasons for students' success or failure to integrate the concepts of the biblical criticism methods into their conceptual framework. We looked at: (a) students' artifacts produced while applying a given biblical criticism method to gospel texts and (b) the general use of method-related concepts when students answered open-ended questions related to their own perception of religious studies.

The concept maps generated from the analysis of a gospel text showed that students had a tendency to build sequences of factual concepts, taken directly from the analyzed texts. This is in contrast to what an expert does, which is built sequences of concepts that synthesized the facts presented in the text at a more abstract level. For example using the feminist interpretation to describe one of the factors indicating the role the analyzed text has on liberating women, a major focus of feminist interpretation, the instructor used the following sequence: "*gender imagery → woman breaks stereotypes by asserting herself → Jesus shifts from male detachment to changing his mind.*" The most common equivalent concepts used by the students in the feminist group for the same analysis were actual descriptors of the woman's attitude: "*woman as unclean,*" "*woman is humble,*" or "*woman appears weak.*"

On the other hand, for the historical criticism method, the one for which student's conceptual networks were found to be, on average, the closest to the expert's conceptual network, the sequences of concepts used in the analysis included several instances that mapped directly to the ones generated by the instructor. For example, the instructor used the sequence: "*embarrassment → Jesus loses argument to a woman.*" Students' interchangeable sequences found in the historical criticism group were: "*embarrassment → Jesus admitting questioner as correct,*" "*embarrassment → it would have been embarrassing for Christians to see Jesus loose this argument,*" or "*embarrassment → the woman questioning and changing Jesus' mind.*"

To expand the analysis of students' conceptual structures beyond the use of biblical criticism concepts in method-related tasks, their answers to two open-ended questions during the exit interview were analyzed. The first open-ended question asked students to define religious studies and then prompted them to clarify if, in their opinion, the same definition applies to both academic and nonacademic settings. Two major themes that reflected the level of integration of biblical criticism ontology were observed in students' answers: (a) religion studies as academic field of study and (b) religion studies as both academic and nonacademic field of study. Most of the students interviewed for this study held a dual model of religious studies, both academic and nonacademic. The academic religious studies were seen as more objective and/or fact based than the nonacademic religious studies. For example, students' perspectives on academic religious studies included either descriptors like "more objective," "a lot more focused," and "open for interpretation" or expressions taken directly from the biblical criticism methods used such as "historical element of how everything came to be" and "open for interpretation."

The second open-ended question asked students to indicate to what degree their understanding of religious studies changed after the gospel part of their course. Students' answers to this second, more reflective question generated two main themes: (a) gained a different perspective on religious studies and (b) got a better understanding of religion studies.

On the positive side, through this qualitative analysis we found that, when reflecting on their gains in understanding from the gospel section of the course, some of the students used concepts that were part of specific biblical criticism methods. For example, students' descriptors of their new understanding of Gospel texts included "how during those time periods, history was recorded," "having multiple attestations," or understating "how characters play against each other and everybody." Inclusion of method-based descriptors in students' reflections suggested strong support for the positive impact of using *The Daily Intelligencer* on lessening students' resistance to these methods.

Overall, answers to both open-ended questions provided evidence of use of biblical criticism concepts and/or conceptual structures in students' answers. Being more reflective in nature, the second open-ended question prompted several students to reflect in more depth on the gains in their understanding of religious studies. However, instances of answers that failed to indicate any evidence for the use of conceptual structures from biblical criticism were found for both open-ended questions.

CONCLUSIONS AND INSIGHTS

This study applied the advancements in Design-Based Research practice to the structure of the instructional and research process and the reporting of findings over two consecutive macrocycles.

Using the DBR process flow we proposed in the beginning of this chapter, Figure 9.9 synthesizes various steps in the two DBR macrocycles described in this case study. While our primary goal in presenting this case study was to illustrate the design-based research process, we also intended to provide insights into the intricate and highly iterative nature this process. For this reason, the mapping presented in Figure 9.9 might not be always exact, as some of the activities crossed the artificial boundaries defined by the theoretical model. For example, while a significant part of the literature review was conducted at the beginning of the DBR process and for each DBR macrocycle, covering both the educational theory and research methodology, supplementary literature review was conducted throughout, as needed. Nevertheless, in the graphical representation it was artificially grouped under the "Review Literature" block.

Reporting followed the process timeline and included research reports on learning outcomes as well as narratives describing the design and redesign tasks. This process was possible mainly because of the instructor's interest and persistence in changing the instructional process beyond superficial or cosmetic adjustments. The instructor's full engagement as a member of the DBR team set the stage for building and nurturing the trust needed to ensure the coherence of the DBR team's activities throughout the entire process. The question still open at the end of that period was: What made the DBR process better than the more traditional approach of conducting two or more successive research studies for a given instructional design solution?

In our experience, the benefits of fully engaging in a Design-Based Research process are twofold. First, by focusing the research on a developmental process (the design process) rather than on the implementation

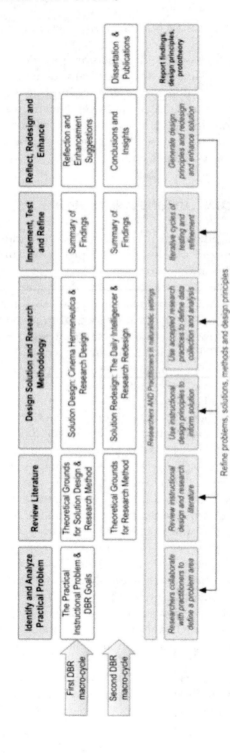

Figure 9.9   Chapter sections mapping to the DBR process.

of an artifact that is the result of that process, the research itself becomes a developmental process bounded by the affordances and the contextual constraints of the design practice. Therefore, the research results are better aligned with the needs for improving the target instructional process.

Second, it leverages DBR's ability to transfer characteristics of the research process to the design process. In our case, for example, the research focus on aligning various measures of students' learning outcomes (e.g., entry-level, online non-Gospel and Gospel essays), produced a more consistent set of metaphors for the design process in the second macrocycle. A more consistent set of metaphors allowed including measures of student's demographics and entry-level knowledge into the flow of students' online tasks. This alignment of theory, treatment, and empirical measurements improves *systemic validity* (Hoadley, 2004, p. 204).

Finally, along with the positive aspects of this implementation of a DBR process, we also observed limitations, mainly due to the virtual nature of students' learning activities in the online learning environment. The major limitations for the first DBR macrocycle were: (a) collection of research data outside the scope of assigned online learning activities that introduced the opportunity for biased student responses and (b) because the research methodology allowed only for a global examination of the impact the online learning environment had on students' performance, the impact associated with specific instructional tasks could be only inferred. For the second DBR macrocycle the major limitations were: (a) the use of a small sample based on voluntary participation; (b) despite the fact that the students had sufficient time to familiarize themselves with the concept mapping software, the novelty of both concept mapping and the software could have affected the quality of students' output; and (c) the research findings dependence on large, heterogeneous population of undergraduate students (first DBR macrocycle) calls for caution when attempting to use this environment with more homogeneous student groups.

To conclude, what made this experience meaningful was the successful combination of several important factors that define the DBR process. First, the activity was part to a real-world context that provided concrete goals. Second, all stakeholders were fully engaged in the DBR process and successfully assumed both principal roles, as subject matter experts in their own field, and secondary roles as consultants for complementary areas. Finally, the research results provided valuable data that, on one hand, created a solid base for the redesign of the online learning environment and, on the other hand, offered information regarding the impact of the proposed designs on students' learning effectiveness.

One corollary of this study that supports the potential impact of a DBR process on the effectiveness of introducing technology in classroom is the further development and success of *The Daily Intelligencer*. Following the completion of this study, the instructor moved to the University of Texas at Austin where, after presenting the prototype and his insights on its impact on students' learning, he obtained funding to transform the prototype into a classroom-ready tool. The changes made to *The Daily Intelligencer* as a result of the second DBR cycle findings were: (a) simplified job application that eliminates the entry-data collection tools used for research purposes, (b) improved graphics that included photos of people that pose as employee who introduce and provide support for students in various stages of their virtual job, and (c) a more elaborated administrator interface that allows a higher level of security for student information and provides detailed information on students' use of the environment.

The latest design of *The Daily Intelligencer* earned the third place in an annual campus-wide competition for Innovative Instructional Technology at the University of Texas at Austin.

REFERENCES

Bannan-Ritland, B. (2003). The role of design in research: The integrative learning design framework. *Educational Researcher, 32*(1), 21–24.

Barab, S. A., Baek, E.-O., Schatz, S., Scheckler, R., & Moore, J. (2008). Illuminating the braids of change in a web-supported community: A design experiment by another name. In A. E. Kelly, R. A. Lesh, & J. Y. Baek (Eds.), *Handbook of design research methods in education. Innovations in science, technology, engineering, and mathematics learning and teaching* (pp. 320–352). New York and London: Routledge, Taylor & Francis Group.

Brown, L. A. (1992). Design experiments: Theoretical and methodological challenges in creating complex interventions in classroom settings. *The Journal of the Learning Sciences, 2*(2), 141–178.

Cernusca, D. (2007). A design-based research approach to the implementation and examination of a cognitive flexibility hypertext in a large undergraduate course. *Dissertation Abstracts International Section A: Humanities and Social Sciences, 70*(4–A), 1245.

Clements, D. H. (2008). Design experiments and curriculum research. In A. E. Kelly, R. A. Lesh, & J. Y. Baek (Eds.), *Handbook of design research methods in education. Innovations in science, technology, engineering, and mathematics learning and teaching* (pp. 410–422). New York: Routledge, Taylor and Francis Group.

Cobb, P., & Gravemeijer, K. (2008). Experimenting to support and understand learning processes. In A. E. Kelly, R. A. Lesh, & J. Y. Baek (Eds.), *Handbook of design research methods in education. Innovations in science, technology, engineering, and mathematics learning and teaching* (pp. 68–95). New York & London: Routledge, Taylor & Francis Group.

Collective, T. D.-B. R. (2003). Design-based research: An emerging paradigm for educational inquiry. *Educational Researcher, 32*(1), 5–8.

Creswell, J. W. (2012). *Educational research: Planning, conducting, and evaluating quantitative and qualitative research* (4th ed.). Boston, MA: Pearson Education.

Demetriadis, S., & Pombortsis, A. (1999). Novice student learning in case based hypermedia environment: A quantitative study. *Journal of Educational Multimedia and Hypermedia, 8*(2), 241–269.

Frey, L. R., Botan, C. H., Friedman, P. G., & Kreps, G. L. (1991). *Investigating communications: An introduction to research methods.* Engelwood Cliffs, NJ: Prentice Hall.

Gustafson, K. L., & Branch, R. (2007). What is instructional design? In R. A. Reiser & J. V. Dempsey (Eds.), *Trends and issues in instructional design and technology* (2nd ed., pp. 16–25). Upper Saddle River, New Jersey: Merrill-Prentice Hall.

Hjalmarson, M. A., & Lesh, R. A. (2008). Engineering and design research: Intersections for education research and design. In A. E. Kelly, R. A. Lesh, & J. Y. Baek (Eds.), *Handbook of design research methods in education. Innovations in science, technology, engineering, and mathematics learning and teaching* (pp. 96–110). New York and London: Routledge, Taylor & Francis Group.

Hoadley, C. M. (2004). Methodological alignment in Design-Based Research. *Educational Psychologist, 39*(4), 203–212.

Jacobson, M. J., & Spiro, R. J. (1995). Hypertext learning environments, Cognitive Flexibility, and the transfer of complex knowledge: An empirical investigation. *Journal of Educational Computing Research, 12*(4), 301–333.

Jacobson, M. J., Maouri, C., Mishra, P., & Kolar, C. (1996). Learning with hypertext learning environments: Theory, design, and research. *Journal of Educational Multimedia and Hypermedia, 5*(3/4), 239–281.

Jang, S. (2000). Effects of Cognitive Flexibility Theory-based instruction on Korean high school history teaching. *Distance Education, 21*(1), 136–161.

Jonassen, D. H., Cernusca, D., & Ionas, I. G. (2007). Constructivism and instructional design: The emergence of the Learning Sciences and Design Research. In R. A. Reiser & J. V. Dempsey (Eds.), *Trends and issues in instructional design and technology* (2nd ed., pp. 45–52). Upper Saddle River, NJ: Pearson Education.

King, L. A. (2010). *The science of psychology: An appreciative view* (2nd ed.): McGraw-Hill.

McKenzie, S. L., & Haynes, S. R. (1999). *To each its own meaning: An introduction to biblical criticism and their application.* Revised and expanded. Louisville, KY: Westminster/John Knox Press.

Merrill, M. D., Drake, L., Lacy, M. J., Pratt, J., & Group, I. R. (1996). Reclaiming instructional design. *Educational Technology, 36*(5), 5–7.

Middleton, J., Gorard, S., Taylor, C., & Bannan-Ritland, B. (2008). The "Compleat" design experiment: From soup to nuts. In A. E. Kelly, R. A. Lesh & J. Y. Baek (Eds.), *Handbook of design research methods in education. Innovations in science, technology, engineering, and mathematics learning and teaching* (pp. 21–46). New York and London: Routledge, Taylor & Francis Group.

Miller, M. J. (1993). Reading the Bible historically: The historian's approach. In S. R. Haynes & S. L. McKenzie (Eds.), *To each its own meaning. An introduction to biblical criticism and their application* (pp. 11–28). Louisville, KY: Westminster/John Knox Press.

Ralph, P., & Wand, Y. (2009). A proposal for a formal definition of the design concept. In K. Lyytinen, P. Loucopoulous, J. Mylopoulos, & W. Robinson

(Eds.), Design requirements workshop (LNBIP 14, pp. 103–136). London: Springer-Verlag.

Schraw, G., Bendixen, L. D., & Dunkle, M. E. (2002). Development and validation of the Epistemic Belief Inventory (EBI). In B. K. Hofer & P. R. Pintrich (Eds.), *Personal epistemology: The psychology of beliefs about knowledge and knowing* (pp. 261–275). Mahwah, NJ: Lawrence Erlbaum Associated, Publishers.

Shuttleworth, M. (2008). *Definion of research.* Retrieved June 12, 2012, from http://www.experiment-resources.com/definition-of-research.html

Soulen, R. N., & Soulen, K. R. (2001). *Handbook of biblical criticism* (3rd ed.). Louisville, KY: Westminster John Knox Press.

Spiro, R. J., Vispoel, W. P., & Schmitz, J. G. (1987). Knowledge acquisition for applications: Cognitive Flexibility Theory and Transfer in Complex Content Domains. In B. K. Britton & S. M. Glynn (Eds.), *Executive control processes in reading* (pp. 177–199). Hillsdale, NJ: Erlbaum Associates.

Spiro, R. J., Coulson, R. L., Feltovich, P. J., & Anderson, D. K. (1988). Cognitive flexibility theory: Advanced knowledge aquisition in ill-structured domains. In *Tenth Annual Conference of the Cognitive Science Society* (pp. 375–383). Hillsdale, NJ: Erlbaum.

Spiro, R. J., & Jehng, J. (1990). Cognitive flexibility and hypertext: theory and technology for the nonlinear and multidimensional transversal complex subject matter. In D. Nix & R. J. Spiro (Eds.), *Cognition, education, and multimedia: Exploring ideas in high technology* (pp. 163–205). Hillsdale, NJ: L. Erlbaum.

Spiro, R. J., Feltovich, P. J., Jacobson, M. J., & Coulson, R. L. (1991, May). Cognitive flexibility, constructivism, and hypertext: Random access instruction for advanced knowledge acquisition in ill-structured domains. *Educational Technology*, 24–33.

Spiro, R. J., Feltovich, P. J., Jacobson, M. J., & Coulson, R. L. (1995). Cognitive flexibility, constructivism, and hypertext: Random access instruction for advanced knowledge acquisition in ill-structured domains. In L. P. Steffe & J. E. Gale (Eds.), *Constructivism in education* (pp. 85–107). Hillsdale, NJ: Lawrence Erlbaum Associates, Inc.

CHAPTER 10

IMPROVING ADHERENCE TO ANTE-RETROVIRAL TREATMENT FOR PEOPLE WITH HARMFUL ALCOHOL USE IN KARIOBANGI, KENYA THROUGH PARTICIPATORY RESEARCH AND ACTION

Caleb J. Othieno, Anne Obondo, and Mathai Muthoni
University of Nairobi

ABSTRACT

Harmful alcohol use has been linked to the spread of HIV in Kenya. It also adversely affects those on antiretroviral (ARV) treatment through poor compliance. This study, using participatory research and action (PRA) methods, sought to understand factors related to alcohol abuse and nonadherence, and to formulate appropriate interventions in a sample of people living with HIV and AIDS (PLWHA) who were also abusing alcohol, at Kariobangi in Nairobi, Kenya.

Action Research, pages 221–235

Through discussions, misconceptions regarding alcohol use were identified. It emerged that alcohol abuse was poorly recognised among both the community and health workers. Screening for alcohol use was not routinely done and protocols for managing alcohol related disorders were not available at the local health centres providing ARVs. The study participants identified improving communication, psychoeducation, and screening for alcohol use as possible action.

We propose that PRA could be useful in improving communication between the health workers and the clients attending primary health care (PHC) facilities and can be applied to strengthen involvement of support groups and community health workers in follow up and counselling. Integrating these features into primary health care (PHC) would be important not only to PLWHA but also to other diseases in the PHC setting. Longer term follow up is needed to determine the sustained impact of the interventions. Problems encountered in the PRA work included great expectations at all levels fostered by handouts from other donors and cognitive impairment that interfered with constructive engagement in some of the PLWHA.

BACKGROUND

There is a high prevalence of HIV infection in sub-Saharan Africa [1]. In Kenya, the majority of HIV infection is through heterosexual transmission [2]. In their report the Kenya National AIDS Council estimated there are 1.4 million people living with HIV in Kenya. The adult HIV prevalence ranges from 0.81% in the North-Eastern provinces to 14.9% in Nyanza with higher prevalence rates ranging from 26% to 58% depending on the testing method used [3]. A range of socioeconomic determinants, systems and resource constraints limit efforts to treat those infected and to reduce new infection [2]. The report noted that over two-thirds of resources are directed towards voluntary testing and counselling while no specific programmes target the PLWHA. It is therefore important to explore and implement programmes that can help to reduce the rate of new infections. One of the interventions that has been suggested is the reduction of harmful alcohol use.

In this study harmful alcohol use means a pattern of use that is causing damage to health, either physical or mental [4]. It is a phenomenon that is widespread in the region. Earlier studies in Kenya showed that approximately 50% of the general population had harmful alcohol use [5, 6]. Further studies have indicated that although an estimated 70% of females and 45% of males in east and southern Africa (ESA) abstain from alcohol, the region had the highest consumption of alcohol per drinker globally [7]. The review further showed that the prevalence of harmful drinking in ESA was more common in those who consumed high quantities per session leading to high frequency of intoxication.

Alcohol use may affect HIV prevention and AIDS treatment in a number of ways. Alcohol use leads to disinhibition through its overall psychodepressant actions on the brain [8]. Although controversial it is thought that the disinhibition from alcohol intake may lead to an increased risk of unsafe sexual behaviours [9]. Alcohol use may undermine adherence to treatment [10, 11], while alcohol interacts in a complex way with antiretrovirals (ARVs) leading to increased hepatotoxicity [12]. In theory, therefore, reduced harmful alcohol intake could lead to improved compliance and reduced risky sexual behaviour thus reducing the rates of new infections and slowing the progression of the epidemic.

The World Health Organisation (WHO) action plan for the prevention and control of noncommunicable diseases [13] and the WHO report by the secretariat [14] proposed certain areas of focus that could be addressed by member states with regard to harmful alcohol use. These included the development of effective services for all people with alcohol-use disorders including those affected by HIV/AIDS. However little has been done in implementing this policy. Almost all the few services for alcohol detoxification and rehabilitation in Nairobi are privately run, with only one public centre based at Mathari Hospital. Thus there is a need to strengthen primary level services and to involve communities in identifying and reducing harmful alcohol use.

Strategies for reducing harmful alcohol use include physician advice, taxation, roadside random breath testing, restricted sales access and advertising bans. Chisolm et al. [15] reviewing cost effectiveness of these different strategies concluded that taxation would be less cost effective in populations with a low prevalence of heavy drinking. They noted that in Africa, since a substantial amount of alcohol consumed is produced and sold through illegal outlets, increasing taxation may actually increase the volume of illicit brew consumed. Offering advice in primary care centres and roadside breath testing were found to be the least cost effective in areas with a high prevalence of heavy drinkers (more than 5%) such as Europe or North America, but more suitable for populations with a concentration of fewer, but heavy, drinkers, such as in Africa. A recent study in South Africa among a small group (n = 112) of South African female alcohol users showed that the women were responsive to behavioural interventions [16]. Cognitive behavioural therapy (CBT) has been shown to be effective in treating people with alcohol use problems in Kenya [17, 18], however its use is still not widespread. Given that in most instances there are few or no effective interventions for managing people with harmful alcohol use and noting the adverse effects alcohol has on those on ARVs we sought to explore the problem using participatory research and action (PRA) methods. Although PRA has been used in Africa in areas such as sociology, social psychology, education, and agriculture its use in medicine and in particular, psychiatry, has been minimal. In Kenya PRA has been used in a health education, sanitation and water project [19].

OBJECTIVE

The purpose of this study is to explore the factors related to harmful alcohol use and identify interventions aimed at improving adherence to antiretroviral drugs treatment among PLWHA who also use alcohol in a harmful way using participatory research and action (PRA) methods.

METHODS

Ethical Approval

We sought and obtained permission from the Kenyatta National Hospital's ethical and research committee as well as the Mathari Hospital administration. Permission was also sought from the Ministry of Education Science and Technology to engage in the community work. Although the PRA process is a noninvasive procedure, confidential details needed to be recorded and therefore the participants were required to sign informed consent documents before enrolment into the project. They were assured that their individual identities would not be revealed in any reports or publications without their consent. The participants consented to being photographed at the meeting.

Participants

The Kariobangi area, in the eastern side of Nairobi City, is densely populated, largely with semi-permanent houses and low income inhabitants. In the area there are various support groups working with PLWHA which had participated in previous PRA work with members of the research team [20] The groups were: Women Fighting AIDS in Kenya (WOFAK), Kenya Widows and Orphans Support Group, Kenya Network of Women—Korogocho group, Maendeleo Afya Kwa Wote (MAKWAK), and the Rehema Day Care and Orphan Projects. In addition there was a group called "I am Worth Defending" and the Kariobangi Health Centre community based care for HIV and tuberculosis (TB).

PRA METHODS

Participatory Research and Action (PRA), also known as Participatory Action Research (PAR) or Action research, has been defined as a research approach that involves active participation of stakeholders, those whose lives are affected by the issue being studied, in all phases of research for the purpose of producing useful results to make positive changes [21]. It stems from the philosophy that human beings are capable of analysing and solving their problems. It is collaborative in nature, and the researchers and participants identify the problem together. It involves learning from each other and understanding one another's perspectives [22] Thus PRA discourages a top down approach in which a researcher or health worker comes with ready solutions. The PRA process goes through three phases. The initial phase involves identifying issues to be addressed (in consultation with the study subjects). This is also known as the "listening phase". This is followed by formulating the actions to be taken and the actual actions. In this study we worked with people living with HIV and AIDS to understand why they abuse alcohol leading to noncompliance and to try to identify the action areas.

Various methods are designed to facilitate the discussions and encourage participation during the PRA process as described by Rene [23] These can be adapted to suit particular situations. The ones used in this project were focus group discussions, brainstorming, role plays, market place discussions, spider diagrams, and Venn diagrams. Additionally, ranking and scoring, and display using star charts helped the participants to identify priority areas.

The contact persons for the organisations described above together with the chief in Korogocho and Kariobangi communities formed the entry points to the community and helped to identify a few PLWHA who agreed to attend the initial meeting. Through snowballing, additional PLWHA were recruited into the project. Additional recruitment was through the health workers at the local clinics who were requested to identify individuals who were on ARV treatment and were also using alcohol.

At the initial meeting, there were 10 PLWHA, 19 participants from the community, and 5 health workers (community nurses from Mathari Hospital and mental health workers from Kariobangi Health Centre). The community participants included social workers, members of community based organisations (CBOs), family members, church leaders, and members of support and counselling groups. The authors facilitated the meeting.

At the first meeting the project leaders explained the purpose of the project and the participatory role each member was supposed to play. Through focus group discussions and the PRA tools the following issues were discussed: perceptions regarding alcohol use in the community, problems associated alcohol use and its effects on compliance to ARV. This was a "listening phase" of the programme.

In a second meeting the same participants (10 PLWHA, 19 participants from the community and 5 health workers) met again. Role plays and case vignettes were used to discuss and draw perceptions on the health problems associated with alcohol use. A "marketplace" approach was adopted to bring out issues of concern. In the market place discussions various issues thought to be important from previous discussions were put up on flip charts around a room (see Figure 10.1). Each chart had a different theme. Participants moved around the room and mingled freely while discussing the issues. At each station there was a person who monitored and recorded the points that arose from the interactions. Before the meeting ended, the participants reflected and collectively analysed the causes and responses to problems identified. Specific persons were then assigned tasks for intervention.

Spider diagrams refer to the figure obtained when a point for discussion is put at the centre on a flipchart and then as the participants discuss various ideas, they are connected to the central body (see Figure 10.2). The strands connecting the ideas with the original theme at the centre form the legs of the spider. Spider diagrams were used to identify the stakeholders working with PLWHA and alcohol dependent individuals.

Venn diagrams were used to map out and visualise the type and strength of relationship that stakeholders working with the PLWHA in the community have with each other (see Figure 10.3). In this method the participants identify the various stakeholders and write the names on small pieces of paper. These are then laid down on the table. The distance, proximity, and strength of the relationships are reflected in how the pieces of paper are laid out.

By the third meeting, held in October 2008, sixty seven PLWHA were now participating in the meeting, as support for the process grew. A final review

Figure 10.1 Participants engaged in "marketplace" discussions.

Figure 10.2   Use of a spider diagram to elicit the participants' feelings on the effects of alcohol on a young man.

Figure 10.3   Participants using the Venn diagram to map out stakeholders working with PLWHA.

meeting was held in July 2009. At this meeting there were 81 PLWHA. Out of these only 41 had been present at the 3rd meeting. Three health workers and two community based workers attended the meeting, with a total of 46 participants together with the 41 PLWHA.

RESULTS

The number of PLWHA that attended the meetings is shown in Table 10.1. The sociodemographic variables are summarised in Table 10.2. The majority of the PLWHA were socially disadvantaged, unemployed, and with low education. A large number were widowed or separated.

Noncompliance among PLWHA

Health workers as well as community members recognised the problems that PLWHA who use alcohol faced, but there were disagreements concerning priority areas. While health workers rated noncompliance with drugs highest, community members considered violence due to stress and legal problems as more important. Both recognised the risk alcohol posed with regard to unprotected sex. For PLWHA on ARVs, the timing of the clinics made it difficult for them to keep all their appointments. They also found the medication frequency inconvenient. Compliance was also poor because after taking medicines they felt hungry and weak and food was either too costly or not available. Whereas some of the latter issues also affected those who were not taking alcohol in that community, the participants felt that alcohol use among the PLWHA compounded the problems. From case studies and vignettes provided during the discussions both health workers and community members could identify the gross forms of alcohol intoxication and dependence, but the concept of alcohol misuse and hazardous drinking did not appear to be commonly

TABLE 10.1   Participatory Research and Action Meetings

	Meeting				
	1st	2nd	3rd	Follow-Up Meeting	Final Meeting
Purpose	Initial recruitment	Setting action areas	Setting action areas	Assessing change	
Number of PLWHA Present	10	10	67	67	81

TABLE 10.2   Characteristics of the PLWHA Included in the Study (N = 67)

Variable	N	(%)
Marital Status		
Never married	11	(15.7)
Divorced	24	(34.3)
Cohabiting	1	(1.5)
Married	9	(12.9)
Widowed	22	(31.4)
Employment		
Never employed	42	(63.0)
Laid off work	5	(7.5)
Retired	1	(1.5)
Education		
None	6	(8.6)
Primary	44	(62.9)
Secondary	16	(22.9)
College	1	(1.4)
Housing		
Own	7	(10.4)
Rented	53	(79.1)
Friends	1	(1.5)
Parents	5	(7.5)
Street	3	(4.5)
Other	1	(1.5)
Religion		
Catholic	47	(70.1)
Protestant	17	(25.4)
Muslim	2	(3.0)
Other	1	(1.5)

or easily understood by community members. It also emerged that the PLWHA had not been screened for alcohol use at the health facilities and that the health workers did not routinely discuss issues of alcohol abuse. The patients felt it was not easy to discuss alcohol related problems with the health workers. They also felt the social problems were not relevant medical problems the health workers could help with. The health workers, for their part, were usually more concerned with the physical aspects of the illness. Thus there was poor communication between the clients and the health workers.

Reasons Given by the PLWHA for Using Alcohol

Stigma and Social Acceptance

The PLWHA linked alcohol use to a desire to be accepted by the community and to prove that they are just like any other person. Some thought using alcohol made them appear sexually attractive. Thus there was peer pressure to drink and alcohol was used to counteract the stigma associated with HIV and to gain confidence to discuss life issues freely.

To deal with psychological problems such as denial, hopelessness, and revenge. Alcohol was seen to make one forget that they are HIV positive. Participants referred to the loss of hope, problems and worries that can be forgotten, temporarily, with alcohol use. Some also felt that PLWHA "drank intentionally to spread the virus." They reasoned that the PLWHA were feeling hurt and wanted to spread the feeling to others as well. They used alcohol drinking to enhance social interaction and entice others into sexual activities with the aim of spreading the viral infection.

Perceived "medicinal value" and physical addiction. People were ignorant of the dangers of using alcohol or thought that since alcohol is "strong" (concentrated) it could kill the HIV virus. It was also noted that ARV drugs made them feel hungry and since they had no food they resorted to alcohol use which numbed their feelings.

Poverty. Lack of money to buy food, easy availability of alcohol, and drinking to get relief from the withdrawal symptoms of alcohol were the other reasons given for using alcohol. The participants were asked to identify important steps in reducing prevalence of harmful alcohol use in the community for PLWHA. Some of the PLWHA said they sometimes engaged in commercial sex to cater for their basic needs. These factors, together with poor health, limited their economic opportunities and security. In this context, alcohol use, noted by PLWHA, community members and health workers to be prevalent in the community, was not only encouraged by poor living and social conditions, but also by cost (it is relatively cheap) and by the social pressure to use alcohol to escape the mental stress caused by poverty. This was exacerbated by social attitudes that did not discourage alcohol use, and misconceptions that in fact encouraged alcohol use, such as that alcohol could kill the HIV virus.

Community resources. Through the use of spider diagrams and Venn diagrams, the participants identified a range of services in the community that could potentially address the problems that were identified. These included nutrition, psychosocial, primary health care (PHC), HIV prevention and treatment services, counseling, as well as social, legal, information, and referral support for PLWHA. However none of these dealt explicitly with the treatment of alcohol and drug related problems in the community, or the needs of PLWHA on ARVs who use alcohol, and their adherence to treatment. The Majengo clinic and the Comprehensive Care Clinics were run by medical doctors whereas Kariobangi and Comboni clinics were run by clinical officers and nurses. The research team leaders AO and MM accompanied by a community nurse visited the community and the clinics to verify the information obtained at the meeting. Discussions with the heads of the various clinics, and the records kept, revealed that alcohol related disorders were not commonly documented. Furthermore none of the health facilities used any screening instruments such as the AUDIT [24].

Action Areas. During the third meeting further discussions on the harmful effects of alcohol took place, exploring reasons why people drink and corrective measures that could be taken. The meetings were used to reinforce the steps people identified that they could take to reduce harmful drinking. Reflecting on the problems identified in the first two meetings, the participants noted that counseling and education were important. The community health nurses together with the authors organised education talks with the staff of the institutions identified earlier. These included the local health centres and the self-help groups. The health workers were taught how to use the AUDIT in identifying problem drinkers and how to recognise and manage alcohol related disorders such as withdrawal seizures. They were also advised to routinely ask questions on alcohol and compliance and to be more sensitive to the patients' social needs. Other aspects on how to improve communication between the care providers and their clients were discussed. For the PLWHA, basic information on the effects of alcohol on the body was provided.

The PLWHA were encouraged to form a registered group which could apply for funding on projects of their choice. The PLWHA and their family members were encouraged to support one another and to identify symptoms of harmful alcohol use among themselves. These were feasible within the network of PHC and community mental health resources in the community, although with additional support from the PRA research team. What was more difficult was implementing interventions aimed at improving the incomes of the affected PLWHA.

DISCUSSION

In our view the use of the PRA methods allowed all the participants to explore the perceptions and feelings of PLWHA and those working with them in the community. Thus we were able to gain new insights into their problem. Furthermore the PRA approach allows the researchers to work together with those affected in finding solutions to their problem. For example, in this community there was clearly much misinformation about the physical effects of alcohol. The perception that strong alcoholic drinks had medicinal value and could kill the virus within the body may have led some PLWHA to drinking. We also found that the health workers and the patients were not communicating well. The clients going to the health centres did not feel free to talk about the social and economic aspects of their illness which was of more concern to them as opposed to the health workers who tended to concentrate more on the physical aspects of the illness. Such information could be useful in formulating interventions in minimising the risks associated with harmful alcohol use and noncompliance. Less easily addressed were the levels of economic and nutritional deprivation that led patients to engage in seemingly irrational behaviour that endangered their health. This calls for attention to the specific nutritional needs of PLWHA who use alcohol as part of their therapy, but also to the wider social and economic determinants that lead to harmful alcohol use. This calls for wider policies for economic and food security in vulnerable communities. Although social support for vulnerable groups is minimal in Kenya, perhaps direct financial support could be initiated for this group of patients.

In our experience the PRA methods need adequate time and patience if one is to support the development of useful information through the work of the group. This could be due to the fact that the participants were used to being passive observers in such situations. They were waiting to be told what to do rather than thinking how they could actively participate in the process. This was further compounded by cognitive impairment in some of the PLWHA. However it would be useful to explore the effectiveness and long term effects of this intervention. If proven successful then the methods could be integrated into PHC approaches to prevention and treatment of other illnesses as well.

LIMITATIONS

The sample of PLWHA was obtained through snowballing so this may not be a representative sample from the community studied. However in this circumstance it was thought to be the best recruitment method considering the stigma that still prevails concerning HIV and alcohol use. Furthermore, the PLWHA who were recruited for the study were not objectively assessed for evidence of alcohol abuse.

CONCLUSION

This action research highlights that wider chronic health and social problems in the community impede uptake of resources for prevention and treatment of HIV and AIDS, and that specific procedures should be put in place, in collaboration with those affected, as part of health services and AIDS programmes. The PRA methods used in this study are one way of identifying needs, noting barriers that prevent meeting those needs, and developing actions that consider both the needs and the barriers.

AUTHORS' CONTRIBUTIONS

CJO conceptualised the study and wrote it, AO and MM participated in the PRA process as facilitators. All authors read and approved the final manuscript.

ACKNOWLEDGEMENTS

We wish to thank the following for their help in this project: the community members of Kariobangi and the neighbouring communities for their cooperation; Rene Loewenson, EQUINET and TARSC for support, funding, training and mentoring for this project, SIDA Sweden for their funding support; the staff of Mathari Hospital especially the Chief Nursing Officer and the community mental health nurses, Lorna Osendi. Teresia Mbugua, Muraya, Wesonga, and community based workers Saidi Ndamwe and Claudi Lugati.

NOTES

1. This chapter is an edited version of a paper published in the journal, *BMC Public Health* (2012, 12, 677). The paper is available online at http://www.biomedcentral.com/1471-2458/12/677. doi:10.1186/1471-2458—12-677

2. The spelling in this chapter reflects international and British conventions rather than American spelling and the editors made no attempt to "Americanize" spelling. Also, the method of formatting citations and listing references is not the format of the American Psychological Association that was used in most other chapters. The editors did not change the citation and reference methods used. When you see a [13], for example, in the paper it is a citation that refers to the thirteenth reference in the list at the end of the chapter.

REFERENCES

1. Joint United Nations Programme on HIV/AIDS. (2010). Global Report: UNAIDS Report on the Global AIDS Epidemic. Retrieved from http://www.unaids.org/globalreport/documents/20101123_GlobalReport_full_en.pdf.

2. National AIDS Control Council. (2009). KENYA HIV Prevention Response and Modes of Transmission Analysis. Retrieved from http://siteresources.

worldbank.org/INTHIVAIDS/Resources/375798-1103037153392/Kenya-MOT22March09Final.pdf.

3. Kwena, Z. A., Bukusi, E. A., Ng'ayo, M. O., Buffardi, A. L., Nguti, R., Richardson, B. Sang N. M., & Holmes, K. (2010). Prevalence and risk factors for sexually transmitted infections in a high-risk occupational group: the case of fishermen along Lake Victoria in Kisumu, Kenya. *International Journal of HIV & AIDS, 21*(10), 703–713.

4. World Health Organization. (1994). *Lexicon of alcohol and drug terms.* Geneva: World Health Organization. Retrieved from http://whqlibdoc.who.int/publications/9241544686.pdf.

5. Acuda, S. W. (1995) International review series: Alcohol and alcohol problems research 1. East Africa. *British Journal of Addiction, 80*(2), 121–126.

6. Shaffer, D. N., Njeri, R., Justice, A. C., Odero, W. W., & Tierney, W. M. (2004). Alcohol abuse among patients with and without HIV infection attending public clinics in western Kenya. *East African Medical Journal, 81*(11), 594–598.

7. Acuda, W., Othieno, C. J., Obondo, A., & Crome, I. B. (2010). The epidemiology of addiction in Sub-Saharan Africa: A synthesis of reports, reviews, and original articles. *The American Journal on Addictions, 20*(2), 87–89.

8. Valenzuela, C. F. (1997). Alcohol and neurotransmitter interactions. *Alcohol Health and Research World, 21*(2), 144–148.

9. George, W. H., & Stoner, S. A. (2000). Understanding acute alcohol effects on sexual behavior. *Annual Review of Sex Research, 11*, 92–124.

10. Cook, R. L., Susan, M., Sereika, S. M., Hunt, S. C., Woodward, W. C., Erlen, J. A., & Conigliaro, J. (2001). Problem drinking and medication adherence among persons with HIV infection. *Journal of General Internal Medicine, 16*(2), 83–88.

11. Jaquet, A., Ekouevi, D. K., Bashi, J., Aboubakrine, M., Messou, E., Maiga, M., Traore, H. A.... Dabis, F. (2010). Alcohol use and non-adherence to antiretroviral therapy in HIV-infected patients in West Africa. *Addiction, 105*(8), 1416–1421.

12. Barve, S., Kapoor, R., Moghe, A., Ramirez, J. A., Eaton, J. W., Gobejishvili, L., JoshiBarve, S., & McClain, J. (2010). Focus on the liver: Alcohol use, highly active antiretroviral therapy, and liver disease in HIV-infected patients. *Alcohol Research & Health, 33*(3), 229–236.

13. World Health Organization. (2008). *2008–2013 Action plan for the global strategy for the prevention and control of noncommunicable diseases.* Geneva: World Health Organization. Retrieved from http://whqlibdoc.who.int/publications/2009/9789241597418_eng.pdf.

14. World Health Organization. (2009). *Strategies to reduce the harmful use of alcohol: draft global strategy.* Geneva: World Health Organization. Retrieved from http://apps.who.int/gb/ebwha/pdf_files/EB126/B126_13-en.pdf.

15. Chisholm, D., Rehm, J., van Ommeren, M., & Monteiro, M. (2004). Reducing the Global Burden of Hazardous Alcohol use: A comparative cost-effectiveness analysis. *Journal of Studies on Alcohol and Drugs, 65*(6), 782–793.

16. Wechsberg, W. M., Luseno, W. K., Karg, R. S., Young, S., Rodman, N., Myers, B., & Parry, C. D. (2008). Alcohol, cannabis, and methamphetamine use and other risk behaviours among Black and Coloured South African women: A

small randomized trial in the Western Cape. *The International Journal on Drug Policy, 19*(2), 130–139.

17. Papas, R. K., Sidle, J. E., Martino, S., Baliddawa, J. B., Songole, R., Omolo, O. E., Gakinya, B. N…..Maisto, S. A. (2010). Systematic cultural adaptation of cognitive-behavioural therapy to reduce alcohol use among HIV-infected outpatients in western Kenya. *AIDS and Behaviour, 14*(3), 669–678.
18. Papas, R. K., Sidle, J. E., Gakinya, B. N., Baliddawa, J. B., Martino, S., Mwaniki, M. M., Songole, R…..Maisto, S. A. (2011). Treatment outcomes of a Stage 1 cognitive-behavioural trial to reduce alcohol use among HIV-infected outpatients in Western Kenya. *Addiction, 106* (12), 2156–2166.
19. Adriance, D. (1995). PRA in a health education, water and sanitation project in Kenya. *PLA Notes, 22*, 41–44.
20. Othieno, C. J., Kitazi, N., Mburu, J., Obondo, A., Mathai, M. A., Loewenson, R. (2009). Use of Participatory, Action and Research methods in enhancing awareness of mental disorders in Kariobangi, Kenya. *International Psychiatry, 6*(1), 18–20.
21. Nelson, G., Ochocka, J., Griffin, K., & Lord, J. (1998). "Nothing about me, without me": participatory action research with self-help/mutual aid organizations for psychiatric consumer/survivors. *American Journal of Community Psychology, 26*(6), 881–912.
22. Lingard, L., Albert, M., & Levinson, W. (2008). Grounded theory, mixed methods, and action research. *BMJ, 337*, 459–461.
23. Rene, L., Kaim, B., Chikomo, F., Mbuyita, S., & Makemba, A. (2006). *Organising people's power for health: Participatory methods for a people-centred health system.* Harare: Training and Research Support Centre (TARSC) with EQUINET. Retrieved from http://www.tarsc.org/publications/documents/PRA%20toolkit%20sample.pdf.
24. Saunders, J. B., Aasland, O. G., Babor, T. F., de la Fuente, J. R., & Grant, M. Development of the Alcohol Use Disorders Identification Test (AUDIT): WHO Collaborative Project on Early Detection of Persons with Harmful Alcohol Consumption—II. *Addiction* 1993, *88*(6):791–804.

CHAPTER 11

ACCESS TO HIV TREATMENT AND CARE AMONGST COMMERCIAL SEX WORKERS IN MALAWI

A Participatory Reflection and Action (PRA) Project Report

Kingsley Chikaphupha, Patnice Nkhonjera, and Ireen Namakhoma
REACH Trust (Lilongwe, Malawi)

Rene Loewenson
Training and Research Center (TARSC, Harare, Zimbabwe)

ABSTRACT

Malawi has over the years intensified its fight against AIDS, through policies, guidelines, services and programmes. Some policies explicitly mention the need for focus on services for commercial sex workers because of their susceptibility to HIV infection and the potential risk they have of spreading the

Action Research, pages 237–268
Copyright © 2014 by Information Age Publishing

virus. The challenge remains to translate these policy commitments into practice, especially given the illegal nature of commercial sex work. One important concern is that commercial sex workers (CSW) themselves have not been included in designing, developing, designing, implementing, and evaluating new policies and programmes affecting them.

This study aimed to explore and address barriers to coverage and uptake of HIV prevention and treatment services among CSWs in Area 25 Lilongwe district, Malawi, using Participatory Reflection and Action (PRA) methods. We set out to introduce and test the power of bottom-up approaches, and particularly community (sex workers) participation and involvement as an approach to increase access to HIV and AIDS services. The research explored barriers to accessing HIV and AIDS treatment and care services amongst CSWs and, in a participatory manner, ways of overcoming the barriers that includes empowerment of a group of CSWs in the study location. The work was implemented within a programme of the Regional Network for Equity in Health in east and southern Africa (EQUINET) that aimed to build capacities in participatory action research to explore dimensions of (and impediments to delivery of) Primary Health Care responses to HIV and AIDS. The programme was co-ordinated by Training and Research Support Centre (TARSC) in co-operation with Ifakara Health Institute Tanzania, REACH Trust Malawi and the Global Network of People Living with HIV and AIDS (GNPP+). TARSC and REACH Trust in particular provided peer review support and mentorship to this work.

INTRODUCTION

An estimated 40 million people now live with HIV globally, 70% in sub-Saharan Africa (SCF, 2004)

- HIV has a high sero prevalence in sub Saharan Africa, with higher than average rates in particular social groups (Buvé et al., 2001). HIV prevalence in Malawi is generally higher amongst females than males, and prevalence in the 15–24 year age group is four times higher in females than in males, at 9% and 2%, respectively (NSO Malawi and ORC Macro
- HIV prevalence levels among sex workers have been found to be as high as 73% in Ethiopia, 68% in Zambia, 50% in South Africa, and 40% in Benin (UNAIDS 2000) In Malawi, while adult HIV prevalence is 12%, it is estimated that 70% of commercial sex workers are HIV positive (nSo 2006). Malawi has experienced an increase in the number of women, including girls as young as 12 years of age, joining the sex industry (WHO 2005).

Knowledge of HIV and AIDS among women and men in Malawi is almost universal, across all age groups, areas of residence, marital status, wealth and education levels (NSO Malawi & ORC Macro, 2005). However, behaviours such as condom use and having multiple sexual partners do not match levels of knowledge. Condom use nationally is below 30% (Njikho, 2008), and levels of unsafe sex are indicated by levels of sexually transmitted infections (STIs) in the past 12 months of 8% in women and 6% in men in 2004 (NSO Malawi & ORC Macro, 2005). STI rates have been found to be higher in urban and semi-urban populations, women and young people (NACP, 2001). Reported rates may underestimate real levels given the asymptomatic nature of many STIs in women, and many people with STIs are reported to seek advice and treatment from friends and traditional healers, respectively (Njikho, 2008).

Malawi has over the years intensified its fight against AIDS, through policies, guidelines, services and programmes. Policies have been developed for AIDS prevention, treatment and care, including Prevention of Mother to Child Transmission (PMTCT), Ante-retroviral (ART) scale up, and strategies for specific sectors. Some policies explicitly mention the need for focus on services for commercial sex workers because of their susceptibility to HIV infection and the potential risk they have of spreading the virus. The National AIDS Commission highlights commercial sex workers (CSW) as a high risk group, and a key group for access to treatment.

The challenge remains to translate these policy commitments into practice, especially given the illegal nature of commercial sex work. The HIV and AIDS policy and strategic framework note that the transport sector is one where CSW interaction with drivers poses risk of infection. The strategy suggests the provision of civic education with involvement of the faith community as an activity to address the problem, while strategies also include lobbying for regulation of CSW and access to condoms. Of concern, CSWs themselves are not included in developing the design, implementation and evaluation of policies and programmes affecting them.

Effective access and uptake of HIV prevention, treatment and care programmes for CSWs in Malawi is affected by wider limits to coverage in the general population and specific barriers for CSWs. Coverage of prevention services is greater than 75% for youth, 25% for CSWs, 51-75% for counseling and testing (VCT) services, 25% for clinical services and over 75% for home based care and orphan care support programmes respectively (UNAIDS, 2008).

There is low uptake of HIV testing nationally, with only 13% of women and 15% of men having had an HIV test and received the results, with the lowest percentage among adolescents (NSO Malawi & ORC Macro, 2005; Malawi Demographic Health Survey, 2004). Knowledge of testing is high, but uptake low. A study conducted in Blantyre and Lilongwe with a sample of 114 youths found that only 14.5% had gone for testing despite 85% knowing where and how to access it (Jiya, 2005),

Government and civil society initiatives offer services to CSWs for VCT, reproductive health, STI prevention and treatment and vulnerability reduction, including income generation, condom promotion and measures to address stigma and discrimination. These programmes have usually been small projects, and not coordinated or integrated into the national response. Two well known interventions targeted at CSWs are those by Banja la mtsogolo (BLM) and the Family Planning Association of Malawi (FPAM). BLM through its TV programme 'BLM talk show' interviews commercial sex workers randomly selected from different pubs across the country and provides or mobilizes for CSWs start-up capital for small scale businesses. FPAM has worked with CSWs in Lilongwe district to build business skills in mushroom growing, hair dressing and tailoring, women football clubs, civic education on prevention, treatment, care and on safe sex negotiation skills and distribution of prevention measures to CSWs in their bars or pubs in Lilongwe.

These initiatives indicate a range of barriers to uptake of services. Poverty is the main motivation behind the choice of commercial sex work, and the CSWs cite their work places as horrible and risky, exposing them to several dangers, including sexual harassment, violence, murder, and contracting HIV. CSWs note when seeking redress for these problems that they experience further abuse from health care workers (HCW) and the police. The principal secretary in the office of the president and cabinet is cited by FPAM as recognizing the poor uptake of services (Calisto, 2009). She cautioned that both CSWs and their clients need to be involved in the options for prevention, treatment and care for HIV and AIDS, and the buyers of the sex, mainly men, need to be recognized as part of the issue.

This study therefore aimed to explore and address barriers to coverage and uptake of HIV prevention and treatment services among CSWs in Area 25 Lilongwe district, Malawi, using Participatory Reflection and Action (PRA) methods. We set out to introduce and test the power of bottom-up approaches, and particularly community (sex workers) participation and involvement as an approach to increase access to HIV and AIDS services. The research explored barriers to accessing HIV and AIDS treatment and care services amongst CSWs and, in a participatory manner, ways of overcoming the barriers that includes empowerment of a group of CSWs in the study location.

The work was implemented within a programme of the Regional Network for Equity in Health in east and southern Africa (EQUINET) that aimed to build capacities in participatory action research to explore dimensions of (and impediments to delivery of) Primary Health Care responses to HIV and AIDS. The programme was co-ordinated by Training and Research Support Centre (TARSC) in co-operation with Ifakara Health Institute Tanzania, REACH Trust Malawi and the Global Network of People Living with HIV and AIDS (GNPP+). TARSC and REACH Trust in particular provided peer review support and mentorship to this work.

Specifically we sought to

- Assess sex workers' knowledge and experience of available HIV prevention and treatment services (with a specific focus on HIV Testing and Counseling (HTC), access to condoms and ART treatment);
- Identify the reported barriers to access and uptake of HIV and AIDS programmes particularly HTC, condoms and ART within and beyond the primary health care (PHC) services;
- Assess health workers' perception of factors within and beyond the PHC services and the community affecting provision and uptake of HIV prevention and treatment services for CSWs; and
- Improve communication between health workers and CSWs on the barriers, identify shared priorities for action and propose, implement and assess actions to overcome barriers and improve PHC oriented provision of HIV prevention and treatment services for CSWs.

Through this we hoped to

- Increase shared knowledge / understanding by CSWs and health workers of the available HIV prevention and treatment services and the barriers to their coverage and use in CSWs;
- Increase report of confidence in health workers in managing prevention and treatment services for sex workers;

- Increase report by CSWs of uptake of HTC and ART services and of quality of care for these services at primary health care facilities; and
- To have both health workers and CSWs report improvements in communication on HIV prevention and treatment services, and on CSW health and health care.

METHODS

The work was carried out in area 25 in Lilongwe (see Figure 11.1). Area 25 is a location/township in the west of Lilongwe city. It has a population of about 77,373 (MoH, 2006). It is a semi-urban area with boundaries on the city, on rural Lilongwe, and with "Kanengo," an industrial site of the city commonly associated with Malawi's tobacco sales at the auction floors.

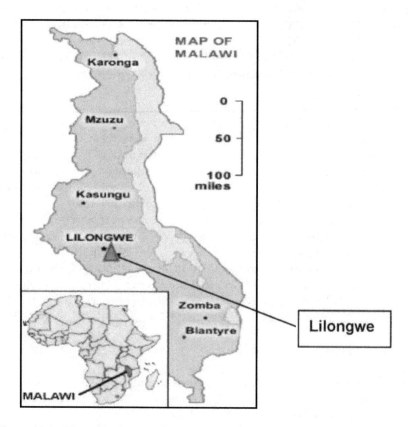

Figure 11.1 Map of Malawi showing the study district, Lilongwe. *Source:* http://www.overlandingafrica.com/malawi.php

The study site was selected due to the availability of interested CSWs and their willingness to reach out to CSW colleagues with health related messages not normally easily accessible to them. This group of CSWs were 'Girls alliance towards Behavioral Change' (GABC), formed by the Youth Development and Advancement organization (YOUDAO). During the time of this study, the tobacco sales underway in the city led CSWs to congregate around Area 25.

The study used a mix of quantitative assessment and participatory action research methods (PRA). The quantitative methods included pre and post intervention questionnaire surveys. The PRA approaches were used to identify needs and develop and guide intervention activities. The PRA approaches were qualitative methods such as key Informant interviews.

Implementation followed the steps outlined below between July 2008 and March 2009:

- Meetings were held with key stakeholders in the study area including local authorities, and health services providers to introduce and consult on the work.
- Qualitative and quantitative tools were used to collect baseline information from the key stakeholders including health workers, commercial sex workers, religious leaders and traditional leaders. A structured questionnaire was used to collect from sex workers, and health providers' information on
  - Knowledge and understanding by CSWs and health workers of the available HIV prevention and treatment services and the barriers to their coverage and use amongst CSWs;
  - health worker confidence in managing prevention and treatment services for CSWs;
  - Perceptions of quality of care at primary health care facilities and reported uptake of HTC and ART services by CSWs;
  - reported adherence to VCT and treatment services by CSWs; and
  - communication on HIV prevention and treatment services between CSws and health workers and participation in mechanisms for communications on health and health care.
- Sixty five questionnaires were administered to 45 CSWs and 20 health providers.
  - The CSWs were sampled using a snowball sampling approach from an initial group of CSWs identified through a youth advancement and development organization (YOUDAO). These CSWs approached colleagues who were willing to be interviewed and introduced them to the study coordinator, who briefed them on the purpose of the study and sought their agreement to participate. Interviews with CSWs were conducted at a place and time convenient to the respondent, some at the offices of YOU-

DAO and some at their respective homes. Twenty respondents from health facilities were purposively selected with the assistance of the facility in-charge according to cadre and their involvement in activities such as reproductive health and AIDS programmes. All interviews were conducted at the facilities. These sample sizes and approaches were largely set by time and resource constraints, by feasibility and the number to work with and measure impact. The quantitative assessment did not aim to collect a representative sample of the respondents but to assess change in the same group through the intervention.

– To support the quantitative tool, four key informant interviews were conducted with community based organization (CBO) leaders and members and one with a traditional leader. They explored issues affecting health care provision and access in CSWs. The sampling of key informants was purposive and the interview used a simple guide derived from the baseline questionnaire with open ended questions. The interviews were conducted by a team from REACH Trust led by the first author (KC).

• A facilitators' team was set up for the PRA work, involving sex workers, health workers, district health officials, community based organization representatives, proprietors of bars or clubs and rest houses, religious leaders, and traditional leaders. Seven facilitators from two community organisations (YOUDAO, GABC), from REACH Trust, the Area 25 Health centre, Dzenza mission health centre, and Gika private clinic made up the facilitation team, who developed the tools with mentoring input from TARSC and trained cofacilitators.

• A PRA meeting involved different stakeholders including CSWs, health providers, staff from the district assembly, and the general community in Area 25. It identified the priority health and health care needs for CSWs from the perspective of the different groups, particularly in relation to HIV; and mapped the services and organizations providing HIV prevention and treatment services for CSWs. It identified the challenges facing health workers in providing HIV services and the issues and barriers facing the CSWs in using these services. The meeting identified also the priority areas for action and developed an action plan to address the priorities identified.

A social map was drawn by participants to outline different services available in the area and the organizations providing them. Ranking and scoring was used to prioritise health needs identified, and a problem tree helped explore their causes. Through a "market place" tool, participants came up with actions that could be taken to deal with these problems. A wheel chart and

Margolis wheel were used to assess perceptions of levels of communication between CSWs and HCWs. These tools are further described in Loewenson et al. (2006).

Finally, the workshop identified major CSW needs and barriers and, together with the health workers, action plans were created.

The action plans developed were implemented over a period of two months, and were monitored and reviewed using progress markers set in the PRA workshop on intended changes.

A quantitative post intervention survey was completed by the same sex workers and health providers as in the baseline to assess change on the parameters surveyed. Further, a final meeting was held of all stakeholders to review the process and changes, to document the lessons learned and to identify the follow up.

We faced a number of limitations. During the pre survey it was found that there was no readily available statistical data on the number of CSWs accessing HIV and AIDS services from the different health facilities, making it impossible to track the number of CSWs accessing these services using information from facility registers. This compromised the exact measurement of the impact using before and after implementation data. However, the pre and post intervention survey, progress markers and reflections by the affected group themselves give some information on the barriers to service uptake and the changes arising from the intervention. The limited resources and relatively short timeframe for the intervention limited to outreach, coverage and PRA skills transfer.

THE FINDINGS

This section reports on the steps of the study and presents the information gathered and analysed. Given the PRA approach the reflections on the findings by participants are integrated within the section.

The Baseline Survey

The 45 CSWs included in the pre and post survey were all female, while 40% of the 20 health workers were male and 60% female. The age of the CSWs ranged from 14–39 years, while that of the HCWs ranged from 22 to 69 years. The CSWs had primary (31%) or secondary (64%) level education, with one each having a college education or no education. The HCWs had higher levels of education, 60% with a college education, 15% with university education and 25% with secondary level education. Most of the CSWs involved in the study were single (42%), although 9% were separated,

40% divorced and 9% widowed. Most of the HCWs were married (80%) with only 10% single and 10% divorced or widowed. The types of HCWs included are shown in Table 11.1.

CSWs have lower education levels and are younger than health care workers. Although most of the CSWs were young, single and of school going age, only five were still studying at the time of the survey, the others reporting having dropped out of school due to death of their parents, early pregnancy and marriage. Those who reported being divorced or separated said they left their husbands because they were abusive, and felt it was better to leave when they could still get another man to marry them. Unfortunately, when this did not happen, they joined the sex industry, seeing friends already in the business earning an income. One CSW said:

> I couldn't have afforded to be just staying with my child, you know I need to take good care of him... and I got fed up with the mockery that I suffered from my friends who had mocked and teased me for a long time telling me that I was wasting time thinking I would get married again. I was convinced and joined them until today I am surviving through this business.

Employment, incomes and livelihood are the main determinants of the choices the CSWs made, and also determine their access to services for HIV and AIDS.

As discussed in the introduction, the baseline survey found knowledge to be high, with 71% of respondents asserting their knowledge on available HIV prevention and treatment services to be high or very high (See Table 11.2). Yet both health workers felt that CSWs faced very high barriers to using health care services that they may know about.

Interviews with stakeholders in the community pointed to barriers such the illegal nature of the business of CSWs, leading to stigmatizing attitudes by the community, and making it difficult for local community based

TABLE 11.1 Characteristics of Healthcare Workers Interviewed in the Pre and Post Survey

Category	Number Interviewed	Type of Formal Training	Period of Providing Services
Nurses	9	Enrolled nurses	1–10 years
Clinicians	4	Medical and clinical	1–10 years
Health Surveillance Assistants (HSAs)	4	HIV counseling and testing, STI treatment	1–5 years
Technicians	3	Environmental health, laboratory	1–10 years

TABLE 11.2 Results of the Baseline Questionnaire to CSWs and HCWs: Rating of Hiv Services

Issue	HCWs Responses (% Total, N = 20)				CSWs Responses (% Total, N = 45)			
	Extremely/ Very High	High	Low	Very Low/ None	Extremely/ Very High	High	Low	Very Low/ None
Knowledge of HIV Services					33	38	27	2
Barriers CSWs Face to Using Healthcare	70	25	5	0	76	22	2	0
Access to HIV Prevention Services	25	40	30	5	2	24	27	47
Access to ART	20	35	45	0	4	51	24	20
Condom Use	5	25	25	45	4	16	7	73
Treatment Default	40	30	30	0	58	20	20	2
Quality of Services	35	40	25	0	27	47	27	0
Level of Communication	5	60	30	5	1	53	31	7
Availability of Communication Mechanisms	20	25	30	25	4	24	27	44

organisations (CBOs) to develop interventions that focus on CSWs. One CBO representative said:

> I recall that at our organization we were talking of identifying women that are either HIV positive or living with AIDS ... but when somebody suggested that we should also try to get some sex workers that are living with the AIDS, the idea was shot down ... they are too difficult to find and work with.

One of the religious leaders bemoaned the tendency by the religious institutions in condemning sex workers as a contributing factor to the social difficulty in CSWs living in society. He said:

> when in that business these people develop an attitude or mentality that they have no one to support them and when they fall sick it is also people of God who despise them and not pray for them saying that's what they wanted. So if they can't get some solace from the church or mosque for prayer who can they believe to say that they will be appreciated and supported ... unless we

change our mindset and attitudes towards sex workers it will remain difficult
to get them back from that business.

Given these barriers, service access was reported to be low, although
health workers had a more favourable perception of this than CSWs. Most
CSWs rated access to HIV prevention services to be low or very low (74%),
although only 35% of health workers had this perception.

This was also reflected in more specific questions on access to HIV testing, and to condoms. Condom use was reported to be very low by 73% of
the CSWs, and by 45% of the health workers. Views on access to ART were
more variable *within* the groups than across the two groups. About half
(51%) of CSWs rated it to be high, and 44% to be low or very low. For the
health workers, 55% rated it to be high or very high, and 45% to be low or
very low. Treatment default was felt by both groups to be high or very high,
rated as such by 70% of health workers and 78% of CSWs.

The mechanisms for dealing with service access were also rated in the
survey. Three quarters, 75%, of health workers rated quality of services to be
very high or high, as did 74% of CSWs. The clinical quality of services provided thus seems not to be a barrier. However the provision for communication between CSWs and health services were rated much lower, with 55% of
health workers and 71% of CSWs rating these mechanisms low or very low.
Yet the level of communication was rated as high by 60% of health workers
and 53% of CSWs. The levels and forms of communication between these
two groups thus merit further exploration.

We were aware of some areas of possible bias in the survey due both to
understanding of the questions and concern about being monitored, and
dealt with these by clearly explaining the questions and assuring confidentiality. We also recognize that the survey was of ratings of perceptions, hence
the evidence is only used as a baseline with the *same* group, both directly affected by the issue under focus, to assess how perceptions and ratings have
changed after the intervention.

The PRA Meetings

The first PRA meeting involved CSWs, health providers, staff from the
district assembly, and the general community in Area 25. It aimed to identify the priority health and health care needs for CSWs from the perspective
of the different groups, particularly in relation to HIV; and to map the services and organizations providing HIV prevention and treatment services
for CSWs. It identified the challenges facing health workers in providing
HIV services and the issues and barriers facing the CSWs in using these

services. Finally the meeting identified priority areas for action and developed an action plan to address the priorities identified.

Social maps of the area were drawn by the PRA workshop participants. They showed the population groups and available HIV prevention and treatment services in the community including but not limited to health services. The groups highlighted places where HIV services are found, and indicated those CSWs frequent most for health care seeking. The participants highlighted that there was only one government facility, Area 25 health centre, serving as the main facility for the area. It is supported by Kamuzu Central Hospital and Bwaila Central Hospital which are referral facilities. Two non state nonprofit facilities exist, Banja la mtsogolo, specializes in reproductive health service including family planning services amongst women and the youth, and a mission facility, Dzenza Mission health centre. Private for profit services mapped included Gika private clinic, Dopa, Lira and Vision Private. The map highlighted support organisations, like YOU-DAO and Kanengo AIDS Support Organization (KASO) providing testing and HIV support services. The sites identified to be frequented by CSOs for services were those offering testing, condom distribution, STI treatment, ART and also those offering privacy, such as in the case of private clinics for STI treatment. For instance, one sex worker had this to say;

> Normally we go to ... because we know that they are open to discussions and keep secrets while in these public hospitals, people are not open and do not keep secrets.

The importance of confidentiality was reiterated by a health worker from one of the health centres which was probably the farthest of all within the location, but one that saw a lot of clients because of the perceived confidentiality of their services.

> Although it is a bit difficult for us to specifically come up with concrete data on how many CSWs we treat with STIs, the average number of 34 STI patients per month that we register speaks volumes of satisfaction that such patients have in our service delivery because even if one is diagnosed with HIV we write a referral letter, conceal it and ask them to take it to area 25 clinic straight to the only person in the ART room and nobody else. This assures confidentiality as without this advice, a lot of patients have been subjected to a lot of abuse as they ended up giving this letter to any HCW they meet there who in the end spread the issue.

To identify the health needs of the CSWs, two groups, one of CSWs and another of HCWs were asked to draw out a list of CSW health needs and rank the needs according to what they felt were the most important. The two lists were then discussed according to the ranks and scores that groups came up with. In plenary after thorough scrutiny of the priority needs as presented by the two groups, a final list of the three priority health needs that were shared and that both groups felt could be intervened upon was agreed upon. These were:

- Lack of early treatment seeking practices amongst CSWs
- Ill treatment of CSWs at health facilities by health practitioners
- Lack of adherence to treatment by most of CSWs.

Triggered by a picture code of a health centre showing a health worker and a CSW, participants discussed and listed the challenges CSWs faced in accessing HIV care, treatment, and support (see Figure 11.3).

The CSWs identified as challenges:

- Poor attitude of and poor history taking by health workers when doing clinical examination
- Being shouted at, ridiculed, insulted and lack of respect by HCWs; over dosing of medication by private clinics; public HCWs not being punctual on starting time of their jobs
- CSWs shyness to express themselves to HCW Stigma by HCWs towards HIV positive CSWs
- HCWs forcing CSWs to have sex with them when they come for health care at the hospital or not treating CSWs they have had sex with

Some of these are further discussed below, from the perception of the CSWs and of the health workers.

Figure 11.3 CSWs discussing barriers they face. *Source:* REACH Trust 2008.

The CSWs pointed to a number of issues affecting quality of care at services: lack of space or rooms at the health facilities, especially in the ART clinic, affecting privacy in the consultation. In the consultation room in one facility patients are seen in twos, also affecting privacy. CSWs reported shortages of drugs, acting as a deterrent to their use of services.

They reported that after HIV testing it took almost two or three years before they went for another test after the first, despite their risk environments, citing poverty and fear for children's welfare as factors restraining them from returning for the test. They felt that knowing their status made little difference to their lives.

A number of reports and allegations were made of disturbing and harsh treatment, sexual harassment and ill treatment, that are recorded here and that the study was not in a position to verify.

One of the CSWs reported that she was ill-treated and rejected at a facility when she went there with several cuts she sustained during a fight. As these were deep cuts, when she was turned back from the hospital and police, the wounds became infected and started to swell. She then returned to the hospital in this condition and recounted the response she got as:

> . . . when I arrived there they started shouting at me saying this is what I wanted and I had for these on my own. They said I wanted to disturb their peace by letting them to touch wounds of prostitutes. I was made to lie down and they stitched my wounds without giving me any painkiller but harshly worked on them while I was crying because I was in great pain. After that they never said anything or gave me drugs and just released me. And because I wasn't sure whether and when to go back for the removal of those stitches and because of the pain on the cut that was in the head, the lining used when stitching caught up with my hair I ended up removing the stitches by myself to an extent that I feel some stitches are still inside me as this part still pains me to date" *(pointing at her upper arm).*

Another sex worker also shared this experience:

> one day when I went to area 25 health I was humiliated by a nurse who was attending to us. This time I had joined one of the research surveys that were being conducted on people on ART. And this day I wanted to request if they could allow to test my kid and possibly take him on the survey as well because I noticed that his health was deteriorating and I suspected he could also be HIV+ and I thought if he is tested earlier the better. Hardly when I uttered a word, the nurse who I think had misplaced her cell phone, angrily started shouting at me that I had stolen her handset. My explanation was never taken heed of and in no time we were at a police station where I was jailed for the whole day.

> Later, I was released in the evening saying that the phone was found. All this happened because the nurse said that I was a sex worker and that she was convinced I had stolen her phone. And so you can imagine how I felt, my

sickly child instead of getting that help I thought he would get was actually left crying all day. So this kind of attitude by HCWs towards us CSWs where they regard us as thieves or people with bad manners always is what puts us off to seek health care at that facility. Unfortunately this is the only biggest and public facility here and although my child is in bad shape now I can't afford to go to private clinics at all. But with the treatment I suffered in the hands of that nurse I can't go back to that facility again. I better die together with my child.

CSWs complained of queuing for hours due to patient numbers and inadequate staff, but also reported favouritism in seeing people later in the queue earlier.

This eventually leaves a lot of people unattended by midday when HCWs break for lunch and since when they go for lunch they also come back very late most of us just walk back home.

They also complained of lack of respect by female nurses in the antenatal clinic and delivery ward, citing a preference for male nurses as they showed respect and compassion.

female nurses are always not respectful of girls and women in general unlike male nurses or clinicians. These male health workers are so understanding and respectful of patients. Female nurses at the labour ward or antenatal clinic speak abusive words at us and they are very cruel when they are handling you especially during labour or delivery. But they needed to be more loving and caring towards their fellow women I wonder why they behave differently?

Some CSWs, however, felt that male nurses and clinicians should be removed from ART clinics and other outpatient services as they were concerned about sexual harassment by male nurses in these services.

While these reports were made by the CSWs, during the PRA workshop the experiences of health workers in providing HIV prevention, treatment and care services were also recounted.

Health workers observed that CSWs do not bring their partners to access STI treatment, undermining their own recovery, despite health workers recommending that they do so. This was of great concern to the health workers as failure to treat both partners of an STI renders the treatment received by a single partner useless and compounds the spread of STIs and HIV.

They reported that CSWs do not adhere to appointment dates, particularly in relation to dates for ART refills and STI treatment checkups. As a result health workers feared that CSWs could develop resistance to treatment. CSWs were seen by health workers to be in a hurry, to avoid being seen by people, when they come for ART refills. This factor was said to be one of the contributors to poor communication between HCWs and CSWs. CSWs did not want people in their location to know their status, and come to the facilities early in the morning hoping to get treatment when the facilities are not full. Yet the services have official opening times. As a result they blame health providers for being late, when in fact CSWs are rather asking for a scenario of care organised around their needs. CSWs shyness or fear to narrate the exact problem they presented to the facility with makes it very difficult for the health workers to address their health problems. For example the health workers reported that CSWs hide having an STI, leading health workers to prescribe the wrong medication. This was confirmed during the role plays when experiences such as CSWs sharing STI medication or reporting headache rather than STI symptoms at the clinic and being given paracetamol were reported.

Health workers observed further health system related challenges as factors affecting the provision of services. These were:

- Inadequate space to operate from
- Shortage of drugs and equipment supplies
- Shortage of expertise in some special cases relating to ART and STIs
- Mismatch between the demand from the high number of cases expecting to be assisted and the few HCWs and resources available

The separate feedback from the CSWs and HCWs on their experience of HIV services for CSWs indicated some areas of shared perception, and some of different concerns. For the CSWs, the way they are treated by service providers was an important issue that health workers did not raise, while health workers raised the poor compliance with service and drug procedures that CSWs did not refer to. Both raised shortfalls in the health care environment and the resources for HIV related services relative to need.

In the short time frame of the PRA process, we did not expect to address all the issues between CSWs and health providers, given that many are structural and deeply rooted and need longer term processes. However we sought to improve communication and trust between the groups as a means of improving uptake and orientation of services, through initiating joint action on the shared feasible priorities they both identified as noted earlier.

From the priority concerns and the issues raised on them, participants developed an action plan that outlined actions that could be taken to address the three priorities identified by both, taking into account areas raised by both with actions for both. Using a market place tool, participants came up with actions that could be taken to deal with these problems. Participants then discussed the flipcharts and wrote their proposals on each. The charts were reviewed by all to identify actions to be taken immediately and those deferred. For the immediate actions, participants then wrote next to the actions who will take them. Again feasible proposals were taken and those that were not were left out. The plan is shown in Table 11.3.

TABLE 11.3 ACTION PLAN DEVELOPED TO ENHANCE CSW UPTAKE OF AND ADHERENCE TO TREATMENT

Problem	Causes	Action	Indicator
Issues and Actions Raised by CSWs on Priority Areas of Action			
Ill-treatment by HCWs	Fatigue on the part of HCWs High expectations of CSWs The way CSWs talk to HCWs Lack of understanding between CSWs and HCWs	CSWs to set up a committee that can liaise with HCWs and take up complaints of abuse	Number of meetings with HCWs over services Minutes of CSWs meetings with HCWs
CSW shyness to express themselves to HCWs	Absence of privacy at the registration place or reception. Friendships or relations with HCWs	Mass awareness campaigns Door-to-door outreach Invisible theatre (i) Hope kits (ii)	Increase in number of CSWs seeking health care at health facilities Increase in number of CSWs joining this group or participating in this initiative
CSW nonresponsiveness to treatment due to default	Reluctance or negligence to take heed of advice Drug sharing	HCWs and CSWs to trace defaulters Counseling for CSWs on drug regimens and advantages to adherence	Reported number of visited defaulters Reported number of CSWs counseled on adherence to treatment
Issues and Actions Raised by HCWs on Priority Areas of Action			
Ill-treatment by HCWs	HCW Fatigue High CSW expectations Poor CSW communication with HCWs Lack of understanding between CSWs and HCWs	Health facilities to form committees to look after the welfare of patients (CSWs) HCWs and CSWs to show more tolerance of one another	Reduced number of conflicts between HCWs and CSWs CSWs and all other patients know where to channel their grievances
CSW shyness to express themselves	Absence of privacy at the registration place or reception Friendships or relations	HCWs to practice confidentiality at all times	CSWs or other patients not presenting with the same problem recurrently
CSW nonresponsiveness to treatment due to default	Reluctance or neglect to take heed of advice Drug sharing	HCWs to inform CSWs on the negative consequences of defaulting treatment HCWs to warn CSWs against drug sharing	CSWs coming for refills in time Improved CSW response to treatment

Several methods were used to select the issues identified for intervention. Invisible theatre uses an interactive drama model to promote behavior change, such as amongst young people. Actors prepare a scenario presenting issues. The scene is performed in public without letting the public know that they are involved in a created performance. Issues are introduced for public debate and awareness.

The hope kit is a tool kit for behavior change amongst young people, by providing solutions and alternatives to behaviors and environments that pose risk for HIV.

After this people split into three buzz groups to identify progress markers or indicators for each action they felt they *must* see achieved in the next two months, that is those that were seen as critical and feasible, as well as for that action they felt they would love to see achieved in the next two months, that is that they would want to achieve but recognize may take longer or have difficulties. In plenary these progress markers were placed next to each action and changes discussed to build with consensus and adopt a final list that would be used to monitor and review progress. This is shown in Table 11.4.

These progress markers were to be reviewed and discussed by the team during and after the intervention to collectively track the progress in implementation.

THE INTERVENTION

Three approaches were identified during the workshop to facilitate participatory mobilization and awareness of commercial sex-workers on HIV

TABLE 11.4 Progress Markers Set

Must Achieve	Would Love to Achieve
• Improved CSW response to treatment • Reduced conflict between HCWs and CSWs • Meetings held between CSWs and HCWs over services • Minutes of CSWs meetings with HCWs • Increase in number of CSWs seeking healthcare at health facilities • Increase in number of CSWs joining this group or participating in this initiative • Reported number of visited defaulters • Reported number of CSWs counseled on adherence to treatment	• CSWs coming for refills in time • CSWs or any other patient not presenting with the recurring problems • CSWs and other patients know where to channel their grievances

and AIDS and these included; Door-to-door, face-to-face talks and group meetings.

Health-workers and CSWs from Girls Alliance towards Behavioral Change (GABC) jointly worked together to reach out to other commercial sex-workers. GABC was responsible for booking appointments with CSWs (see Figure 11.4). CSWs were visited either at home or at brothels. For brothel visits, GABC got consent and booked appointment with bar owners. We learned during the study that some bar proprietors are alleged to provide CSWs with accommodation for which CSWs pay only utility bills. The CSWs in their turn attract male customers to drink at the place. The CSWs had an identified leader, and the CSW leader and proprietor boss were visited with information with their consent, and these leaders informed the rest of the CSWs at that particular bar on the objectives of the intervention and the planned visit by the PRA team to discuss health with them. The approach was recommended by the bar owners, who indicated they were moved by the concept. An agreement with the bar owners and the CSWs was reached and a date for the talks was set.

In the door-to-door campaign, the team provided counseling to CSWs, encouraging early reporting to services for illness. As a result of observing some problems with the health of CSW children (see Figure 11.5), essentials like soap, iodized salt, and sugar, among others, were also distributed to support some additional health promotions on hygiene and oral rehydration for children, while noting that this demands follow up intervention by the team.

As a result of the door-to-door visits, face-to-face talks and group meetings:

Figure 11.4 Sex workers coming for testing and treatment. *Source:* REACH Trust 2008.

Figure 11.5   CSW rooms and children at a local bar.

- Over 60 CSWs underwent HIV testing and counseling, 25 CSWs were tested in their brothels and 35 reported for testing after the door-to-door activities. One of the CSWs who had expected her result to be positive but was actually found to be HIV negative, left after the test for her home village the same day, in her response to being not infected after being in the business for several years.
- Nine CSWs were referred for ART treatment.
- Thirty four sex workers were screened, diagnosed and treated for STIs.
- Forty hospital officials in the facilities around the area of intervention were sensitized on the issues identified affecting uptake of and adherence to services.
- Thirty CSWs came for group therapy sessions at GABC, adding to the original members in the group.
- Thirty five CSWs were counseled in the door-to-door and community outreach activities.
- A suggestion box was introduced at Dzenza health facility.

The other actions taken for each area are summarised in Table 11.5.

Further to this information, to improve conmmunication and monitor the progress of the activities, a committee was set comprising health workers and CSWs. This committee met weekly to discuss the progress of the activities. The monitoring also involved the GABC and the GABC and health workers involved in this process submitted reports on all activities conducted. The committee's weekly meetings worked as a review of the progress of activities and findings were reported during these meetings, and the tools and processes of implementation reviewed to tackle emerging issues. Members of the PRA taskforce were also provided notebooks to

TABLE 11.5 Summary of Interventions Implemented

Objectives	Method	Action Points Identified	Activities Done to Address Action Points	Results
To improve CSWs access to HIV and AIDS services	PRA workshop with 30 people comprising CSWs and HCWs	CSWs shyness to express themselves to HCWs CSWs nonresponsiveness to treatment due to treatment defaulting	35 door-to-door one-on-one discussions with CSWs counseling them on importance of drug adherence 3 outreach campaigns with CSWs in 3 pubs encouraging early uptake of health care HIV counselling and testing (HCT) and STI treatment to CSWs in the 3 visited pubs 10000 male condoms distributed to the CSWs visited in brothels to share Female condoms given to 8 CSWs	More CSWs seeking care 25 CSWs access HCT and STI services 9 CSWs tested HIV + and referred for WHO staging 16 tested HIV- but still treated for STIs. Over 60 CSWs taught on correct, consistent use of male and female condoms
To improve communication between CSWs and HCWs	Suggestion boxes installation in facilities Set up committee to oversee the sustainability of the intervention Facility meetings and briefings by PRA team discussing challenges revealed by CSWs	Ill-treatment by HCWs	1 suggestion box installed at Dzenza Health centre Committee holding weekly meetings and separate visits to facilities to monitor progress and review implementation Briefing for departmental and facility meetings held to discuss issues of communication between HCWs and CSWs in facilities.	Channeling of views through the suggestion box and feedback by the health care providers to the clients Early attention to emerging challenges and suggestions to the smooth implementation of the intervention HCWs and CSWs appreciating each other's perspectives and communication improving.

record their observations of the process and the management of it by the team, and these observations were also discussed during the weekly meetings. This monitoring of both the process and the self-monitoring acted as a double check in the implementation of the intervention.

ASSESSMENT OF THE CHANGES
AFTER THE INTERVENTION

During the monitoring of implementation of the project, all except the first two progress markers on the MUST achieve column were felt by the whole group to have been met by the time the study phase ended. According to respondents during the evaluation survey, conflicts still occurred and there was still some ill-treatment reported of CSWs at facilities. The "would" love to be achieved markers had not been achieved by the end of the intervention, although progress had been made towards them.

The post intervention assessment was conducted between December 2008 and January 2009, with the same 65 CSWs and HCWs from the pre survey.

Comparing the pre- and-post intervention survey results (See Table 11.6) The findings were:

For the CSWs:

- Rating of knowledge increased.
- Rating of barriers fell from 76% rating as extremely or very high in the pre survey to 38% in the post survey.
- Rating of access to services improved, from 2% rating access to HIV prevention as extremely or very high in the pre survey to 54% in the post survey; and 4% rating ART access as extremely or very high in the pre survey to 47% in the post survey.
- Perceived condom use increased from 4% rating as extremely or very high in the pre survey to 42% in the post survey.
- Treatment default was seen to have fallen, from 58% rating this as extremely or very high in the pre survey to 18% in the post survey.
- Communication was felt to have improved greatly, from 1% rating this as extremely or very high in the pre survey, to 56% in the post survey; while presence of communication mechanisms went from 4% to 11%, respectively.
- A decline was reported in perceived quality of services, from 27% rating this as extremely or very high in the pre survey to only 4% in the post survey.

Differences were thus recorded in the level of access and use of HIV prevention and treatment services, a finding verified by the data

TABLE 11.6 Pre and Post Intervention Survey Results

Knowledge of:	HCW Responses (% Total N = 20)								CSW Responses (% Total N = 45)							
	Pre Intervention				Post Intervention				Pre Intervention				Post Intervention			
	Extremely/Very High	H	L	Very Low/None	Extremely/Very High	H	L	Very Low/None	Extremely/Very High	H	L	Very Low/None	Extremely/Very High	H	L	Very Low/None
Barriers CSWs Face	70	25	5	0	60	30	10	0	33	38	27	2	89	11	0	0
Access to ART	20	35	45	0	35	60	5	0	76	22	2	0	38	38	24	0
Condom Use	5	25	25	45	10	90	0	0	4	51	24	20	47	44	4	4
Treatment Default	40	30	30	0	5	40	55	0	4	16	7	73	42	42	13	2
Quality of Services	35	40	25	0	45	50	5	0	58	20	20	2	18	27	51	4
Level of Communication	5	60	30	5	50	50	0	0	27	47	27	0	4	62	33	0
Availability of Communication Mechanism	20	25	30	25	20	40	40	0	1	53	31	7	56	24	16	4

Note: H = High; L = Low

collected during the door-to-door surveys and facilities during the project implementation. For example, it was reported from Dzenza health centre that the average number of clients treated for STIs in a month rose from 34 before the intervention to approximately 50 after.

For the health workers:

- Rating of barriers fell to a lower degree, from 70% rating as extremely or very high in the pre survey to 60% in the post survey.
- Rating of access to services improved slightly, with the same levels rating access as extremely or very high in the pre and post survey, and an increase in those rating this as high; Further 20% rated ART access as extremely or very high in the pre survey rising to 35% in the post survey.
- Perceived condom use increased from 5% rating as extremely or very high in the pre survey to 10% in the post survey.
- Treatment default was seen to have fallen, from 40% rating this as extremely or very high in the pre survey to 5% in the post survey.
- Communication was felt to have improved greatly, from 5% rating this as extremely or very high in the pre survey to 50% in the post survey, while presence of communication mechanisms remained level at 20% in both surveys.
- An improvement was reported in perceived quality of services, from 35% rating this as extremely or very high in the pre survey to 45% in the post survey.

Health workers thus similarly reported improvements in the areas noted by the CSWs, although their rating of improvements was generally a little more modest than the CSWs. It may be that the greater impact was felt by the CSWs, noting that this is a subjective rating. It is however interesting that both groups perceived positive impact, triangulating the evidence on the reported trend.

Facilities reported CSWs coming to the clinics after referral by the PRA counselor, for testing and if positive initiation of ART. Word spread through the CSWs and services, but not always accurately. More CSWs were reported to have gone to area 25 health centres for staging. Due to some poor coordination and communication between the referral authority and the receiving facility, some CSWs went home unattended for two consecutive days, as they came on days that staging is not conducted, unlike their colleagues who had come on the right day for staging of patients for ART.

There are two areas that pose cause for concern for sustaining the progress noted. The CSWs recorded a decline in their rating of quality of services post intervention, possibly given their higher knowledge and expectations after the PRA meeting and intervention, and their greater willingness to speak about their views of services. If they do not perceive services to provide the quality they need they may revert to non use and default. Further, some respondents cautioned that the favourable outcomes were a feature of the recent timing of the intervention and the desire to impress or keep the implementers involved, and we understand that much deeper and longer term changes are needed to make a difference to the livelihoods and environments needed to sustain good practice.

DISCUSSION

From an initial baseline of high knowledge but poor rating of access and uptake, due to both barriers in the community and in the services themselves, the intervention has changed the perceptions of both CSWs and health workers, and the reported uptake of services by both CSWs and facilities. The PRA process was able to draw out experiences of the barriers faced, with priorities identified as:

- Lack of early treatment seeking practices amongst CSWs,
- Ill treatment of CSWs at health facilities by health practitioners, and
- Lack of adherence to treatment by most CSWs.

The separate feedback from the CSWs and HCWs on their experience of HIV services for CSWs indicated some areas of shared perception, and some of different concerns. For the CSWs, the way they are treated by service providers was an important issue that health workers did not raise, while health workers raised the poor compliance with service and drug procedures that CSWs did not refer to. Both raised shortfalls in the health care environment and the resources for HIV related services relative to need.

In the short time frame of the PRA process, we did not expect to address all the issues between CSWs and health providers, given that many are structural and deeply rooted and need longer term processes. The PRA process itself raised issues of gender violence and abuse that CSWs face (including through attitudes and practices in health care services) that de-humanise them, and perpetuate their own harmful behaviours. It is possible to be fatalistic about any positive change in this context, even though change is necessary to address the more powerful drivers of risk practices, including from male clients. As one CSW said, "If you tell us to use condoms always and yet it is the sex without condom that fetches big monies, what is it that you are going to provide to us to really change our lives for the better"?

However, the group of CSWs and health workers as a whole identified interventions that were immediate and feasible to address the three barriers they prioritized. An intensive intervention, involving door to door counseling, engagement at places of work, formation of joint committees between CSWs and health workers and sensitization of health workers was implemented, steered and reviewed by the team with the CSWs and health workers themselves. The findings suggest that the process used has some effect on addressing these barriers and mobilizing demand for and uptake of HIV prevention and treatment services in CSWs.

We were not able in this intervention to address deeper structural issues of laws, policies, employment, incomes, health service infrastructure and resourcing, and inadequate human resource capacity that we found also block CSW access to services. These need attention by government and its local and international partners if the declared universal access to HIV and AIDS prevention, treatment, care, and support is to be achieved. In a context where alarming increased numbers of girls join the sex industry annually, engaging CSWs and HCWs is essential to address these drivers of commercial sex work and bring services close to affected communities.

We were however able to address those local level factors that undermine the communication and effective interaction between providers and communities, when services do exist. This calls for public health to guide service provision on this area, so that CSWs are able to access to prevention and care programmes to reduce and eventually stop the spread of HIV for all. Unless we build a PHC oriented programme framework that provides for active and meaningful participation of these marginalized, most affected groups, like CSWs, we will not be able to achieve goals of universal access to HIV prevention, treatment and care in some of the groups where the greatest public health demand exists. This includes enabling CSWs to not only know and recognize their risk, but to see themselves as having the means and skills to take feasible actions and use services to reduce that risk.

A PRA intervention appears to have offered a means to achieving this. Our intervention indicates that civil society is well placed to provide the sort of bridging activities needed, and we suggest that government and international agencies collaborate more effectively with civil society to hear and engage CSWs' on their concerns and health needs.

IMPLICATIONS FOR PHC ORIENTED PREVENTION, TREATMENT, AND CARE FOR CSWS

While great progress has been made in shaping and delivering HIV and AIDS prevention, treatment and care services, including the syndromic management of STI in state and non state primary health-care units, to reach and ensure uptake in CSWs, this study suggests that there is need to go a step further:

- To take a public health approach, to recognize, listen to, involve and build capacity in CSWs and ex-CSWs, and the civil society organisations that work with them, as a primary group for reaching and mobilizing uptake of services in CSWs
- To ensure messages for health promotion that are locally relevant to the barriers CSWs face to healthy behaviours and health service uptake, and invest in mechanisms, skills and tools for enhancing communication between health workers and CSWs and within CSWs as peers on issues such as adherence and compliance with treatment regimes
- To acknowledge the presence of stigma and sexual harassment within health services and put in place training, guidelines, mechanisms and actions to check it
- To ensure that HIV and AIDS services integrate through relevant linkages to issues of sexual abuse and gender based violence on groups like CSWs
- To ensure that services reach out through civil society, leaders from affected groups, to places where CSWs are found, and involve key stakeholders in those environments in enabling this outreach.

LESSONS LEARNED ON USING PRA APPROACHES

While PRA approaches were valuable in achieving the communication needed to prioritise and build consensus on barriers and actions, sometimes unearthing painful and harsh realities, they provided both learning and challenge for the team. The PRA approach was effective in drawing out experience and views about the things CSWs and health workers felt affected their well-being or ability to provide services; and was also a safe constructive means to address concerns about each other that were barriers to service uptake and sources of sometimes violent conflict. It built not simply individual but collective empowerment, and so as a process affirmed other interventions aimed at tackling gender violence by groups as a whole supporting affected individuals, including formal authorities. The time taken may be an important investment if it acts as a base for further intervention. For example the work reported here provides an entry point for further work on the issue of concurrent partnerships that will through working with CSWs give greater focus to men who are mostly buyers of sex.

Yet the process is demanding, particularly of time and leadership. We recognize that CSWs are the best people to reach their fellows, and that PRA processes are time intensive and demand facilitation skills that will be difficult to spread rapidly in the many CSWs in Lilongwe, and nationally.

NEXT STEPS

A dissemination workshop was conducted after the intervention and three major steps resolved during this meeting as follow up to this work and the evidence and learning from it:

GABC pledged its commitment to continue the door-to-door campaigns to signal the seriousness of the initiative with the CSWs, and would build HIV counseling and testing skills in those CSWs able to take this on.

Further it was proposed that the group engage the district health office on intensifying the outreach provision of testing and counseling, ART and sexual reproductive health services like family planning close to the sex workers' environment. The group, co-ordinated by REACH Trust, proposed to consult authorities and mobilise resources to follow up on these steps.

On the deeper issue of economic empowerment and employment, the meeting resolved that with REACH Trust coordination, the technical working group formed during this project, should link the CSWs with institutions that lend capital to women, and with those that provide vocational skills.

It would not be possible to discuss a PHC oriented approach to HIV related services without recognizing the need to take on the wider environments of deprivation that both lead to commercial sex work, and that expose CSWs and their families to risk. We observed children with malnutrition and living in extremely poor living environments in confined and shabby rooms (shown earlier) that pose a threat of many health problems, including sexual harassment and future commercial sex work. A comprehensive PHC approach must give attention to addressing these social determinants not only of the health of the CSWs, but of their children.

ACKNOWLEDGEMENTS

We hope the report will contribute to ongoing discussion and debate and will be enriched by other methods of assessing evidence as well as other research questions that will further the issues raised and give attention to the means that CSWs merit in achieving equitable access to HIV and AIDS services. The authors acknowledge EQUINET, TARSC, and REACH Trust colleagues for peer review support and SIDA Sweden for financial support. We are indebted to the representatives of different institutions that made a broader stakeholder group for the study. Special mention to the HIV and AIDS unit from the Lilongwe District Health Office (DHO), Lighthouse clinic, Banja La mtsogolo, Family Planning Association of Malawi (FPAM), Area 25 Health Centre, Gika private clinic, Dopa Private clinic, Dzenza mission health centre, YOUDAO, GABIC and all the CSWs from Area 25 for the providing valuable input to the project. We thank also the media and in particular the state broadcaster Malawi Broadcasting Corporation Radio 1 for dissemination of the project's findings to the public.

Equity in health implies addressing differences in health status that are unnecessary, avoidable and unfair. In southern Africa, these typically relate to disparities across racial groups, rural/urban status, socio-economic status, gender, age and geographical region. EQUINET is primarily concerned with equity motivated interventions that seek to allocate resources preferentially to those with the worst health status (vertical equity). EQUINET seeks to understand and influence the redistribution of social and economic resources for equity oriented interventions, EQUINET also seeks to understand and inform the power and ability people (and social groups) have to make choices over health inputs and their capacity to use these choices towards health.

EQUINET implements work in a number of areas identified as central to health equity in the region:

- Public health impacts of macroeconomic and trade policies
- Poverty, deprivation and health equity and household resources for health
- Health rights as a driving force for health equity
- Health financing and integration of deprivation into health resource allocation
- Public-private mix and subsidies in health systems
- Distribution and migration of health personnel
- Equity oriented health systems responses to HIV/AIDS and treatment access
- Governance and participation in health systems
- Monitoring health equity and supporting evidence led policy

EQUINET is governed by a steering committee involving institutions and individuals co-ordinating theme, country or process work in EQUINET: R Loewenson, R Pointer, TARSC, Zimbabwe; M Chopra MRC, South Africa; I Rusike, CWGH, Zimbabwe; L Gilson, Centre for Health Policy, South Africa; M Kachima, SaTUCC; D McIntyre, Health Economics Unit, Cape Town, South Africa; G Mwaluko, M Masaiganah, Tanzania; M Kwataine, MHEN Malawi; M Mulumba U Makerere Uganda, S Iipinge, University of Namibia; N Mbombo UWC, South Africa; A Mabika SEATINI, Zimbabwe; I Makwiza, REACH Trust Malawi; S Mbuyita, Ifakara Tanzania

For further information on EQUINET contact:
Training and Research Support Centre
Box CY2720, Harare, Zimbabwe
Tel + 263 4 705108/708835 Fax + 737220

Email: admin@equinetafrica.org
Website: www.equinetafrica.org

For REACH Trust
P. O. Box 1597
Lilongwe, Malawi
Tel + + 266 (0) 1 751 247
Email: info@reachtrust.org
Website: www.reachtrust.org

Series editor: R Loewenson

NOTES

1. Through institutions in the region, EQUINET has been involved since 2000 in a range of capacity building activities, from formal modular training in Masters courses, specific skills courses, student grants and mentoring. This report has been produced within the capacity building programme on participatory research and action (PRA) for people centred health systems following training by TARSC and IHI in EQUINET. It is part of a growing mentored network of institutions, including community based organisations, PRA work and experience in east and southern Africa, aimed at strengthening people centred health systems and people's empowerment in health.
2. The spelling in this chapter reflects international and British conventions rather than American spelling and the editors made no attempt to "Americanize" spelling.

REFERENCES

Buvé, A., Caraël, M., Hayes, R. J., Auvert, B., Ferry, B., Robinson, N. J., Anagonou, S.... Laga, M. (2001). Multicentre study on factors determining differences in rate of spread of HIV in sub-Saharan Africa: methods and prevalence of HIV infection. *AIDS, 15*(4), S5–14.

Calisto, S. (2009, February 11). Chigwiri sex workers' hope. *The Nation* (newspaper, Malawi).

Njikho, H. Y. (2008). *Needs assessment for media reporting on key health issues in Malawi.* Unpublished paper, Lilongwe, Malawi: Ministry of Health.

National AIDS Control Programme. (2001). *HIV and STI sentinel surveillance report.* Lilongwe, Malawi: National AIDS Control Programme.

Jiya, W. (2005, April). Knowledge, attitudes and practice among youths regarding voluntary counseling and testing in Machinjiri and Mitundu. Lecture presented at the National HIV/AIDS research and best practices conference (Lilongwe, Malawi Institute of Management)

Loewenson, R., Kaim, B., Mbuyita, S., Chikomo, F., Makemba, A., & Ngulube, T. J. (2006). *Organising people's power for health: Participatory methods for a people-centred health system.* Retrieved from http://www.tarsc.org/publications/documents/PRA%20toolkit%20sample.pdf.

National Statistical Office Malawi (NSO) and ORC Macro. (2005, December). *Malawi Demographic Health Survey 2004.* Retrieved from http://www.measuredhs.com/pubs/pdf/FR175/FR-175-MW04.pdf.

NSO. (2006). *Malawi behaviour surveillance survey.* Zomba Malawi: National Statistical Office.

Save the Children Fund. (2004). *Children in a world of AIDS.* Retrieved from http://www.savethechildren.org/atf/cf/%7B9def2ebe-10ae-432c-9bd0-df91d2eba74a%7D/World_of_AIDS_1004.pdf.

UNAIDS. (2000). *AIDS epidemic update: December 2000.* Retrieved from http://www.unaids.org/en/media/unaids/contentassets/dataimport/publications/irc-pub05/aidsepidemicreport2000_en.pdf.

UNAIDS. (2008). *Malawi HIV and AIDS Monitoring and Evaluation Report 2007.* Retrieved from http://www.unaids.org/en/dataanalysis/knowyourresponse/countryprogressreports/2008countries/malawi_2008_country_progress_report_en.pdf.

World Health Organisation (WHO)/UNAIDS (2006) *HIV country profile Malawi December 2005.* Geneva: World Health Organization.

CHAPTER 12

COOPERATIVE INQUIRY REVISITED

Reflections of the Past and Guidelines for the Future of Intergenerational Co-Design

Mona Leigh Guha and Allison Druin
University of Maryland

Jerry Alan Fails
Montclair State University

ABSTRACT

Since its creation, the Cooperative Inquiry method of designing technology with and for children has been refined, expanded, and sometimes questioned. Cooperative Inquiry has been adopted and used widely throughout the world, and it continues to evolve and grow to meet current needs. This paper examines the origins of Cooperative Inquiry, discusses how it has changed since its original inception, and clarifies the intent of its techniques. This chapter concludes by presenting how Cooperative Inquiry can support designing with and for today's international, independent, interactive, and information ac-

Action Research, pages 269–299
Copyright © 2014 by Information Age Publishing
All rights of reproduction in any form reserved.

tive children in the context of the developing world, mobile computing, social computing, and the ubiquity of search.

INTRODUCTION

Children can have a voice in the design of new technologies. We have spent the past 15 years designing technology for children with children, and we continue to do so today. In this paper, we discuss our experiences designing with children, clarify seven assumptions about design partnering with children, and set forth new ideas for designing with and for today's international, independent, interactive, and information active children [1] in the context of the developing world, mobility, social computing, and the ubiquity of search.

Design Partnering Through the Years

In 1999, we published an introductory article on our methods of designing with children [2]. Cooperative Inquiry, which suggests on-going inclusion of children in the design process, is grounded in human–computer interaction (HCI) research and theories of cooperative design [3], participatory design [4], contextual inquiry [5], activity theory [6], and situated action [7]. Cooperative Inquiry is unique from these previous design methods in that it is specifically intended to inform the design process of teams that include adults and children. Although many of the techniques may have similarities to those in other design theories, they have been specially modified to meet the needs of an intergenerational design team [8]. Additionally, Cooperative Inquiry is a method of design partnering in which adults and children work together. The intense involvement of adults and children together in Cooperative Inquiry sets this method apart from informant design with children [9] and [10]. The involvement of adults with children differentiates Cooperative Inquiry from Children as Software Designers [11] in which children work either alone or with their peers.

Since our initial publication, not only has our own team gone on to expand and situate the discussion of these methods [8], [12], [13], [14] and [15], but other researchers have discussed their adoption and use of Cooperative Inquiry with a wide range of participants in a variety of contexts including schools [16], [17], and [18] and homes for children with disabilities [19]. Researchers utilizing Cooperative Inquiry also develop a wide variety of technology, from educational software [17] to alternative and augmented communication systems for children with special needs [19].

COOPERATIVE INQUIRY

Cooperative Inquiry offers a set of techniques that can be used by teams of adults and children together throughout the design process. In Cooperative Inquiry, "design" includes all of the steps necessary to conceive, develop, and produce a technology—essentially all of the work from start to finish in the creation of technology, including brainstorming, coding, building, iterating, and testing. This is intentionally a broad use of the term "design" as Cooperative Inquiry is a process which encompasses a long timeline in design. Cooperative Inquiry design techniques include using *Bags of Stuff* and large sheets of paper to prototype; *Sticky Notes* to critique; journals, videos, and white-board discussions to reflect; and role playing to problem solve.

Bags of Stuff is a prototyping technique in which children and adults use big bags filled with art supplies such as glue, clay, string, markers, socks, and scissors to create low-tech prototypes of technology [8] (see Figure 12.1). This is based on one of the oldest cooperative design methods used in Scandinavian countries [20]. In Cooperative Inquiry, the team sits on the floor to engage in low-tech prototyping, which is different from the original Scandinavian low-tech prototyping technique. We also always break into small groups when creating low-tech prototypes. Due to the small group prototyping, the process of sharing ideas is more structured.

Figure 12.1 Children and adults working together using bags of stuff.

After the low-tech prototypes are created by groups of two to three children and one to three adults working together, each group presents their ideas to the whole team. We designate one adult team member to take notes on the *Big Ideas* on a white board during these presentations. As each team presents, the note-taker writes down the ideas that are surprising, most repeated among groups, or ideas that receive the most reaction from the whole team (see Figure 12.8). After the presentations, the team discusses these ideas and decides which to pursue. We have found that using a bag of art supplies can strongly support bringing children into the design process.

We have found value in tailoring the materials with which to prototype to specific projects. For example, we now often brainstorm on large sheets of paper, which allows numerous design partners to gather around a table or floor space to collaboratively work on one idea (see Figure 12.2). This two-dimensional brainstorming technique has been especially useful when working on screen-based interfaces. The advantage of the large paper versus a small sheet of paper is the collaboration and elaboration that can occur by gathering around one large workspace. We have also learned that it is sometimes necessary to tailor the contents of the Bags of Stuff to a specific project. For example, when exploring technology involving music, it is necessary to include auditory supplies—such as bells and noisemakers.

Sticky Noting is a Cooperative Inquiry technique for critiquing an existing technology or the prototype of a new one. The technique begins with

Figure 12.2 Children and adults brainstorming together using large sheets of paper.

all adults and children using a technology. As they are working, all partners write down on Sticky Notes what they like or dislike about the current technology, and any suggested changes to the technology. Each like, dislike, or design idea is written on a separate sticky note. As the notes are written, they are gathered and given to an adult researcher who places them on a large wall space (see Figure 12.3). One or more researchers then groups the notes in categories (e.g., likes, dislikes, design ideas) as well as subcategories which emerge from the sticky note comments. For example, many partners might like where the buttons are placed, or possibly lots of partners dislike the audio used. The outcome is a kind of informal frequency analysis [21] which shows possible trends that can inform directions for the next iteration of a technology.

One of our most recent techniques is *Layered Elaboration* [22]. In Layered Elaboration, design partners either create or are provided with a base design on which to elaborate and iterate. As each small group elaborates on the original design, a sheet of clear acetate is laid over the original design. Additional sheets of acetate can be added so that each group can add their ideas without "destroying" the original, or the work of other groups. Between iterations, we hold *stand up meetings* in which design partners quickly explain their ideas before the design is passed on to another group for further elaboration.

At various times during the design process, we ask all partners to reflect on their experiences by writing or drawing in journals, videotaping activities, and having large group discussions [12]. We find that reflecting in this way can help all members, adults and children alike, to clarify ideas and continue the elaborative creative process. These reflective experiences can

Likes	Dislikes	Design Ideas

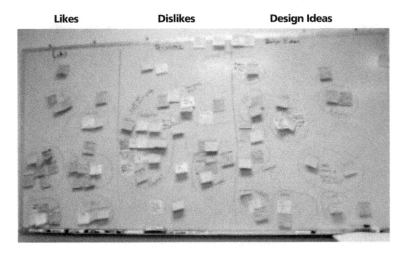

Figure 12.3 Sticky notes clustered into big ideas within likes, dislikes, and design ideas.

be adapted for use with all ages as children who cannot yet write can draw or speak about their ideas. If a child chooses to draw, an adult team member will sit with that child, and with his/her permission, annotate the drawn reflections in writing to provide clarification for later analysis. Likewise, if a child prefers, he/she can tell his/her ideas to an adult design partner who will enter them into the child's journal (see Figure 12.4).

Changes to Cooperative Inquiry Over the Years

Through the years, Cooperative Inquiry has continued to change and grow. As we created a set of methods that worked well for children, we discovered that "children" was too broad an age range. The children on our longstanding design team are 7–11 years old; however, we have worked with children both older and younger than this range, and found that each has their own unique needs.

When working with older children (ages 10–13), for example, the children needed more specific guidance when low-tech prototyping [23]. When working with younger children (ages 4–6), we discovered they needed more support to effectively collaborate [13]. This ultimately led to the creation of a new Cooperative Inquiry technique called *Mixing Ideas*. In Mixing Ideas, individual team members each begin with an idea and then follow a step-by-step method of combining the ideas into one big plan [14]. The support given in the combining process through Mixing Ideas is often enough to support the fragile egos of young children and help them see their influence on the final product. Helping the team to explicitly see the

Figure 12.4 Adults and children reflecting and recording in journals.

combining of ideas by using the Mixing Ideas technique also can help to build cohesion on the team.

Over the years, we have also found it necessary on occasion to modify how we work with children in the design process to meet our evolving needs. For example, in the early days of our intergenerational design partnerships, we did a lot of *technology immersion* with children in order to better understand how they used technology [24]. While observing children in the long-term use of a technology can be valuable, we have found this particular activity to be time-consuming, and the results we were getting seemed to be less helpful than we had hoped in that the information gathered from these techniques did not contribute significantly enough to the design of new technology to support the amount of time needed to complete them.

In designing with and for children, we recognize three underlying dimensions of the roles of children in the design process; they are *the relationship to developers, the relationship to technology,* and *the goals for inquiry* [8]. Each of these dimensions encompasses a continuum of possibilities based on the role the child plays in the design process [8] (see Figure 12.5). In keeping with our philosophy of continually revisiting our method to ensure that it is the best that it can be, later in this paper, we will explore how these dimensions can be expanded upon to meet the needs of today's children.

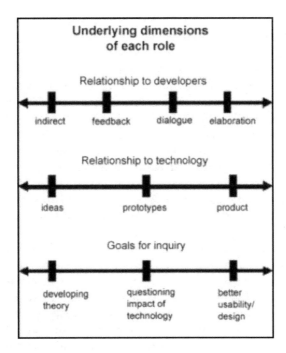

Figure 12.5 Dimensions of roles in the design process.

Cooperative Inquiry and Idea Elaboration

We have found that the most important goal of any design partnership between adults and children is idea elaboration [8]. Idea elaboration begins when one team member (adult or child) shares an idea with the team. From this idea, a new thought or direction may be inspired by another adult or child. When these ideas build upon each other to create new ideas, ultimately it may be difficult to remember whose ideas they were originally. Many of our techniques directly support idea elaboration. Both adults and children share in the process together so that all views are incorporated.

It can be said that the elaboration process is the hallmark of a good design team with or without children. However, idea elaboration is often quite difficult for young people—and can become more so when they are expected to elaborate with adults. More commonly, adults conceive of ideas and either teach them to children or ask for feedback. The notion of elaborating on each other's ideas in a team that consists of adults and children is more difficult, and therefore these teams should use design techniques created to encourage and enhance elaboration. Since elaboration is so central to the design approach of Cooperative Inquiry, this goal of elaboration influences all that we do in our design partnerships.

Cooperative Inquiry in Practice

We are often asked to explain how Cooperative Inquiry looks in practice. While each team may conduct their activities differently depending on the context and resources, what follows offers a snapshot of our experience.

Our sessions run twice a week, after school, in our lab at the university. While this lab space is shared by all researchers in our lab, the space is kid-friendly—it includes a floor-level table, comfortable chairs, couches, and inviting places to sit (Figures 12.1–12.4, 12.6, and 12.8 show work in our lab). Before these twice-weekly sessions, which run through the academic year, we have a two-week design team boot camp each summer in which our researchers and child design partners participate in two intensive weeks of daily, day-long design partner activities.

When the children arrive for a design session, they eat a snack together with the adults participating in that day's design session. This helps to ease children and adults from their everyday lives into their role as design partner. While all child design partners join every session (barring sickness or vacation), adult design partners attend sessions relevant to their research. We generally have 6–8 children and 3–4 adults at a session.

After the snack, we begin the work of a session. We could be using Bags of Stuff to design the iPod of the future. We might be using Sticky Notes to critique a newer version of a partner's website. We might go outside to test a new mobile technology built by one of our graduate students. No matter what the activity, we end by coming together to have a large group discussion, share our ideas, and think about future directions. At the end of the session, the children leave, and the adults remain to debrief and discuss the day's activities, outcomes, and what's next.

ASSUMPTIONS ABOUT COOPERATIVE INQUIRY

Although Cooperative Inquiry has been adopted and widely used, some researchers have questions concerning the specific techniques and the value of working with children during the design process. By discussing and addressing the following seven assumptions about Cooperative Inquiry, we hope to support the growth and evolution of codesign with children. It should be noted that although some of these assumptions reference published papers, others have been brought to our attention through informal means such as conversations with our colleagues. Our intent in this section is to address these issues in a manner intended to clarify the intent and implementation of Cooperative Inquiry. These clarifications are based on our experience working with children using the Cooperative Inquiry method on a continual and regular basis twice every week of the school year, and for two full-time weeks over the summer, for nearly 15 years.

Assumption One: Adults Are Acceptable Proxies for Children In the Design Process

Some colleagues have asked us why we work with children, and why we do not just work with adults as proxies for children in the design process. Despite the fact that we were all seven-year-olds once, no adult member of our team is a seven-year-old today. The technological complexity and richness of a child's environment today is different than the childhood environment in which today's adults grew up [25] and [26]. Today's children are experts at what it means to be a child today.

Beyond this, it is often argued that adults with training in child development, such as teachers or psychologists, should be able to represent the needs of the children they work with. This approach has been used especially in cases where the target population is considered "difficult"—such as children with autism [27]. While there are additional challenges to working with difficult children as design partners, there are those, ourselves included, who advocate partnering with children with special needs [28] and [15]. We have often found that adults who work with children are influenced by the way in which they work with children, and that many times, even given the best intentions, they are thinking of their own needs (e.g., classroom organization, discipline) as opposed to the needs of the child.

An example of the way in which children are able to voice their technological requirements in a way that adults cannot came many years ago. We were given a technology which was a shared surface on which adults could collaborate. It was intended for office use. In order for the technology to work, users had to sit on a magnetic foam pad for their finger to be recognized on the computing surface. In our effort to redesign the technology so that children could "finger paint" on the screen [13], we quickly discovered that not a single child would sit still when they went to draw on the surface.

These children had been talking for months about magic keys for use with computers of the future—keys that could open up treasure boxes and let you play special games. Our team realized that the magnetic pads did not need to be for sitting—they could become magic keys. We mounted the surface vertically and cut the pads into the shape of keys for the children to hold in order to make the Magic Wall work. If users did not hold the magic key, then there would be no magic, and thus, no drawing. Working with these children streamlined our process to quickly come up with a kid-friendly solution to a potentially development-halting issue.

Assumption Two: Existing Power Structures Between Adults and Children Cannot be Overcome

We once asked one of our young design partners to help us figure out how to help adults become better listeners. He was eight years old and had been a design partner for over a year. After some brainstorming of ideas such as "microphones that help make children's voices louder" and "checking adult's ears" to be sure they could hear, our young design partner grew quiet, wondering if anything on this list could "really work". Finally, he simply said, "You just have to be patient with them, since they only know what adults know. But when we're patient you can learn from adults and they will learn, too. We all need to talk together and listen together. Sometimes people have to remember to hear first and then talk" [29, p. 8]. This young design partner has taken an issue that concerns many researchers and turned it on its head—instead of adults having to patiently listen to children, he saw it as his job to allow the adults their shortcomings, and to work with the adults despite the challenges. Still, many researchers question whether the pre-existing power differentials inherent between children and adults can be adequately modified to produce a true partnership [25], [30] and [9], or if they are simply too socially engrained to be overcome. While we agree that these power issues exist, we would argue that they can be resolved, especially in the context of design partnering. Others have pointed out how important it is to do this, especially in cultures where the power differentials between adults and children are especially pronounced [31]. Overcoming power differentials in any context takes time and specific techniques.

The issue of time is unique to each team. Given the long-term commitment of our child design partners at the University of Maryland, time is a luxury that we have. We find that most children at first are not entirely comfortable with allowing us to change their idea of power structures, but, over time, they become comfortable with the idea of the adults on the team as their design peers.

There are numerous techniques that we use to change these perceptions of power differentials, including wearing informal clothing, using informal language, not raising hands to speak, everyone being on a first-name basis, eating together, and sitting on the floor together (see Figure 12.6) [32], [2], [12], [26], and [22]. We also find that during our summer two weeks which kick off our research year, informal fun time together is important for building relationships. We do this through adults and children participating together in activities like playing outside, visiting the campus farm, and participating in scavenger hunts (see Figure 12.6). These activities, which seem simple, have great influence when undertaken by adults and children together.

Additionally, we "pay" our child design partners with a small technology gift, such as an iPod shuffle or robot dog, at the end of each year [32]. Offering our children the kind of pay that we can, given child labor laws, shows them that they are valued contributors to the group. Other teams have gone so far as to involve children in the grant-writing process and to involve them even in decisions on how they will partner with adults [33].

However, the power pendulum can swing too far, and, if adult partners are not mindful, the children can end up dictating the sessions. It is quite

Figure 12.6 Changing the power structures between adults and children: left, informal play (scavenger hunt) activities; right, adults and children sit together on the floor.

typical that a new adult who joins our team will be so concerned that the children have a voice in design sessions that they essentially offer no input. This is not the way an intergenerational design team using Cooperative Inquiry should function. As mentioned earlier, one of the most important goals of Cooperative Inquiry is idea elaboration, in which adults and children build on each other's ideas.

There are some roles in Cooperative Inquiry in which adults do maintain typical adult responsibilities. For example, adults on a design team must provide structure to the design sessions and keep sessions on pace to accomplish the design tasks. This means adult design partners must plan the basic flow of design sessions before the children arrive. Occasionally, an adult will need to step into a caregiver role, for example if a child needs to use the rest room we will walk into the hallway to ensure they safely make it there and back, or if two child design partners are clearly not getting along we might need to intervene to help mitigate an argument between a seven-year-old and a nine-year-old before feelings are hurt. It is important at any time that an adult is fulfilling these typically adult roles that we maintain our roles as partners—and that we treat children at all times with the same respect we would afford adults.

We do not try to change all pre-existing adult/child relationships, merely the ones that exist in the context of the design process. We have never had a report from a child, parent, or teacher where overcoming power structures within our lab have caused a child to behave inappropriately in school or at home. We find that children are able to differentiate between contexts and how to behave differently in different contexts.

Assumption Three: There Are Specific Characteristics That a Child Must Have in Order to be a Design Partner

One concern often brought up is that child design partners must be academically and/or technologically advanced. Researchers may worry that to be effective design partners, children need to be extremely expressive [34]. We have found that being smart or tech-savvy does not necessarily equate to being able to collaborate well. In fact, it may be more difficult for an academically smart child to collaborate since he or she may have less of a need to do so on a regular basis. As we are situated in a university setting, people often wonder if we work with particularly smart children. We have no such criteria. If we are looking for any specific characteristic in our design partners, it is to create a more diverse team. Thus, we strive for a rough balance of gender, age, and ethnicity.

For design teams working in schools, museums, or other settings beyond the direct control of the researchers, the idea that certain criteria need to be met in order to be a design partner can be hard to overcome. Often, a school will want to "impress" the researchers by offering only their "best" students as design partners [31]. In our own research, the ability to choose design partners has sometimes been usurped by the school or setting [35]; however, we do not define a set of preconditions for children other than being able to commit to participating on the team.

Assumption Four: There Is No Distinction Between Informant and Design Partner

A common question we have been asked is to clarify the difference between the levels of involvement children can have in the design process, most notably the distinction between informant and design partner [8] (see Figure 12.7).

Informant design came to prominence in the late 1990s [9] and [10]. Informant design advocates working with children in the design process at specific points during the design process when their input is considered to be the most valuable [36]. On the other hand, with design partnering, children are involved in the design process at all stages [2]. The continuity of child involvement is the essential difference in the two methods. Informants are called in when their thoughts and advice are needed. Design partners are equal stakeholders throughout the design process. The relationship to adult designers for a child informant is one of having a dialogue, whereas the relationship to adult designers for a child design partner is one of elaboration (Figure 12.5).

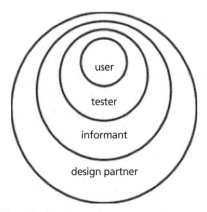

Figure 12.7 Design roles assumed by children [8]. This figure shows the increasing involvement that children can have in the design process.

As children who are involved as design partners enter into a long-term agreement, there is time at the beginning of their tenure as a design partner to train them. At any given time, our team includes both new and veteran child design partners. We have found that it often takes months for a child to become a true design partner—one who understands and can use our methods and techniques, and who is not afraid of offering opinions and communicating ideas.

Some of the confusion in the distinction between informant and design partner likely stems from the fact that though the involvement of the children is different, some of the techniques, such as low-tech prototyping, are the same. Although the technique may be the same, what the child is able to contribute to in the design process may be fundamentally different. With informant design, the goal is for children to have a dialogue with and provide feedback to adults, whereas for design partnering, the primary goal is elaboration, which is a fundamental difference in the underlying dimension of how children relate to adults (see Figure 12.5) [8]. The role of an informant can be likened to that of a consultant [37], brought in at the time when his/her input is the most needed. The goal of building the idea together (design partner), as opposed to having a dialogue and then adults going back to work to create the ideas (informant), is quite different. This is not to say one is better than the other, only that these roles of informant and design partner are different.

Assumption Five: Children Come Up With Ideas That Are Fantastical—And Unusable

We need to value the imaginations of children, because young people can remind us of the obvious and teach us to consider the impossible. We need to empower children to share their ideas in ways that enable adults to truly hear and appreciate what they are saying [8]. Much of what is exciting about design partnering with children is the fantastical ideas that are proposed. Without these cutting-edge, often visionary ideas, our technology process would stagnate. More than once the adults on our team have been puzzled by an issue, taken it to the design team, and been overwhelmed by the onslaught of obvious solutions the children help us to imagine.

During brainstorming, our teams will often design ideas that we clearly cannot build—for example, a rocket ship with a teleportation device. Part of the process of working with children as design partners is to have creative, thoughtful adults who are able to hear what children are saying and pull out the Big Ideas that are workable for the technology—all as a part of the elaboration process (see Figure 12.8) [38]. The key is to realize

Figure 12.8 Top: Artifacts from a bags of stuff activity; Bottom: The big ideas gleaned from group discussion of the low-tech prototypes.

that it is not the rocket ship or the teleportation that the children thought we could build tomorrow—rather a mobile technology (rocket ship) that could socially network with their friends (teleportation). These underlying truths are often discovered in large group discussions at the end of sessions in which adults and children ask critical questions to each other about designs, such as "Why does it need to be a rocket ship?" and "We can't build a teleportation device by next week. What would be the next best thing?"

Some have voiced concerns, as a premise rather than a conclusion, that technology created through the intergenerational design process is not carried to fruition nor is the resultant technology better than it would have been without the input of child design partners [39] and [40]. While we cannot prove empirically that the resultant technology is "better", over the years of working with child design partners, our design team has produced numerous and varying types of technology. Together, we have explored making new storytelling worlds [41] and [42]; travelled to new outdoor places with mobile technologies [43]; taken new digital library journeys [12] and [44]; and built bridges between children from different cultures [45].

Assumption Six: The Children Involved in Design Teams Are Limited Representatives

We are often asked how so few children can represent the needs of all children. People worry that the input given by children will be skewed to the specific children involved in the process [34]. We believe this to be no truer of a team using Cooperative Inquiry than with any design team, made up of adults or children. We strive to recruit children who are diverse in socioeconomic status, gender, ethnicity, and age, in order to gain the most diverse views possible when designing, as we also do with adults.

Additionally, we feel that the issue of generalizability is misplaced in reference to child design partners. The children we partner with are design partners—not testers of technology. Though we strive for diversity in both adult and child design partners, a statistically representative sample is not necessary for the design process. Ensuring a representative sample is necessary for instances when we are empirically testing a product [21], not for when we are designing. We do, however, sometimes find the need to consult with a larger group of children than our design partners. At that point, we ask other children to participate as users, testers, or informants [8] to supplement the work of our design team.

Another issue that has been raised is that, once children are trained as design partners, they may no longer represent the views and needs of children as a user group [46]. Over the years of working with children to become design partners, we have found that design partnering does not fundamentally change who children are or their world views. They still care about the same things that they cared about before—but now they have the skills and tools necessary to communicate their wants and needs as designers and as a part of a team with the power to create technology.

Assumption Seven: Design Teams Need to Follow the Cooperative Inquiry Method Exactly to be Successful

Cooperative Inquiry is a method that can be applied in many different design situations. While teams have different resources (e.g., time, funding, access to children), we believe that most teams can use and benefit from using some part of Cooperative Inquiry. Certainly many factors need to be taken into account when choosing how best to work with children in the design process, including time and funding available [15]; however, others have found the costs of participatory design in certain situations to be modest [47]. It is important to remember that, at its core, Cooperative Inquiry is a method made up of a collection of techniques used in conjunction with a philosophy of partnership and elaboration. Not all techniques must be used by all teams, and all techniques can be adapted and modified to best fit for a team's specific needs. As explained in the initial Cooperative Inquiry paper, "These techniques do not necessarily offer a magic formula for working with children, but rather a philosophy and approach to research..." [2, p. 594]. Numerous researchers around the world have design partnered with children in varying ways to best meet their needs. Some use an overall "scaled-down" model of Cooperative Inquiry [48]. Others adapt it to a context other than a university lab—such as a museum [30], school [25] and [49], or field trips [39]. Other modifications include changing the adult to child ratio [50] and [49], and time of day [25]. Cooperative Inquiry is a widely applicable method that allows children and adults to work together to design technology.

Challenges of Design Partnering

While we believe in the value of partnering with children, at times these techniques can be difficult, time-consuming, and even frustrating. More than one of our sessions has included yelling children and frustrated adults. However, more often than not, we walk away with a surprising idea that could have never come from just adults or children.

There are incontrovertibly challenges inherent in design partnering. Schedules must be accommodated—not only those of school-age children with other extracurricular activities, but also of graduate students, staff, and faculty members trying to balance research, classes, and other responsibilities. As mentioned earlier, the time it takes for a child to become truly comfortable as a design partner can often be a matter of months. During this time, children may be less likely to offer insightful ideas in the design process. Time and longevity are vital—we have rarely found a child who walks through the door on day one and is ready to participate as a full-fledged design partner. They need time to learn the method and its techniques and to get used to the process.

Likewise, there is a learning curve for adults in becoming design partners. Over the years, our team has included adults from a wide range of fields. We find that there tend to be field-specific challenges for adults in learning to design with children. Educators need time to get used to the idea of working with children as opposed to teaching them. Computer scientists and engineers often need time to learn how to talk with children. Given time, most adults who are invested in producing quality technology for children and who believe in the process can develop into effective design partners.

DESIGN PARTNERING TODAY AND IN THE FUTURE

Through the years, we have continually modified, extended, and expanded the Cooperative Inquiry method as contexts and times change. Together with our child design partners, we have created technologies we believe were developmentally appropriate for the children of their time. These technologies range from storytelling robots [26] to online digital libraries [51]. Fifteen years into designing with children, we see that the children of today are no longer the children we began design partnering with before the turn of the twenty-first century. While today's world poses new trends in designing with and for children, it is important to note that the underlying roles that children can play in the design process have not changed; rather, the underlying dimensions of roles are expanding due to new technologies and contexts.

We find that there are four salient characteristics of children today: they are internationally aware, independent, interactive, [1] and information active. As technology and progress continue to shrink the world by making it more accessible, and as children are becoming more internationally aware, there is a need to partner with children across the country and globe including what is considered as the developing world. Today's children's independence can be supported by designing for mobility. Social computing addresses the interactive nature of today's children. Finally, the information activity of today's children begs us to address the ubiquity of search. In this section, we look at each of these in turn, including considerations and guidelines for how to design with and for children given each characteristic.

The Shrinking and Developing World

As children grow up and ultimately enter the workforce, they will find it necessary to collaborate and communicate with their peers not only in their immediate physical workplace, but also in the global workplace. Children are becoming aware that not all people are equally advantaged—not only in their own country, but around the globe. Therefore, partnering with children who are far away and in part of the developing world is important to encourage our children's empathy, community, and future well-being. Our efforts to engage in distributed design in our own research include partnering with children across the country and the globe in our digital libraries research, as well as with the United Nations Children's Fund, which works to advance children's rights internationally (http://www.unicef.org/). We have worked in the area of the developing world in working with the People in Need Website which connected children in American with children in Haiti [52].

Considerations for Design Partnering With Children in the Shrinking and Developing World

The immediate issue in design partnering with children in the shrinking and developing world is how to do it. The initial Cooperative Inquiry techniques were developed with the assumption that all researchers, child and adult alike, would be physically colocated. Working with partners half-way around the world adds to the dimension of a child's relationship to developers—we no longer need only to think about the kinds of interaction that children will have with adults, but we also must consider partner location which can range on the continuum from colocated to entirely distributed. Furthermore, we should consider whether our partners are in developing or industrialized countries, and what this means for their access to technology, both socially and physically.

In designing with and for children in the developing world, there are practical considerations to manage. We need to be more hardware agnostic and consider accessibility and per device cost. Additionally, deployment matters [51]. The ability to get technology into the hands of children cannot be overlooked. It is our belief that the HCI community should consider the immediate impact of what we develop on users today. We must also consider technology, latency, and maintenance problems as the developing world has different issues in technology than the industrialized world. Finally, designers must consider more than just the technology. The politics or social impact of getting people to use what we are creating can often be challenging. We must make changes in what we are creating based on these considerations.

Guidelines for Design Partnering With Children in the Shrinking and Developing World

In partnering with children in distributed locations, we have found that updating some of our techniques made it possible to engage in distributed codesign. The technology available to researchers today enables us to overcome the geographical distance that may exist between partners. We have found that, even in emerging countries, we may be able to locate the technology we need to support this kind of collaboration.

A technique that we have found useful when working with groups that are geographically disparate is to design online. Our team has created a tool to support distributed codesign, DisCo [53]. Using an easy-to-understand interface that runs on computers with access to the internet, DisCo supports asynchronous codesign in which child and adult design partners may be geographically non-colocated. The eventual goal of DisCo is to connect children across the globe, including those in the developing world.

Mobile Technology

Mobile devices—including cell phones, personal digital assistants, and now tablets—are inundating the world [54] and [55]. According to one estimate [55], on average, more than four of every five people worldwide have access to mobile phones. In the United States, approximately 87% of adults have a cell phone, and of those 46% have a smartphone [56]. With this proliferation of mobile devices, children are using them more often [57] and [58]. Almost three quarters of the top selling apps in the iTunes store are for preschool or elementary-aged children [59]. Parents are upgrading their mobile devices and giving their old technology to their children to play with [60]. Beyond the wide accessibility of mobile devices, these smaller devices are more natural for young children as they can more readily be used while in motion—and most children are active. Physical movement and play involve mobility, which are inherent characteristics important for the social and cognitive development of young children [61]. Indeed, mobile devices are becoming an even more integral part of the lives of adults and children.

Considerations for Designing Mobile Technology

While designing mobile technologies for children, there are a few considerations that need be made. First, mobile device usage is generally spontaneous for short bursts of time [36]. Rarely are mobile devices used for hours on end; instead, they are used for short periods of time to look up an address or phone number, send a text message, check email, or play a game. Mobile technologies can interrupt users as several of these provide alerts which can distract the user from other tasks and compete for attention. We call the interplay between the virtual and physical worlds *Digital/Physical Switching*. We do not see this trend in technology use as inherently good or bad because we are still learning about its impact on a child's world. What we can say is that it is something we only minimally saw in the early days of computing because children were stationary at desktop computers, tethered to mice and keyboards. We expect as mobile technologies become even more common than traditional computers, more Digital/Physical Switching may lead children to more multi-tasking in learning and social situations.

Guidelines for Designing Mobile Technology

Mobile devices can be used in many contexts. Because of the importance of context, mobile technologies should be designed in the context for which they are intended. For example, in designing technologies for field trips, we found it necessary to have children not only use these systems outside of a laboratory setting, but also do design activities within that outdoor setting [43]. Since technologies will be used in a real-world environment, evaluation of technologies should be in their native context. Traditional lab usability tests miss the richness and chaos of a real-world setting [62]. Lastly, mobility should be viewed as a purpose and not just a feature of a particular device. Most mobile technologies have the added benefit of being easily carried by a child from place to place. By instilling a reason for the child to use the device in real-world context, these devices can encourage active learning. For example, a mobile collaborative story application [63] can spur children to explore their environment and encourage exploration, elaboration, and learning. Such an application has the purpose of mobility—where children must be moving to make the best use of the application, instead of simply being able to carry their device wherever they go.

Social Computing

Many technologies today, for children and for adults, focus on what we think of as social computing—that is, technology that brings people together. There are many forms of social computing. Online, people are brought together through online social sites like Facebook. Physically, people can be brought together using mobile devices designed to encourage collaboration. We must consider all types of social computing—virtual and physical, collocated and disparate—when designing for today's children.

Considerations for Social Computing

When designing for social computing, we should keep in mind whether the resultant technology is intended for colocated or distributed use. Even though we believe that social computing can be fun, motivating, and possibly even educational, when designing online environments for children, we must be mindful of their safety. Children are inherently social beings and they enjoy interaction, sometimes leading to divulging of inappropriate information. At the same time, we need to be respectful that children are important and self-aware, and often want to be in control. Walking the line of keeping children safe and allowing them the necessary freedom and challenge to grow in online social situations is an important consideration.

Additionally, we need to remember that not all of children's collaborations involving technology are with other children. Intergenerational collaboration occurs often around technology—with a father showing his daughter a new app for finding sports scores on the iPhone, to a grandfather reading a story online with a grandson. These intergenerational interactions offer opportunities for growth for both partners. Finally, as mentioned earlier, we must not always think of the virtual and physical worlds as entirely separate. They have already begun to overlap, in technology such as Webkinz, where a technologically enhanced stuffed animal has another life online. The popularity of social computing applications that encourage an interaction between the virtual and physical world will continue to grow.

Guidelines for Designing Social Computing

In designing social computing applications for children, there are some guidelines we should remember. Finding an appropriate setting in which to observe a child interacting in social computing is difficult. If we bring children into a lab setting, we more than likely change the manner in which they interact with the technology. A child on his/her bed at home with a laptop is likely to have a different comfort level and different behaviors than one asked to sit in an adult chair in front of a desktop at a lab. As much as possible, when gathering design requirements for social computing, we should be venturing out into the child's world, rather than forcing them into ours.

Additionally, the design process should reflect the eventual product. For example, when designing products to encourage non-colocated interaction, researchers should consider online codesign such as DisCo. Likewise, if a product is intended to support intergenerational interaction, then participants of each age group should be involved in the design process. Finally, and most practically, we should be mindful that codesign for multiple devices are hard to deploy. It is ideal to have the same number of devices as designers—which is not always possible, especially in the early prototyping stages. This can be ameliorated by using low-tech design techniques as much as possible at the beginning of the design process.

Ubiquity of Search

Today, children are often online. Rideout et al. [64] report that 84% of children between the ages of 8 and 18 go online at home. Extending beyond the home, Lenhart et al. [65] report that 95% of children between the ages of 12 and 17 go online in some setting. Children today search the internet, and expect to find a wealth of information. The kinds of searching that children do vary greatly [66], from simple searches at home (i.e., searching for game sites) to complex searches at school (i.e., composing a paper over the course of a few months). Given this ubiquity of search and the variety of search tasks, it is important that we think of children as we design search engines for them—not only remembering the developmental and cognitive levels of children, but also thinking of the whole child including the social and affective implications of search design [67] and [66].

Considerations for Ubiquity of Search

Children enter queries into search tools such as Google in natural language, as questions, and, less frequently, as keywords. While search engines have gotten better at handling the varied queries from children over time, they cannot handle complex searches that require breaking a search apart into smaller pieces [66]. Once past the keyword search, children often find results pages challenging [66] and [68], having difficulty discerning that results are clickable [68], knowing which sources are reliable, or having the required reading proficiency to understand the website snippet provided [66]. Therefore, when designing search engines for children, researchers must pay special attention to the results pages and ensure that they are navigable, understandable, and usable by children.

Finally, we should consider that most searches no longer occur within a self-contained information space. In the past, children's searches involved mainly finite data sets, such as those included on a CD encyclopaedia or DVD-Rom [69], or on preselected category search sites, such as Yahooligans! [70]. Today, children routinely search the internet with its boundless available information.

Guidelines for Designing for Ubiquity of Search

Due to the pervasive nature of the internet and search engines for children, using finite data sets is no longer an optimal way to design and research. In the past, creating small data sets simply for the purposes of research was valid. However, as children today search tremendous amounts of information on the internet, in order to understand how children search and filter results, it is imperative that they are working with authentic available data.

When designing for the ubiquity of search in our own foray into studying children's search practices on the internet [71] and [66], we discovered that in-context design and testing is crucial. Children search in their home or school environments, not in contrived lab settings. Rideout [64] reports those youths are more likely to go online at home (57%) than at school (20%) or other places such as the library or friends' homes (14%). Their performance at home is necessarily affected by all of the distractions inherent in daily life—just as it would outside of the study context. Therefore, working with children in their natural environment(s) is imperative to guiding real-world design. Finally, industry is listening. Our partner for our search engine study is Google. They are invested in providing children with optimal search engines, and it is our job as designers to investigate how to do this.

CONCLUSION

Over the years, through our research we have both created new technologies for children [43], [12] and [42] and developed new ways to work with children in the design process [13], [14] and [53]. Today, we continue our efforts in collaborating with young people, pushing the boundaries of designing technologies with and for children. Today, we need to consider design partnering with all children, including those in the developing world. Today, we need to consider design methods that can support the design of mobile and social technology, that support the endless curiosity of children as they search for what matters. We feel that Cooperative Inquiry fulfills these needs as it meets its original goals and intents and as it continues to expand and evolve.

ACKNOWLEDGMENTS

This paper, and in fact all of our work, would not be possible without the help of our child design partners, to whom we are forever grateful. We thank our numerous adult design partners who work tirelessly with those child design partners. Thank you to our colleagues Juan Pablo Hourcade, Franca Garzotto, and Beth Foss for insightful comments and feedback on early drafts and ideas for this paper. In addition, there have been countless organizations that have funded our work over the years, and to each and every group we are thankful. In particular, we would like to acknowledge the National Science Foundation, the Institute of Museum and Library Services, the World Bank, Microsoft Corp., the National Park Service, Discovery Communications, and Google.

NOTES

1. This chapter is a modified version of a journal paper. The citation is: Guha, M., Druin, A., & Fails, J. (January, 2013). Cooperative Inquiry revisited: Reflections of the past and guidelines for the future of intergenerational codesign. *International Journal of Child-Computer Interaction, 1*(1), 14–23.
2. APA citation and reference formats were not used in the original version of the journal article. The original formats for citations and references have been kept in this revised version of the paper.

REFERENCES

1. Druin, A. (2009). *Mobile technology for children: Designing for interaction and learning.* Amsterdam, Netherlands: Morgan Kauffman.
2. Druin, A. (1999, May). Cooperative inquiry: Developing new technologies for children with children. In Proceedings of the SIGCHI conference on Human Factors in Computing Systems, Pittsburgh, PA (pp. 592–599). New York: ACM.
3. Greenbaum, J., & Kyng, M. (Eds.). (1991). *Design at work: Cooperative design of computer systems.* Hillsdale, NJ: Lawrence Erlbaum.

4. Schuler, D., & Namioka, A. (Eds.). (1993). *Participatory design: Principles and practices*. Hillsdale, NJ: Lawrence Erlbaum.

5. Beyer, H., & Holtzblatt, K. (1998). *Contextual design: Defining customer-centered systems*. San Francisco, CA: Morgan Kauffman.

6. Nardi, B. (Ed.). (1996). *Context and consciousness: Activity theory and human–computer interaction*. Cambridge, MA: MIT Press.

7. Suchman, L. (1987). *Plans and situated actions: The problem of human-machine communication*. Cambridge, UK: Cambridge University Press.

8. Druin, A. (2002). The role of children in the design of new technology. *Behaviour and Information Technology, 21*(1),1–25.

9. Scaife, M., Rogers, Y., Aldrich, F., & Davies, M. (1997, March). Designing for or designing with? Informant design for interactive learning environments. In *CHI '97: Proceedings of the SIGCHI conference on Human factors in computing systems*. Paper presented at SIGCHI Conference on Human Factors in Computing Systems: Looking to the Future, Atlanta, GA (pp. 343–350). New York, NY: ACM.

10. Scaife, M., & Rogers, Y. (1999). Kids as informants: Telling us what we didn't know or confirming what we knew already? In A. Druin (Ed.), *The design of children's technology* (pp. 27–50). San Francisco, CA: Morgan Kaufmann Publishers.

11. Kafai, Y.B. (1999). Children as designers, testers, and evaluators of educational software. In A. Druin (Ed.), *The design of children's technology* (pp. 123–145). San Francisco, CA: Morgan Kauffman.

12. Druin, A. (2005). What children can teach us: Developing digital libraries for children with children. *Library Quarterly, 75*, 20–41.

13. Farber, A., Druin, A., Chipman, G., Julian, D., & Somashekhar, S. (2002, June). How young can our design partners be? In T. Binder, J. Gregory, & I. Wagner (Eds.), *Proceedings of the 2002 Participatory Design Conference*. Paper presented at Participation and Design: Inquiring into the Politics, Contexts and Practices of Collaborative Design Work, Malmo, Sweden (pp. 272–276). Palo Alto, CA: CPSR.

14. Guha, M. L., Druin, A. Chipman, G., Fails, J. A., Simms, S., & Farber, A. (2004, June). Mixing ideas: A new technique for working with young children as design partners. In *IDC '04 Proceedings of the 2004 conference on Interaction design and children: Building a community*. Paper presented at IDC 2004: 3rd International Conference for Interaction Design and Children: Building a Community, College Park, MD (pp. 35–42). Baltimore, MD: ACM.

15. Guha, M. L., Druin, A., & Fails, J. A. (2008, June). Designing with and for children with special needs: an inclusionary model. In *Proceedings of the Seventh International Conference on Interaction Design and Children*. Paper presented at IDC 2008: 7th International Conference on Interactive Design and Children, Chicago, IL (pp. 61–64). New York, NY: ACM.

16. Rhode, J., Stringer, M., Toye, E. F., Simpson, A. R., & Blackwell, A. F. (2003, July). Curriculum-focused design. In S. MacFarlane, T. Nicol, J. Read, & L. Snape (Eds.). *Small users, big ideas: Proceedings of interaction design and children 2003*. Paper presented at IDC03: Interaction Design and Children, Preston, England UK (pp. 119–126). New York, NY: ACM.

17. Robertson, J. (2002, July). Experiences of designing with children and teachers in the StoryStation project. In S. MacFarlane, T. Nicol, J. Read, & L. Snape (Eds.). *Small users, big ideas: Proceedings of interaction design and children 2003.* Paper presented at IDC03: Interaction Design and Children, Preston, England UK (pp. 29–41). Amsterdam, The Netherlands: IOS Press.

18. Takach, B. S., & Varnhagen, C. (2002, August). Partnering with children to develop an interactive encyclopedia. In M. M. Bekker, P. Markopoulos, & M. Kersten-Tsikalkina (Eds.). *Proceedings of the International Workshop "Interaction Design and Children."* Paper presented at the International Workshop on Interaction Design and Children, Eindhoven, The Netherlands (pp. 129–143). The Netherlands: Shaker.

19. Hornof, A. (2008, June). Working with children with severe motor impairments as design partners. In *Proceedings of the Seventh International Conference on Interaction Design and Children.* Paper presented at IDC 2008: 7th International Conference on Interactive Design and Children, Chicago, IL (pp. 69–72). New York, NY: ACM.

20. Bjerknes, G., & Ehn, P. (1987). *Computers and Democracy: A Scandinavian challenge.* Aldershot, UK Avebury: Gower Publishing Company Ltd.

21. Druin, A., Bederson, B., Hourcade, J. P., Sherman, L., Revelle, G., Platner, M., & Weng, S. (2001, June). Designing a digital library for young children: An intergenerational partnership. In *Proceedings of the 1st ACM/IEEE-CS joint conference on Digital libraries.* Paper presented at JCDL'01: 1st ACM/IEEE-CS Joint Conference on Digital Libraries, Roanoke, VA (pp. 398–405). New York, NY: ACM.

22. Walsh, G., Druin, A. Guha, M. L., Foss, E., Golub, E., Hatley, L., Bonsignore, E., & Franckel, S. (2010, April). Layered Elaboration: A new technique for codesign with children. In E. D. Mynatt, D. Schoner, G. Fitzpatrick, S. E. Hudson, W. K. Edwards, & T. Rodden (Eds.). *Proceedings of the 28th International Conference on Human Factors in Computing Systems.* Paper presented at CHI '10: CHI Conference on Human Factors in Computing Systems, Atlanta, GA (pp. 1237–1240). New York, NY: ACM.

23. Knudtzon, K., Druin, A., Kaplan, N., Summers, K., Chisi, Y., Kulkarn, R., Moulthrop, S., Weeks, A., & Bederson, B. (2003, July). Starting an intergenerational technology design team: a case study. In S. MacFarlane, T. Nicol, J. Read, & L. Snape (Eds.). *Small users, big ideas: Proceedings of Interaction Design and Children 2003.* Paper presented at Interaction Design and Children 2003, Preston, England (pp. 51–58). New York, NY: ACM.

24. Druin, A., Stewart, J., Proft, D., Bederson, B., & Hollan, J. (1997, March). KidPad: A design collaboration between children, technologists, and educators. In *CHI '97: Proceedings of the SIGCHI conference on Human factors in computing systems.* Paper presented at SIGCHI Conference on Human Factors in Computing Systems: Looking to the Future, Atlanta, GA (pp. 463–470). New York, NY: ACM.

25. Large, A., Bowler, L., Beheshti, J. & Nesset, V. (2007). Creating web portals with children as designers: Bonded design and the zone of proximal development. *McGill Journal of Education, 42*(1), 61–82.

26. Montemayor, J., Druin, A., & Hendler, J. (2000). PETS: A personal electronic teller of stories. In A. Druin & J. Hendler (Eds.) *Robots for kids: Exploring new technologies for learning* (pp. 73–108). San Francisco, CA: Morgan Kauffman.

27. De Leo, G., & Leroy, G. (2009, June). Smartphones to facilitate communication and improve social skills of children with severe autism spectrum disorder: Special education teachers as proxies. In *Proceedings of the Seventh International Conference on Interaction Design and Children.* Paper presented at IDC 2008: 7th International Conference on Interactive Design and Children, Chicago, IL (pp. 45–48). New York, NY: ACM.

28. Gibson, L., Gregor, P., & Milne, S. (2002, July). Case study: designing with 'difficult' children. In S. MacFarlane, T. Nicol, J. Read, & L. Snape (Eds.). *Small users, big ideas: Proceedings of interaction design and children 2003.* Paper presented at IDC03: Interaction Design and Children, Preston, England UK (pp. 42–52). Amsterdam, The Netherlands: IOS Press.

29. Druin, A., Hammer, J., Kruskal, A., Lal, A., Schwenn, T.P., Sumida, L., Wagner, R., Alborzi, H., Montemayor, J., & Sherman, L. (2000). How do adults and children work together to design new technology? *ACM SIGCHI Bulletin, 32*(2), 7–8.

30. Roussou, M., Kavalieratou, E., & Doulgeridis, M. (2007, June). Children designers in the museum: applying participatory design for the development of an art education program. In T. Bekker, J. Robertson, & M. B. Skov (Eds.). *Proceedings of the Sixth International Conference for Interaction Design and Children.* Paper presented at IDC07: International Conference on Interaction Design and Children, Aalborg, Denmark (pp. 77–80). New York, NY: ACM.

31. Kam, M., Ramachandran, D., Raghavan, A., Chiu, J., Sahni, U., & Canny, J. (2006, June). Practical considerations for participatory design with rural school children in underdeveloped regions: early reflections from the field. In *IDC '06 Proceedings of the 2006 conference on Interaction design and children.* Paper presented at IDC06: 5th International Conference on Interaction Design and Children, Tampere, Finland (pp. 25–32). New York, NY: ACM.

32. Alborzi, H., Druin, A., Montemayor, J., Sherman, L., Taxen, G., Best, J., Hammer, J., Kruskal, A., Lal, A., Schwenn, T.P., Sumida, L., Wagner, R., & Hendler, J. (2000, August). Designing StoryRooms: interactive storytelling spaces for children. In D. Boyarski & W. A. Kellogg (Eds.), *Proceedings of the 3rd conference on Designing interactive systems: processes, practices, methods, and techniques.* Paper presented at DIS '00: Designing Interactive Systems 2000, Brooklyn, NY (pp. 95–104). New York, NY: ACM.

33. Randolph, J., & Eronen, P. (2007). Developing the learning door: A case study in youth participatory program planning. *Education and Program Planning, 30*(1), 55–65.

34. Moraveji, N., Li, J., Ding, J., O'Kelley, P., & Woolf, S. (2007, April). Comicboarding: using comics as proxies for participatory design with children. In *CHI '07 Proceedings of the SIGCHI Conference on Human Factors in Computing Systems.* Paper presented at SIGCHI conference on Human factors in computing systems: Reach beyond, San Jose, CA (pp. 1371–1374). New York, NY: ACM.

35. Druin, A., Weeks, A., Massey, S., & Bederson, B. (2007, June). Children's interest and concerns when using the International Children's Digital Library: a

four-country case study. In *JCDL '07 Proceedings of the 7th ACM/IEEE-CS joint conference on Digital libraries*. Paper presented at JCDL '07 Joint Conference on Digital Libraries, Vancouver, British Columbia, Canada (pp. 167–176). New York, NY: ACM.

36. Rogers, Y., & Price, S. (2009). How mobile technologies are changing the way children learn. In A. Druin (Ed.), *Mobile technology for children: Designing for interaction and learning* (pp. 3–22). Amsterdam: Morgan Kauffman.

37. Hourcade, J. P. (2008). Interaction design and children. *Foundations and Trends in Human–Computer Interaction, 1*(4), 277–392.

38. Druin, A., Guha, M. L., & Fails, J. A. (2008, April). Giving children a voice in the design of new technology: What's new and old but still works. Invited tutorial presented at CHI '08: CHI Conference on Human Factors in Computing Systems: art. science. balance, Florence, Italy.

39. Kelly, S. R., Mazzone, E., Horton, M., & Read, J. (2006, October). Bluebells: A design method for child-centered product development. In A. Morch, K. Morgan, T. Bratteteig, G. Ghosh, & D. Svanaes (Eds.), *Proceedings of the 4th Nordic Conference on Human-Computer Interaction: Changing Roles*. Paper presented at NordiCHI 2006: The 4th Nordic Conference on Human-Computer Interaction, Oslo, Norway (pp. 361–368). New York, NY: ACM.

40. Mazzone, E., Horton, M., & Read, J. (2004, October). Requirements for a multimedia museum environment. In *Proceedings of the third Nordic conference on Human-Computer interaction*. Paper presented at NordiCHI: Nordic Conference on Human-Computer Interaction, Tampere, Finland (pp. 421–424). New York, NY: ACM.

41. Benford, S., Bederson, B., Akesson, K.P., Bayon, V., Druin, A., Hansson, P., Hourcade, J.P., . . . Taxen, G. (2000, April). Designing storytelling technologies to encourage collaboration between young children. In *Proceedings of the SIGCHI conference on Human factors in computing systems, 2000*. Paper presented at CHI'00: Human Factors in Computing Systems: The Future is Here, The Hague, The Netherlands (pp. 556–563). New York, NY: ACM.

42. Montemayor, J., Druin, A., Chipman, G., Farber, A., & Guha, M.L. (2004). Tools for children to create physical interactive StoryRooms. *Computers in Entertainment: Educating Children Through Entertainment, 2*(1), 12–24.

43. Chipman, G., Druin, A., Beer, D., Fails, J. A., Guha, M. L., & Simms, S. (2006, June). A case study of tangible flags: a collaborative technology to enhance field trips. In *IDC '06 Proceedings of the 2006 conference on Interaction design and children*. Paper presented at IDC06: 5th International Conference on Interaction Design and Children, Tampere, Finland (pp. 1–8). New York, NY: ACM.

44. Hutchinson, H., Bederson, B., & Druin, A. (2006, June). The evolution of the international children's digital library searching and browsing interface. *In IDC '06 Proceedings of the 2006 conference on Interaction design and children*. Paper presented at IDC06: 5th International Conference on Interaction Design and Children, Tampere, Finland (pp. 105–112). New York, NY: ACM.

45. Komlodi, A., Hou, W., Preece, J., Druin, A., Golub, E., Alburo, J., Liao, S., Elkis, A., Resnick, P. (2007). Evaluation of a cross-cultural children's online book community: Lessons learned for sociability, usability, and cultural exchange. *Interacting with Computers, 19*(4), 494–511.

46. Taxen, G. (2003). *Towards Living Exhibitions*. (Doctoral dissertation). Retrieved from Karlstads Universitet http://urn.kb.se/resolve?urn=urn:nbn:se:kth:diva-1616.

47. Taxen, G. (2004, July). Introducing participatory design in museums. In *PDC 04 Proceedings of the eighth conference on Participatory design: Artful integration: Interweaving media, materials and practices—Volume 1*. Paper presented at PDC 2004: The eighth biennial Participatory Design Conference: Artful Integration: Interweaving Media, Materials and Practices, Toronto, Canada (pp. 204–213). New York, NY: ACM.

48. Taxen, G., Druin, A., Fast, C., & Kjellin, M. (2001). KidStory: A technology design partnership with children. *Behaviour and Information Technology, 20*(2), 119–125.

49. Niemi, H., & Ovaska, S. (2007, June). Designing spoken instructions with pre-school children. In T. Bekker, J. Robertson, & M. B. Skov (Eds.), *Proceedings of the Sixth International Conference for Interaction Design and Children*. Paper presented at IDC07: International Conference on Interaction Design and Children, Aalborg, Denmark (pp. 133–136). New York, NY: ACM.

50. Large, A., Nesset, V., Beheshti, J., & Bowler, L. (2006). Bonded design: A novel approach to intergenerational information technology design. *Library & Information Science Research, 28*(1), 64–82.

51. Druin, A., Bederson, B., Rose, A., & Weeks, A. (2009). From New Zealand to Mongolia: Codesigning and deploying a digital library for the world's children. *Children, Youth and Environment: Special Issue on Children in Technological Environments, 19*(1), 34–57.

52. Ellis, K. (Producer & Director). (2009). Edutopia: Kids and adults design new tech tools [video]. Retrieved from http://www.edutopia.org/digital-generation-kidsteam-dana-video.

53. Walsh, G., Druin, A., Guha, M.L., Bonsignore, E., Foss, E., Yip, J., Golub, E., Clegg, T., Brown, Q., & Brewer, R. (2012, June). DisCo: A codesign tool for online, asynchronous distributed child and adult design partners. In *IDC '12 Proceedings of the 11th International Conference on Interaction Design and Children*. Paper presented at IDC '12 The 11th International Conference on Interaction Design and Children, Bremen, Germany (pp. 11–19). New York, NY: ACM.

54. Gartner Newsroom. (2011). Gartner says worldwide mobile connections will reach 5.6 billion in 2011 as mobile data services revenue totals $314.7 billion [Press release]. Retrieved from http://www.gartner.com/it/page.jsp?id=1759714.

55. International Telecom Union (ITU). (2012). Information Communication Technologies (ICT) data and statistics [Data file]. Retrieved from http://www.itu.int/ITU-D/ict/statistics/.

56. Smith, A. (2012, March 1). Nearly half of American adults are smartphone owners. Retrieved from http://pewinternet.org/Reports/2012/Smartphone-Update-2012.aspx.

57. Goldberg, S. (2010, April 27). Parents using smartphones to entertain bored kids. *CNN.com*. Retrieved from http://www.cnn.com/2010/TECH/04/26/smartphones.kids/index.html?hpt=Sbin.

58. Tracey, L. M., Smith, A., Well, A. T., & Wellman, B. (2008, October 19). Networked Families: Parents and spouses are using the internet and cell phones to create a new connectedness that builds on remote connections and shared internet experience. Retrieved from http://www.pewinternet.org/~/media//Files/Reports/2008/PIP_Networked_Family.pdf.pdf.

59. Shuler, C., Levine, Z., & Ree, J. (2012, January 12). iLearn II: An analysis of the education category of Apple's app store. Retrieved from http://joanganzcooneycenter.org/upload_kits/ilearnii.pdf.

60. Yu, R. (2012, March 8). Families trading up to give older iPads to kids, parents. *USA Today*. Retrieved from http://www.usatoday.com/tech/news/story/2012-03-06/apple-ipad-family/53390232/1.

61. Hughes, F. P. (1999). *Children, play, and development.* Needham Heights, MA: Allyn & Bacon.

62. Rogers, Y. (2011). Interaction design gone wild: striving for wild theory. *Interactions, 18*(4), 58–62.

63. Fails, J. A., Druin, A., & Guha, M. L. (2010, June). Mobile collaboration: Collaboratively reading and creating children's stories on mobile devices. In *IDC '10 Proceedings of the 9th International Conference on Interaction Design and Children.* Paper presented at IDC '10: The 9th International Conference on Interaction Design and Children, Barcelona, Spain (pp. 20–29). New York, NY: ACM.

64. Rideout, V., Foehr, U. G., & Roberts, D. F. (2010, January). Generation M2: Media in the Lives of 8–18 year olds. Retrieved from http://www.kff.org/entmedia/upload/8010.pdf.

65. Lenhart, A., Madden, M., Smith, A., Purcell, K., Zickuhr, L., & Rainie, L. (2011, November 9). Teens, kindness, and cruelty on social network sites: How American teens navigate the new world of Digital Citizenship. Retrieved from http://pewinternet.org/Reports/2011/Teens-and-social-media.aspx.

66. Foss, E., Hutchison, H., Druin, A., Brewer, R., Lo, P., Sanchez, L., & Golub, E. (2012). Children's search roles at home: implications for designers, researchers, educators, and parents. *Journal for the American Society of Information Science and Technology, 63*(3), 558–573.

67. Bilal, D. (2005). Children's information seeking and the design of digital interfaces in the affective paradigm. *Library Trends, 54*(2), 197–208.

68. Jochmann-Mannak, H., Huibers, T., Lentz, L., & Sanders, T. (2010, July). Children searching information on the internet: performance on children's interfaces compared to Google. In F. Crestani (Ed.), *Proceedings of the 33rd international ACM SIGIR conference on Research and development in information retrieval.* Paper presented at Sigir '10: The 33rd International Acm Sigir Conference on Research and Development in Information Retrieval, Geneva, Switzerland (pp. 27–35). New York, NY: ACM.

69. Large, A., Beheshti, J., & Breuleux, J. (1998). Information seeking in a multimedia environment by primary school students. *Library and information science research, 20*(4), 343–376.

70. Bilal, D. (2002). Children's use of the Yahooligans! web search engine. III. Cognitive and physical behaviors on fully self-generated search tasks. *Journal of the American Society for Information Science and Technology, 53*(13), 1170–1183.

71. Druin, A., Foss, E., Hutchinson, H., Golub, E., & Hatley, L. (2010, April). Children's roles using keyword search interfaces at home. In *Proceedings of the SIGCHI Conference on Human Factors in Computing Systems*. Paper presented at CHI '10: CHI Conference on Human Factors in Computing Systems, Atlanta, GA (pp. 413–422). New York, NY: ACM.

CHAPTER 13

TRANSITIONS IN WELL-BEING AND RECOVERY

Cooperative Inquiry Involving Older Adults With Lived Experience of a Mental Illness

Kathleen Thompson
Northern Kentucky University

ABSTRACT

This chapter summarizes Action Research involving Cooperative Inquiry (CI). The CI discussed in this chapter focused on understanding the factors that support the well-being and recovery of older people living with a serious mental illness from the perspective of older adults themselves. The 16-month study involved a group of nine adults ranging in age from 46 to 67, who all live with a serious mental illness. The coresearchers created a qualitative questionnaire and obtained data from adults living with a mental illness. The interviews explored: (a) the impact of a mental illness, (b) the roles of family, friends, and the community, and (c) supporting well-being and recovery. The inquiry found that: the impact of being diagnosed with a severe mental illness is significant and life-altering; the support of friends, family,

Action Research, pages 301–326
Copyright © 2014 by Information Age Publishing

301

and mental health professionals is important in accepting one's illness and maintaining a sense of well-being; and recovery is best supported through part-time work, community involvement and meaningful activities or hobbies. The study highlighted the importance of adopting a social justice and human rights orientation rather than focusing primarily on improving clinical and in-patient services. The findings indicate the most meaningful way to support the well-being and recovery of older adults living with a serious mental illness is to act in ways that strengthen the capabilities individuals have to improve their own well-being and support their own recovery. The findings of this study are distinctive. While qualitative studies on recovery are common, how recovery was focused on was pre-determined by the researcher. The extended epistemology of CI allowed for a focus on well-being and recovery that was determined entirely by the coresearchers.

Cooperative Inquiry (CI) focuses on authentically sharing decision-making power with the research subjects, who are considered coresearchers. In the spirit of authentically conducting CI, the nine coresearchers took ownership for the inquiry and created the research questions early in the study. The feature that differentiates this form of Action Research from other participative methodologies is that CI offers an extended epistemology, as the following pages describe. In this inquiry, the outcome of the focus on well-being and recovery was an emphasis that all coresearchers were genuinely interested in. The final research questions represented issues that were authentically of interest and importance to each of the nine coresearchers. By seeing their own experiences reflected in the research questions, the coresearchers were able to use their experiences as a lens for exploring the research questions, which represents the fundamental principle of CI—to do research *with* rather than *on* people.

This research was designed to provide insight, from the perspective of older adults themselves, into the factors that support the well-being and recovery of older adults living with a mental illness. I was interested in the topic because my work in the mental health field over previous decades helped me appreciate the high levels of stress that aging caregiving parents of adults with lived experience of mental illness are experiencing. While working as the Executive Director of a provincial nongovernmental agency providing direct service to citizens and families impacted by mental illness, I worked directly with numerous families from across the province and around the country that were in severe distress due the advanced aging or death of elderly caregiving parents. I had studied Action Research (AR) in my PhD methods course and a close colleague/friend was using AR in his study of the health issues facing pregnant women in his homeland of Ghana. I was aware of AR's ability to support authentic work with vulnerable and marginalized individuals. As well, a colleague of mine in the mental health field was interested in my study and we discussed my evolving research question. She recommended AR. Then, a committee member, who ultimately became my supervisor, suggested I explore CI. As well, Tim Pyrch (2007; 2004) led me in a summer research class to explore the fit further. Once I started exploring the inspiring work of Heron and Reason, I knew the fit was obvious. The CI premise that supporting human flourishing is a valuable outcome was a fit for expanding my knowledge of the factors that would support the long term well-being of a cohort I was used to working with—older adults with lived experience of mental illness who are facing the advanced aging and death of caregiving parents. I was particularly attracted to Heron's (1998) assertion that cooperative decision-making is the foundation for an inquiry group to affect human flourishing. A methodology implemented through cooperative and participative decision-making felt like a solid way to generate meaningful knowledge about supporting the long-term flourishing of older adults with lived experiences of mental illness.

DEFINITION OF TERMS

A term that is used in this document is serious mental illness, which, clinically, is described as an illness that is (at times) debilitating and that is persistent. This definition specifically involves diagnoses from the Fourth Edition of the Diagnostic and Statistical Manual of Mental Disorders, the DSM-IV (American Psychiatric Association [APA], 1994) such as schizophrenia (and related diagnoses such as schizoaffective disorder), clinical depression, and bipolar depression. For the purpose of this study, people were sought who had been ill for at least 10 years so that participants would be able to speak to the impact of living with a serious mental illness over a significant period of time. For the purpose of this study, people in the age range of 40 to 54 years were defined as middle-aged. Older persons were defined as people 55 years of age and older, recognizing that 65 is the official retirement age in Canada because that is when citizens become eligible for Old Age Security and (usually) Canada Pension Plan.

Cooperative Inquiry

Cooperative Inquiry or CI is a person-centered inquiry with the ultimate goal of fostering human flourishing. CI was founded by John Heron and evolved out of the era of civil rights, the anti-war movement, and the second wave of feminism (1970; 1971; 1996; 1998). Concepts and philosophies that guide CI include:

- Freedom—the self-creating person
- Existentialism—the self as a reciprocal agent
- Kantian philosophy—human freedom; autonomy and rational agency
- Humanistic philosophy (Maslow & Rogers)—self-actualization (Heron, 1996; 1998; Heron & Reason, 2004)

CI is based on participative, democratic, technocratic and experiential values. A cooperative inquiry seeks to engage coresearchers in reciprocal relations that use the full range of human sensibilities to obtain holistic knowledge. What distinguishes CI from other process-oriented Action Research is that CI is committed to participative research decision making both politically and epistemologically. The political wing of the participative paradigm of CI maintains that supporting human flourishing is intrinsically worthwhile and a valuable end. Cooperative decision-making provides a foundation for an inquiry group to affect its flourishing (Reason, 1998). The methodology of CI is implemented through participative and cooperative decision-making. In other words, the coinquirers are fully informed and fully involved in sharing power over decisions about the research content, the focus of the inquiry, what the inquiry is seeking to find out and what to achieve.

The specific procedures of CI involve repeatedly cycling between four phases. The outcomes of CI correspond with four ways of knowing. The following sections describe the Four Phases of CI and the Ways of Knowing

THE FOUR PHASES OF CI

The CI process includes four phases which coresearchers cycle through repeatedly (see Figure 13.1). Phase One involves the initial relationship building in that coresearchers agree to the focus of the study and the procedures for gathering and recording data from the research experience (Heron, 2004). The strategy begins with a plan of action to allow the first action phase to explore an aspect of the topic of the inquiry (Heron, 1996). The group of coresearchers creates a launching statement of the inquiry topic in this first phase.

Phase Two involves the coresearchers becoming cosubjects as everyone engages in activities agreed to in Phase One. The second phase also involves recording observations and experiences as well as outcomes of the experiences. The application of an integrated range of inquiry skills begins

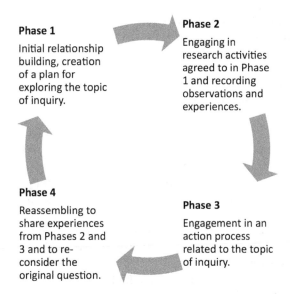

Phase 1

Initial relationship building, creation of a plan for exploring the topic of inquiry.

Phase 2

Engaging in research activities agreed to in Phase 1 and recording observations and experiences.

Phase 4

Reassembling to share experiences from Phases 2 and 3 and to re-consider the original question.

Phase 3

Engagement in an action process related to the topic of inquiry.

Figure 13.1 Four phases of an AR Cycle. Adpated from Heron, 1996, p. 54–55.

to occur in the second phase of CI (Langton & Heron, 2003). Creating records of the experiential data generated is another activity that inquirers are involved in during the second phase of the inquiry.

Phase Three is full immersion in the action phase (Heron, 1996). With a spirit of openness, inquirers may break through into new awareness (Heron & Reason, 2004). The third phase is the hallmark of the CI method as it is during this time that coresearchers become fully engaged in the experience through full immersion. The goal is that a degree of openness is achieved that is free enough of preconceptions that inquirers can see the research issues in new ways. The hope is that superficial understandings of the research questions become elaborately developed.

The second and third phases involve an agreed time period with an end point, leading to Phase Four. The group of inquirers reassembles in this fourth phase to share experiential data from Phases Two and Three and to reconsider the original research question in light of the action that was experienced individually and as a group (Heron & Reason, 2004). This fourth phase allows for the dialectic of CI to unfold, meaning the cycle between reflection and action. Figure 13.1 depicts a four-phase AR research cycle.

The cycle between reflection and action is then repeated several times. Ideally, the four cycles are repeated six to ten times. In subsequent cycling, a variety of intentional procedures are used during reflection. Special skills, described in the next section on rigor, are employed in the action phases so that several aspects of the inquiry topic can converge. At the end of the cycling, a major reflection phase occurs so that threads can be pulled together and the outcomes clarified. At this point a decision can be made by the group about whether or not to collaboratively write up a cooperative report.

Heron (1996) articulates four ways of knowing: experiential, presentational, propositional, and practical.

- *Experiential* knowing involves the belief in one's sense of presence and the transformations of personal being that unfold through the process of fully engaging in the inquiry.
- *Presentational* reports involve insights about the inquiry domain that are creatively represented through expressive modes such as drawing or dance.
- *Propositional* reports are informative about the inquiry domain, meaning they describe and explain what was explored and describe the inquiry method.
- *Practical* knowledge is defined as the belief in one's developing skill. The highest value in CI is given to practical knowing. Heron's view is that the intellect is only useful if it is practically helpful.

Figure 13.2 is Heron's depiction of the ways of knowing, with practical knowledge appropriately situated at the top.

As inquirers begin cycling through the four stages of a cooperative inquiry they first gain experiential knowing which leads to presentational

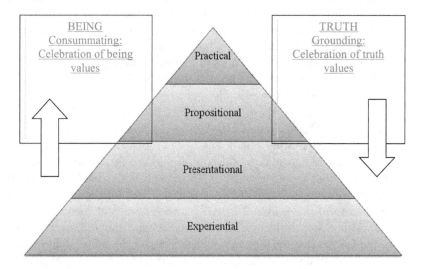

Figure 13.2 Ways of knowing in co-operative inquiry. Adapted from Heron, 1998, p. 239.

and propositional knowing, particularly as coresearchers experience convergence of concepts in Phase Four. Phase 1—creating the CI research plan—involves primarily propositional knowing—describing the domain of inquiry. Phase 2—engaging in research activities—has mostly to do with gaining and using practical research skills and the belief in one's skills, but also involves experiential knowing. Phase 3—engagement in an action process—involves primarily gaining experiential knowledge, and presentational knowing where sharing results is part of the Phase 3 action process. Experiential knowing involves transformations of personal being that unfold through the process of fully engaging in the inquiry. Phase 4 involves primarily propositional knowing, summarizing the research done and planning the next Phase 1 (unless the inquiry is complete).

The central difference between CI and a constructivist or a critical theory approach to research is that a cooperative inquiry sees practical knowledge as being of intrinsic value in itself. Critical or constructivist approaches are more concerned with propositional knowledge. CI seeks to generate social emancipation. Practical knowing is grounded in and consummates other ways of knowing, providing a link between the political and the epistemological (Reason, 1998). A key to effective CI is recognizing the limits of propositional and conceptual ways of knowing. CI generates outcomes that are not only "valid" but that can be self-transcending.

THE SETTING

The study occurred during a 16-month period beginning in the fall of 2006. The setting in which the study occurred was ideal. Weyburn is located in southern Saskatchewan in Canada. In 2006 the population of the city was just under 10,000 people. (Statistics Canada, 2006). Initially the local economy was based on agriculture and the area is now in the midst of an economic boom fueled by local oil fields.

From a mental health perspective, Weyburn was an interesting location to conduct CI given the city's rich history in psychiatry. The Souris Valley Psychiatric Hospital, located in Weyburn, was one of the province's largest psychiatric facilities from the 1920s to the 1980s. Most citizens of Weyburn have family members who either were employees or patients of Souris Valley. The substantial facility, which was one of the largest buildings in Saskatchewan during its heyday in the 1940s and 1950s, had been abandoned for several years by the time we started the CI. Weeds had grown over the old buildings. The City of Weyburn worked hard to find another use for the building. When lengthy negotiations with a Chinese firm broke down, the City regrettably made the decision to tear down the aged facility.

The CI occurred during the end of the era of Weyburn's psychiatric hospital and thus the history and future of psychiatric care in the city was prominent on the minds of the city's citizens. It was a dynamic and an exciting city to conduct mental health research as every person I encountered—from hotel managers and restaurant owners to print shop staff and bakers—was enthusiastic about supporting the inquiry. The staff of the hotel where we held our meetings took great pride in serving our group delicious, fresh, nutritious, home-cooked meals following each of our session. The setting was ideal for CI.

THE PROBLEM

A rationale for creating a CI project involving older adults with lived experience of a mental illness was that the extended epistemology of CI generates knowledge *with* people that supports human flourishing from the perspective of coinquirers. Historically, mental health practitioners have assumed that people with a serious mental illness, such as schizophrenia, are not reasoning human beings. Consequently, there has historically been a lack of research from the perspective of people living with a serious mental illness. There is also a shortage of knowledge from the perspective of older adults with lived experiences of mental illness (Davidson, 2006; Thompson, 2003; Hatfield, 2000; Anthony, 1993). A focus on older persons is significant given the overall aging of the Canadian population and the large number of older adults who have a serious mental illness and who are currently supported by elderly caregiving parents. The demographics of the aging Canadian population means there will be increasing numbers of middle-aged and older adults who have a mental illness in the coming years. It is important to understand recovery from the perspective of older adults and to establish recovery-oriented policies and programs to meet the increasing numbers of older people living with a serious mental illness in Canadian society.

Yet, there is a need for research from the perspective of older adults themselves given the overall aging of the North American population. Demographically, Canada's overall population is aging (Human Resources and Skills Development Canada, 2012). Accordingly, a significant increase in the numbers of elderly individuals living with a serious mental illness is expected over the coming decades (Thompson, 2003; Hatfield, 2000; Levine, 1999; Cohen, 1995). For an aging population—from a health and social perspective—people with serious mental illness are a vulnerable older subset of the population. The quality of life of older people living with a mental illness is an important consideration in planning for the future. It is important to identify the policy and service implications that are anticipated over the coming decades related to predicted increases in the proportion of the population that will be seniors in the next 10 to 20 years. In Canada and in the United States, it is estimated that aging family members care for 50% to 70% of older adults living with schizophrenia, with an estimated 50% living in a parental home (Forsyth, 2001; Lefley & Hatfield, 1999).

Older individuals who have a serious mental illness are at-risk for poverty, isolation, poor physical health, homelessness, degenerative neurological diseases such as dementia, and suicide (Whyte, 2004). Suicide is the leading cause of death of people diagnosed with serious mental illness in all age categories (Pinikahana, Happell, & Keks, 2003; Radomsky, Haas, Mann, & Sweeney, 1999). It is important that policy makers and practitioners are aware of and prepare for the growing numbers of older adults that are anticipated over the coming decades.

NARRATIVE

The inquiry involved nine coresearchers who were between the ages of 46 and 67. The criteria for being involved in the study were based on age, diagnoses and living status. Coresearchers who met the following criteria were invited to participate in the study: (a) over the age of 40 years, (b) diagnosed with a serious mental illness, and (c) not living with caregiving parents. When conducting research with psychiatrically disabled individuals, it is reasonable to expect a 50% attrition rate. The ideal size for a cooperative inquiry is six to twelve individuals. The initiation and establishment of an inquiry group occurred through two open forums I held in Weyburn. The forums involved explaining the research project and inquiring with attendees about interest in participation. A total of 18 individuals came to the two forums. The outcome was that nine coresearchers signed on for the study. The nine coresearchers all participated fully in every state of the inquiry. No individuals dropped out of the study; the group was fully engaged in the inquiry until the end of the project.

Diagnostically, seven of the nine coresearchers were living with a schizophrenia spectrum disorder. Two of the coresearchers had dual diagnoses related to depression and/or addiction issues. Five of the nine coresearchers were men while four of the coresearchers were women. Only one of the coresearchers was not Caucasian, which was (unintentionally) representative of the demography of the region.

WHAT HAPPENED AND HOW

The coresearchers and I went through ten complete CI cycles during a dynamic and engaging 16-month period. The first cycle was preceded by several meetings, which involved open-ended, free-flowing brainstorming. Given the extended epistemology of CI, it was important that the coresearchers develop a research focus they all identified with and saw merit in studying.

The first four cycles of the inquiry involved: (a) self interviews to allow coresearchers time to individually reflect on their experiences related to the research questions; (b) small group interviews on the same preliminary topics; (c) creating and piloting an instrument, a qualitative questionnaire; and (d) gathering data by interviewing community members who also have lived experiences with mental illness. The fifth cycle focused on analyzing the interview data. In the sixth cycle the group prepared to share the research result in the community. Cycles 7–9 saw the group host a series of community-based Roundtables. The final and tenth cycle involved debriefing, reflecting and wrapping up. Subsequent to the tenth cycle, the coresearchers and I presented the findings at four conferences, one provincial, two national, and one international.

The process involved ten cycles:

> Cycle 1: Self interviews to allow coresearchers time to individually reflect on their experiences related to the research questions
> Cycle 2: Small group interviews on the same preliminary topics
> Cycle 3: Creating and piloting an instrument, a qualitative questionnaire
> Cycle 4: Gathering data by interviewing community members who also have lived experiences with mental illness
> Cycle 5: Analyzing the interview data
> Cycle 6: Group preparation for sharing the research result in the community
> Cycles 7, 8, & 9: Community-based Roundtables
> Cycle 10: Debriefing, reflecting and wrapping up

Cycle 1

The first four cycles generated new knowledge for the coresearchers and me. Cycle 1 generated considerable propositional knowledge. Practical and experiential knowledge were generated in Cycles 2–3. The data collection phase, Cycle 4, involved gathering practical knowledge through conducting interviews with peers of the coresearchers.

The extended epistemology of CI meant that while I positioned myself at the start of the inquiry with a proposed research question, I was committed to sharing power around decision-making related to the focus of the research and the methodology. It is useful that I was grounded in the openness required of a CI practitioner because an ethical issue occurred when it became clear very early in the reciprocal and engaging brainstorming that preceded Cycle 1. The issue was that the topic I brought to the inquiry was not of interest to the coresearchers. The suggested research topic focused on supporting individuals living with mental illness to navigate transitions in caregiving including the advanced aging and death of caregiving parents. I had to set aside the investment I had made in the old topic, including the months of preparation I had put into a literature review on caregiving. Yet, as an ethical CI practitioner, I knew the only rigorous way to navigate the inquiry was to authentically position the inquiry topic within the decision-making domain of the coresearchers (Thompson, 2009). Thus, I embraced the new topic, which emerged from the focus group and early engagement: *What are the factors that support the well being and recovery of people with lived experience with mental illness?*

Cycle 1 began with a study domain determined which was to explore the experience of being diagnosed with a mental illness and strategies that individuals use on a day to day basis. A coresearcher presented the group with a questionnaire she had done in a previous workshop which she found useful. When the group reviewed photocopies of the questionnaire, there was widespread support. "I like it!" one person said. "Me too" piped in another. Thus, the initial data collection instrument the group used was one a coresearcher brought to the group during the first cycle.

Since we had already discussed the different methods for conducting AR (secondary analysis, drama and video-making, case studies and stories, interviews, focus groups, photovoice, etc.), the group was familiar with the concept of interviewing. It was determined that people would self-interview using the agreed-to interview questions. The action of Cycle 1 involved a focus group to discuss the results of the self-interviews. That session was the beginning of many powerful and practical discussions between the coresearchers about practical knowledge over how to support their well-being and recovery. The conversation focused on the significant (and generally negative) impact of receiving a diagnosis of mental illness. In the cointerviews several people reported their fears about relapsing and how they felt that living with a mental illness limited their potential as human beings. Concerns about the side effects and limitations of psycho-active medications were also discussed. With respect to strategies that support their well-being, the coresearchers reported that it was useful to think about the future, "not thinking of the past but looking forward." Other topics covered included the importance of the support of friends and (para)professionals. One person said this of their friends, they "keep me on the right path." Another said their friends "offer a foothold." The importance of supportive professionals and (para)professionals was also discussed. Other supportive factors discussed in the first cycle were community involvement, exercise, artistic endeavors and appreciation. A term that was often used in the study emerged in Cycle 1: "persistent action." The term was immediately adopted as a useful way of expressing the process of actively pursuing well being in the face of living with a mental illness.

Cycle 2

Cycle 2 began excitedly as the coresearchers spontaneously spoke about their gratitude in being able to talk with one another about their experiences, symptoms and strategies. "It's great to be able to talk to other people about my illness!" one coresearchers said with a full smile. I will forever remember the excitement and warmth this individual displayed in their facial and body movements as full appreciation was expressed for being able to learn from others. "Ya," said another. "I've never been able to talk to other people about their symptoms. This is really helpful." The comments were met with a round of nodding and expressions of agreement.

I was surprised that the group therapy sessions the coresearchers had been in for years did not involve conversations about symptoms. "Haven't you been talking in your groups about your symptoms and how to manage them?" I asked. There was silence for a few seconds until heads began to shake. "No," one person said. "When we have group sessions the topic is decided for us," the person said.

"I am surprised that so many people have similar experiences," a coresearcher said. "Yeah, me too. I'm not the only one with these problems," another coresearcher stated. Later that evening as I wrote in my own research journal in my hotel room, I wrote "What are they doing in group therapy sessions in the mental health system if people are not being given time and space to talk about their experiences with 'being' ill?" It was encouraging to be part of an experience of generating a substantial amount of experiential and practical knowledge that was clearly helping people on a day-to-day basis. The experience of Cycle 2 highlighted for me that part of the power of CI is its capacity to generate practical knowledge that supports human flourishing—which is a valid pursuit in and of itself. To this end, it felt as though the CI had already achieved successes, even though it was early in the inquiry. Nonetheless, people were benefiting from the dialogue!

In the second cycle the coresearchers created an open-ended qualitative questionnaire and interviewed one another. The excitement was high as people moved into their first interview experience. Three groups of three were set up so that one person could be taking notes, while one was interviewed and one was the interviewer. "I'm excited about what I'll learn," said one person. "Me too," exclaimed another with a broad smile. "Thank you for letting us share," one person said to me. "Yes, thanks so much. We really need this," another exclaimed. I reciprocated by letting the group know how much I was learning from them and how grateful I was for the new knowledge we were cocreating. Practically, topics such as avoiding relapses, knowing the signs of de-compensation (meaning a possible episode of psychosis), experiences with institutionalization and the impact of psychosis on one's personality were the focus in Cycle 2. The cycle wrapped up with an inspiring journal reflection offered by one coresearcher on the merit of having explored the difficulties they have endured in their life: "I am grateful for the darkness—it's the only time the stars come out."

Cycle 3

Cycle 3 involved deciding precisely whom to interview as well as creating and then piloting the instrument. The cycle began by turning the research concept into a question. We went over the Ways of Knowing in CI (Figure 13.2) and repositioned ourselves in the propositional knowing we had generated so far. Rather than focusing on "avoiding relapses" as we had been, the focus shifted to "supporting well being and recovery." It was exciting to watch the coresearchers create their own research question and that everyone was interested in the topic that had spontaneously evolved. The use of the two phrases was seen as being important because using only the term recovery was seen as problematic. "We're not always recovering" one coresearcher said and added, "Some days I am just trying to get through the day and to fight off my hallucinations and stay out of the psych ward!" A consensus was easily achieved that the study should also look at factors that support a feeling of well-being even in the face of serious illness and troublesome symptoms.

Cycle 3 ended enthusiastically as there was unanimous excitement and curiosity about what the study would uncover. As the cycle ended, I complimented the group on being the most consistently prepared and professional group of individuals I had worked with. Before the cycles, I equipped everyone with a box of office supplies including a binder to bring to the meetings and for holding our meeting paperwork. Every one of the coresearchers had attended each meeting to date, brought their paperwork (and binders in this case) and came to the meetings with their 'homework' completed. I will forever remember the broad smiles that I received as the cycle concluded; my compliments were genuine.

Cycle 4

The fourth cycle saw the group diverge into exploring different topics with respect to the agreed-to research questions of "What factors support the well-being and recovery of people living with a mental illness." Three topics that were explored were: (a) Supported Housing and Group Homes; (b) Mental Health Professionals; and (c) the soon-to-be-implemented smoking ban at the Weyburn Hospital, which houses the in-patient psychiatric services. For each topic, I conducted a short literature review and provided the group with background information. For the housing issues, we reviewed the Adult and Youth Group Home Regulations (Government of Saskatchewan, 2005). The group was interested in fully understanding the rights of residents of group homes as well as knowing the regulations regarding the training and required professionalism. As a result of reviewing the regulations governing group homes, the coresearchers decided to include some questions about housing rights in the interview. Regarding the second issue, the group was interested in exploring the topic of "burn out" amongst mental health professionals. Brainstorming sessions before the cycles began had highlighted the commonality of encountering mental health professionals perceived to be burned out, meaning lacking in patience, flexibility and compassion. In the end the group decided to study themselves and things they are experts on, namely their own experiences with pursuing well-being and recovery.

The topic of the proposed smoking ban at the Weyburn hospital, including the psychiatric ward, offered a powerful experience for the group and me about the influence our work was having on the community. I brought research, a short literature review, of evidence on the topic. We recognized that there was more literature on the importance of quitting smoking than there was for positions in favor of continued provision for smokers who are resident in in-patient psychiatric wards. Nonetheless, our discussion in this area had an impact for at least one coresearcher told at least one local psychiatrist that our group was considering studying the negative impact of the impending smoking ban on the well-being of psychiatric patients in Weyburn and area. Soon after, it was reported to our group that there would be provisions made for psychiatric patients in Weyburn such that the hospital smoking ban would exclude the designated area for psychiatric patients. The group felt elated with the news that the mere discussion of our possibly doing research around the smoking issue had impacted the policy. The change in smoking ban policy was the first example for the group of the tangible nature of the power of our inquiry and our activities. We celebrated the news and enjoyed an elated discussion with all of us smiling happily. It was an honour to be part of such a transformative experience where a group of individuals who once felt powerless were enjoying the reality of having their voices heard in their community.

We converged back to the research question and added sub-questions based on our discussions:

A. What is the impact of living with a mental illness?
B. What roles do family, friends and (para) professionals play in supporting well-being and recovery?
C. What activities support well-being and recovery?

Another question was added: "How can action occur to improve the well-being and recovery of older adults living with a mental illness?"

The next stage was to create and pilot the instrument after which time we moved directly into the climax of Cycle 4—the data collection. Each coresearcher interviewed one peer, and an older adult with lived experience with mental illness. Constancy of conditions were maintained during the data collection phase of the study. All of the interviews were conducted in the same small business room at the Weyburn Inn. I acted as the note-taker and transcribed the interview verbatim, with the interviewee sitting next to me such that they could see the screen and check for accuracy of the transcription. The interview process was always the same with my initiating the dialogue and going through and acquiring a signature for the ethics form. Then, the interviewer, a coresearcher, would conduct the semi-structured interview.

Cycle 5

The fifth cycle was also engaging in part because it was interesting and exciting to go through the interview data together. The coresearchers were already adept at coding and categorizing qualitative data from the work we'd done thus far. They began to analyze the data even before the meeting formally began. Each coresearcher was given a copy of all of the data for the purpose of the analysis. As well, each interviewee received a copy of their individual interview so they could check the reliability of the transcription and to add any additional comments.

Unintentionally, the demographics of the interview group paralleled the coresearch group. Four of the interviewees were women and five were men. The ages of the interviewees were evenly distributed, ranging from 27 to 60 years of age. The mean age of the nine adults interviewed was 46.7. The median age was 49 and the mode was 50. None of the interviewees were new residents in the city of Weyburn. The range of years of Weyburn residency was 8 to 39. On average (mean), interviewees had lived in Weyburn for 21 years. The median and mode of residence in Weyburn was 15 years.

The interviewees were all Caucasian. The ethnicity of the interviewees was representative of the demographics of Weyburn which is 95% Caucasian (Weyburn Community Profile, 2006). In terms of ethnic backgrounds, two of the nine respondents described themselves as Canadian / Anglo-Saxon

/ Caucasian. The other seven interviewees cited European roots: French; Swedish; Scottish; Scottish and French; Scottish and Norwegian; German and Norwegian; and German and Scottish.

ANALYSIS: IMPACTS, SUPPORTS, WELL-BEING AND RECOVERY

As we moved from reading through the data into analyzing it, I found it powerful and rewarding to watch the coresearchers read and absorb the propositional and practical knowing the interviews contained. Having read the data through slowly, line by line, I suggested we move into the data analysis, specifically coding and categorizing the data. We reviewed the basics of coding and categorizing qualitative data. I found people had already coded much of the data as they read through it initially. As with previous qualitative analysis, a focus group was used in the analysis once people had looked at the data individually and done some preliminary coding. The data analysis process involved categorizing the coded data and discussing the general themes that emerged from the data. The experiences of analyzing the brainstorming, self-interview, and group interview data meant the process of coding and categorizing the data was becoming instinctive to the coresearchers. Without my needing to talk about codes and categories, the coresearchers would already be talking about themes represented in the data. I was challenged to keep pace with the coresearchers and was often surprised at how quickly people processed new knowing/knowledge both individually and as a group. Analyzing the interview data together was an engaging process.

The *impact* of developing a mental illness, living with an untreated mental illness, and being diagnosed, is significant and life-altering. One person involved in this study remembered being ill as early as age seven yet the youngest age of diagnosis reported was age 26. For all of the coresearchers and interviewees, the impact of having a mental illness is serious. One of the most detrimental impacts reported was the chronic poverty of relying on social assistance. Feeling stigmatized and discriminated against is another negative impact that was reported. Coresearchers and interviewees reported the impact of developing and being diagnosed with a mental illness decreased their sense of well-being with respect to negative impacts on work, socioeconomic status, friendships, and family members.

Each coresearcher and interviewee agreed that the *support* of other human beings who believed in them and who stood by them was critical to both their well-being and their recovery. Friends who also had a serious mental illness were reported to be the most common form of support. Family (of origin) was also commonly reported as being very important except for a few of the people (4/18). Community (e.g., CMHA) and institutional supports (e.g., Social Assistance and Mental Health Service) were stressed by everyone involved as being important. The Weyburn office of the CMHA came out as being particularly helpful and the most popular with most people citing one or two especially supportive staff members by name. The strength of the support for the Weyburn CMHA emphasized how important it is to have one or two supportive people in the community to communicate with on a regular basis.

The study revealed a variety of common strategies that support *well-being* and *recovery*. However, the group did not break down activities or strategies into categories of "well-being" and "recovery." Rather, coresearchers felt they could not articulate for interviewees whether or not something such as dancing was promoting well-being or recovery. "It could be helping you with both" expressed one coresearcher when I asked about how to handle the two categories. Thus, the concepts analyzed below are deemed to support well-being and/or recovery, depending on the reality of the individual.

Activities such as being involved in art through painting or writing were commonly reported as were activities such as dance and exercising. Another enjoyable activity-related theme was being with pets either through exercise or in play. Community involvement was also described as being helpful. Community activities ranged from being involved in programs at the local CMHA, library, or church. Work was also described as an activity that is helpful to people on a day-to-day basis.

We moved into experiential and propositional knowing as we wrapped up our coding and categorizing of the interview data and began to talk about our overall impressions of the findings. "What do you think of these findings compared to what you discovered about yourselves and our group?" I asked the coresearchers. One person said, "This is so much like what we learned from our own interviews." "Yeah really," exclaimed another. "It's kinda freaky how this is so much like what we said," exclaimed another coresearcher. It was rather stunning to us all how similar the finding from data were between the previous data (self- and group interviews) and the interviews with community members. "I guess I assumed it would be different," one person said, to which others agreed. It was, therefore, surprising that there seemed to be no major difference between the data sets. I talked to the group about the concept of replicating research results and how the similar results speak to the reliability and validity of our results. As we reflected on the cycle after analyzing the interview data, coresearchers expressed gratitude for all they have learned through the interview process. "This is so cool!" one person said of the learning experience. "I agree," said another with a big smile.

The group concluded the five factors that support the well-being and recovery of older individuals with lived experience of a mental illness are:

- Positive Coping Strategies
- Community and Community Based Organizations
- Paid Employment
- Supportive Friends and Family
- Human Services, Mental Health, and Social Services

While all five factors are important, the value of paid work was highlighted as being the most significant given the focus of the study. Furthermore, the subsequent Roundtables supported this emphasis because participants stressed the importance of poverty reduction as a key strategy towards supporting the well-being and recovery of older adults with lived experience of a serious mental illness.

Each cycle ended with a group reflection/journaling section. Three questions were posed: (a) What am I learning? (b) What did I learn at today's meeting? and (c) What questions do I have? The reflections expressed at the end of Cycle 5 are below.

- What am I learning?
  - How similar our problems are
  - That I am like other people
  - How to cope better
  - That I need my friends
  - It is good to be involved in the community
  - I am never alone
  - That we all have a lot in common
- What did I learn today?
  - That we should be proud of ourselves because we did a good job
  - What questions do I have?
  - What now?
  - Will this make a difference?

Cycle 5 ended with another glorious feast of fine food from the Weyburn Inn. I again congratulated the coresearchers on a job very well done. "I feel good!" one coresearcher exclaimed, speaking both of the good food and our success with the interviews and analysis. "I can't wait to tell the docs!" another proudly exclaimed. We were all excited about the upcoming cycles focusing on disseminating our knowledge to the community.

Cycle 6

Cycle 6 involved preparing to disseminate the data through a series of three Roundtables. It is important to highlight how reticent the coresearchers were at the onset of the study to speak publicly. Yet, by the beginning of Cycle 6, all members were engaged and enthusiastic about sharing the results with the community. It was an exciting time of the inquiry! The first group Roundtable included the staff, volunteers and board members of the Canadian Mental Health Association (CMHA)—Weyburn Office. It was a small Roundtable of supportive individuals and was, in part, designed to build strength and confidence for the ultimate session, the Community Roundtable.

Cycle 7

The climax of the inquiry occurred during Cycle Seven, which involved the actual Community Roundtable, held on September 21. To the pleasure of the coresearchers and the researcher, a wide range of mental health sector leaders and engaged community members attended and actively participated in the roundtable. The event went better than planned and was a highlight of the project. It provided coresearchers the opportunity to share the interesting and timely research findings and, at least for the duration of the roundtable, to dialogue with practitioners and to shift power relations. More people attended than expected: all of the seats were full and we ran out of handouts. Executive and middle management of the local mental health and addictions branch of the health region attended along with two local psychiatrists. Other practitioners such as nurses, psychologists, and social workers were in attendance, along with some nursing students doing internships at a local hospital. Community members and family members of people who live with a serious mental illness also attended the roundtable.

The presentation went well and as planned. Each coresearcher was fully engaged and skillfully delivered the agreed-to section of research results to an enthusiastic and impressed audience.

The lively dialogue that occurred after the presentation (and subsequent refreshment break) was powerful and instructive. The practitioners expressed that they were impressed with the research. The dialogue at the roundtable following the presentation focused on the importance of poverty reduction and in the support of family, friends and the community (including the mental health community). One psychiatrist initiated a useful discussion on the merit of prioritizing the concept of reducing stigma over reducing poverty. Reducing poverty serves to reduce stigma, the practitioner stressed. Others in attendance expressed comments supporting poverty reduction, particularly the staff of community-based organizations such as the CMHA.

The September 21st event was a highlight of the project for the coresearchers and me.

Cycle 7 wrapped up with a brief group reflection/celebration involving the coresearchers in the roundtable room after the attendees departed. It was a short, smile-filled interaction that involved spontaneous expressions of a sense of satisfaction and appreciation that the event was so successful.

Shortly after the event, an executive member of the Weyburn Branch of the CMHA called the researcher in her Weyburn hotel room to excitedly expressed gratitude for bringing together all of the key players in the regional mental health sector (e.g., senior management, psychiatrists, practitioners, community leaders) for a productive discussion. "I've been trying to do that for 20 years!" the person excitedly told the researcher. The call was a validation of the transformative power of CI—we had experienced a powerful cooperative experience that shifted energies within a community.

The seventh cycle involved all ways of knowing: propositional, practical, experiential, and presentational. We presented our knowledge resulting from the inquiry, most of which was practical. The dialogue which occurred after our presentation provided new insights and knowledge. The event itself was transformational for a group of individuals who all stated at the onset of the project that they would "never be able to present in public," to quote one coresearcher. Each of the coresearchers who presented, eight in total (since one individual chose to remain anonymous and did not attend), can now call themselves experienced public speakers. Presentational knowing resulted from the dialogue that occurred with attendees as we shared our new knowledge with the people who attended the event. The overall success of the event was a peak experience for those of us who presented at the event.

Cycles 8, 9, and 10

The Action/Reflection dialectic of CI continued in the final cycles. Cycle 8 involved debriefing and reflecting on the powerful Cycle 7. Cycle 9 saw the coresearchers present the research findings to the interviewees. The discussion following the presentation again focused on the pivotal significance of poverty reduction. Cycle 10 felt like a mixed blessing as it was nice to summarize and reflect upon the inquiry process. Yet, it was difficult to wrap up the inquiry, which had engaged us all for so many months.

GROUP AND PERSONAL INSIGHTS

What Changes Occurred

The inquiry led to numerous, significant changes in social policy, perceptions of professionals, coresearchers, and interviewees and for me as well.

The study findings were included as support for a wider effort by the provincial disability sector to successfully strengthen provincial income support policies for individuals living with significant and long-term disabilities. The policy change occurring in Saskatchewan was one of the most substantial and progressive changes occurring currently in North America. After many years of community building and lobbying on behalf of provincial, disability sector Non-Government Organizations (NGOs) and subsequent policy development with government, the Saskatchewan Assured Income for Disabilities (SAID) was established in 2011. SAID is a separate provincial income support program for people with disabilities that allows provincial citizens accepted into the program a significantly higher level of income as well as a higher level of dignity and stability. The results of this study added to the impetus for the development of this significant program.

The coresearchers and all other provincial residents who are now on SAID are receiving at least $250 more a month in addition to being able to earn up to $100 extra. Moreover, the research I am leading for the provincial disability sector stands to increase the rates that people on SAID will receive into the future. Thus, it is easy to conclude that the tangible and quantifiable outcomes of the CI addressed in this chapter are significant and longstanding at provincial and local levels. Up to some 7,000 residents are expected to come onto SAID over the next two years along with thousands more over the coming decades. Most of the coresearchers and interviewees should qualify for SAID. Thus the lives of the individuals involved in this study are tangibly improved. On a personal level, my career is more meaningful and more impactful now that I am clear on how my efforts and energies can best support individuals with lived experience of mental illness.

The experience of sharing CI with the coresearchers was transformative for me in that the coresearchers helped me to understand that my efforts to strengthen the well being of people impacted by mental illness are better focused on human rights and social justice perspectives rather than on clinical interventions. "An appointment with a psychiatrist does not help you if you are hungry," one coresearcher said when we were discussing the issue of prioritizing poverty reduction over increasing access to (costly) mental health services. It is appropriate that the study concluded by emphasizing that meaningful poverty reduction and a social justice orientation are pivotally important in supporting the well-being and recovery of people living with a mental illness. The study proposed that efforts by practitioners, policy makers and politicians to support individuals diagnosed with a mental illness should focus on building upon the untapped capabilities that individuals hold for improving their own well-being and supporting their own recovery.

My previous professional efforts approached responses to serious mental illness through a clinical or medical lens. As a result of participating in this

CI study, I changed the direction of my professional efforts towards advancing human rights and reducing poverty. Consequently, I am currently working on doing research with the provincial disability sector to support the implementation of SAID.

On a more serious personal level, my husband tragically died unexpectedly of a heart attack while I was writing up my dissertation. I was devastated and was ill-prepared for widowhood. After taking more than a year off of working on my dissertation, I was forced to return to the task of completing and defending the document given that I was up against a firm timeline to complete my degree. Words are not adequate to describe how helpful the data and knowledge accrued during the inquiry supported my personal recovery from grappling with the sorrow of my husband's death. Digging deeply into the wisdom of the coresearchers about how they advance their well-being and recovery in the face of devastating experiences was substantially supportive to my healing journey and recovery from the trauma of losing my late partner suddenly. In this sense, the inquiry supported my own recovery, unexpectedly.

Perceptions and Beliefs of Individuals and Groups

The inquiry changed the perceptions of everyone involved. I stopped focusing on caregiving for people with lived experience of mental illness and focused instead on supporting the recovery of individuals. Plus, my career changed toward a focus on human justice and human rights away from clinical pursuits. The coresearchers and interviewees were changed through the process of the inquiry, most substantially in their belief in their own capacities to create change. The transformational aspect of the study could be described as providing evidence of catalytic validity, as described by Lather (1991). Research with catalytic validity is described as moving those it studies to understand the world and the way it is shaped in order to be able to transform it. The coresearchers gained self-understanding about their experiences with a mental illness through months of meaningful dialogue on the impact of diagnoses and coping with symptoms. The experience of deciding upon topics to study and then actually studying a variety of issues through the repeated cycling process helped the coresearchers develop self-direction. Subsequent to the study, coresearchers have published letters to the editor in the local paper and report being more interested in community and group activities. The self-understanding and self-direction coresearchers achieved throughout the course of the study relate to Lather's concept of catalytic validity. Finally, the professional community changed its perceptions with respect to the capacity of individuals to work together to articulate their needs and develop opportunities for action.

Organizational and Operational Power Shifts

The most substantive power shift of this inquiry was the establishment of SAID and the reality that each month people are receiving more money, and have less administrative burdens. On a local level, the inquiry shifted the power dynamics between practitioners, the community, and individuals with lived experience. Thus, the study can be considered a success on multiple fronts. With respect to knowledge generation, the inquiry generated the four forms of knowing at various cycles in the inquiry as Table 13.1 below highlights.

WHAT WOULD I DO DIFFERENTLY?

A regrettable and costly error that I made early in the inquiry was not working with a supervisor who was an AR practitioner. Instead, I tried to work with a supervisor who had never worked with AR and whose work in the mental health field dated back twenty years. The combination of the supervisor not having current experience clinically, being unfamiliar with AR, and also being inaccessible, resulted in substantial delays in completing my degree. Fortunately, when I got back to work on my dissertation after my husband died, my AR experienced Committee Member, Dr. Tim Pyrch, took on the role of Supervisor. Subsequently, I defended the research and completed my degree. Just as other practitioners (Lather, 1991; Maguire, 1987) have found that AR could be difficult to move through academia, I too found that not all academics are proponents of AR. It is critical for students doing theses or dissertations using AR to work with supervisors who are familiar with AR and who philosophically support the goals of AR.

Another shortcoming of the study is that I have delayed in putting up practical descriptions of the inquiry on the Internet, through the CMHA

TABLE 13.1 Primary Ways of Knowing Generated and Actions

Cycle	Primary Ways of Knowing Generated	Actions
1	Propositional	Self-interviews, small and large focus groups
2	Practical & Experiential	Interviews, focus group
3	Practical	Created questionnaire, small & large focus groups
4	Practical	Conducted interviews
5	Presentational	Focus groups
6	Practical & Experiential	Focus group
7–9	Presentational & Experiential	Three roundtables
10	All forms, mostly practical	Focus group

website, of the inquiry for the coresearchers to access at their convenience. There is an article available in the *Transitions* journal (Thompson, 2008). *Transitions* is a bi-annual publication available on-line through the CMHA— Saskatchewan Division. The article was created before the research was fully completed so it is more of a partial summary of the study with provisional conclusions. Now that the study is complete, it would also be useful to use some Internet space to clearly lay out the study and its findings both for individuals and families with lived experience of mental illness and for potential action researchers. It is important for AR researchers to allocate monies and time towards disseminating our work since the experiences are often powerful and impactful.

CONCLUSIONS

To conclude, this chapter has highlighted that CI is a powerful tool for working with individuals and communities towards progressive practical and social change. Working directly with people dealing with an issue, in this case mental health, resulted in a change to the basic research question to one that was more directly useful to the participants. The participants and researchers improved their understanding about themselves and the research question. Participants gained knowledge, experience and confidence is conducting interviews, analyzing data and making presentations. The study recommendations were used as part of efforts to develop a new provincial income support program for people with disabilities. The results of the study influenced the direction of the researcher`s work and showed the coresearcher participants that their views and involvement could make a real difference.

REFERENCES

American Psychiatric Association. (1994). *Diagnostic and statistical manual of mental disorders* (4th ed.). Washington, DC: American Psychiatric Association.

Anthony, W. (1993). Recovery from mental illness: The guiding vision of the mental health service system in the 1990s. *Psychosocial Rehabilitation Journal, 16*(4), 11–23.

Cohen, C. I. (1995). Studies in the course and outcome of schizophrenia later in life. *Psychiatric Services, 46*(1), 877–879.

Davidson, L. (2006). What happened to civil rights? *Psychiatric Rehabilitation Journal, 30*(1), 11–14.

Forsyth, P. (2001). Who will be there? Families worry what will happen to ill children when parents are gone. *Schizophrenia Digest, 8*(1), 16–19.

Government of Saskatchewan. (2005). *The Adult and Youth Group Home Regulations.* Regina: Ministry of Social Services.

Hatfield, A. (2000). The older caregiver's quandary: Who will care when we are not there? *The Journal, 11*(3), 6–8.

Heron, J. (1970). The phenomenology of social encounter: The gaze. *Philosophy and Phenomenological Research, 31*(2), 243–264.

Heron, J. (1971). *Experience and method: An inquiry into the concept of experiential research.* Surrey, UK: University of Surrey, Human Potential Research Project.

Heron, J. (1996). *Co-operative inquiry: Research into the human condition.* London: Sage Publications.

Heron, J. (1998). *Co-operative inquiry: Research into the human condition.* Thousand Oaks, CA: Sage Publications.

Heron, J. (2004). *A revisionary perspective on human inquiry.* Auckland, New Zealand: South Pacific Centre for Human Inquiry. www.humaninquiry.com [Retrieved on October 19, 2008].

Heron, J., & Reason, P. (2004). The practice of co-operative inquiry: Research 'with' rather than 'on' people. In P. Reason & H. Bradbury (Eds.), *Handbooks of action research: Participative inquiry & practice* (pp. 179–188). Thousand Oaks, CA: Sage Publications.

Human Resources and Skills Development Canada. (2012). Indicators of Well-being in Canada: Canadians in Context —Aging Population. http://www4.hrsdc.gc.ca/.3ndic.1t.4r@-eng.jsp?iid=33. Accessed July 5, 2012.)

Langton, B. & Heron, J. (2003). *Cookbook of dyadic inquiry.* Available: www.human-inquiry.com/cookbook.htm

Lather, P. (1991). *Getting smart: Feminist research and pedagogy within the postmodern.* New York: Routledge.

Lefley, H., & Hatfield, A. (1999). Helping older parental caregivers and mental health consumers cope with parental aging and loss. *Psychiatric Services, 50*(3), 369–375.

Levine, K. J. (1999). *Older adults with severe mental illness: Characteristics and levels of care.* Keene, NH: Antioch New England Graduate School.

Maguire P. (1987). *Doing participatory research: A feminist approach.* Aherst, MA: The Centre for International Education, School of Education, University of Massachusetts.

Pinikahana, J., Happell, B., & Keks, N. A. (2003). Suicide and schizophrenia: A review of literature for the decade (1990–1999) and implications for mental health nursing. *Issues in Mental Health Nursing, 24*, 27–43.

Pyrch, T. (2007) Participatory action research and the culture of fear: Resistance, community, hope and courage. *Action Research, 5*(2), 199–216.

Pyrch, T., & M. T. Castillo (2004). The sights and sounds of Indigenous Knowledge. In Reason, P., & Bradbury, H. (Eds.) (2004). *Handbooks of action research: Participative inquiry & practice.* Thousand Oaks, CA: Sage Publications.

Radomsky, E., Haas, G. L., Maan, J. J., & Sweeney, J. A. (1999). Suicidal behavior in patients with schizophrenia and other psychotic disorders. *American Journal of Psychiatry, 156*(10), 1590–1595.

Reason, P. (1998). Co-operative inquiry as a discipline of professional practice. *Journal of Interprofessional Care, 12*(4), 419–436.

Statistics Canada (2011). Source Statistics Canada—Community profiles http://www12.statcan.gc.ca/census-recensement/2011/ (Accessed July 5, 2012.)

Thompson, K. (2003). Stigma and public health policy for schizophrenia. *Psychiatric Clinics of North America, 26*(1), 273–294.

Thompson, K. (2008). Transitions toward recovery: The Weyburn research project. *Transitions, (Fall 2008)*. Regina: Canadian Mental Health Association (Saskatchewan Division) Inc.

Thompson, K. (2009). Transitions toward recovery: Ethical considerations in working with older people living with a serious mental illness. In W. J. Spitzer & K. Neuman (Eds.), *Senior services delivery: Ethical issues and responses* (pp. 47–64). Petersburg, VA: The Dietz Press.

Whyte, J. (2004). *Iceberg on the horizon: Mental health among older adults—social, intellectual, spiritual.* Regina, SK: Canadian Mental Health Association (Saskatchewan).

ABOUT THE EDITORS

Jerry Willis is a faculty member in the St. John Fisher College executive leadership doctoral program. He has written many papers and books on conducting applied research that address real world problems and a number of his doctoral students have used or adapted one of the models of action research discussed in this book for their dissertation research. In his own research he has used many of the methods of action research to develop and apply an instructional design model based on constructivist and participatory principles. This type of action research is designed to create educational plans, curricula, resources, and materials. His email address is jwillis@aol.com

Claudia Edwards is a faculty member in the St. John Fisher College executive leadership doctoral program. She used action research in her dissertation at Fordham University. She studied the role of the public in public education and wrote the book, *Who Stole Public Education*, which was published in 2011. The book was based on her dissertation. In addition to her work as a faculty member she is Director of a community action project that focuses on the improvement of public education in urban settings. Her email address is cledwards@sjfc.edu

Action Research, page 327
Copyright © 2014 by Information Age Publishing

ABOUT THE CONTRIBUTORS

Maria Casamassa is currently Coordinator of Literacy and Funded Programs at the East Meadow Union Free School District in New York. Her dissertation at Teachers College, Columbia University was an interpretive action research project that focused on the issue of the situated literacies of home and school, and how parents and teachers can work together to foster a child's literacies. Her email address is mtc4255@aol.com

Dan Cernusca is a professor at Missouri University of Science and Technology. While affiliated with the University of Missouri, Columbia, he led an action research project that focused on the development of a new, technology-enhanced version of a course on biblical criticism. The method he used is called design-based research or DBR. It is an emerging method of focusing on the development and evaluation of instructional resources, courses, or materials. His email address is dcernusca@mst.edu

Kingsley Chikaphupha is employed by the Research for Equity and Community Health Trust (REACH) in the Training and Research Support Centre (TARSC). REACH is located in Lilongwe, Malawi. Dr. Chikaphupha is active in applied research to achieve equity in health care and in the conduct of research to influence policy. The chapter he coauthored describes a project to improve HIV treatment and care for sex workers in Malawi. The work was based on an action research model called PRA or Participatory Reflection and Action which is described in detail in the chapter. His email address is kingray2307@yahoo.com

Action Research, pages 329–332
Copyright © 2014 by Information Age Publishing
329

Allison Druin is a Professor in the College of Information Studies at the University of Maryland, College Park. From 2006 to 2011 she was Director of the Human-Computer Interaction Lab (HCIL). She currently works in HCIL with a team of colleagues who use a method she pioneered to create useful technology for children. Her research papers and books have introduced many to a model of design based on a collaborative partnership between children and adults. The chapter she coauthored in this book is an overview of how the concept of using cooperative inquiry as a foundation for intergenerational codesign developed and how it has changed over the past 15 years. Her email address is allisond@umiacs.umd.edu

Jerry Alan Fails is currently a faculty member in the Department of Computer Science at Montclair State University in New Jersey. Prior to Montclair State he was a doctoral student at the University of Maryland where he worked for six years in the Human-Computer Interaction Lab. He continues his work on involving children in the design and development of technology and he coauthored a book on the topic with colleagues at HCIL that was published by Now Publishing in 2014. In the book you are reading now he coauthored a chapter on using cooperative inquiry as a foundation for the intergenerational design of technology. His email address is jerry.fails@montclair.edu

Mona Leigh Guha is a Research Associate in the Human-Computer Interaction Lab (HCIL) at the University of Maryland, College Park. Dr. Guha's work since graduate school has been the use of cooperative inquiry and participatory design as a foundation for development and deployment of technology resources for children. As she and her coauthors said in their chapter, "Children can have a voice in the design of new technologies." That chapter then goes on to illustrate how teams of adults and children cooperate to design very interesting and useful products that are better because of the cooperative aspect of the approach HCIL uses. Her email address is mguha@umd.edu

Ioan Gelu Ionas is a faculty member at the University of Missouri Columbia where he teaches in the Department of Industrial and Manufacturing Systems Engineering. He is a coauthor with Dr. Dan Cernusca of the chapter on design-based research as a form of action research. In addition, he has published several papers on instructional design and on the development of innovative college courses. His email address is ionasig@missouri.edu

Rene Loewenson is based in the Training and Research Center (TARSC) in Harare, Zimbabwe. Dr. Loewenson is an epidemiologist by training and has worked in several African nations over the last 20 years. She was a faculty member at the University of Zimbabwe Medical School for ten years, and during the 1990s she organized a health department for the Zimbabwe Congress of Trade Unions where she also worked. More recently her base of operation has been TARSC in Harare where she has been involved in many projects as well as coordinating the Southern African Network on Equity in Health (EQUINET). The chapter she coauthored describes a project to improve HIV treatment and care for sex workers in Malawi. Her email address is rene@tarsc.org

Anna Mathai Muthoni is a lecturer in the Department of Psychiatry, School of Medicine, College of Health Sciences, University of Nairobi. Her specialty area is social psychiatry and one of her interests within the field of human sexuality is gender and AIDS. She is a coauthor of the chapter about using participatory action research methods to improve the likelihood that alcohol abusing community patients who are HIV positive will consistently follow their ante-retroviral treatment regimen. Her email address is mathai@web.de

Ireen Namakhoma works at the Research for Equity and Community Health Trust (REACH) in Lilongwe, Malawi. Her published research includes many papers on topics related to the treatment of AIDS and reducing the rate of new infections in several African countries. She coauthored the chapter in this book about using participatory reflection and action (PRA) methods to enhance the care and services for commercial sex workers in Malawi who have AIDS.

Patnice Nkhonjera works at the Research for Equity and Community Health Trust (REACH) in Lilongwe, Malawi. She is a social scientist and Knowledge Management and Communications Manager for Research at REACH. Dr. Nkhonjera has published a number of studies related to the diseases of poverty and the influence of both gender and equity on the availability of health care. The chapter she coauthored describes a project to improve HIV treatment and care for commercial sex workers in Malawi.

Anne Obondo is a Senior Lecturer in Social Work in the Department of Psychiatry, School of Medicine, College of Health Sciences, University of Nairobi. In collaboration with colleagues in the department she has studied ways of improving patient adherence to treatment for several serious illnesses. She is one of the coauthors of the chapter in this book that describes the use of participatory action research to increase adherence to treatment plans by HIV patients in the community who are also alcohol abusers. The participatory action research team included both community health professionals and the HIV patients. Her email address is nnobondo2@gmail.com

Caleb Othieno is a faculty member in the Department of Psychiatry, School of Medicine, College of Health Sciences, University of Nairobi. With his colleagues

Dr. Othieno has conducted a number of participatory action research studies on how to improve the treatment of serious health problems in Kenya. His chapter in this book is about the efforts of a team from the University of Nairobi to improve adherence to an ante-retroviral treatment regimen by patients with HIV as well as alcohol abuse. His email address is cjothieno@uonbi.ac.ke

Shankar Shankaran is currently a faculty member at the University of Technology in Sydney, Australia. Prior to that he was a senior manager in the Singapore branch of an international global engineering company based in Japan. His action research project, which used virtual action learning, was designed to help prepare managers in Singapore for major changes in the way the branch operated. His email address is shankar.shankaran@uts.edu.au

Carol Anne St. George teaches at the University of Rochester. Among her scholarly and professional interests are literacy development and parental involvement. Her action research study involved an exploration of how parents and teachers can collaborate through parent-school partnerships to enhance literacy development. Her email address is cstgeorge@warner.rochester.edu

Wenying Shi works in the College of Education at the University of Alberta. Before coming to Canada she was a faculty member at a Chinese university where she taught English as a Second Language. As an immigrant herself she experienced many of the difficulties and barriers immigrant graduate students face. Her action research study focused on those barriers and issues as well as ways of overcoming them. She used an emancipatory action research model. Her email address is *cathy.shi@ualberta.ca*

Kathleen Thompson is an Assistant Professor in the Department of Counseling, Social Work, and Leadership at Northern Kentucky University. Before coming to NKU she was a social worker in Canada for many years and completed her PhD in social work at the University of Calgary. Her professional interests include the needs of adults with serious mental health issues and how the support system can better meet their needs through collaboration and cooperation. Her chapter in this book is about an action research study she did for her dissertation. The study used cooperative inquiry as a method for helping older adults with the lived experience of mental illness influence the services and resources available to them. Her email address is thompsonk20@nku.edu

La-Kicia K. Walker-Floyd teaches at the University of Phoenix. Her action research project used a participatory action research journal to help her better understand and improve her online teaching. Her email address is judicial1@hotmail.com